Indian Political Thought and Its Contemporary Relevance

Edited by
Lopamudra Sengupta

Foreword by
Sekhar Bandyopadhyay
Professor of Asian History
Victoria University of Wellington

ATLANTIC
PUBLISHERS & DISTRIBUTORS (P) LTD

ATLANTIC
PUBLISHERS & DISTRIBUTORS (P) LTD
7/22, Ansari Road, Darya Ganj, New Delhi
Tel.: +91-11-4077 5252, 2327 3880
E-mail: orders@atlanticbooks.com
Web: www.atlanticbooks.com

Published by Atlantic Publishers & Distributors (P) Ltd., 2024
Reprint 2024

Printed & bound in India by Atlantic Print Services

Dedicated to

In loving memory of

Dr. Rajasri Basu

A versatile Scholar

Department of Political Science

Rabindra Bharati University

Foreword

Modernity arrived in India through the conduit of colonial rule, as British Empire's mission was to modernize India following a European Enlightenment model. The view of Europe that was presented was an exaggerated one, while the view of India that was constructed was based on stereotypes that justified the empire as a civilizing mission. Thus, classical India was believed to be the golden age—it was Europe's past—which had degenerated in the medieval period that was an age of decline for the Indian civilization. It was from this state of degeneration that colonial rule was to deliver the Indians and lead them into the path of enlightenment and modernity, teach them the art of self-governance. In political terms this modernity would mean various things, like a public space, rule of law, democracy, equal citizenship, civil society and so one.

Recent scholarship has however questioned these stereotypes and critiqued scholarly writings that were influenced or inspired by such colonial knowledge. We acknowledge today that not everything was golden in ancient India, nor was medieval period an age of total darkness or stasis, particularly so far as intellectual developments were concerned. We once used to believe that Indian social and political reformers only imitated the European post-Enlightenment rationalism and its idea of progress. Today we recognise that they also tried to relate those ideas to their own indigenous traditions and ontologies, and tried to evolve a modernity that would be modern, but not Western. The dominant project of the Indian social and political thinkers in the nineteenth and twentieth centuries has been to craft such an alternative modernity by relating European ideas to the intellectual traditions that they had inherited from their own past.

I am glad to see that in this volume the history of this complex intellectual journey has been put to critical scrutiny by a group of eminent historians and political scientists. They not only look at the structure of thoughts of a number of Indian political thinkers from ancient, medieval and modern times, but also discuss the relevance of their ideas to some of the contemporary political problems such as empowerment of women, protection of minorities, respect for human rights, identity politics, and concerns for environment and ecology. These dispassionate as well as divergent readings of political modernity through the writings of some of the intellectual stalwarts of modern India will be of use not only to students of political science and history, but to all concerned general readers. I congratulate the editor for bringing together such a useful volume.

Sekhar Bandyopadhyay
Professor of Asian History
Victoria University of Wellington

Preface

One of our pious duties is to introduce our students to the broad canvas of Indian Political Thought and relate it to the relevance we still have today. Often it is noted that students study these areas as part of the nationalist movement, and fail to relate them with contemporary political scenario.

This book arises out of the necessity to focus on the underlying philosophical principles essential in studying Indian society and politics. From the postcolonial era to this age of globalisation there has been sweeping changes in economy and forms of governance. The book therefore tries to focus on the universality of social principles that are still considered by the States as essential for smooth functioning of a political system.

The contributors through their articles have discussed and analyzed the political thought of Indian political thinkers, activists and mass leaders who have introduced path breaking ideas to usher in change and lead towards progress with a bent to *Indigenous Modernisation*.

The language maintained is lucid since a vast number of our students study only in their respective vernacular languages and may not feel comfortable to study this book if written in difficult language.

The contributors through these articles have essentially expressed their opinions in their respective essays and I have merely compiled them to bring out this a volume.

If the students find it beneficial we will know that our goal has been reached.

Lopamudra Sengupta

Acknowledgements

An Edited book is the outcome of a concerted effort by all the contributors. I take this opportunity to acknowledge my indebtedness to all my professors, colleagues and friends for helping me to bring out this book. I am grateful to all my teachers and colleagues for their scholarly suggestions and necessary guidance.

I express my deepest gratitude to Dr. Chittabrata Palit, Dr Sobhanlal Datta Gupta, Dr Debi Chatterjee, Dr Sibranjan Chatterjee, Dr. Sumit Mukerji, Dr Partha Pratim Basu and Dr. Hitendra K. Patel for their unconditional support and cooperation.

I express my deepest gratitude to Dr Rajasri Basu who is unfortunately not with us any longer but will remain in our minds and heart forever.

My sincerest thanks to Dr. Raj Kumar Kothari, Professor of Political Science, Vidyasagar University, Midnapore, West Bengal for extending his support and cooperation for the publication of this book.

I am thankful to all my contributors, who readily agreed to write for this book despite their busy schedule. Without their cooperation this book would not have been possible.

A special thanks to Dr. Sarbani Guha Ghosal and Dr Kashshaf Ghani for providing timely and necessary suggestions.

I acknowledge my sincere thanks to my student Aniruddha Basu who inspired me to write this book for the students and helped me in providing information for the book.

I am thankful to the staff, Ramkrishna Mission Institute of Culture (Library) Golpark, Kolkata for giving me access to all the materials required.

I am grateful to Partha Pratim Bose (Librarian), Department of International Relations, Jadavpur University for his support and cooperation.

I am thankful to all my Colleagues of Bangabasi College for their valuable suggestions. A special thanks to Sujit Chatterjee my colleague, Bangabasi College (Librarian) for providing all the necessary books and information's whenever needed.

I am thankful to my son Arjyadeb for providing me with the technical assistance without which the book would not have obtained a 'print' existence.

I am fortunate to have the support of my family, my parents who continue to inspire me till today and my husband, Abhik who constantly urged me to look for further references and complete the project despite many obstacles.

I acknowledge my profound indebtedness to Atlantic Publishers & Distributors for their earnest cooperation in publishing this book within time.

Lopamudra Sengupta

Contents

SECTION III
Social and Political Ideas of Reformist Thinkers

SECTION IV
Social and Political Ideas of the Thinkers of Modern Period

Contributors

Anurag Bannerjee is the Founder and Chairman of Overman Foundation. At the age of twenty, Anurag penned a biography of Dilip Kumar Roy titled *Achinpather Dibyapathik* (thus he became the youngest Indian to pen a biography) and at the age of twenty-one he translated one hundred poems of Sri Aurobindo into Bengali titled *Debotar Shrom*; both the books were published in 2008. His first book in English, *Nirodbaran: The Surrealist's Journey*, was published in December 2006 when he was twenty-two years old. In the past few years, he has established himself as a poet, essayist, researcher, biographer and translator. He was an Associate Professor at NexGen Institute of Business and Technology, Kolkata. He was also a faculty at Sri Aurobindo Centre for Advanced Research (SACAR), Pondicherry, where he conducted the course on Integral Management developed by him. He has lectured in several national symposiums and seminars organized by Sri Aurobindo Centre for Advanced Research, Sri Aurobindo Bhavan (Kolkata), National Council of Education and Jadavpur University. He is a Trustee of Sri Aurobindo Sakti Centre Trust which runs the "Sri Aurobindo Bal Mandir" School at New Alipore, Kolkata. In April 2011 Anurag was felicitated with the 'Nolini Kanta Gupta Smriti Puraskar' by 'Srinvantu' and Sri Aurobindo Bhavan, Kolkata.

Dr. Chittabrata Palit Professor (Retd.), Department of History, Jadavpur University. Kolkata MA (Cal) Ph.D. (Cantab) Fras (London), Founder and Director of Corpus Research Institute, Director, Institute of Historical Studies (Kolkata). He is specially acknowledged as an authority on economic history and history of science. His book on *Authentic Gandhi* deserves special mention.

Dr. Chitrita Chaudhuri Associate Professor, Department of Political Science, Vidyasagar College, University of Calcutta. She has extensively worked on Rammanohar Lohia and her book *Rammanohar Lohia and the Indian Socialist Thought* (Calcutta Minerva Associates 1993) deserves special mention.

Dr. Debi Chatterjee Professor (Retd.), Department of International Relations, Jadavpur University. Her special areas of interest includes Dalit Studies, Marxist ideas and movements in India. She has authored a number of books which includes *Dalit Rights/Human Rights*, Rawat Publications, Jaipur, 2011, *Ideas and Movements Against Caste in India: Ancient to Modern Times*, 2nd Edition, Abhijeet Publications, New Delhi, 2010, [1st Edition, print-o-graph Publishers, Calcutta, 1998], *Up Against Caste: Comparative Study of Ambedkar and Periyar*, Rawat Publications, Jaipur, 2004. *Sociology of National Integration*, Minerva Associates, Calcutta, 1993. Chatterjee Publishers, Calcutta 1985, Colour Volcano (a book on racism on South Africa). Founder Editor: *Voice of Dalit* [biannual journal on Dalit issues being published since 2008].

Dr. Hitendra K. Patel Associate Professor, Department of History, Rabindra Bharati University.

His research interests centre on the intellectual, social and political history of colonial and post-colonial India. His books *Communalism and Intelligentsia in Bihar 1870-1930* (published by Orient Black Swan, Delhi 2011), *Role of Intellectuals and Hindu Muslim Divide, in Mujibur Rehman ed., Communalism in Post-Colonial India: Changing Contours*, Routledge, London, *The Intelligentsia and the Making of Hindi Movement in Bihar in Indian Historical Review*, Volume 38, No 1, June 2011, Sage Publications, Delhi, 139-162, *Khudiram Bose: Revolutionary Extraordinaire* (Publication Division Delhi 2008).

Dr. Karabi Mitra Associate Professor, Department of History, Bijoy Krishna Girls College, Howrah. Her research interest includes intellectual history, local history, gender studies and South East Asian studies. She has contributed number of articles in national and international journals and is presently working on UGC sponsored Minor Research Project on the role of voluntary and government organisations in Women's Development, Published Maratha Saga, a view from colonial Bengal.

Dr. Kashshaf Ghani Assistant Professor, School of Historical Studies, Nalanda University.

His fields of interest includes Sufism, Islam in South Asia and Muslim Societies with a focus pre-modern India.

Dr. Kingshuk Chatterjee Associate Professor, Department of History, Calcutta University.

His area of research is Middle East and Political Islam. His doctoral work was on the Intellectual origins of Islamic Revolution of Iran, at the Calcutta University. He is a guest faculty at the Institute of Foreign Policy Studies, Calcutta University and secretary, Foreign Policy Study Circle, at the American Centre. Among his publications *Ali Shari'ati and the Shaping of Political Islam in Iran* (New York: Palgrave Macmillan, 2011), 'Explorations of the Self: From Iqbal to Sharia'ti' in S. Maswood et al. (eds) *Between Tradition and Modernity: Aspects of Islam in South Asia*, Calcutta University Monograph Series (Calcutta: K.P. Bagchi, 2011), 'Too Tight a Grip?: Between the Centre and the Periphery in the Islamic Republic of Iran', in S. Das and S. Chakrabarti (ed) *Challenges of Nation Building in Developing Societies: Vignettes from West and South Asia* (K.P. Bagchi, Calcutta, 2010). He was Fulbright Scholar-in-Residence, US Naval Academy, Annapolis, Maryland, USA (2006-2007).

Kumkum Chattopadhyay Associate Professor (Retd.), Political Science Bethune College, Kolkata. She has extensively worked on Tagore Studies. Her article on Tagore's views on Decentralised Development: An Alternative Model in edited book *Decentralising Rural Government and Development* edited by Anil Kumar Jana published by Rawat Publications deserves special mention.

Dr. Lopamudra Sengupta Associate Professor, Department of Political Science, Bangabasi College, University of Calcutta. Her principal area of research has been Human Rights, on which she has obtained her Ph.D. from Jadavpur University,

Kolkata. She was a guest faculty at the MPhil course on Women's Studies at Burdwan University and M.A. course on Human Rights in the Department of South and South-East Asia, Calcutta University. She has published papers in the areas of Human Rights, Gender Studies and Feminism, primarily in the socio-cultural milieu of South Asia.

Her recent work on India's Third Gender will be published shortly. She has been awarded with the first prize for her article on "*Manabadhikar, Prasanga Brihannala*" by *Sahitya Kahan*, a literary journal in 2006. She has also been conferred best paper award on her paper India's Third Gender at Cross Roads: A Human Rights Perspective by Management Development Research Foundation at 2nd National Conference on Politics and Governance, 3rd August 2014 in New Delhi.

Dr. **Mahasweta Das Sharma** Associate Professor, Department of History, Asutosh College, University of Calcutta. Her area of interest includes Medieval and Modern Indian History specially 18th century.

Dr. **Nandini Bhattacharya** Associate Professor, Department of History, Calcutta Girls College, University of Calcutta. Her areas of interest includes extensive research on Soviet and Post-Soviet Tajikistan, its society, culture and identity. She is the author of the book *Duelling Isms: Soviet and Regional Identity in Central Asia*, Shipra Publication, Delhi, 2007. She has successfully completed two minor research projects under UGC and has successfully completed a project on Indo-Tajik cultural link in the past and present in collaboration with Maulana Abul Kalam Azad Institute of Asian Studies, Kolkata.

Dr. **Partha Pratim Basu** Professor, Department of International Relations, Jadavpur University, Kolkata. He received his Ph.D. in Political Science from University of Calcutta. He has also served as Departmental Chair; Director, School of Media, Communication and Culture; and Coordinator, PG Diploma Course on Human Rights at Jadavpur University. His publications include *Press and Foreign Policy in India,*

North-South Relations: A Postcolonial Research Agenda (co-author), *Revisiting Rammohun Roy's Political Agenda, Democracy and Democratization in the 21st Century* (co-editor), *Locating Cultural Change* (co-editor) apart from several book chapters and articles contributed to edited volumes and national and international journals of repute.

Dr. Peu Ghosh Assistant Professor, Political Science, Lady Brabourne College, Kolkata. Her area of interest is International Relations and Theory. Her books *International Relation and Indian Government and Politics* published by PHI Learning Private Limited, New Delhi deserves mention.

Late Dr. Rajasri Basu Associate Professor, Department of Political Science & Director Women's Studies Centre in Rabindra Bharati University. Her principal areas of research and interests were Political Theory, Gender Studies and Theoretical Public Administration. She played a crucial role in establishing the UGC sanctioned Women's Studies Centre in Rabindra Bharati University, 2009, of which she was the director till her tragic death in an accident in June, 2015.

Sarbani Guha Ghosal Associate Professor, Political Science Bijoy Krishna Girls College University of Calcutta. Her areas of interest includes Political Theory, Political Sociology & Gender Studies. At present working in UGC sponsored Minor Research Project on 21st Century Civil Society Movement of Kolkata (2014-2016). Previously she had completed UGC sponsored Minor Research Project on Domestic Violence and had published a number of articles in ISBN/ISSN numbered books/journals.

Dr. Sibranjan Chatterjee Associate Professor (Retd.), Department of Political Science Maulana Azad College, Kolkata (University of Calcutta), is a Member of West Bengal College Service Commission, Government of West Bengal. He has delivered a number of lectures on Swami Vivekanada in national seminars.

Dr. Sobhanlal Datta Gupta Professor (Retd.), Department of Political Science, University of Calcutta. His area of interest is Marxian Political Theory. His published works include

The State of Political Theory: Some Marxist Essays [co-author] (1977), *Justice and the Political Order in India 1978*, *Komintern and the Destiny of Communism in India 1919-1943*, *Dialectics of a Real and a Possible History* (2006; revised and enlarged edition, 2011) [German version of the book has been published under the title *Komintern and Kommunismus in Indien: 1919-1943*, Berlin: Dietz Verlag 2013], (ed.) P.C. Joshi, K. Damodaran, *A Documented History of the Communist Movement in India*. Select materials from archives on Contemporary History, School of Social Sciences, Jawaharlal Nehru University, New Delhi, Vol. I: 1917-1922, Vol. II: 1923-1925 (2007); (ed), Ryutin Platform (Stalin and the Crisis of Proletarian Dictatorship) (2010), Marxism in Dark Times: Select Essays for the New Century (2012).

Dr. Sumit Mukerji Professor, Department of Political Science, Dean of Arts and Commerce, Kalyani University. His area of interest includes Modern History and Politics. He has extensively written on Netaji Subhas Chandra Bose. His books include *Gorkhaland: The Dormant Volcano,* APH Publishing House, New Delhi, 2014, *Subhas Chandrer Jibone Rabindra Nather Provab:* Collection of essays on Subhas Chandra Bose in Bengali, N.E. Publishers, Kolkata, 2008 and Subhas Chandra Bose: *The Making of the Warrior Philosopher* (1921-1941), N.E. Publishers, Kolkata, 2006. He has been conferred the author of the year 2014 by University of Kalyani. He has been the recipient of First Prize in a National Eassy Competition Organized by Bharat Pathik, New Delhi, 1994. He stood sixth in West Bengal Civil Service Examinations, 1987.

Introduction

Lopamudra Sengupta

(I)

Political thought constitutes a significant and fascinating domain in the study of political philosophy. It is possible for a student and a scholar of political thought to know the political thinking of an important personality belonging to particular space and time and from there to conjure up the thinking of the human community living at that time, at that particular place. The study becomes more intriguing when the scholar delves into the ancient, medieval and modern period and tries to locate the political thinking of that period with the changes undergoing in the contemporary era. It helps in reconstructing our knowledge about the people living in that period and helps in understanding the cardinal principles working behind the activities of the state and society.

The book on *Indian Political Thought and Its Contemporary Relevance*, provides a radical re-thinking of the dominant ideas and thought that have been produced in India by ancient, medieval and modern thinkers. Indian political thought is characterised by an *"Indigenous"* tradition of its own.

Though these ideas that were advocated by the thinkers arose under specific historical, social, political and economic conditions yet the underlying elements of their thoughts have far reaching impact on the minds of the people. It broadened visionary horizon in understanding the cardinal principles of rights, equality, liberty and freedom in the face of domination and oppression within the state and society. These thinkers were broadly concerned with "*how* people feel, think and behave, but *why* they feel, think and behave as they do, and *with what consequences* for themselves and for others" (Myrdal: 1968).

This belief in how good life can be attained in the best society and state still acts as the driving force for analysing the activities of the state, in adoption of public policies, techniques of coordination between the state and man's survival with "dignity" in the society.

This book tries to explore the insights of the existing thoughts from a wider perspective of "*Social Justice*". It critically analyses how the tenets of their ideas that have been practiced almost six decades before (from the time when India became a new nation in the history of diplomatic affairs in 1947) and even before that is highly effective at a purely pragmatic level till now and for decades to come.

This book has focused on the ongoing studies that have developed in the post independence period which has tried to link up the ideas with the major contemporary issues that have arisen at the beginning of the 21st century with changed political, economic, social and global conditions.

It highlights the emerging areas of Indian political thought in the post independence period that has tried to grapple with issues emerging from environmental movements, empowerment, human rights issues pertaining to man's dignity, sustainable development, women's movement, feminist issues, socialist ideas, civil society, etc.

These emerging areas however, are thought as categories greatly championed by the West. For quite some time now social science scholarship in India has been critical of the Eurocentric view of studying social sciences. This was primarily because of India's contact with the Western culture. As eminent scholar Tapan Roy Choudhuri argues in his book *Europe Reconsidered—Perceptions of the 19th Century West*, that the West acted as a major catalyst that triggered off responses which was unprecedented in all spheres of life.[1] One cannot ignore the fact that our political thinkers were largely exposed to ideas of the West. From Raja Rammohun Roy to Rabindranath Tagore, (except Vidyasagar) to Gandhi and Subhas Chandra Bose, Nehru, Ambedkar, Jinnah, Jayaprakash Narayan, among many others had resided in the West or had received Western education. Therefore it cannot be denied that they had infused Western liberal ideas largely into the feudalistic and archaic social system that dominated Indian socio-cultural scenario at that point of time.

But what is particularly 'relevant', even today is their method of applying these ideas in the Indian social system. Recently there has been repeated emphasis on the need for 'indigenising' social sciences in the face of uncritical acceptance and application of concepts and theories derived from the West. There is in a way a search to find out what might be described as '*Indiana*', to analyse and discuss these issues today.[2] The need to look into these practices has become more significant in the face of global changes and challenges. While the economic condition is still staggering far behind the other developed countries, the need to politically be one and equal with other developed States in the world has struck an imbalance in the values and culture of our lives. This again calls for the restoration of the values that were prevalent and laid emphasis by these thinkers in their attempt to build a strong society of individuals even at the face of dehumanisation and jeopardising of rights, equality and justice by the Colonial State.

(II)

Indian political thought has a fairly long and fascinating history that began even before the period of *Kautilya* and *Manu*. The age of the Ancient thinkers extends from the Vedic Age to the death of emperor *Harshavardhana* in 647 A.D. It includes the political thoughts discussed in the four *Vedas*, the *Dharma Sutras*, the *Smritis*, the epics (*Ramayana and Mahabharata*), the *Puranas*, the *Nitisastras*, the works of *Panini* and *Patanjali* (*Ashtadhyayi* and *Mahabhashya* respectively), the *Arthashastra* of *Kautilya*, etc. They touch on a wide range of issues concerning both state and society. Their works provide a very accurate reflection of the social reality of the historical period of their creation. The epics like The *Ramayana*, The *Mahabharata*, The *Vedas*, The *Upanishads*, and The *Purana's*, were upholders of man's basic relation to the society. The two central concepts that conceptualised political life revolved around the twin concepts of *Danda* and *Dharma*. The term *Danda* means discipline, force restraint, constraint or punishment (Parekh 1986).

In the Indian social and philosophical thought, all rights were treated as a part of *Dharma*. The word *Dharma* which comes from the Sanskrit root "*dhr*" which means 'to hold together', 'to sustain' concerns not only the moral but social and cosmic orders which are relevant even today. The ideal society therefore has all along been the *Dharma* society which embodies innocence and assures the individual of innocent existence while striving for liberation. The *Dharmic* society essentially is one where the life and personal dignity (worth) of individuals in a society has a proper value, which can neither be dissolved in nor derived from anything else but from the doctrine of *Dharma*. The ability to live "humanly" was the prime concern of *Dharma*. *Dharma* was thus created for the purpose of binding all "classes" (in the broader sense of the term) endowed with diverse characteristics and varying degrees of intellectual, physical, political and economic powers, which sustains, unifies, develops and strengthens the human society as one organic system. The need was then felt to formulate *Dharma* in accordance with the requirement of the common man in different spheres of his activity. Thus while *Kautilya's* '*Arthashastra*' was an attempt to take *Dharma* into the sphere of polity and economy. '*Manusmriti*' is an attempt to bring out the application of Dharma in the ethical and religious spheres. The various '*Dharma*' – *Sutras* concern themselves with both secular and religious laws.[3] *Dharma*, with its various dimensions vis. as duty, conscience, customary morality, reflective morality, justice etc. was considered as the ideal social order and was accepted in India, not only by the Hindus but even by the Jains and the Buddhists too. Hence the Indian social and religious philosophy recognised an organic vision of society where all functions were recognised as essential parts of one order.[4]

The age of the Medieval thinkers starts with the end of the centralised authority of emperor *Harshavardhana* on his death in 647 A.D. The Medieval period extends from 647 A.D. to 1757 A.D (i.e. it ends with the advent of British rule in India after the Battle of Plassey). Though there are quite a few significant thinkers in this age like *Kabira, Dadu, Tulsidasa, Vallabhacharya, Ziauddin, Barani, Abul Fazal,* etc. This book extensively discusses the views of *Barani* and *Abul Fazal* as has been included in the syllabus. This period reflects a great mingling of the indigenous thoughts of Hindu thinkers along with the theories brought in by philosophers from outside the

Indian sub-continent. The medieval period, particularly before the advent of the Mughals marked a deterioration in the Indian Hindu society. People had grown a parochial outlook. As eminent historian KM Pannikar, observed that society became static.[5]

This degeneration continued even after the disintegration of the vast Moghul empire and its aftermath. By the time the East India Company established its rule over parts of India both the Marathas and the Mohammedan Nawabs had exhausted their resources, economic and military and the nation as a whole had become demoralised. The Hindu society in particular was beset with superstitions and evils of various kind eg. sati, untouchability, intolerant caste distinctions and taboos of various kinds.

A living society ought to have both the power and continuity and the ability to change. As Professor Radhakrishnan writes– In the history of every community a time comes when radical changes in the social order becomes obligatory, if the community is to exist as a being force and continue to progress.[6]

At this juncture in our cultural history, India produced a member of path breaking scholar-reformers who sought to give a new orientation to socio-religious thought and institutions of the people. This marked the advent of a 'Reformist Era', in India also popularly known as the "Indian Renaissance", that witnessed the advent of illustrious men like *Raja Rammohun Roy*, *Iswar Chandra Vidyasagar*, *Vivekananda*, *Rabindranath Tagore, Jyotirao Phule, Tarabai Shinde*, *Bankim Chandra chattopadhyay, Sir Shed Ahmed Khan, Bal Gangadhar Tilak, G.K. Gokhale, Tarabai Shinde, Pandita Ramabai Saraswati, Sarala Devi Chaudhurani*, etc. There were many others like *Dayananda Saraswati, Dadabhai Naoroji, Pheroze Shah Mehta, Madam Mohan Malaviya, Sarojini Naidu, S.N. Banerjee,* but in this book we have discussed only the ideas of those theorists mentioned in the previous sentence due to the boundaries set by the syllabus and constraint of time. The Reformist thinkers were basically concerned with the restructuring and renovation of Indian society.

The era of Modern thinkers begins with very significant thinkers like Sri *Aurobindo*. About the same time as *Aurobindo,* we find the largest political figure of Modern India: *Mohondas Karamchand Gandhi*. After that there are other very important thinkers like *Manabendra Nath Roy, Jawaharlal Nehru, Vinayak Damodar Savarkar, Maulana Abul Kalam Azad, Md. Ali Jinnah, Bhimrao Ramji Ambedkar, Subhas Chandra Bose, Narendra Deva, Jayaprakash Narayan, Rammanohar Lohia*, etc. Though some others like *Keshav Baliram Hedgewar, Shyama Prasad Mukherjee, Md. Ali, Motilal Nehru, Chittaranjan Das, Kamaladevi Chattopadhyay* and *Suhasini Chattopadhyay*, among others but we have dealt only with the thought of those theorists mentioned in our syllabus, and lack of academic assistance.

The modern period as referred in this book, mainly highlights the dynamic role played by the nationalist leaders of our country and their adherence to pursue goals of Freedom Liberty Justice and Equality.

In addition to the adherence to these goals, the facts that deeply lies underneath the political thought of all the thinkers from ancient to modern period put emphasis on

(i) nation building,

(ii) building a strong society of individuals separate from the existence of State, and

(iii) develop a World outlook that connects National identity with International vision.

In post colonial India, Western democracy which had imitated the style and formal practices of Westminster democracy could not address the social equality as was expected. On the contrary certain sections of people with vested interests, made matters worst. Incidents of violence and 'dehumanising political practices' have become a part of common political culture. The concept of a larger societal whole that was prevalent in ancient society became a myth. It became a reflection of complex existence of interplay of different segments and sections of people. Together with this the market economy and excessive materialism have deeply affected the social fabric and has called in for a restoration of the traditional values that were advocated by these thinkers.

Their thought which have been considered idealist and utopian have again gained relevance. One may be engaged into a dialogue on Minority Rights, Identity Politics, Multiculturalism Women's Empowerment and Human Rights, but what is important for a social scientist is the need to appreciate the value of "survival" which itself is the greatest need of this hour. Elements of "how" to survive despite being a multicultural, multi lingual and multi religious country had captured the attention of these thinkers. How to differentiate the "personal" from "political" and "public" from "private" pervaded the realms of their ideas. The method of dissolving "cultural differences", was at the heart of their thoughts. They taught the "end" of political virtue and not the "means" of political "dispassionateness" where political irrationality kills all ethical virtues. They were critical to injustices when and where raised yet vigilant and critical about its own culture.

They had "explored" the ways in which cultural traits and traditional practices can be utilised for social and economic upliftment, and had identified individuals in terms of "existing skill" who have tremendous potential for up gradation, and can act as important 'agents' of social change.

Finally, how differences of ideas among themselves can be transformed by each other into a strong democratic will, have been reflected in their ideas.

This book primarily looks into these contemporary issues as has been portrayed in their ideas.

(III)

Keeping the chronology of events in mind the book has been divided broadly into four sections:

(1) Ancient Thinkers

(2) Medieval Thinkers

(3) Reformist Thinkers

(4) Modern Thinkers

Each Chapter contains three segments (i) Introduction or a brief biography, (ii) Basic Tenets of their Thought, (iii) Relevance of their thought in Post Independent India.

The first section of the book contains three chapters.

The First Chapter written by Rajasri Basu traces the gradual development of human civilisation in the ancient period from New Stone or Neolithic culture to the Chalcolithic culture, to the Bronze age urbanisation of the Indus Valley civilisation to the early Vedic Aryan culture, and the age of Jainism and Buddhism. The writer focuses on the gradual development and domination of territorial states, the beginning of the history of the Deccan and the subsequent spread of civilisation in the eastern part of India till the empire building under the Guptas. Besides referring to the various features of the ancient society she also pointed out to the political economic and social changes that took place from seventh century onwards which ultimately led to the transition to the medieval society.

The Second Chapter written by Peu Ghosh deals with *Kautilya*s theory of the state which is magnificently exposed in the *Arthashastra*, a treatise that lay down the rules of statecraft, public administration, diplomacy, war strategies and economic policies. After a discussion on *Kautilya*'s Saptanga Theory of the state, Dandaniti and Diplomacy she urges that modern-day diplomacy for example the Chinese design of 'String of Pearls', resembles strongly with that of *Kautilya*'s theory. Moreover further similarly between *Kautilya*'s and Machiavellian's thought has also been referred to. She concludes by referring to the universal element of statecraft present in *Kautilya*'s thinking, the agenda of "national interest", that still acts as the primary factor in national and international politics.

The Third Chapter written by Rajasri Basu exposes the views of *Manu*, the legendary author of one of the *Smritis* or law code, the *Manusmriti*, which is also popularly known as *Manusamhita* or *Manava Dharma*shastra. In order to establish *Dharma*, and welfare of humanity *Manu* advocated a society based upon caste divisions. The author points out that though *Manu*smiriti is regarded as one of the first law books in the world yet its views against women and Dalit are derogatory in nature and have largely been condemned both by both Indian Liberal feminists as well as by Dalit scholars and leaders including BR Ambedkar, one of the great champions of social justice and crusader against caste hierarchy.

The second section also contains three chapters.

In the Fourth Chapter Kashshaf Ghani traces the main features of Medieval Indian Political thought, that stretches roughly from the thirteenth to the late eighteenth century. He brings into focus the major influences of non-Indian cultures and civilisations especially the advent of Islam that provided a new direction to an existing political culture. The author pointed out the basic principles which governed all subsequent political thinking in Muslim societies. The most remarkable feature of Indo-Islamic political thought is their adaptability to Indian conditions.

The Fifth Chapter is written by Kashshaf Ghani on *Ziauddin Barani*, the most important political thinker of the Delhi Sultanate. He discusses how Barani's political ideology aimed at advising the ruling community, particularly the Sultan, in the correct ways of ruling his State. His Fatwa-i Jahandari upholds the elements of good statecraft for the Muslim Kings. He emphasised on the adherence to *Sharia* in establishing an ideal Muslim State, but also relied on secular law with the principles of Sharia that revealed the political pragmatism of his thought.

The Sixth Chapter is written by Kingshuk Chatterjee on *Abul Fazl Allami*, who laid down the intellectual parameters of the theory of sovereignty inspired by the doctrine of *Wahdat al-Wujud*.

In the third section there are eight chapters in all.

In the Seventh Chapter, Partha Pratim Basu, traces the thought of the first conscious modern political thinker Raja Rammohun Roy. The article exposes Rammohun Roy's critique of Hindu idolatry practices and the changes he brought in the Hindu religion for the sake of the social and political good of the people. The article upholds Rammohun Roy's ideas of constitutional Government based on separation of powers. Basu, also extensively elaborates on Rammohun's belief in preserving individual rights and especially that of women and point out the steps taken by Raja Rammohun Roy to ameliorate the socio economic position of women thus ushering in "Social Justice", with the active intervention of the state.

In the Eight Chapter, Nandini Bhattacharya upholds the vision and insights of Syed Ahmed Khan, who started the process of modernisations among the Muslims of India through a series of constructive efforts, with the benevolent support of the colonial authorities.

In the Ninth Chapter, Lopamudra Sengupta recollects the contribution of Iswar Chandra Vidyasagar, who fought against the inhuman practices which were 'invoked' by '*Desachar*', and not '*Shastra*' at that time. In the article the writer points out his pivotal role in spreading Mass Education in the society and focuses on the nature of women's freedom or *swadhinata* that was more attuned to the needs of humanistic considerations.

In the Tenth Chapter, Mahasweta Das Sharma traces the thoughts of the reformist thinkers, Phule, Ranade, Tilak and Gokhale. She traces extensively the various ways adopted by these thinkers to get rid of the 'social evils' like the Emancipation of Shudra and ati-Shudras, and movement against untouchability and women's emancipation thereby evoking a new dimension in the realisation of 'social justice'.

The Eleven Chapter is written by Sarbani Guha Ghosal on Bankimchandra Chattopadhyay, the Bengali Linguist and Nationalist. She has pointed out how Bankim Chandra Chattopadhyay, was utterly frustrated at the degeneration of the Indian society and culture under the British rule and sought to review the nationalist and patriotic feelings through the spread of popular education among the masses. This he did by promulgating his ideas through Bengali Language and Literature. The author has portrayed how Bankimchandra Chattopadhyay could effectively provide a linkage between India's glorious past as well as emphasise on the innovations of survival in the future.

In the Twelfth Chapter, Karabi Mitra traces the genesis of feminist ideas in India in the late nineteenth century, from the works of three educated women. *Tarabai Shinde*, *Pandita Ramabai Saraswati* (Maharastra) and *Sarla Devi Chaudhurani* (Bengali). Inspired by the social reform movement, that was triggered by *Rammohun Roy* and *Iswar Chandra Vidyasagar* in the early decades of the nineteenth century, those thinkers clearly raised issues related to subjugation of women under patriarchal domination. The author draws attention to the fact that how these thinkers identified the "agents" of exploitation and seek to establish themselves as "the individual being", capable to assert herself in a patriarchal order.

In the Thirteenth Chapter, Kumkum Chattopadhyay traces the path of nationalism and Nation Building as was envisioned by Rabindranath Tagore. She also pointed out to Tagore's attempt in building a strong society in which people will be awakened to recognise their identity. She traces extensively the ways by which Tagore tried to fulfill his vision of nation building. His ideas of rural reconstruction, education and culture has been specifically looked into. Elements of contemporary thought like Tagore's vision on *Chhatraswaraj*, Environment have also been looked into.

In the Fourteenth Chapter, Sibranjan Chatterjee analyses Swami Vivekananda's idea of freedom and individual liberty. The author pointed out Swamiji's increasing concern about the role of masses, who constitutes the backbone, of a nation. Swamiji's idea of socialism, democracy as well as his ideas of "social justice", have been discussed in a new perspective.

The Fifteenth Chapter is the first chapter of the fourth section that discusses the ideas of Mohandas Karamchand Gandhi, the first thinker of the modern period. Prof. Chittabrata Palit aptly narrates how Gandhiji was deeply influenced by the philosophy of Ruskin and Tolstoy, which had cast a deep spell on his activities that he undertook throughout his life. Apart from Gandhiji's role in some of the major nationalist movements, the author drives our attention to the unique methods that Gandjhiji had adopted to bring in a new thrust in India's economy, politics and society. Gandhiji's crusade against untouchability and his increasing concern for environment in the context of global pollution and ecological imbalance leading to lethal diseases have been extensively analysed and discussed.

In the Sixteenth Chapter, Anurag Banerjee dwells on the uniqueness of Sri Aurobindo's Nationalist ideas that revolved around the concept of a religion or Santana *Dharma*, in which the Indians were required to live.

In the Seventeenth Chapter, Hitendra K. Patel tried to capture the "shifts" in Jinnah's ideas that changed from 1920 till post 1947. Essentially a liberalist who believed in tradition of moderate politics at the beginning of his political carrier, Jinnah ideas gradually changed owning to the realities of politics. His formulation of 'Fourteen points', and his advocacy of Two Nation Theory remained for a long time the main plank of Muslim politics in India.

The Eighteenth Chapter deals with the political ideas of Vinayak Damodar Savarkar. Professor. Chittabrata Palit explores Savarkar's vision of a Hindu State and highlights the various controversies that surround his concept of '*Hindutva*' and seeks to examine its nature.

In the Nineteenth Chapter Sobhanlal Datta Gupta traces the evolution of Manabendranath Roy's ideas from militant Nationalism to Radical Humanism. He critically examines the positions taken by both Indian Marxists and by the defenders of Roy' Radical humanism as regards to M.N. Roy's contribution to Indian political thought. Finally why Roy's ideas could not become a popular ideology inspite of its optimistic vision of the future has been extensively analysed and discussed.

In the Twentieth Chapter, Rajasri Basu discusses the political ideas of a great Indian scholar and leader of the national movement, *Abul Kalam Azad*. The author throws light on how *Abul Kalam Azad* freed himself from the shackles of his orthodox ways of life and was initiated into politics by a Bengali revolutionary. The author narrates how Azad tied his concept of secularism with that of nationalism. Inspite of many differences with Gandhi and Nehru, Azad continued to strive for India's awakening especially by placing his conviction on the necessity of providing basic education to all especially of the women of India, who have the ability to transmit it into next generation. The author thus highlights the role of education in human development, that is particularly relevant in today's world.

In the Twenty First Chapter, Sarbani Guha Ghosal upholds the socialist ideas of Narendra Deva, who was often idealised as an 'ethical socialist' due to his primacy of moral values. The author points out his faith in the working class as the vanguard in the struggle for liberation and describes his keen interest in agrarian reconstruction of India and his views on secularist nationalism with special emphasis on national social planning.

In the Twenty Second Chapter, Lopamudra Sengupta highlights the lofty ideals of Jawaharlal Nehru which he tried to translate into reality after he became the first Prime Minister of India. The author tries to bring into focus the elements of his thought, the scientific and rational temperament, his diplomatic manoeuvres and his advocacy of democracy, socialism and humanism that runs deeply in his political thought.

In the Twenty Third Chapter, Debi Chatterjee describes the life of one of the greatest leader in modern India, that of Bhimrao Ramji Ambedkar, and highlights the difficulties he 'encountered', while growing up due to his birth in Mahar caste family, which was considered as untouchable in India. The author upholds the main tenets of Ambedkar's ideas which was a clear synthesis of Indian philosophical ideas and Western liberal thinking. His belief in liberal democratic institutions and their capabilities of bringing about 'social justice' has been extensively discussed in this chapter.

In the Twenty Fourth Chapter, Sumit Mukerji, highlights the spectacular role played by Netaji Subhas Chandra Bose in the freedom struggle of India, particularly his contribution in the formation of India National Army (INA) where he particularly assigned special role to women. The author has pointed out that Netaji advocated reconstructing post independent India along scientific lines and his emphasis on intermingling of various communities irrespective of caste or religious distinction had great impact in bringing harmony among the Hindus and Muslims. The author also brings into focus Netaji's ideals of nationalism and socialism, which emphasised on the need to be shaped according to the social ideal and politics of one's own country. The author has significantly highlighted the mystery that surrounds the death of Netaji Subhas Chandra Bose.

In the Twenty Fifth Chapter, the author Sibranjan Chatterjee traces the "uniqueness", of Jayprakash Narayan's political ideas as regards to socialism and partyless democracy. The author intricately discusses Jayprakash Narayana's concept of 'Total Revolution', that seeks to change the society on all aspects—economic, social political, cultural, moral—spiritual ideological and educational. The author while discussing on the Relevance of his thought today, also captures some of the dilemmas his thought suffered from.

In the Twenty Sixth Chapter, Chitrita Chaudhuri unfolds the thought of another 'Socialist' leader, Rammanohar Lohia. The author pointed out that thought he subscribed to the major principles of Marxism and Leninism, he was not a blind supporter of communism particularly as was practised in Soviet Russia. Jayaprakash Narayan rejected the linear view of history as it placed the Western Countries of Europe in an advanced position in the ladder of civilisation. He however adhered to a more simplistic division of world history which have been elaborately discussed by the author in this chapter. Chitrita Choudhuri draws our attention to Lohia's concept of 'socialist civilisation', which had a completely different flavour from capitalism and communism and instead embraced the entire humanity, devoid of classes and castes in composition, thus advocating his views of a 'world state', which is distinctive in all respect.

(IV)

The Twenty Six Chapters that have been discussed in the present volume, illuminates the genesis of various contemporary issues that were reflected in the thoughts of Indian Political Thinkers.

Essence of issues like that of Human Rights, Man's Dignity, Women's Empowerment, Environment, Ecology, Human Development can be largely traced back in their ideas. Gandhiji's commitment to individual freedom in the face of organised and concentrated violence of the state pointed out that he was totally in favour, of protecting the 'individuals', from the onslaughts of the State, which is also the starting point of Human Rights Declaration. Only a great philosopher like Gandhiji could realise the demerits of 'unrestricted' individual freedom which might be dangerous for social harmony. In his Weekly, *Harijan*, of 31 March 1946, he wrote that both individual liberty and interdependence are both essential for life in society. "Willing Submission" to social restraint for the Sake of the well being of the whole society enriches both the individual and the society of which one is a member.[7] In a world which is torn by atrocities and systematic violence, Gandhijis concept of 'Ahimsa' and 'Non-Violence', are increasingly becoming relevant for the re-construction of a healthy society, that are largely upheld Worldwide.

Emphasis on the need to promote village industries, as a part of rural reconstruction which Gandhiji had long ago emphasised are now considered as important elements of "good governance", that acts as major ideal in serving the welfare of the citizens. Moreover Gandhiji's concept of 'Khadi', a cloth made out of natural fibre and spun by one's own hands is the most sought after material suitable for making garments, that captures the fancy of the rising urban educated class who are increasingly becoming conscious of adopting only 'eco-friendly' products for their daily needs and usages.

Thus emerging concepts related to Environment, and Ecology had largely occupied the minds our thinkers. Rabindranath Tagore wrote songs and verses and repeatedly emphasised on the need to protect the environment. His idea of '*Halakarshan*', or furrowing '*Vriksharopan*', or tree planting festivals in *Santiniketan* bears testimony to this. *Visva Bharati* became a garden university. The school classes were held in *Amrakunja* or the mango grove in the open air. This was his idea of communion with nature.[8]

In '*Hind Swaraj*', Gandhiji too criticised the British industrial society which devastated nature in its attempt to maximise its thrust of gorging consumer goods.[9] The relevance of these words are of great significance especially in this age of 'Global Warming'. Issues related to women's well being were also largely thought in those days. Though the newly emerging term 'Feminism', which is nowadays used like a buzzword and occupies a central force in explaining women's condition in this society, it should be pointed that the nature of Feminism in India was vastly different than what was is being practised in western countries. The concern of the Indian thinkers from *Raja Rammohun Roy*, *Iswar Chandra Vidyasagar*, *Bankim*

Chandra, *Vivekananda*, *Tarabai Shinde* and others were to raise women's legal, political, and social status, but not strictly as something equal to those of men in the society, (as is popularly understood by Feminism in the West). Their approach was more '*humanitarian*', and emphasised greatly on 'Capacity Building', and in expanding the "Substantive Freedoms".[10] For this they relied more on 'education', as the only "means' of endowing individual freedom that will give their women the ability to live the kind of life they value for themselves. This equally advocated the essence underlying the concept of 'Women's Empowerment' today.

Moreover, concepts of like that of 'Development', had been largely expressed in their ideas. In 2005, UN Secretary General Kofi Anan in report 'In Larger Freedom', stated that

(i) freedom from want, i.e. eradication of hunger and poverty
(ii) freedom from fear, i.e. abolition of wars and
(iii) the freedom to lure in dignity, the respect for human rights should be the goal in order to proceed towards 'Development'[11]

These words are reminiscence of what Swami Vivekananda had once uttered:

"...Bread! Bread! I do not believe in a God, who cannot give me bread here, giving me eternal bliss in heaven. Pooh! India is to be raised, the poor are to be fed, education is to be spread, and the evil of priest craft is to be removed...more bread, more opportunity for everybody..."[12]

Vivekananda was conscious that mere political freedom, without social justice is an empty declaration that will not be able to fill up the void.

Indian political thinkers therefore consistently advocated Development, along economic social and cultural lines. They had also realised the need for a fair distribution of wealth that civil reduce the gap between the rich and poor and the increasingly placed emphasis on planning the economy on socialistic lines that will not be a blind imitation of Marxism.

In the midst of changing governments, and shifting "policies" about religion, and its major implications on the society and the role of state in a multicultural, multilingual and multi religious society, the need to look into the vision of these leaders has become increasingly relevant. Gandhiji's idea of *Sarva-Dharma-Samabhava* (Equal approach to all religions), Swami Vivekanada's Universal Religion or Tagore's 'Religion of Man' reveals an unique approach to be followed in this society.

The book on Indian Political thought: Its Contemporary Relevance thus introduces a "holistic" approach in studying the contemporary problems that studies the complex interplay of all the social factors that contribute in making a just society.

This book is an attempt to encompass and provide inputs from optimal references and is written in a lucid language for the benefit of the students. The topics discussed in this book are based on the cross section of the syllabi provided by the leading Universities nationally. However, as pointed at the outset due to constraint of time we could not include some thinkers in this volume. However keeping in mind the growing need to understand certain important issues like womens movement and education we have particularly traced back to some of the writings like that of Vidyasagar, Maulana Abul Kalam Azad, and Three Faces Of Feminist Thought that are not included in most syllabi of leading Universities. Moreover there has not been any systematic effort to delineate between political thinkers, mass leaders, or those actively engaged in the Nationalist movement. The chronology has been followed simply as we find them within the historical time and space. The contemporary relevance of the ideas of these thinkers in many chapters are not proportional in length as their impact in the Indian society do varied, across time and space in the Indian society for example the contribution of Jawaharlal Nehru in Indian politics cannot be same as Jinnah, as the latter, lived only a year after independence.

Nevertheless a modest attempt has been made to locate their importance in terms of its impact. I sincerely belief that this book will help the students and all those who are interested to develop an insight in studying contemporary political thought and develop their own ideas in comprehending Indian Political Thought based on the history and politics of our country. Inspite of our effort to bring in accuracy of facts,.their might be gross mistakes and serious omissions of facts for which the editor requests readers to point out which can be corrected in the subsequent editions. Opinions reflected in each chapter are the contributors own and the editor has merely compiled them to make this an useful volume.

Notes

1. Roy Choudhuri, T. (1988) '*Europe Reconsidered*': Oxford University Press, p. 231.
2. I am benefitted, greatly from Gayatri Chakravorty Spivak's, Key note address on "Theory as Practice", delivered at XVII International Conference, 21-24 December 2014, at International Centre, Goa. Speaking on the Gandhi-Ambedkar debate, at the inception of the new nation she draws our attention to raise the quality of education for the children and not only quantity – quotas and years.
3. Velassery Sebastian (2005), *Casteism And Human Rights: Towards Onthology of the Social Order*: London Marshall Cavendish Academic, p. 108.
4. *Ibid*., p. 134.
5. Pannikar, KM. (1960) '*A Survey of India History*': Bombay, Asia Publishing House reprinted, p. 106.
6. *Ibid*., p. 114.
7. Pantham, T. (1986) '*Beyond Liberal Democracy: Thinking with Mahatma Gandhi*'. In Pantham T & Deutsch K L ed(s) Political Thought in Modern India, New Delhi, Sage of Publication, p. 339.
8. Palit, C. (2013) '*Authentic Gandhi*', New Delhi, Kunal Books, p. 100.
9. *Ibid*., p. 101.
10. This notion is something in common with the essence of Amartya Sen's concept (1999) of capability that relates to "Substantive freedoms" of individuals to live the kind of life they value and have reasons to value.
11. For details refer to Sen, Amartya. (1999) '*Development as freedom*': New Delhi, Oxford University Press.
12. Ganguly, A.K. (2013) 'Social Justice & the Constitutional Dispensation', in Radharaman Chakrabarti (ed) *The Quest for Human Unity: A Multi-Layered Approach*, Kolkata: Ramkrishna Mission in Culture, Golpark, p. 152.
13. Khan, A.W. (2013) 'The Power of Peace: Using the Tool of Information & Communication'. In (ed) *The Quest for Human Unity: A Multi-Layered Approach*, Kolkata: Ramkrishna Mission in Culture, Golpark, p. 170.

SECTION I

Ancient Indian Political Thought

1

Ancient Indian Life and Thought —A Chronological Framework

Rajasri Basu

Introduction

The study of ancient Indian political thought is particularly important for several reasons. First, it gives us an idea of when and how people developed one of the earliest civilizations of the word. Secondly, by studying ancient political thought, one gets an idea about gradual development of human civilization—from nomadic life to a settled life, from pastoral economy to agricultural economy, from band and kin-based social and political organizations to the rise of the territorial state—took place. Thirdly, it also enables us to trace the roots of different languages that we spoke today and different scripts that we use today as it has more or less been established by the linguistic anthropologists that the languages that we see today have their roots in ancient days and have developed through ages.

At the same time, it is difficult to comprehend and locate the features of ancient Indian political thought as there have been several sources spread across different parts of India and also the 'ancient' period is spread over a long-time line. Ancient India is vast in terms of both space and time. Its spread is for about two millennia and its extent is from Baluchistan in the western part of the Indian subcontinent (now in Pakistan) to Kamrup in eastern India (modern day Assam), Himalayas in the north to deep down in the Deccan. It is, therefore, very difficult to identify its nature or to mention certain characteristics as its features. The society, obviously, underwent and witnessed many changes, which again had their reflection in the archaeological, and more so in the literary sources. That is why, whenever, we want to mention certain features, the time period comes into picture and the features are always to be mentioned in the context of time frame. The entire period witnessed the gradual development of human civilization from New Stone or Neolithic culture to the Chalcolithic culture, to the Bronze age urbanization of the Indus Valley civilization to the early Vedic Aryan culture, the later Vedic Aryan civilization, the age of Jainism and Buddhism, the gradual development and domination of the territorial states, dawn of history at the Deccan and the spread of civilization in the eastern part of India, and finally empire building under the Guptas.

This vast period of ancient India naturally displays several features. The features have been mentioned here separately taking the different periods into consideration.

The Neolithic Civilization of the Mehrgarh

From the world perspective, the Neolithic age began in 9000 BCE. However, the only known Neolithic settlement in the Indian subcontinent is attributed to Mehrgarh civilization, which stretches roughly from 8000 BC to 3500 BCE. Mehrgarh is situated in Baluchistan, a province of the modern day Pakistan. It was one of the largest Neolithic settlements in the area between the Indus and the Mediterranean. The following features could be noticed from this settlement:

1. Initially, it displayed pastoral economy, where the settlers raised and domesticated goats, cattle and sheep.
2. People knew the art of agriculture and people produced wheat and barley from the outset. It is the earliest known site of agriculture in South Asia.
3. Compartmentalized mud brick structures have been excavated indicating existence of granaries, where cereals were stored. This indicates that cereals were produced in substantial quantities.
4. Later Mehrgarh people knew the use of Bronze and Copper or, in other words belong to the Chalcolithic age (4800-3500 BCE).

5. Expansion of agriculture and pottery could be noticed in the later part of the Mehrgarh civilization that is, during 4500-3500 BCE.

Apart from Mehrgarh, three important Neolithic settlements could be noticed in the Indian subcontinent although they belonged to a much later period. These three areas are Kashmir in the north-west, the hills of Assam and the Garo hills of the Meghalaya and the settlement of southern part of India, which is to the south of the Godavari.

The Chalcolithic Culture

The Chalcolithic period follows the Neolithic culture. The Chalcolithic age signifies the use of metals—and the use of copper, to be precise as it was the use of copper, that came first amongst all the metals. Along time line, this period precedes the bronze-age Harappan culture but in many parts of India they came in the later part of the mature Harappan culture. The Chalcolithic settlements were mostly found in south-eastern Rajasthan, western part of Madhya Pradesh and in western Maharashtra. The principal features of the Chalcolithic settlements in India may be mentioned below:

1. The Chalcolithic civilization of India was predominantly a rural civilization.
2. The Chalcolithic people mostly used tiny tools and weapons made of stone and copper.
3. Pottery was in extensive use and there is enough indications that they knew the use of potter's wheel.
4. Tools and weapons excavated from the sites of Chalcolithic culture indicate that the people were expert coppersmiths and skilled craftsmen.
5. Regional differences in social structure, economic activities and political organizations apparent. While the people settled in eastern part of India grew rice, people in Maharashtra produced barley.
6. The settlement pattern and the burial practices indicate not only regional differences but also the beginning of social inequalities.

7. Terracotta figures of women suggest that the Chalcolithic people worshipped mother goddess.

The Bronze Age Urban Civilization of the Indus Valley

The archaeological excavations at Harappa and Mohenjodaro in the north-western part of the Indian subcontinent are great discoveries, which broaden man's knowledge of the past. This civilization is older than the Chalcolithic civilization of India but as the people of this civilization used bronze along with copper and iron, the civilization is regarded as succeeding the Chalcolithic civilization. It is also to be noted that the Harappan civilization is far more developed than the preceding civilization.

The Indus Valley Civilization from 3500 BC displays a civilization with the following features:

1. The Harappan people developed a highly developed urban civilization having knowledge in town planning and efficient municipal governments, which placed a high priority on hygiene. This site had probably the world's first known sanitation system.
2. People belonging to Harappa and adjoining places were mostly traders and artisans. They had economic and diplomatic relations with far off countries. The Indus civilization's economy appears to have depended significantly on trade, which was facilitated by major advances in transport technology. A touchstone bearing gold streaks was found, which was probably used for testing the purity of gold.
3. There were large and small dwelling places in Harappa and Mohenjodaro, which indicated a kind of stratification in society, but the fact all the houses had access to water and drainage indicate a kind of egalitarianism, too. Given the similarity of artefacts, it seems that there was a large state throughout; however, there were multiplicity of power-structures. It seems that there were many rulers in a large state indicating a kind of complex decision-making.

4. The people of the Indus civilization achieved great accuracy in measuring length, mass, and time. They were among the first to develop a system of uniform weights and measures.
5. People of the Indus valley civilization, from the early Harappan periods, had knowledge of proto-dentistry. The oldest (and first early Neolithic) evidence for the drilling of human teeth *in vivo* (i.e., in a living person) was found in Mehrgarh. Eleven drilled molar crowns from nine adults were discovered in a Neolithic graveyard in Mehrgarh that dates from 7,500-9,000 years ago. It indicates a highly developed form of medical science.
6. Religion or religious practices of the Harappan people are difficult to establish. Some Indus valley seals show *swastikas*, which are found in other religions worldwide. In view of the large number of figurines found in the Indus valley, some scholars believe that the Harappan people worshipped a Mother Goddess symbolizing fertility.

The Aryan Civilization

The decline of such a highly advanced urban civilization and the rise of the early Vedic civilization overlap to an extent, as from 1500 BCE onwards, we come across in north-western part of India a civilization, which was able to establish itself—firmly called the Vedic civilization or the Aryan civilization. The Vedic period was a period in history during which the *Vedas* were composed. The time span of the period is uncertain. Philological and linguistic evidence indicates that the *Rigveda*, the oldest of the *Vedas*, was composed roughly between 1700-1100 BCE, and this period is also referred to as the early Vedic period. The Vedic period heralded the period of Aryan culture in India, which although first settled in the north-western part of India, Gradually spread to the Ganga-Yamuna doab. The Aryans were wandering herdsmen without the settled lifestyle, permanent architecture, and systematic urban planning observed in the Indus Civilization. They invaded India, imposing their social and philosophical ideas and introducing a pattern of life that was to persist for centuries. During this time period two groups of religious scriptures came into existence—the *Vedas* and the *Upanishads*—which had a profound effect on the development of Indian culture, thought, and religion. Transmission of texts in the Vedic period was by oral tradition or in *shruti* and a literary tradition set in only in post-Vedic times. Despite the difficulties in dating the period, the *Vedas* can safely be assumed to be several thousands of years old.

The Vedic period, that is the period from 1500 to 600 BCE displays the following features:

Tribal Assemblies (Vidatha)

The term *vidatha* is mentioned several times in the *Rigveda* and seems to be the most important assembly in the *Rigvedic* period. The *vidatha* was an assembly meant for secular, religious and military purposes. The *Rigveda* only once indicated the connection of woman with the *sabha* whereas *vidatha* is frequently associated with woman.

Women actively participated in the deliberations with men. It seems that the *vidatha* was the earliest folk assembly of the Indo-Aryans, performing all kinds of functions—economic, military, religious and social. Produces were distributed in the *vidatha*.

The members discussed the exploits of heroes, and conducted war against the hostile tribes. The *vidatha* also provided common ground to clans and tribes for the worship of their gods.

Sabha

The term *sabha* denotes both the assembly and the assembly hall. The latter sense comes from the later Vedic texts. This assembly was also attended by woman who was called *sabhavati*. It was basically a kin-based assembly and the practice of women attending it was stopped in later Vedic times.

A passage in the *Rigveda* speaks of the *sabha* as a dicing and gambling assembly. It was also associated with dancing, music, witchcraft, and magic. It discussed pastoral affairs and performed political and administrative functions and exercised judicial authority.

Samiti

All the six references to *samiti* come from the latest books of the *Rigveda* showing that it assumed importance only towards the end of the *Rigvedic* period. It is generally agreed that the early *samiti* was a folk assembly in which people of the tribe gathered for transacting tribal business.

According to Ludwig it was a core comprehensive conference, which included the common people (vis), the *brahmanas* and the rich patrons. Probably, it was a general tribal assembly. It discussed philosophical issues and was concerned with religious ceremonies and prayers.

A reference in the *Atharvaveda* suggests that the *samiti* was identical with the tribal military unit (*grama*) whose collection was called *samgrama*. However, the political functions of the *samiti* were far more prominent. References suggest that the king was elected and re-elected by the *samiti*.

In the beginning, there was no difference between the *sabha* and the *samiti*. Both are said to be daughters of *Prajapati*. The *Atharvaveda* shows that both were mobile units led by chiefs who kept moving along with the forces.

The only difference between *sabha* and *samiti* seems to be the fact that *sabha* performed judicial functions, which the *samiti* did not. Later, the *sabha* became a small aristocratic body and *samiti* ceased to exist.

Gana

Gana, the technical word for the republic, has been interpreted in most of the *Rigvedic* references in the sense of assembly or troop. A careful study shows that it was a sort of gentile organization of the Indo-Aryans. The leader of the *gana* is generally called *ganapati* and at some places *ganasya* raja.

Parisad

The early *parisad* seems to be a tribal military assembly, partly matriarchal and partly patriarchal. However, the variety of the references to the *parisad* in the *Rigveda* may also have been due to the non-Vedic character of the *parisad*. In later Vedic period it tended to become partly an academy and partly a royal council dominated by the priests, who functioned as teachers and advisers.

Political Organisation

The political units during the *Rigvedic* or the early Vedic period comprised of *Grama* (village), *Vish* and *Jana*. The biggest political unit was that of *Jana*, after which came *Vish* and then, *Grama*. The leader of a *Grama* was called *Gramani*, of a *Vish* was called *Vishpati* and that of *Jana* was known as *Jyeshta*. The *Rashtra* (state) was governed by a *Rajan* (King) and he was known as *Gopa* (protector) and *Samrat* (supreme ruler). The king ruled with the consent and approval of the people. There were four councils, namely *Sabha, Samiti, Vidhata* and *Gana*, of which women were allowed to attend only two, *Sabha* and *Vidhata*. The duty of the king was to protect the tribe, in which he was assisted by the *Purohita* (chaplain) and the *Senani*.

However, the concept of territory was completely absent. The tribal chief or the *rajan* was the leader of the people belonging to a particular tribe and not the ruler of any territory. This is why he was known as *janasyagopa* or *gopatijanasya*. The terms for territory are not common in the *Rig-Veda*. Although the term *Jana* which means tribe is used 275 times, the term *Janapada* does not occur even once.

The *Rigvedic* king, it is believed, was one of the equals whose hereditary position was not unquestioned. Several references suggest that the king owed his office to the choice of the people. Most references to the election of the king by the tribesmen (visa) are found in the *Atharvaveda*, but the practice must have begun much earlier. Some stray references to it are found in the *Rigveda* as well. This clearly shows that the tribe elected its chief.

However, some references suggest that kingship or chief ship was confined to certain families, even though the actual examples do not confirm the practice of royal succession in one family for more than three generations. Thus, it is quite doubtful if the law of primogeniture was sharply defined.

This lack of strong hereditary succession came in the way of chief to become the most powerful person. His authority was also curtailed by the tribal assemblies called *sabha*, *samiti*, *vidatha*, praised and *gana*. The *Vrajapati* the *Kulapa* (head of the family) and the *gramani*, all appear to have functioned as military leaders. The only functionary who had some permanent responsibility for defence was purpatis (commanders of mud forts or strongholds).

The *Rigvedic* kings employed spies called *spasa* to keep an eye on the conduct of the people. *Ugra* and *Jivagribha* were officials probably meant for dealing with the criminals and the *madyamasi* seems to have acted as a mediator in disputes.

Society

The four-fold *Varna* system of social division, which is the hallmark of the later Indian society, was virtually absent in the *Rigvedic* period. The two classes that were mentioned in the early *Rigveda* were only two—the *arya* and *dasa*. We have rather evidence of threefold social differentiation in the *Rigveda* as *Brahma*, *Kshatra* and *Vish*, which was primarily a functional division. Other division was based on colour for which the term *Varna*, was used.

Towards the end of the *Rigvedic* period *Brahmana*, *Kshatriya* and *Vish* became distinct groups. At this time the egalitarianism of the early tribal society gave way to class differentiation, which became distinct in the later Vedic period. Numerous social changes took place during the later Vedic period. The concept of *Varna*, along with the rules of marriage, was made quite stiff. Social stratification took place, with the *Brahmins* and the *Kshatriyas* being considered higher than the *Shudras* and the *Vaisyas*. Cows and bulls were accorded religious significance. The importance of agriculture started growing. The families became patriarchal and people began praying for the birth of a son.

During the early *Rigvedic* period, women were to free to move. They could participate in many rituals alongside men. We come across some very educated women like *Ghosha*, *Apala*,

Gargi, Maitreyye, Lopamudra and others who could be placed on an equal footing with men, so far as education is concerned. But gradually, the position and place of women in the society underwent changes and the began to be confined within the four walls of the house. They were deprived of education and were solely treated objects of child-bearing and child-birth.

The basic social unit in the *Rigvedic* society was the patriarchal family which consisted of members belonging to three or four generations. In some instances the family may have included the parents of both the bride and the groom. The family was also the primary unit of production and consumption.

However, some scholars have taken an opposite view that the *Rigvedic* family, as reflected in the earlier stratum of the text, was nuclear or 'elementary' consisting of not more than two generations and the joint family system emerged only towards the close of the *Rigvedic* phase (*kula*, the term for family, is rarely mentioned. *Griha* seems to be a more popular term for family. The eldest male member of the family was known as *Kulapa* (protector of the family).

The social structure was based on kinship, which was rather simple. Terms for father, mother, brother, sister, son and daughter existed distinctly but nephews, grandsons and cousins were known by a common term *naptri.* Father's father and mother's father were known by a common term.

Purohita was another powerful person who accompanied the king to battle and boosted his morale with prayers and spell. Because of the constant wars, the tribal chief or the king commanded the services of a large number of slaves (*dasas*). This, along with the acquisition of large number of cattle, made the chief a wealthy person.

About half a dozen functionaries such as *mahisi* (literally the powerful one, was the crowned queen), the *purohita,* treasurer, the charioteer, the *tankan* (carpenter) and the *duta* (messenger) are mentioned. We do not hear of any code of law nor do we meet with any category of officers to administer justice.

Economy

Economy in the *Rigvedic* period was sustained by a combination of pastoralism and agriculture. There are references, in the *Rigveda*, to levelling of field, seed processing, and storage of grains in large jars. War booty was also a major source of wealth. Economic exchanges were conducted by gift giving, particularly to kings (*bali*) and priests (*dana*), and barter using cattle as a unit of currency. While gold is mentioned in some hymns, there is no indication of the use of coins. Metallurgy is also not mentioned in the *Rigveda*.

The *Rigvedic* king did not have elaborate administrative machinery because the nature of the *Rigvedic* economy could not support it. An economy in which the surplus was very small, the king and his officials received only *Bali*, i.e. offering to a prince or to a god. This tribute was received in kind from the clansmen of the chief and from the conquered people. However, these tributes were neither regular and nor stipulated and hence cannot be called a tax. Similarly, the terms *senani* and *sena* (used 20 times in *Rigveda*) do not show the existence of a regular standing army. The military functions were invested in the Vedic assemblies.

The transition of Vedic society from semi-nomadic life to settled agriculture in the later Vedic age lead to an increase in trade and competition for resources Agriculture dominated the economic activity along the Ganga valley during this period. Agricultural operations grew in complexity and usage of iron implements (*krishna-ayas* or *shyama-ayas*, literally black metal or dark metal) increased. Crops of wheat, rice, and barley were cultivated. New crafts and occupations such as carpentry, leather work, tanning, pottery, astrology, jewellery, dying, arose. Apart from copper, bronze, and gold, later Vedic texts also mention tin, lead, and silver.

Vedic Religious Practices

The Vedic forms of belief are the precursor to modern Hinduism. *Rishis*, composers of the hymns of the *Rigveda*, were considered to be divine. Sacrifices and chanting of verses started gaining significance as the principal mode of worship.

An essential element was the sacrificial fire—the divine *Agni*—into which oblations were poured, as everything offered into the fire was believed to reach God. People prayed for abundance of rain, cattle, sons, long life and gaining 'heaven'. The main deities were *Indra*, *Agni* (the sacrificial fire), and *Soma*. People also worshipped *Mitra—Varuna*, *Surya* (Sun), *Vayu* (wind), *Usha* (dawn), *Prithvi* (Earth) and *Aditi* (the mother of gods). Yoga and *Vedanta* became the basic elements of the religion.

The Age of Jainism and Buddhism

The *Ganga* plain in the northern part of India witnessed the rise of numerous religious sects during the 6th century BCE. Of which the Jain and the Buddhist sects turned out to be the most prominent. The root behind the rise of Jainism and Buddhism can be traced to the later Vedic and post Vedic society, which was highly hierarchical and unequal. Naturally, there was tension in the society and the downtrodden and the socially underprivileged tried to break this stifling and static social structure. Besides, with the expansion of an agricultural economy, large scale settlement began in the middle-*Ganga* plain. The agricultural economy based on the iron ploughshare required bullocks for ploughing. However, the Vedic rituals and sacrifices required killing of the cattle's. Finally, the Vedic society with its emphasis on the *varnashrama* did not hold the *Vaishyas* in high esteem and the *Vaishyas* were accorded a place only after the *Brahmanas* and the *Kshatriyas*. But their economic position was quite high. So they required a religion which is suited to their needs. All these get manifested in the two most predominant religions of the time—the Jainism and the Buddhism.

The features of Jainism are mentioned below:

1. It was a first serious attempt to mitigate the evils of the hierarchical Vedic society.
2. Jainism rejected Sanskrit as it was the language of the Brahmins and instead used *prakrit* language, which saw its growth during this time.
3. It abhors violence and propagates non-violence against all living creatures.

4. But it also gradually turned into a rigid, inflexible religious order.

The features of Buddhism may now be mentioned:

1. It did not recognise the existence of God or soul, which may be regarded as a kind of revolution in the realm of religion, not only at that time but even today.
2. It attacked the *varna* system and the downtrodden, lower caste people was very much attracted to it. It had its appeal to the people of non-Vedic origin and area too.
3. It calls for equality not only of castes but also of gender too. Women were allowed to be members of the *sangha*, which is also of huge importance, particularly, in view of the fact that in the later Vedic society, women lost all their earlier honour and prestige.
4. It was remarkably a liberal and democratic doctrine, which was unthinkable not only at India at that time but difficult to find one at that time in other cultures and countries too.

The Existence and Domination of the Territorial States

The use of iron from the beginning of the Chalcolithic age led to the gradual advancement and progress of human civilization culminating into the rise of territorial states replacing the earlier band or kin-based political organizations from 6th century BCE onwards particularly in the modern day UP and Bihar regions. The extensive use of iron enabled the warrior class to use armoury made up of iron, on the one hand and the peasantry to produce enough food grains, on the other. This while helped the warrior class to engage themselves in war and to extend the boundary of the kingdom and at the same time the state began to have surplus food grains which could a large army. Fortified kingdoms with cities and towns evolved. The notion of geographical territory became important and instead of allegiance to the kin-group or to a person, people started to show their allegiance to the territory or to the *janapada*.

By third century BCE, there were around 40 *janapadas* in the northern and north-western India. But what is more significant is that some of them grew to be bigger territories or the *mahajanapadas*.

During the period of domination of Buddhism, there were 16 *mahajanapadas* or what is called *shoroshmahajanapada*. Of these *Kasi*, *Vatsa*, *Kosala* and *Magadha* in northern India and *Gandhara* and *Kamboja* in north-western India were large and powerful kingdoms. From 6th century BCE onwards, the history of India was the history of struggle and war are amongst these kingdoms for supremacy. By the end of the 4th century BCE, *Magadha* emerged as the most powerful of these kingdoms.

Dawn of History and Extension of Civilization in Other Parts of India

The transition of the pre-historic period was marked by rural settlements with agricultural produce, production of agricultural surplus, emergence of territorial states, and introduction of writing and written literature, division of society into classes. All these happened in the northern and north-western part of India and the southern Deccan and the eastern India remained outside this process at least till 2nd century BCE. Extension of civilization in these two regions was made possible by the development on the part of the local people, on the one hand and the migration of the people of northern India to these regions, on the other.

In the Deccan three kingdoms were important—the *Pandya*, the *Chola* and the *Chera*. The *Pandya* kingdom occupied the southernmost and the south-eastern part of the India peninsula; the *Chola* kingdom was situated to the north-eastern part of the *Pandyas* and the *Chera* kingdom was at the modern-day Kerala. The principal features of this part of civilization are the following:

1. They were engaged in warfare amongst as also with Sri Lanka indicating the process of expansion of their geographical territory.

2. As it was a relatively later day civilization, it was not just agriculture that dominated their economy. Trading was a very important aspect contributing to the economic flourish of these kingdoms.
3. Spices, particularly pepper, ivory from the tusks of elephants, and pearls from sea shells were important trading items. They had trade links with the West too.
4. Weaving reached a very high level and weaving of complex silk and cotton were important components of trading activity.
5. Division of society into classes with *Brahmanical* dominance gradually evolved and became an important feature of these kingdoms.

In this respect, it may be mentioned that the beginning of civilization in the forms of settled human community, development of an agricultural economy and formation of scripts and writing ability in eastern part of India came much late around fourth to fifth century AD. The civilization of this region displayed more or less the same features that we find in the civilizations of other parts of India. Land based agricultural economy became prominent with signs of advanced economy at some places. A fairly organised state structure evolved with the division of society into classes.

Rise of the Empire

Although ancient India witnessed the rule of the Maurya dynasty during the third and second century BCE, which was a vast empire, the rule of the Gupta dynasty during 335 to 455 AD is politically significant for several reasons. First, although the Gupta empire was smaller in comparison to the Mauryan empire, the Guptas were able to unite the northern India, politically, which is no mean a task. Secondly, with the passage of time, it becomes difficult to unite such a large territory as different areas exhibited different cultures with different kinds of human settlements. Thirdly, there were many lesser kings and feudatories in the Gupta empire, which clearly indicated the Guptas' suzerainty. The Gupta empire displayed certain features, which may be mentioned below:

1. The army was certainly modern as compared to the earlier armies as the Gupta empire's army had cavalry as its core.
2. The judicial system was far more developed under the Guptas than in the ancient times. Several law books were compiled and for the first time civil and criminal administration were clearly demarcated.
3. Decentralised administration could be noticed, which in fact is a hallmark of modern day governance. Provincial and local administration was highly developed.
4. Long distance trading activities were on decline while agricultural economy with signs of feudalism could be noticed. A large part of virgin land came under agriculture but the benefits of these mostly went to new emerging priestly landlord class while the peasants were on the decline in the social and economic hierarchy.
5. The earlier *varna* system was gradually replaced by a *jati* system, that is, the earlier four castes were subdivided into several sub-castes. Two apparently contradictory features informed the caste system of the Gupta period. First, the position of *shudras* improved a bit. As they were allowed to perform certain religious rituals as also to listen to the *Ramayana* and the *Mahabharata*. Secondly, the number of the untouchables increased and their plight also deteriorated.
6. With the rise of establishment of feudalism, the position of women deteriorated a lot. With men investing more on land, they became interested in increasing their family, they became more polygamous and women were treated no more than a property.
7. Religious toleration could be noticed during the rule of the Guptas. Although the society was hierarchical and unequal, there was no record of religious persecution.
8. Finally, art and literature developed and reached a new height. Although art was largely driven by religion literature was remarkably secular.

Conclusion

Gradually, during seventh century onwards, some changes could be noticed in the political, economic and social order which ultimately led to the transition to the medieval society, a few centuries later. A different kind of society came into existence dominated by the landlords who now stood between the state and the peasants. They now began to run the administration which was so long manned by the officials of the state. Similar type of development and changes also occurred in Europe from the sixth century AD. Unlike in the West, Indian ancient society did not employ slaves in the production and slavery was not an institutionalised system in India. In India the onus of production and paying of taxation fell upon the peasants, artisans, traders and agricultural labourers, who principally belonged to the *vaishyas* and *shudra* castes. There were signs of revolt from these castes and land began to be granted on a large scale to the Brahmans and temples just as they were granted in Europe to church. The rise of the landlords as a very powerful economic and social class ultimately paved the way for transition from an ancient to a medieval society.

Further Reading

Altekar, A.S. (2002). *State and Society in Ancient India*, Delhi: Motilal Banarsidass.

Sharma, R.S. (1989). *Origin of the State in India*, Bombay: University of Bombay.

——— (1996). *Aspects of Political Ideas and Institutions in Ancient India*, Delhi: Motilal Banarsidass.

——— (2005). *India's Ancient Past,* New Delhi: Oxford University Press.

——— (2009). *Rethinking India' Past,* New Delhi: Oxford University Press.

Thapar, Romila (2000). *History and Beyond*, New Delhi: Oxford University Press.

2

Kautilya and The Theory of State (371-283)

Peu Ghosh

I
INTRODUCTION

Kautilya (371-283 B.C.) was the chief advisor and minister of Chandragupta Maurya and the author of the treatise titled *Arthashastra*. Though there are disputes regarding the actual identity of *Kautilya* as *Chanakya* or *Vishnugupta* and also the authorship of the *Arthashastra* yet it is undeniable that *Arthashastra* is a magnificent exposition of statecraft, public administration, diplomacy, war strategies and economic policies. There is also confusion about the actual time period of *Arthashastra*. Usually the traditional view opines that it was written towards the end of fourth century BC. While some modern thinkers put the date before the *Mauryan* period while some refer to much later period. Commonly, it is accepted that *Arthashastra* was written between fourth century B.C. and two century B.C. *Arthashastra*, the text disappeared only to be rediscovered by R. Shamasastry in 1904 who brought out Sanskrit translation in 1909 and English translation in 1915.

Usually *Arthashastra* is referred to as 'science of politics', 'science of material gain', 'science of polity', and 'treatise on polity'. Some scholars refer *Arthashastra* as 'science of political economy' (Boesche 2003). This Indian treatise is a remarkable contribution towards Ancient political thought in India. The *Arthashastra* comprises fifteen *Adhikaranas* (books). Book I is 'Concerning Discipline', Book II is on 'The Duties of Government Superintendents', Book III is 'Concerning Law',

Book IV is on 'The Removal of Thorns', Book V is on 'The Conduct of Courtiers', Book VI is on 'The Source of Sovereign States', Book VII is on 'The End of the Six-Fold Policy', Book VIII is 'Concerning Vices and Calamities', Book IX is on 'The Work of an Invader', Book X is on 'Relating to War', Book XI is on 'The Conduct of Corporations', Book XII is on 'Concerning a Powerful Enemy', Book XIII is on 'Strategic Means to Capture a Fortress', Book XIV is on 'Secret Means' and Book XV is on 'The Plan of a Treatise'.

However, Kautilya's powerful exposition on the *Saptanga* theory of the state, *Dandaniti* and Diplomacy need special mention among other concepts and ideas which he propounded.

II
KAUTILYA'S POLITICAL THOUGHT

Saptānga Theory

Arthashastra comprises not only *rāja-nīti* (conduct of Kings) or *danda-nīti* (science of punishment), but it contains an exclusive elaboration of what can be said a categorization of the various elements that compose the kingdom. For Kautilya, a *rājya* (the State) or the body-politic consists of seven *angas* (limbs) or *prakrtis* (constituent elements). It is because of these seven *angas* a *rājya* is described as a *Saptānga* organism. Scholars classify this as an abstract and juristic conception of state.

The seven *angas* or *prakrtis* as contained on Chapter I of Book I can be underlined as:

[1] *Svāmin* or *rāja* (the sovereign); [2] *Amātya* (the ministers); [3] *Janapada* or *rastra* (the rural countryside and its people/ territory and its population; [4] *Durga* (forts and fortified towns including small township); [5] *Kośa* (treasury or exchequer); [6] *Danda* or *bala* (army) and [7] *Mitra* or *suhrt* (friends and allies).

The seven *angas* need an elaboration to get an idea of the complete scheme of a *rajyas* (the state).

[1] *Svāmin*—He is the sovereign owing allegiance to none. He should work towards maintenance of Dharma which would help retain the social order based on the family, property and

caste. Welfare of the people, *Yogakshema*, would be his primary objective. To prepare himself to become fit for kingship Kautilya has given an elaborate account of the strict regime of discipline for the King and Princes in Book I 'Concerning Discipline' in Chapter V and VII he talks about the education of the Princes and restraint of the organs of senses, i.e., shaking off of the aggregate of six enemies, namely, lust, anger, greed, vanity *(mána)*, haughtiness (*mada*) and overjoy (*harsha*). Kautilya prescribes that a Prince should maintain celibacy till the age of sixteen and after that he shall observe the ceremony of *tonsure* (*godana*) and marry. Kautilya also speaks about day to day even hour to hour education, restraint and discipline that should be observed by the Princes and Kings. They ought to keep company of aged and receive education in *Purana, Itibritta* (history), *Akshyaika* (tales), *Udaharana* (illustrative stories), *Dharmasastra, Arthashastra* and *Itahasa.* A well educated and disciplined King will be in power unopposed. The duty of a King is to preserve the *varnashrama* by preventing people to swerve from their respective duties and imposing punishment (*danda*) on those violating their duties. Kautilya says in the happiness of his subjects lies his happiness and in their welfare lies the welfare of the King. Whatever pleases the King should not be considered as good but whatever is pleases his subjects will be considered good. Therefore, a King shall be active and discharge his duty and with these he can achieve both the desired ends and abundance of wealth.

In a nutshell, in Book VI—Chapter I concerning the source of sovereign states, Kautilya talks about the best qualities of a King. Born of high family, possessing valour, virtuous truthful, not addicted to procrastination, powerful to control his neighbouring kings, having an assembly of ministers of high quality and possessing self discipline are some of the right qualities of a King among others qualities mentioned by Kautilya. An unrighteous King with vicious character even though he may be an emperor can fall prey to the wrath of his subjects or even his enemies. On the other hand, a wise King trained in politics even though he may possess a small territory can expand his territory and may not be defeated.

[2] *Amātya*—This refers to the ministers, counselors, adhyaksas or heads of secretarial departments including offices of higher or lower ranks and even the clerical staff—the whole bureaucracy who have devotion towards the *Svāmin*. Kautilya says that sovereignty (*rájatva*) is only possible with assistance. A single wheel can never move so the King must employ ministers and listen to their opinion. Kautilya talks about the qualities of persons who are to be employed as Councillors or Priests. Only persons who were good, honest, sincere and free from vices and were persons of dignity, character, foresight and integrity were to be appointed as ministers. However, above all qualification and capacity to perform one's work was most important in case of ministerial appointments.

The King assisted by the Prime Minister (*Mantri*) and his High Priest should examine the character of his ministers (*amātya*) appointed in government departments. He will offer them religious allurement, monetary allurement, love allurement and allurement under fear (Book I, Chapter 10) and test their integrity and purity of character. The Prime Minister/s (*mahámátra*) will also be tested by him similarly. Of the tried ministers, those tested under religious allurements shall be employed in civil and criminal courts, those tested of monetary allurements shall get employed as revenue collectors and chamberlain, those tested of love allurements can be employed to superintend pleasure grounds and those tested under allurement of fear can be employed to immediate services. However, those who have been tested of all these allurements shall be appointed as Prime Ministers (*mantrinah*). The King will set the spies into operations to find out the purity and impurity of the characters of his ministers (*amātya*).

[3] *Janapada*—This term is sometimes used interchangeably. Sometimes it is used to mean territory and sometimes it is used to mean population. Therefore, it can be said that Kautilya may have used it to mean the territory and its population. He talked about constructing villages on new sites or old ruins either by inducing foreigners to immigrate or by moving excessive population from thickly populated areas of his own Kingdom.

The villages so formed will have population of not less than hundred families and not more than five hundred families of agricultural people with boundaries and capable of protecting each other. There shall be a *stháníya*, a fortress of that name in the centre of eight-hundred villages, a *dronamukha* in the centre of four-hundred villages and a *khárvátika* in the centre of two-hundred villages. There would be a sangrahana in the midst of a collection of ten villages.

[4] *Durga*—Kautilya talks about construction of forts on all four quarters of the four boundaries of the Kingdom. He suggests about four kinds of forts a water fort (*audaka*), a mountainous hill fort (*párrvata*), a desert fort (*dhánvana*) and a forest fort (*vanadurga*). Water and mountain fortifications were ideal for defending populous centers and forest fortifications are habitations in wilderness. For him fort is a vital part of the kingdom. Kautilya opines that whoever between the two kings builds an impregnable fort which will be inaccessible by nature and involve less expenditure, will register a better position than the other. He gives details about the construction of forts in Book II, Chapter III.

[5] *Kośa*—is the treasury is another important element of the state. A healthy treasury would ensure the prosperity of a state as well as maintenance of internal and external independence of a state. Kautilya says that justly obtained through inheritance or acquired by self, a rich treasury capable to withstand calamities of a long duration is the best treasury.

[6] *Bala*—This refers to army and Kautilya mentions six types of armies. He mentions six types of armies—hereditary forces, hired troops, soldiers of fighting corporations, troops belonging to an ally, troops belonging to an enemy and soldiers of wild tribes.

Kautilya categorizes the army into *maula* (the standing army), *bhrita* (the territorial army), *sreni* (the militia), *mitra* (the ally's army), *amitra* (alien forces), and *atavi* (tribal forces). Of these six types—*sreni* refers to mercenaries and the first three were drawn from the citizens of the country. The last two, *amitra* and *atavi*, were deemed untrustworthy and unreliable, plunder being their only goal, and hence to be used only as a last resort or as disposable troops.

[7] *Mitra*—This is an ally and the seventh component of a *rājya*. Kautilya classifies allies as *sahaja* and *kritrima*. *Sahaja* is traditional ally whose friendship came down from the time of father and grandfather and his kingdom was situated near the territory of the immediate neighbouring enemy. *Kritrima* was an ally whose friendship was acquired for the protection of wealth and life of one's kingdom. Kautilya always preferred *sahaja* ally than the *kritrima* one. Kautilya talks about enemy too. Thus, it can be said that Kautilya looked at the state both externally and internally. By discussing ally or *mitra* and enemy or *ari*, he thinks in the international sphere too.

The seven elements of sovereignty or the *saptanga* are like seven pillars of the Kingdom, each one an indispensable pillar and the source of sovereignty of the state.

Kautilya propounds a state which aims at not only maintenance of law and order but maintenance, protection, preservation and promotion of a social order that is identified as *Varnashramadharma* (class, stage system). Kautilyan state also aims at optimization of use of resources for the benefit of the state and its citizens. The nature of state he articulated was that of a welfare state. The State was to be involved in *Yogakshema* or promotion of happiness and welfare of the citizens. Therefore, the main function of the state was maximization of welfare.

The primary functions of state as upheld by Kautilya were:

(1) Upholding the social order which was maintenance of *Varnashramadharma* (class, stage system) through the observance of *Dharma* (duty).

(2) *Yogakshema* (welfare of the citizens) which implies well-being, prosperity and happiness.

(3) Maintaining common law for all citizens as contained in ancient customs and usages of the land.

(4) Protecting the society from internal disturbances by preserving internal order and protecting it from external aggression.

(5) Maintenance of public works, consular and diplomatic services with the help of different departments of the state.

(6) Saving society from natural disaster as well as supernatural calamities.

Moral, spiritual and material conditions of people came within the purview of *Yogakshema.* All round public welfare was the primary objective of the state through the promotion of *Dharma* (by fostering feeling of piety), *Artha* (by encouraging trade, industry and agriculture) and *Kama* (by ensuring peace and order and by encouraging fine arts). The duty of the king was to maintain *Dharma* and to protect his subjects and give security and justice. Therefore, among other duties of the king like upholding social order, enforcement of *Svadharma* (doing one's duty), maintenance of public works, protection of state and society and the like, the primary duty of the king was *Yogakshema.* Kautilya maintains that *Danda* (force) is needed to promote proper and equitable distribution of social gains for material prosperity and spiritual enhancement of a kingdom (Kohli 1995).

Dandaniti

For Kautilya, there were only four sciences from where all that concerns about righteousness and wealth can be learnt, namely, *Anvikshaki*, the triple *Vedas* (*Trayi*), *Varta* (agriculture, cattle breeding and trade i.e., economics) and *Dandaniti* (science of government). Kautilya is slightly different from his predecessors Manu and even the school of *Brihaspati.* While Manu acknowledges three (the triple *Vedas*, *Varta* and the science of government), the school of *Brihaspati* accepts the existence of two sciences (*Varta* and science of government).

Anvikshaki comprises the philosophy of *Sankhya, Yoga* and *Lokayata*. *Anvikshaki* consists of the whole body of scholastic philosophy which bestows the goodness of foresight, speech and action and helps in developing a steady mind. A King with the full knowledge of *Anvikshaki* can execute the triple *Vedas*, or *Varta* and even *Dandaniti* with great skill because *Anvikshaki* is often identified as the science of logic and reasoning.

Triple *Vedas* determine the duties of the four castes and of the four orders of religious life. The king shall be cautious that no four castes should deviate from their duties which will bring in happiness and progress.

Varta is concerned with the economic activities which constitute the prosperity of a kingdom and it brings grains, cattle, gold, forest produce and free labour which enrich the royal treasury. It is through *Varta* that the king exercises his control over his and his enemy's party.

To Kautilya however, the well being and progress of these three sciences depends upon the cardinal principle of *Danda* or punishment and *Dandaniti* is the law of punishment or may be classified as science of government. The King by using *Dandaniti* can secure his acquisitions and improve them too. To keep this world going the sceptre (*udyatadanda*) must be kept raised as this sceptre will help to keep the people under control. *Dandaniti*, Kautilya observes, is the right path to gain the respect of the people as when *danda* or punishment is awarded with due consideration, the people become devoted to righteousness and works towards production of wealth and enjoyment. When a ruler imposes severe punishment he creates repulsive behaviour among people and when a ruler imposes mild punishment he becomes contemptible. When a punishment is ill-awarded due to greed, anger or ignorance, there might be possibility of public fury even the most peaceful of all people like the hermits or ascetics there can be resentment. In the absence of *Dandaniti*, there will be absolute anarchy and a situation which can be identified as *matsyanyayamudbhavayati* where the strong prevails over the weak.

Danda, therefore, can be the only thing which can secure life and safety and this in turn is dependent on discipline (*vinaya*). A student, after investiture with scared thread was supposed to learn the triple *Vedas*, the science of *Abhikshaki*, the science of *Varta* and the science of *Dandaniti*. Education in such fields was to be imparted through specialist teachers and practitioners (Bhaduri 2007).

Diplomacy

Kautilya had also given a rigorous thought about conducting of foreign policy. A great part of the *Arthashastra* is devoted to the conduct of war, diplomacy, foreign policy, elaborate spy system and covert operations to achieve the ends of a state.

Kautilya gives us a unique arrangement of twelve kingly *prakrtis* or primary kings forming the statul circle or *dvādaśa-rāja-mandala*. The *mandala* was supposed to comprise:

[1] *vijigīsu* (aspirant conqueror) who is to be at the centre, [2] *ari* who is situated immediately on the border area of the conqueror, [3] *mitra* is the king who is situated close to the enemy but is separated from the conqueror and is a friend of the conqueror, [4] *ari-mitra* (enemy's friend), [5] *mitra-mitra* (friend's friend), [6] *ari-mitra-mitra* (enemy's friend's friend). This comprises the frontal area of the conqueror. In the rear the arrangement consists of [7] *pārsnigrāha* (the rearward enemy), [8] *ākranda* (rearward friend who can come forward to help *vijigīsu* at his call, [9] *pārsnigrāhasāra* who is the friend and ally of rearward enemy and [10] *ākrandasāra* is the friend and ally of rearward friend, [11] *Madhyama* king, or the neutral king is the one who is close to both the *vijigīsu* and his *ari* and he is able to show his strength to both, [12] *Udāsina* king is the most powerful neutral king who is very highly placed in strength and resources (Mukherjee 2004).

The conqueror, his friend, and his friend's friend are the three primary kings constituting a circle of states. As each of these three kings possesses the five elements of sovereignty, such as the minister, the country, the fort, the treasury, and the army, a circle of states consists of eighteen elements. Thus, there are four primary circles of States, twelve kings, sixty elements of sovereignty, and seventy-two elements of states. Each of the twelve primary kings shall have their elements of sovereignty, power, and end. Strength is power and happiness is the end. Strength is again of three kinds—intellectual strength, strength of sovereignty arising from a prosperous treasury and a strong army and physical strength. The end is also of three types attainable by intellect, strength of sovereignty and physical strength. Possession of power and happiness makes a King superior or inferior. Thus a King should always work towards augmenting his power and elevating his happiness. This can be done by adopting a six-fold policy as proposed by Kautilya.

Diagram

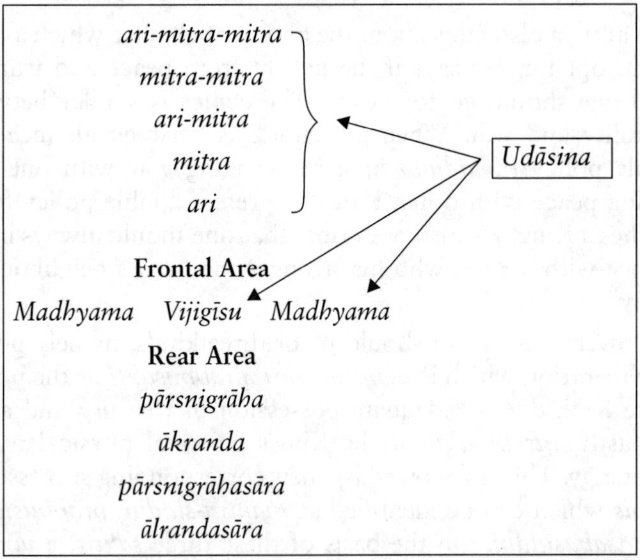

Statul Circle or *dvādaśa-rāja-mandala*

The Circle of States is the source of six-fold policy. Kautilya in Chapter I of Book VI stated six fold causes of political action in diplomacy (*sādgunya*) which can be identified as peace (*sandhi*), war (*vigraha*), expedition or campaign for conquest (*yāna*), neutrality (āsana), dubious attitude (*dvaidhibhāva*) and alliance (*samāṣraya*). He sees four strategies of exercising power namely, *saama* (peace/conciliation), *daana* (gift), *bheda* (dissension/rupture) and *danda* (force). If war was fought then Kautilya prescribes three kinds of warfare like open war fought traditionally, concealed war which is fought using guerilla tactics and silent war which can be fought using covert actions against the enemy. The way prosperity and security (*Yogakshema*) of the community as far as Kautilya is concerned depended upon the peaceful calmness (*śama*) and adventurous energy (*vyāyāma*) of the King.

Upon consideration of one's resources and strength of the enemy, the King has to decide whether he wants peace or war. Therefore, a king in the circle of sovereign state shall adopt the six-fold policy and make an effort to move on from the policy of deterioration to stagnation and finally to progress.

Kautilya also talks about the nature of alliance which a King should opt for. He says if the benefit from peace and war are equal one should go for peace. The choice is similar between neutrality and war. When the choice is between alliance and double policy (*dvaidhibhāva*), i.e., waging war with one and making peace with other, Kautilya prefers double policy for it enriches a King. He also prescribes that one should always make alliance with a King who his stronger than one's neighbouring enemy.

Power to Kautilya should be of three kinds, namely power of deliberation which is *mantra-śakti, prabhuśakti* or the power of the King due to adequate possession of treasury and army and lastly, *utsāhaśakti* or the King's personal physical power and energy. This is followed by their corresponding successes or *siddhis* which can be identified as *mantra-siddhi, prabhusiddhi* and *utsahasiddhi.* On the basis of these three *saktis,* a *vijigīsu* king who is equal to his enemy is called *sama*, when stronger than enemy then called *jyayan* and when weaker than enemy then he is called *hina.* An intelligent application of *sādgunya* or diplomacy will lead attainment of target. The *vijigīsu* king with proper application of *sādgunya* can cross over the state of deterioration (*ksaya*) to that of stagnation (*sthāna*) and then gradually from the state of stagnation to that of augmentation or progress or *vriddhi.* However, before adopting a particular policy of *sādgunya*, the *vijigīsu* king must weigh his options among the six-fold diplomatic actions his strengths in comparison to his enemy. A king must first find out whether he is equal, superior or inferior in wealth, resources, strength, arms and the like and then adopt a particular diplomatic posture. Depending upon his strength he can enter into *sandhis* or alliances in the nature of *hīnasandhi* with the enemy. The king may also enter into alliances with allies of superior, equal or inferior status to confront a powerful enemy. Kautilya obviously sees sharp intellect more powerful than real warfare. He prescribes covert means of hitting the enemy like using of secret methods of sowing dissension among the hostile chiefs, engaging beautiful women for creating mutual jealousy, engage spies, application of poison and other covert means to bring destruction to the enemy (Basak 1967).

II
RELEVANCE

Kautilya made a great contribution towards Indian political thought and it was not only that he became relevant during his time but his relevance is still undeniable today. The real politics in contemporary scenario may not purely correspond to Kautilya's exposition of political ideas about state, foreign policy and economic activities, yet their significance cannot be totally erased off. Rule of law is the cardinal principle in running most of the democratic countries. Welfare of the citizens is regarded as a goal in democratic countries though welfarism has undergone change after globalization took over the economic activity. Regarding conducting of foreign policy diplomacy still is the most viable option. The considerations which Kautilya had given for adopting a particular posture discussed above is still relevant in relations/politics among nations. Even if one tries to cite India-Pakistan relation and play of real politic, diplomacy and the options chosen to deal with one another cannot be said to be dramatically different from Kautilya's scheme, only that the situation is different. The mandala theory may not be quite similar to the concept of balance of power yet is a commendable scheme of statul arrangement to be conceived so many years ago. National power on the basis of one's resources is a determining factor in international relations and this basic truth was propagated by Kautilya long ago—a concept so contemporary.

If one visualizes the Chinese design of 'Strings of Pearls'*, it can be said to be a modern day exposition of mandala

*Strings of Pearls—A Chinese strategy to encircle India by building or developing relations with States around India and isolate India in South Asia and limit her extension of activities beyond this region and also check India's activities in the South China Sea, Indian Ocean and Arabian Sea.

theory even in the minimum sense of it but definitely is an exposition of balance of power between China and India. China is aware that it has to limit growing India's influence in South Asia, Southeast Asia, Central Asia and Persian Gulf to ensure China's energy security supplies and political and strategic preponderance in this entire region. China wants to achieve this by establishing economic and military nodes in various countries by using diplomacy and economic packages. China has targeted countries like Myanmar, Bangladesh, Nepal, Sri Lanka, Maldives, Mauritius and Seychelles, Thailand and Cambodia and above all Pakistan. Strategic investments are being made by China in Hainan Island in the South China Sea, the Straits of Malacca, port developments in Chittagong in Bangladesh, Sittwe, Coco, Hianggyi, Khaukphyu, Mergui and Zadetkyi Kyun in Myanmar, Laem and Chabang in Thailand and Sihanoukville in Cambodia.

The problems discussed in *Arthashastra* are of the most practical kind faced by the Kings and solutions suggested are still relevant and practicable in the modern administrative world. Espionage and the liberal use of provocative agents are recommended on a large scale in Chapter XI of Book I on The Institution of Spies. Murder and false accusations were to be used by a king's secret agents without any thoughts to morals or ethics. There are chapters for kings to help them to keep in check the premature ambitions of their sons, and likewise chapters intended to help princes to thwart their fathers' domineering authority too [Book I on Concerning Discipline]. Kautilya is a political realist of par excellence. The Political Realism, a dominant school of thought in International Relations can be said to have its roots in the classical thinking of Kautilya manifested in *Arthashastra*.

The de-glorified or heinous methods of conducting statecraft may have to be accepted with a critical eye but nature of politics and control of power have not changed much. Kautilya needs more readings and thorough critical research and definitely his propositions if accommodated and moulded with the changing times will give a new dimension to statecraft, diplomacy, war, strategic thinking, public administration, urban planning, public finance and economic planning and various other fields.

Many a time parallels are drawn between Kautilya and Machiavelli. Though both lived during different times, almost 2000 years apart, yet striking similarities can be found in their writings. Both aimed at unification of Kingdoms destructed by external aggression or internal strife. Kautilya wrote against the backdrop of Alexander's invasion of India and ensuing unstable political conditions. Machiavelli wrote during troubled period in Italian history post reformation and renaissance when Italian city states were in a chaotic condition. Both Kautilya and Machiavelli though totally did not disregard ethics yet both understood that unscrupulous and ruthless measures had to be taken to suppress internal disruptions and external aggressions.

Machiavelli does not set his Prince such high standards as Kautilya does yet both wrote almost on similar terms. While Chanakya strongly drew from Hindu philosophy and sees the world through the spectacles of Hindu cosmology, Machiavelli describes the world through human nature but the ends both advocate being quite similar.

Kautilya talked about virtue in politics and restraint of senses and passions as prescribed in Book I Concerning Discipline. Machiavelli considered people to be greedy, selfish and cruel and only understood force. Therefore, Machiavelli prescribed strong political force to restrain deviant behaviour and virtue to him meant that the Prince could resort to unprincipled means not sanctioned by religious or ethical standards and still be virtuous for the sake of maintaining his sway over the state and his subjects. Yet, as country's security and integrity was top a priority and for that both proposed all kinds of fraud and use of violent methods and Kautilya went as far as using poisonous powder for attaining political goal. While Machiavelli acknowledged the role of fortune Kautilya believed in *Karma*. Though both used method of observation yet Kautilya did not make an exhaustive reference to ancient Indian history while Machiavelli used lot of examples from Roman history. Kautilya's *Arthashastra* seems to work out and explain every minute details of statecraft and is far more exhaustive than Machiavelli's work. Both have earned notoriety because of their pessimistic propositions. However, it is undeniable that diplomacy is a mixture of hard and soft policies and approximately corresponds to the methods and forms explained by Kautilya years ago or for that matter Machiavelli. Years ago Kautilya talked about civil service and welfare state which are concepts quite modern.

As long as states remain as prime actors in international relations and national security tops agenda of national interests of all states, Kautilya's dictums will stand the test of time. Though in whole part the Kautilyan principles cannot be applied in the present context of national and international politics yet Kautilyan assumptions, saptanga theory, concepts of diplomacy, idea about civil service, duties of a ruler and a full-fledged espionage system will be respected even in contemporary politics.

References

Basak, R.G. *Some Aspects of Kautilya's Political Thinking*. Burdwan: The University of Burdwan, 1967.

Bhaduri, Nrisinghaprasad. *Dandaniti*. Kolkata: Sahitya Sansad, 2007.

Boesche, Roger. January 2003. "Kautilya's *Arthaśāstra* on War and Diplomacy in Ancient India". *The Journal of Military History*, 67(1): 9-37.

Kautilya, *Arthashastra*, Translated into English by R. Shamasastry, https://archive.org/details/Arthasastra_English_Translation

Kohli, Ritu. *Kautilya's Political Theory: Yogaskhema—the Concept of Welfare State*. New Delhi: Deep & Deep Publications, 1995.

Mukherjee, Bharati. *Pracheen Bharatborsher Rashtranoitik Chinta*, Kolkata: Sri Bhumi Publishing, 2004.

Suggested Readings

Ghosal, U.N. "A History of Indian Political Ideas: The Ancient Period and the Period of Transition to the Middle Ages". *American Historical Review* 66 (4), 1961.

Sharma, R.S. *Aspects of Political Ideas and Institutions in Ancient India*. Delhi: Motilal Banarasidass, 1991.

Varma, Vishwanath Prasad. *Ancient and Medieval Indian Political Thought*. Agra: Lakshmi Narain Agarwal, 1961.

3

Manu and Ancient Indian Society

Rajasri Basu

I
INTRODUCTION

The name of Manu appears, in different ways, on different occasions, if one studies the ancient Indian political thought. In Hindu mythology, Manu is regarded as the first man. According to legends, Kasyap and Aditi, who were born asexually from Brahma, the creator of the world, were the first husband and wife of this world. *Surya* or the Sun was born from the womb of Aditi and Manu was born from the womb of *Usha* who was the wife of *Surya*. Manu was the son of *Surya* and he is called *Vaivasvata* as *Vivasvan* is another name for *Surya*. The entire mankind or the *Manabjati* is born from Manu. The name has an etymological connection with the Sanskrit verb *man*, "to think." Manu is also regarded as the legendary author of one of the *Smritis* or law code, which is called *Manusmriti*. The name of Manu appears in the *Vedas* or the *Srutis*, which are prior to the *Smritis*, as the performer of the first *yagna* or sacrifice. He is also known as the first king, and most rulers of ancient India traced their genealogy back to him, either through his son (the solar line) or his daughter (the lunar line).

It has again been mentioned in *Arthashastra* by Kautilya that overtaken by a state of anarchy, people elected *Vaivasvat Manu* as their king and undertook to pay 1/6th of their, 1/10th of their articles and apportion of god. In return for these, the King guaranteed social welfare of the people by undertaking to suppress acts of mischief afflicting the guilty with taxes and coercion. It may be regarded as a contract by which the King arose as a supreme source of authority, who cannot be disregarded.

However, there is a lot of confusion surrounding the identity of Manu—whether he is a mythical figure or not, his contribution, whether there was a single or several Manus and so on. The Vedic texts—the earliest written sources of ancient Indian polity are primarily religious in nature. It becomes a bit difficult to decipher and isolate facts of polity from it. That is why, according to most of the scholars of ancient India, *Dharmasutras*—also known as *Dharmashastras* are the earliest written books throwing light on the duties of the king, laws regarding taxation, protection of property and so on. The *Dharmasutras* were written in prose. In other words, *Dharmasutras* are important literary sources of ancient Indian polity.

These *Dharmasutras* gradually developed into *Smritis* or the corpus of *Smriti* literature, which also deal with different facets of the polity but they are written in verse. *Smriti* denotes tradition in the sense that it portrays the traditions of the rules on *dharma*, especially those of lawful virtuous persons. With regard to legal texts, scholars have commonly translated *Smriti* as "tradition". It is believed that *Smriti* does not have divine origins. *Smriti's* literal translation, "to remember" explains this. In a sense, *Smriti* consists of the memories of wisdom that sages have passed on to their disciples. These memories consist of traditions. It is these memories that make up the second source of dharma and consequently have been recorded to become a written source.

The oldest and the most significant and important *Smriti* is that of Manu. It is popularly called *Manusmriti*, but also labelled as *Manusamhita* or *Manava Dharmashastra*. Noted Indologists assigned its period to 200 BC-200 AD. The text presents itself as a discourse given by Manu, the progenitor of mankind (Manu>Manab=mankind) to a group of seers, or *rishis*, who asked him fervently to tell them the "law of all the social classes". The Sanskrit text was edited in 1913 by P.H. Pandya and in 1920 by J.R. Gharpure. The text was first translated into English (from manuscripts) in 1794 by Sir William Jones. Chapter VII of this text titled *rajdharma* is the most important from the political standpoint as it deals with the duties of the king, lays down the principles of taxation and highlights the importance of the coercive authority of the state.

The text shows the obvious influence of previous *Dharmasutras* and *Arthashastras*. The *Manusmriti* was the first to adopt the term *vyavaharapadas*. These eighteen "Titles of Law" or "Grounds for Litigation" make up more than one fifth of the work and deal primarily with matters of the king, state, and judicial procedure. The *dharma* class of texts were noteworthy because they did not depend on the authority of particular Vedic schools, becoming the starting point of an independent tradition that emphasized *dharma* itself and not its Vedic origins.

The original narrative was subdivided later into twelve chapters. The book is written in simple verse as opposed to the metrical verse of the preceding *dharmasutras*. Manu also introduced a unique "transitional verse" which denoted the end of one subject and the beginning of the next. The treatise is written with a frame story, in which a dialogue takes place between Manu's disciple, *Bhrigu*, and an audience of his own students. The story begins with Manu himself detailing the creation of the world and the society within it, structured around four social classes. *Bhrigu* takes over for the remainder of the work, teaching the details of the rest of Manu's teachings. The audience re-appears twice more, asking first to ask about how Brahmins can be subjected to death, and second to ask the effects of action.

The *Manusmriti* is compiled with a focus on the "doables" of dharma rather than on the actuality of everyday practice in India after the decline and collapse of the Maurya Empire. Thus, it has a normative framework, in the sense that it discusses what should be done to establish dharma rather than on what is being done. Still, its practical application cannot be underestimated. Through intermediate forces such as the instruction of scholars, the teachings did indeed have indirect effect on major segments of the Indian population. It is also an invaluable point of common reference in scholarly debates.

It seems likely that the book was written in a manner which was very mindful to the dangers facing the *Brahmin* community during a time of much change and social upheaval. A renewed alliance between the *Brahmin* and *Kshatra* communities is clearly a goal reflected in the introduction of the *vyavahapadas*. The emphasis which this topic receives can be seen as an offering of solidarity from the religious community to the ruling class.

II
MANU'S CONTRIBUTION IN MEDIEVAL INDIAN POLITICAL THOUGHT

Manu's work or *Manusmriti*, along with being an important literary source of ancient Indian polity, has been viewed as the major law-book for establishing the supreme, sovereign and coercive power of the King, for establishing the stringent social hierarchy in the society and for reaffirming firmly subordinate and submissive role of women in society, which no doubt had been established since the later days of the *Rigvedic* period.

To Manu, unlike Kautilya, the coercive power of the state of force is more important than the welfarist aspect of the state. As Altekar says that to Manu, it is the *danda*, which governs the people, protects all and is the custodian of dharma. The element of justice within *danda* becomes gradually extinct and force has overtaken the place of justice. Moreover, to Kautilya, the importance and value of the seven elements or the *saptaangas* of the State are to be considered as gradually declining. To Manu, however, *svami* or the King and *danda* or the coercive force are more important than the others as these two are necessary for preserving the society and the state against all odds. Manu, however, pointed out that *danda* should be exercised by the king according to law. But there is no doubt that the element of *danda* took considerable significance in post Maurya times, when centrifugal forces had been set in motion due to foreign invasions and internal dissents.

The element of dharma assumes, however, more importance when we come across the narrative regarding how *danda* had been used to check the warring classes within the society. It has been mentioned in the *vayupurana* that the castes or the *varnas* in the society did not perform their respective duties and came into mutual conflict with each other even after the duties of the respective castes or *varnas* in society were settled. In this version, Manu was not the first king but created two first kings, when approached by people—*Priyavrata* and *Uttanapada*, who were vested with *danda* or the rod of authority. Thus, *danda* was used not only to create the state but also to check the mutual struggle amongst the *varnas*. In this way, we come across not only the growing importance of *danda* but the gradual and the stringent division of society into classes.

To Manu, the establishment and preservation of *dharma* were most important duties of the King. For establishing *dharma*, the preservation of the family and prevention of adultery were necessary, which naturally were important duties of the King. Another important duty of the King, according to Manu was the preservation of the caste or the *varna* system. In his view, the kingdom prospers only so long as the purity of the castes was maintained. Otherwise, the kingdom perishes altogether along with the population. In fact, the maintenance of the purity of the castes was the most important duty of the King as it is an indispensable element of *dharma*. The king is there to protect and preserve *dharma*. And if *dharma* is violated, there is bound to be a *pralaya* or the dissolution of the whole social order. A kingdom can prosper only so long as the purity of *varnas* is maintained.

Some of the illustrative codes from *Manusmriti* may be mentioned, which unequivocally established the fact that Manu fervently believed and wanted to establish a society based upon caste divisions for establishing *dharma*.

For the welfare of humanity the supreme creator Brahma, gave birth to the Brahmins from his mouth, the *Kshatriyas* from his shoulders, the *Vaishyas* from his thighs and *Shudras* from his feet. (Manu's code I-31)

God said the duty of a *Shudra* is to serve the upper *varnas* faithfully with devotion and without grumbling. (Manu I-91)

The Brahmin should never invite persons of other *varnas* for food. In case, the latter begs the Brahmin for food, the Braḥmin may give them some left-over. Even these left-over must be served not by the Brahmin but by his servants outside the house. (Manu II-2)

A *Shudra* is unfit of receive education. The upper *varnas* should not impart education or give advice to a *Shudra*. It is not necessary that the *Shudra* should know the laws and codes and hence need not be taught. (Manu IV-78 to 81)

The hierarchical stratification of the society according to castes and the issue of unpaid labour to be provided by the *Shudras* perhaps indicated the development and flourishing of an agrarian society following the pastoral economy. This can also be established from the fact that King was, for the first time, was referred to as *mahipati* or lord of the land by Manu. This established the claim of the King on earth or soil. In some later texts, the world has been described as the wife of the King, that is, with whom the King can enjoy his life with pleasure. In other words, the King became not only the owner of the land but could utilize according to his own wishes. This indicated the existence of an agrarian, feudal, land-based society, the beginning of which could be found during the time of *Manusmriti*.

III
RELEVANCE OF MANU'S THOUGHT

Highly prescriptive and rigid in its thinking, *Manusmriti* not only confirmed and rationalized the caste hierarchy, but also commented and expressed reservations about the capabilities and position of women. However, many would have argued that Manu actually accorded honour and dignity for women but did not believe in the freedom of women. In fact, till the period of colonial India, and at times, even today, Hindu apologists consider the *Manusmriti* as the divine code of conduct and, accordingly, the status of women as depicted in the text has been interpreted as Hindu divine law. At the same time, there is no denying the fact that Manu reserved an inferior and unequal status to women, which are quite clear from many of his laws.

Anthropologists and Indologists through various sources have come to the conclusion that the position and status of women in ancient India varied greatly. For instance, during the early Vedic period, wife enjoyed full rights and regularly participated in religious ceremonies with her husband. We find *Gargi* and *Maitreyi* distinguishing themselves in *Brahmavidya*, the highest knowledge. *Apala* and *Atreyi* were also knowledgeable. Matrimony was not mandatory for women. Unmarried educated, knowledgeable of *Vedas* women were referred to as a *vidushis*.

However, the situation underwent radical changes during the later Vedic period and during the period of the *Smritis*, women were held in lowest esteem and can be compared with the *shudras*. Pre-puberty marriage came to be practiced. According to Manu "Bride should be one third the age of the groom thus a male of twenty-four should marry a girl of eight year. *Manusmriti* laid down various restrictions regarding the traditional rights of women. According to Manu, women are not allowed to do any work independently either inside the house or outside the house Women could perform sacraments and samskars, but these were to be performed silently and no vedic mantras were to be recited. Women were passive observer rather than active participants. She could not even conduct any fast and *vartas* without her husband's permission.

The theory of *Anuloma* and *Pratiloma* was based on such prejudices "Women have desire for ornaments, passion, anger, dishonesty, malice, bad conduct and the like. Women do not care for beauty, nor is their attention fixed on age; they give themselves to the handsome as well as the ugly, just for that he is a man." According to this theory if a woman is chaste, it is because she has not found a proper man, place, or opportunity. It has been mentioned that a women are possessed of love of scandals and the lust for sex. A woman deprived of sex grows old. Though her possession for man, her unstable temper and inherent heartlessness they become disloyal to their husband, however carefully they may be guarded, in this world. She was to be guarded in by her father in her childhood, by her husband in youth and by her sons after the death of her husband (V. 148-49). Thus, the life of an adult woman revolves around her father in her childhood, by her husband in her youth and by her sons in her old age.

As stated earlier, some who believed in the so-called "golden era" of India's past argue that women are treated well and respected by Manu. They ask the modern feminists to take examples from *Manusmriti*. But Indian Liberal feminists and Dalits view the *Manusmriti* as anti-women and anti-Dalit text, where women and Dalits are degraded. Ambedkar in his article "The Rise and Fall of Hindu Women" argues that Hindu religion through its religious texts, such as the *Manusmriti* always degraded women. Sita Agarwal's analysis of the degradation of women in the Vedic period, argues that the continuation of the Vedic religions which collectively referred to as Brahminism is the reason for degradation of women. Ruth Manorama, a Dalit Christian feminist scholar and social activist from Tamil Nadu, traces the roots of the degradation of Dalits and Dalit women to the *Manusmriti*. Surendra Jondhale observes that the ancient Hindu text Chaturvanya treated women as Dalit. Undeniably, in the ancient Hindu religious texts, the "entire Dalit society including men and women did not have equal economic rights. Lower caste women are doubly discriminated: caste and gender. Manu considered women as slaves. Surendra Jondhale has the same criticism of *Manusmriti* for making the women and Dalits inferior to other people; thus the psychological, social and cultural proscriptions unleashed by Manu restricted her autonomy. This lower status of women continued even in the 1000 years of the Muslim rulers and through the Medieval India.

The laws of Manu still are practiced at present time. As Sonia Mahey observes, the horrendous Laws in the *Manusmriti* were incorporated into Hinduism because they were favourable only to the upper castes which form the majority of India. Even today, in modern times, we see the severe oppression and exploitation of Dalit women. Certainly, the Indian social order has been built upon the pillars of the *Manusmriti* says Kumud Pawde.

Since the code of Manu intermingles with the Indian culture and Hindu religion, it is very hard to remove those anti-Dalits and anti-women texts in *Manusmriti*; people consider it as sacred. Therefore, Sita Agarwal suggests: Since such passages cannot be deleted in modern times, nor can the *Vedas* be modified, it hence follows that all Indian feminists must fight against any and all forms of Vedic religion. Unless they do so, Indian women shall forever remain enslaved to Vedic tyranny.

Apart from the Indian feminists, *Manusmriti* has been highly criticised by those, who believe in egalitarianism and in social justice. Dr. B.R. Ambedkar, one of the great champions of social justice and a crusader against caste hierarchy, publicly staged a protest movement against *Manusmriti* when he along with his supporters burnt a copy of *Manusmriti* at the second Conference of the Depressed Classes on December 27, 1927 at Mahad, a small town in Maharashtra. Ambedkar in his decision of burning *Manusmriti* pointed out that it is a religious document of Hindus and is perceived as the constitution by Hindus. Starting from those, the dalit movement in India is based upon *Manuvad*. The burning of *Manusmriti* heralded the birth of protest against *Brahminism* and the beginning of dalit assertion in the Indian polity.

There are some, however, who point out that Manu did not prescribe a caste system based upon birth. He in fact called upon a stratified social system based upon qualities, action and nature of the individual. In fact, this is a *varna* system, which is totally different from a caste system based upon birth. The defenders of Manu point out that the biggest proof of *Manusmriti* proposing *varna* system and not caste system is that in the first Chapter of *Manusmriti*, there is mention of the origin of four *varnas* and no mention of castes or *gotras*. Had caste or gotra been important, Manu would have mentioned which castes belong to *Brahmins*, which to *Kshatriyas*, which to *Vaishyas* and which to *Shudras*.

Notwithstanding this defence, *Manusmriti* is regarded as the principal source, which openly proclaimed casteism and gender discrimination in the Indian society. However, Friedrich Nietzsche, the great German philosopher of the late 19th century eulogised Manu's law book on the ground that it has an affirmation of life. Manu's law book, according to Nietzsche permits oneself to get the upper hand, to become perfect, and to be ambitious of the highest art of living. So, even today, *Manusmriti* remains an enigma; it has been supremely criticised for its gender discrimination and prescription for a caste hierarchy. Still, it has been a very important source of ancient Indian history and remains one of the first law books in the world.

Further Reading

Altekar, A.S. (2002). *State and Society in Ancient India*, Delhi: Motilal Banarsidass.

Sharma, R.S. (1989). *Origin of the State in India*, Bombay: University of Bombay.

——— (1996). *Aspects of Political Ideas and Institutions in Ancient India,* Delhi: Motilal Banarsidass.

——— (2005). *India's Ancient Past,* New Delhi: Oxford University Press.

——— (2009). *Rethinking India' Past,* New Delhi: Oxford University Press.

Thapar, Romila (1960). *Aśoka and the Decline of the Mauryas,* New Delhi: Oxford University Press.

——— (2000). *History & Beyond*, New Delhi: Oxford University Press.

Young, Julian (2010). *Friedrich Nietzsche: A Philosophical Biography*, Cambridge: Cambridge University Press.

SECTION II

Medieval Indian Political Thought

4

Medieval Indian Political Thought: Key Ideas

Kashshaf Ghani

In the history of Indian political thought the medieval or pre-modern era stretching roughly from the thirteenth to the late eighteenth century forms an interesting period, primarily due to the influences from various non-Indian cultures and civilizations. Such influences did not remain limited to the sphere of superficial interactions, but had deeper dynamics which resulted in imparting this period with an individuality of its own, in many ways distinct from its earlier history. The most important element which contributed towards shaping the political ideology of this era was the advent of Islam. The coming of Islam brought with it the richness of Arab and Persian culture and society, which was decisive in providing new direction to an existing political culture. However such influences did not mean a complete overhaul of the indigenous political traditions. It remains undeniable that each society has a personality and receptivity of its own. It can attract and absorb external influences to a degree to which it can assimilate. When such influences become overpowering, leading to disorder in the socio-political balance, it leads to decay of the political culture. The story of medieval India reads no different.

In political and military terms the advent of Islam to Indian shores can be traced to the conquests carried by the Arab commander Muhammad bin Qasim, starting from the coast of Sind deeper into Multan, in the early 8th century. Taking this as the early medieval period, coinciding with the earliest Muslim invasions, the medieval era in Indian history is supposed to begin from the time Muslim conquests resulted in permanent political fortunes in north India, precisely after the victory at the Battle of Tarain in 1193 AD. This led to the foundation of the Delhi Sultanate in 1206 AD. This was followed by the empire of the Mughals which begun after their victory in the Battle of Panipat in 1526 AD. Muslim political domination came to an end with the formal dissolution of the Mughal political structure by the British in 1857 AD.

Political ideas in Islam converged from both the non-Islamic Semitic tradition, and the tradition of Muhammad, the Prophet of Islam. However the roots of political ideas and institutions in Muslim societies remained deeply attached to Islamic religion. Islam in its early stages was an exclusive political doctrine, based on the Koran as its supreme directing, motivating and compelling force. Muslims believed in one God and in their Prophet Muhammad. After the time of Muhammad, the political structure of Islam began to develop and take shape under the institution of the Caliphate held by different dynasties across time and space. As Islam spread across continents, cultures and civilizations its political ideology began to crystallize, though not uniformly, aided both by external influences and various Muslim political theorists. The influences of Plato and Aristotle, especially their moral concerns, are also abundant in the Arabic sources.

Islamic political thought was not merely expressed by the founder but was embodied in the political system he created. Since Muhammad's divine mission was integrally related to state building, it left Muslims obsessed by the idea of communal solidarity and political legitimacy. In the years after the Prophet Muhammad, political theorists framed their ideas around the office of the Caliphate based on the principles of the *Shariat*. It was argued that the Caliphate originated, flourished and existed with the primary aim of ensuring that the *Shariat* is evenly followed throughout the realm, and affairs are conducted in accordance with its principles.

Three basic principles which governed all subsequent political thinking in Muslim societies were:

(a) The *Shariat* or the divine law based on the Quran,
(b) Historical tradition of the early years of Islamic caliphate,
(c) Consensus and solidarity of the Islamic community.

Therefore the framework of political thinking rested firmly on the religious law of Islam. No rule departing from the *Shariat* was justified. The purpose of the state was in principle to serve the *Shariat*. In Islamic political theory the state was considered not only as a necessary organ to check man's natural aggression, but a supreme organisation to regulate life. It was believed that a good king was better than a bad king and a bad king was better than anarchy.

The Islamic concept of sovereignty rests on the Quranic message 'Obey God and the Messenger and those among you in authority'.[1] This message held little ambiguity in the lifetime of the Prophet as his personality combined those of the Messenger and also the one in authority. Lack of clarity arose in the period after the Prophet on the idea of the one in 'authority'. Consensus was achieved when the Caliph, as the representative of the Prophet, was made to combine in himself all forms of authority—political and religious. He depended on the traditions of the Prophet along with the authority of the Quran in his day-to-day governance. With the incorporation of non-Muslim communities within the Caliphate complications began to arise regarding the formulation of legal codes of conduct and the nature of Muslim political authority.

From ninth century onwards scholars in the Islamic world came forward with theories concerning the nature and character of an Islamic state and its ruler. Al Farabi (870-950 AD) argued that the necessity of a political order arose from a mutual collaboration among the common masses who wished to be saved from anarchy and statelessness. For him rulers should be from among those who have qualities of leadership. Such individuals should have certain qualities like, physical beauty, perseverance, sharp memory, erudition, control over senses, fearlessness, truthfulness, etc. He proposed a group of learned advisers who would guide the ruler in all forms of crisis, thereby aiding in good and responsible governance. Al Mawardi (974-1058 AD) was a legist who believed that an Islamic state system should be run through efficient administrative departments who would look after collection of taxes, security of the region, judiciary and local administration. Nizam ul Mulk Tusi (1017-1091 AD) believed that political authority is God-given, which should be used to maintain law and order in society along with security. Well-being and prosperity of subjects is also a responsibility of a ruler. Abu Hamid Al Ghazali (1058-1111 AD) argued that the State is an important institution which provides security to the common masses and helps in maintaining law and order in the society. It is in order to tide over the state of lawlessness in society that common masses come together and entrust the ruler with power and authority. For Ghazali, the State is an outcome of individuals collaborating in various capacities and entering into a contract with the ruler.

When Islam arrived in India it carried with it much of the above principles. Its followers brought with them the concept of Islamic brotherhood and preached the doctrine of equality, which encouraged the ideal of freedom through communal existence. They dismissed indigenous practices like idolatry and social inequality, which pointed out clearly to the fundamental differences between Islam and various other sects and creeds of India. Such ideas projected Islam as a more dynamic and radical doctrine. The foundation of the Delhi Sultanate in 1206 AD and its acceptance of various political theories saw the development of the belief that a king or an emperor is the representative of God on earth.

Taking cue from the above, many are driven to believe that the State in medieval India was a theocracy where the Sultan merely acted as the vice-regent of God, the supreme ruler of the State. All earthly rulers are appointed by the will of God, and their duties rest with carrying out the will of God according to the instructions laid down in the texts of Islam. The subjects, on the other hand, have little choice but to obey whoever is the royal authority. Since the Koran commands its believers to 'Obey God and the Messenger and those among you in authority.' Projecting themselves as the vice-regent of

God on earth gave the rulers of Muslim India the authority to ignore even the Caliph. Though some of the earlier Sultans received robes of honour from the Caliph in Baghdad, the fall of the Abbasid Caliphate in 1258 led the Sultans of Delhi to ignore the position of the Caliph altogether. One of the earliest was Balban who styled himself as *Zil-ullah* or the shadow of God, which was later emulated by Muhammad bin Tughluq. Mubarak Khilji even went to the extent of declaring himself the Caliph. Throughout the period of Muslim rule in India succession to power was decided purely through military might aided by political and religious conspiracies of the aristocracy/ nobility and *ulama*.

The roots of this dissociation can be located in the title taken by Muslim rulers—Sultan, which imparted an idea of an independent political sovereign. This was in contrast to the office of the Caliph, which was meant to be a representative of the Prophet combining political and religious responsibilities. In course of time the political institution of the Sultanate developed certain characteristics of its own—First, its functioning rested on the collection of regular taxes, both agricultural and non-agricultural, as a means of fuelling the expenses of the State. Secondly, tax collectors were appointed to carry on this responsibility in various parts of the empire. Thirdly, the authority of the Sultan to arbitrate on various matters and pass judgments based on the *Shariah*. This restored order within the realm, brought mischief-makers to law and hence helped in the spread of Islam. In order to carry out such responsibilities the Sultan was required to submit himself completely to the will of Allah and live a pious life divorced from all luxuries and immoral practices.

In all practical terms however the State in medieval India stopped short of operating as a complete theocracy. The reason being majority of the rulers across all ruling houses resisted the domination of the religious scholars (*ulama*) in State affairs, thereby maintaining a distance between political and religious realms. During the period of the Delhi Sultanate and the Mughals the state, in most cases, took an indifferent attitude towards imposing Islam forcefully on its subjects. Even the *Shariat* was not completely adhered to in many instances, where the laws promulgated by the ruler, to work out solutions from practical problems, were taken to be final. The *ulama* was not always consulted in the framing of laws, though it was kept in mind not to contradict the *Shariat* blatantly. Laws were formulated keeping its mind the best possible solution to a problem, thereby maintaining stability within the social structure, rather than the sentiments of the *Shariat*.

Important changes were particularly noticeable from the reign of the Khiljis from 1290 AD when the power and involvement of the nobility and aristocracy were curtailed to a great extent. Exclusive dominance of the high-born Turks were done away with. Instead Indian Muslims, Hindus, Taziks were made part of the political structure. This multi-ethnic character of the political elite became more prominent during the reign of the Tughluqs and became the cause of dissent among the traditional aristocracy, like Ziauddin Barani. However this shift in the social composition was significant in terms of the political maturing of medieval ruling houses.

Nizam al-Arudi, a twelfth century jurist, contributed towards developing the idea of political thought in Islam by suggesting certain modifications within the original doctrines. He held that Prophet Muhammad will be represented in the farthest parts of the Islamic world by his lieutenants or *naiban*. And the powers exercised by these *naibs* will be in the capacity of being representatives of the Prophet and after him, the Caliphs. By doing this the political authorities in farthest corners of the Islamic world made themselves part of the lineage where the source of authority stretched back to God through the Caliph and the Prophet. Therefore the Sultans, though they ruled independently, exercised supreme powers on behalf of the Caliph and eventually God—the real sovereign.

This doctrine also came to be utilised skillfully to legitimize the position of the Sultan in the eyes of his subjects, and thus secure their obedience. As a result the Delhi Sultans never hesitated to accept titles and robes of honour from the Caliph, even when he was almost a prisoner in the hands of the Buwahids. Iltutmish (1211-36) took pride on receiving the certificate of investiture from the Caliph whose name even appeared in the *khutba* and on the coins minted by the Sultanate. As a result he had no difficulty in styling himself as *Nasir i-Amir ul-Muminin*, or the lieutenant of the defender of the faithful. Such was the strength, even if symbolic, of the office of the Caliph in the mind of his Muslim subjects that even after the Abbasid Caliphate came to an end in 1258, rulers like Sultan Jalaluddin Khilji (1290-96) continued to inscribe the name of the Caliph on his coins. Alauddin Khilji and Ghiyasuddin Tughluq too styled themselves as *Nasir i-Amir ul-Muminin,* or the lieutenant of the defender of the faithful.

The most remarkable feature of Indo-Islamic political thought presented itself through its adaptability to Indian conditions. Muslim rulers in India, in Sultanate as well as the Mughal period, paid only formal obeisance to the Caliph in Baghdad. A more generous political approach can be noticed among the Mughal rulers than among those of the Delhi Sultanate, who refused to look outside their domain of rule for political inspiration and symbols of legitimization. The shifting tenor in Indo-Islamic political theory, across centuries and ruling houses can be gauged through the differences in ideas between Fakhr i-Mudir the author of *Shajara* at the court of Qutubuddin Aibak and Abu'l Fazl the author of *Ain i-Akbari* in the court of Akbar. The former postulated the God-Prophet-Sultan triad, while the latter remarked 'it is communicated by God to kings without the intermediate assistance of anyone and men in the presence of it bend the forehead of praise toward the ground of submission.'

Political theorists of this period were divided between those who believed that the Sultan had a duty to convert Hindus to Islam and those who advocated that Hindus were *Zimmis* or people who should be protected if they perform certain duties such as non-construction of new temples, non-rebellion and respect Muslims, etc. However by the time of Akbar's reign the Mughal State was acting upon policies like political pluralism towards subjects which resulted in liberal toleration. Majority of Muslim rulers were uninterested in following the over-zealous religious scholars and their idea of a *Dar ul-Islam*

(Land of Islam). As a result there hardly exists any historical record of forceful conversion carried as part of the State policy. Subjects were left to follow their own religious beliefs and social customs, which they continued to follow even after converting to Islam. Such a situation of holding on to ones cultural roots even after accepting a new faith resulted in mixed traditions where non-Islamic and Islamic traditions got fused within a single individual, often spreading to large communities. It can be argued that Indo-Islamic political thought aimed at a deeper understanding of inter-community relations between Muslims and Hindus.

Such a degree of socio-cultural and religious freedom in medieval Indian society brings us to the idea concerning the duties of the Sultan centred on the primary responsibility of protection to his subjects. This covered a wide range of activities consisting of, but not limited to, protection of life, faith and belief, protection of property, enforcement of law in the land and the protection of the kingdom from foreign invasions. The Sultan was the guardian of his realm and his subjects. Thus, it was his responsibility to uphold the eternal and divine laws that governed his domain. In more than one occasion he acted unscrupulously, and with extreme ruthlessness in times of emergency with the specific aim of maintaining law and order with the aim of protecting the society.

In spite of their despotic attitude towards governance, every Sultan accepted the interpretation of the divinely ordained code of conduct (*Shariat*) and acted accordingly. He also strived hard to ensure the proper application of this code in all spheres of his reign, sometimes ruthlessly. Since in a heterogeneous society like that in thirteenth century India, it was impossible to govern only on the tenets of the *Shariat*. In an age where the sacred order was precariously positioned, it became mandatory on the part of the ruler to be ruthless in his administration for the proper maintenance of the code of conduct. This was to ensure that the society did not degenerate into immorality and rebellion. But such ruthlessness was never meant to compromise the eternal essence of the Islamic faith expressed in peace, justice, along with a liberal and humanist outlook.

Scholars like Barani were of the opinion that a Muslim ruler should follow the path of truth and be accountable to God for his conduct. This accountability was extended to ensure the well-being of subjects through responsible governance, peace and safety in daily life, regulating prices of food grains and other necessary items. Elements of responsible governance, for Barani, meant that the ruler should ensure transparent administration, and abstain from whimsical behavior, deceit, vengeful attitude and wrong doing. This was prescribed as a means to uphold the moral character of society and maintain law and order.

Abu'l Fazl while enumerating the responsibilities of a just ruler argued that the necessity for a just ruler arose from a situation where lawlessness and exploitation of resources was rampant. As a result in order to quell rebellions and restore order a ruler is important. He will consult only the wise and noble-minded. A ruler should treat talented individuals and scholars with respect but need not depend too much on them. Neither will the ruler worry about those individuals who lack talent and those who stay away from harming others. However the ruler should punish those who live in luxury and lack concern for others and even harm other people. And for the worst individuals who harm others the most and hence disrupt the social system, the ruler should banish them from his kingdom. If the need be such people should be given exemplary physical punishment short of death sentence, since human life is created by God.

Abu'l Fazl further elaborates that a good ruler is one who protects good, does away with evil, and promotes justice, truthfulness, responsible governance and good ethics. A bad ruler is characterized by conceit, egotism, decadence, greed and flattery which result in instability, lack of security, violence, rebellion and theft in his realm.

The rich contribution of Islamic law and world view, their ideas about justice and equality entered legal and various other institutions, reinforced by adoption of Urdu and Persian as court languages across various political dynasties. If we fail to keep the above in perspective we shall not be able to properly understand the evolution of modern Indian psyche. Islamic political thought rested mainly on Greek and Persian antecedents. The traditional Indian ideas about social order, justice, kingship, equality which might have profoundly influenced Greek thought of Hesiod, Plato and Aristotle came back home in a new form via Persia through Islam. There was a close resemblance between these ideas and those of Ziauddin Barani on his discussions concerning the traditional notions of good and evil and the need for moderation and justice in a well governed state. To this we turn now.

Endnote

1. Quran 4:62. For a detailed discussion on Islamic political thought along with duties and responsibilities of a Muslim ruler, see, Tamara Sonn (1996), "Political Authority in Classical Islamic Thought", *American Journal of Islamic Social Sciences*, 13, 3, pp. 309-24.

5

Ziauddin Barani (1285-1357)

Kashshaf Ghani

I
INTRODUCTION

The foundation of Muslim rule in the Indian subcontinent dates back to the early thirteenth century. The early Turkish Empire of Delhi gradually carved out a political domain for itself together with an attempt at formulating a political theory on which rested their rule in the days to come. The primary political thinker of the Delhi Sultanate was Ziauddin Barani, whose works were instrumental in shaping the political theory of the kingdom. Muslim religious and legal scholars of the age contributed much in laying down the principles of political thought in the larger Islamic world. This came to form the basis of rule in the lands of the Islamic Caliphate. The Delhi Sultanate, though not strictly a part of the Islamic Caliphate, nonetheless, could not avoid the influence of theories propounded by Muslim scholars. In our analysis of Ziauddin Barani's political ideas we will witness his mind at work, with respect to the Indian surroundings, along with influences of Muslim scholars from outside the Indian subcontinent.

II
BARANI SHAPING THE POLITICAL IDEOLOGY OF THE MEDIEVAL TIMES

Ziauddin Barani is remembered primarily as the leading historian of the Delhi Sultanate. His contribution towards shaping the political ideology of his age remains significant, brought forward through his works, the *Tarikh i-Firoz Shahi* and *Fatwa-i Jahandari*. Both these works were written by Barani with the aim to educate the ruling community of the age, the Sultans of Delhi. Through his works Barani aimed at inspiring the Delhi Sultans to formulate a coherent political ideology for the State, which from time to time had to cope with political uncertainties. In course of shaping the political ideology of the Delhi Sultans, the primary aim of the *Fatwa-i Jahandari* was to inspire those Sultans who have not been blessed with innately virtuous dispositions to strive hard to rule as true Islamic kings. He calls upon rulers to imbibe the qualities of God, especially combine within their character the twin qualities of benevolence and wrath, and at the same time know when to apply which quality in relation with their subjects. Through such an advice, Barani furthers his aim of witnessing the establishment of such a socio-political order where the words and commands of God are held in supreme respect. Those who dare to deny those commands are made to suffer punishment, subordination or even death.[1]

Barani believed that only persons of high birth and lineage should be entitled to occupy positions of power and authority. Thus only individuals who were born into the ruling elite, and were familiar with the working of the bureaucracy should be in a position to undertake responsibilities of governance and administration. Barani's obsession with ensuring the authority of the high-born stem from his personal experience as part of the aristocracy. His family served the three main ruling houses of the Sultanate—the Ilbaris, the Khiljis and the Tughluqs.[2] As a result Barani could never distance himself from the corridors of power and patronage, which was reflected in his writings, where he chose to take a top-down approach towards understanding society and politics. Thus his works speak little of the masses and their involvement in the governance of the Sultanate. He chose to read the political climate of the age through the lenses of aristocracy, which he could never overcome till the last days of his life. Thus in the age of Muhammad bin Tughluq when a new class of officers and bureaucrats arose from the lower strata of the society, like Laddha, Najba, Manka, Babu Naik,

Peera, etc. Barani was completely disillusioned.[3] He could never reconcile himself to the fact that winds of change had begun to blow in the corridors of power. Such a change eventually witnessed a suppression of the older aristocracy by the new ruling class rising from below. The collapse of the prestige of the older aristocracy, of which Barani himself was a part, was unacceptable to him, though he was bestowed with great honour and prestige in the court of Muhammad bin Tughluq.

Such were the reasons, conditioned by an increasing degree of fluidity in the political composition of the Sultanate that conditioned Barani's political ideology. In a period of uncertainty and political turmoil Sultans became more and more dependent on the slave bureaucracy. Even when the Turks, in a later period, regained their position at the royal court a constant source of tension was the differences between the hereditary ruling community and the need for competence and loyalty in the political structure of the Sultanate. Barani focused much of his attention on analyzing how such tensions affected the functioning, and hence the fortunes of the medieval State and its ruler.

Barani's political ideology aimed at advising the ruling community, particularly the Sultan, in the correct ways of ruling his State, thereby achieving stability within the domain. The first step which Barani suggested towards this means was to achieve a balance between various components of the ruling community—the crown and the nobility. A similar balance was also suggested in loyalty and competence within the bureaucracy. This became important due to the changes in the composition of the nobility—the rise of the low-born into positions of higher responsibility. A policy started by earlier Sultans was encouraged by Muhammad bin Tughluq who broke the dominance of the older aristocracy by introducing elements from the lower rung of the society.

Such a policy of the State also affected Barani's fortunes adversely, who refused to tolerate the loss of honour and prestige of the hereditary nobility. In the words of Barani, it was the philosophers, the 'enemies of stability and respectability', who were responsible for this change in the State ideology.[4] They were responsible for proposing the idea of social equality in the bureaucracy, which resulted in the influx of commoners and hence created instability within the political structure. Along with the above, in the *Fatwa-i Jahandari* Barani also advocates a non-philosophical approach towards governance. Philosophy for him does little good to take into consideration the complexities of the political situation and suggest a pragmatic solution towards ensuring the stability of the State structure.[5]

At the same time Barani also suggested a complete dissociation of the lower classes from any benefits enjoyed by the higher classes. The former must be deprived from educational opportunities, and be kept in perpetual ignorance. This would limit their participation in the affairs of State and society.[6] As a result the reins of governance would continue to remain entrusted in the hands of the hereditary aristocracy who in turn will ensure stability in the political structure and hence within the society at large. In the *Fatwa-i Jahandari* Barani traces the dominant elements in the Khilji nobility. The early supporters and officials formed the Alai nobility who remained in power till 1300. They were followed by a new group of nobles composed of middle-ranking officials and Indian Muslims. This group was subverted in the closing years of Alauddin Khilji's reign by individuals from the lower sections of the society. Barani condemned the latter as total outsiders and considered them responsible for making the Sultanate unstable.

As a result Barani makes an impassioned appeal towards maintaining the position and authority of the aristocratic ruling families, without making too many changes in them. Change for Barani, was the main cause for political and social instability within the Sultanate. A hereditary continuation in the aristocracy would ensure virtues such as political acumen, administrative skill and statesmanship—which cannot be acquired by the low-born. Protecting the lives and properties of the traditional Muslim aristocracy would in the words of Barani protect the political structure of the Sultanate itself in the long future.[7]

Many of Barani's explanations in the *Fatwa-i Jahandari* impart a sense of contradiction, which affects the clarity of his political ideology. Two cases may be discussed as examples. The rise of the low-born in the political structure of the Sultanate is seen by Barani as a conflict between 'Faith' and 'Infidelity'. The former being the immigrant political aristocracy, while the latter being the low-born converts to Islam. Since the latter have already undergone conversion, therefore it becomes impossible to characterize them as infidels. To overcome this contradiction Barani puts forward the theory that conversion among low-born is always imperfect and incomplete. However much they try, they cannot reach the standards of a Muslim by birth, in this context the high-born aristocracy. Thus he addressed them as hypocrites.[8] Barani's theory understandably has a worldly context, related to equations of power and authority, with little or no religious significance attached to it. Barani even fails to substantiate his theory from any religious authority.

Those who have chosen the nobler occupations, from them alone come forth goodness, kindness, generosity, valor, purity of vision, justice, equity, gratitude and fear of God. They alone are worthy of offices and posts in the realm and under the government. Whenever vices have been inserted into the minds of those who choose mean occupations, immodesty, falsehood, perfidy, sins, wrongs, lies, ingratitude, conceit and godlessness appear. They are called lowborn, base, mean, worthless, shameless and of impure birth. The promotion of the low and the lowborn brings no advantage in this world (*Fatwa-i Jahandari*).

Barani's treatment of Muhammad bin Tughlaq too reflects contradictions and confusions. The Sultan treated the scholar with much respect and kept him as his companion for seventeen years, in recognition of Barani's exceptional scholarship and personality.[9] In return Barani showered praises on the Sultan elevating him to the Pantheon of Prophets and saints. Barani's heart bled and he wept while describing the passing away of Muhammad bin Tughluq. At the same time in a span of few pages, Barani takes a completely different approach and starts condemning the Sultan in severe terms, finding in him traits of Nimrod and the Pharaoh.[10] He is depicted as undertaking foolish, ill conceived projects which ruined his kingdom and weakened his authority. The rebellions which occurred during his reign reduced the Sultanate to chaos. In judgment Muhammad bin Tughluq never recognized the proper occasions for severity and leniency. All this in the eyes of Barani resulted from the pool of unworthy aides which the Sultan had gathered around him. The philosophers he patronized provided him with all the wrong advice, like the appointment to offices based on talent and not high-birth. Such advice, for Barani, carried seeds of instability within them, which manifested when the projects of the Sultan started to fail miserably. Therefore for Barani, for the proper functioning of the Sultanate, philosophers must be expelled from the domain, or else suppressed.

Whomsoever God has chosen and has honoured with excellence, greatness and ability in proportion to his merit should be singled out and honored by kings. But if the ruler out of natural inclination and lack of wisdom honors a scoundrel then the ruler holds God in contempt. Such a ruler is not worthy of the Caliphate of deputyship of God. For opposition to the wisdom of creation he will be punished in the next world (*Fatwa-i Jahandari*).

The death of Muhammad bin Tughluq not only signaled a shift in the political ideology of the Sultanate, but also in the fortunes of Barani. Though the Sultan had been instrumental in recruiting low-born individuals to political offices, yet it remains undeniable that Barani received his highest respect and honour during the reign of Muhammad bin Tughluq. Thus the praises on the Sultan were an expression of gratitude from the scholar. However when his fortunes began to fade with the rise of a new class of bureaucrats, Barani could not hold back his disappointment and frustration, which vented itself by condemning the Sultan.[11] A capable scholar he was, Barani made every attempt to foil such contradictions in his writings. For which he took recourse to a dogma which he developed in the *Fatwa-i Jahandari*, that Sultans should be a mixture of qualities and know when to employ them. At the same time, Sultans should also know to take a balanced approach to the affairs of his kingdom. Barani argued that it was only when Muhammad bin Tughluq failed to take such a balanced approach in his administration, that Barani took up the pen to record the atrocities of the Sultan.[12]

Barani largely drew his principles of political ideology from pre-Islamic Sassanid Persia, whose heroes provided him the ideals of kingship.[13] So that when Barani chose to advice Muhammad bin Tughluq on his policies, the former borrowed his analogies from the Iranian folk hero Jamshid as an ideal of how Sultans should function in various situations. Once on the issue of capital punishment Barani, borrowing from Jamshid, adviced the Sultan that capital punishment was justified for apostasy, willful murder, adultery between married people, conspiracy, heading a revolt, aiding and abetting king's enemies and acts of disobedience which affected the stability of the realm. However Jamshid opted for the appointment of able ministers who would devise ways to avoid the shedding of subjects' blood. To this Muhammad bin Tughluq replied that gone are the days when order could be restored without bloodshed. In his age subjects have become more violent and less submissive, which makes bloodshed mandatory. On another occasion Barani adviced Muhammad bin Tughluq that earlier rulers had decided to abdicate in favor of their wazir, when relations between the ruler and the ruled became irreparable as a result of the realm being engulfed in endemic revolt. However Muhammad bin Tughluq chose to inflict punishment on his rebel subjects rather than abdicate his throne for a better successor.[14] Thus, it is evident that there were times when the Sultan relied on his own decisions, and chose not to follow the political advice of his counsels.

Great kings have observed many conditions and have been very cautious in the matter of consultation. The opinion of their counselors has seldom erred. The counselors ought to be properly appointed. They should be nearly equal to each other in their experience, in their loyalty, and in their status before the king. If one counselor is perfect in intelligence and the other defective, there will be a danger of incongruity in the decision (*Fatwa-i Jahandari*).

In the *Fatwa-i Jahandari* Barani's political ideology is built on the premise that God has entrusted power in this material world to form a working partnership between prophets and kings. The Islamic theory of government is based on the idea that religion and kingship are inseparable in a State system. Therefore the office of any temporal authority is a divine institution. However, Barani argues that these powers cannot be combined singularly under the authority of the king. And kings must not abuse the dignity conferred upon them by God by using their office to further their material desires. For Barani the ideal kingship came to an end with the first four 'rightly guided' Caliphs. Abu Bakr, Umar, Uthman and Ali were successful in following the *sunna* of the Prophet Muhammad, avoiding pomp and pride, and in combining, in correct degrees, personal poverty, humility towards God and the duties of kingship.[15] After that age the institution of kingship became more corrupt and increasingly dependent on force and violence. As a result of which rulers moved away from the above desired qualities and took recourse to pomp and grandeur, might and majesty to win over their subjects and keep them under control.[16]

God is the real king and earthly kings are the playthings of His decree and Divine Power. He is the real king and to Him alone is kingship proper.

Religion and temporal government are twins, that is the head of religion and the head of the government are twin brothers. There must be both prophets and kings in this world so that mankind's business in both the worlds may be carried through in accordance with God's wishes. Almighty God has adorned prophets and kings with inborn virtues and praiseworthy qualities (*Fatwa-i Jahandari*).

In the light of such excesses done by later rulers, Barani opined that the only way to uphold the God-given dignity and value of kingship is to encourage and ensure the spread of Islam. Alongside it is also the duty of Muslim rulers to create and ensure social peace and stability within their domain which would allow the flourish of Islam. Precisely, scholars like Barani in the *Fatwa-i Jahandari* advised and hence expected the Sultan to take up responsibilities and assume functions in the Muslim community previously allotted to the Caliph. Thus a true Muslim Sultan, for Barani, is one who enforces the *Sharia* in his domain, weeds out unorthodoxy and suppresses the infidel, in this instance the Hindus in his kingdom.[17] Alongside the Sultan must also dispense strict justice and avoid un-Islamic punishments. In cases where the *Sharia* does not suggest capital punishment, death must be the last option, only if the stability of the domain and the peaceful spread of Islam is affected. A true Sultan must avoid the company of evil persons, and appoint only pious Muslims to office. The implication of this advice became evident later when Barani identified the philosophers as evil and enemies of the political order, and low-born Muslims as 'infidels' appointed to office. In case the Sultan is not a hereditary ruler, he should refrain from killing the supporters of the earlier Sultan.[18]

The greatness of a king who protects religion is beyond description, for it is through his protection and promotion of the faith that Muslims give themselves to obedience towards God and the performance of their religious duties. That the mandates of the *Sharia* of the Prophet may become operative over different realms...and the banners of Islam may reach unto the highest heavens (*Fatwa-i Jahandari*).

Drawn towards the practical realizations of his time and age, Barani admitted that as a result of the unbelief and innovations that has come to prevail the idea of kingship in later Muslim kingdoms, the possibility of ruling the domain according to the *sunna* (model practice) of the Prophet and the Muslim community at the time of the four 'rightly-guided' Caliphs (632-61) has become an impossibility. In spite of his orthodox beliefs Barani did not hesitate to admit the impossibility of enforcing the laws of the *Sharia* in the administration of the Sultanate. Along with the fact that the political realism of the age demanded an adherence to state laws (*zawabit*).[19] Such a reading not only brought forward the impracticality of applying *Sharia* laws to all political orders across Muslim societies; yet at the same time it also reflected Barani's deep understanding of the evolution of Islamic polity and the practical requirements of the Sultanate. Though Barani intended that *zawabit* be accepted as a complement to the *Sharia* with the aim to reinforce the latter rather than to severe the two.[20]

III
RELEVANCE OF ZIAUDDIN BARANI

Along with the ideals of kingship, Barani also borrowed the class-consciousness of pre-Islamic Sassanian society which he applied while advocating that political authority should be the preserve of the high-born who are better equipped to maintain a stable socio-political structure. At the same time influences of Greek political thought, studied from the writings of Al Farabi and Nasiruddin Tusi, can be discerned from Barani's writings. In keeping with this tradition, Barani stated that a just ruler is he who treated every individual on merit and quality and entrusted him with the responsibility for which he is fit.[21] For Barani, Sultans and Kings are mortal beings. Hence their human nature is made up of contradictions comprising both good and evil. As a result it is mandatory for rulers to know when to apply his qualities for the interests of his subjects and for the spread of Islam. Towards those who are obedient and submissive to Islam, the Sultan ought to be kind and generous. Similarly, those who are unbelievers and mischief-mongers, the Sultan needed to treat them with terror and punishment.[22] Barani backed it up with his theory that a man's occupation is an index to his moral and religious status in the eyes of God. Thus, he concluded that an ideal Muslim ruler was he who had the ability to understand the different dispositions of men and apply the appropriate method of treating them. An ideal ruler should honour and favour those who have been honoured and favoured by God with many virtues, and disfavour those who have been thrown into vices by God.[23] The application of such a political ideology on part of Barani became evident later in his career when he set out to evaluate the reign of Muhammad bin Tughluq and his political decision-making discussed above.

All the subjects of the ruler are dependent upon him and he is the Lord and judge over all. Wrath and grace, power and compassion, severity and sympathy, pride and humility, harshness and softness, anger and forbearance, mercy and hardness of the heart, which are opposing qualities should adorn the king in the most perfect manner and should be employed at proper times and on appropriate occasions. With these perfect dispositions the king can deal with thousands of men who are different in their qualities and dispositions, temperaments and natures (*Fatwa-i Jahandari*).

In the *Fatwa-i Jahandari* Barani poits out certain requirements for the maintenance of a stable political structure[24]—

1. A strong and contended army,
2. A well-filled treasury,
3. An equitable system of taxation,
4. An efficient espionage system for communication of information related to the subjects of the State.

On the above points Barani also elaborates on the effective ways of conducting the business of kingship. These include the ways of managing the army and treasury, intervening in economic life to stop scarcity and price rise thereby saving subjects from economic distress, appointing wise counsels for correct advice, along with appointing truthful spies to keep the ruler informed of the happenings in his kingdom, and protect him from lies, deceit and dangers. For Barani the counsels of the Sultan must be of noble origin and should not be unworthy men. Barani considered the noble character of an individual to be more of a moral, than social status. In whatever the Sultan does he must exercise a correct resolve, set before him higher aspirations while fulfilling his obligatory responsibilities towards Islam. All this needs to be done before the Sultan immerses himself in vain glory and grandeur.[25]

Along with this, the ruler, for Barani, in spite of his external pomp and grandeur must conform to humility and submission before God and His chosen ones if he wishes to carry on his responsibility.[26] Barani sets out to prove his theory through a study of the fate met by the family of Alauddin Khilji. Barani argues that Alauddin's glory and success would seem to the worldly eye to be a result of his personality and actions as a Sultan. Rather, seen with proper degree of perception it will be evident that the Sultan owed his success to the presence of Shaykh Nizamuddin Awliya, the Chishti Sufi saint in his kingdom, and the latter's spiritual blessings on Alauddin.[27] Barani rues that the Sultan never gave much importance to his presence. Neither did he ever seek the blessings of the Chishtia master. As a result of which both Alauddin and his family had to pay a heavy price. First, the Sultan died of suspected foul play. Malik Kafur, Alauddin's military commander blinded Khizr Khan and Shadi Khan, and imprisoned Mubarak Khan, all sons of the Sultan. Having removed these obstacles, Malik Kafur threatened to exterminate Alauddin's entire family.[28] With this narration Barani intends to point out that worldly success in political affairs hold little permanence, if not firmly grounded on complete submission to God and reverence towards His chosen subjects, the Sufis. Only by serving the cause of Islam with a pure heart and performing religious duties continuously, without lapses, Barani argues, can a ruler expect to draw the beneficence of God along with respect and dignity from his subjects.[29]

Real belief in God and certainty and firmness in true faith remain conspicuous in only a small number of individuals... never will be the power and authority of the caliphate be asserted and become well constituted without the terror and majesty and pomp of temporal rulership.

Servitude to God is the necessary condition of religion. And conditions of this servitude are submission, supplication, poverty, self-abasement, abjectness and humility. On the other hand, the requirements of kingship are haughtiness, pride, aloofness from others, luxurious living, lack of civility, grandeur and might... it is the duty of religious kings to fear and regret such actions as a danger to religion, to ask for divine forgiveness during the night with weeping and lamentations (*Fatwa-i Jahandari*).

From a pragmatic point of view Barani emphasized on the necessity of despotism in order to integrate the ruling community. And in the rise of a despotic monarchy the importance of force cannot be ignored. Thus, Barani in his own way advocated the use of force towards the establishment and sustenance of a despotic authority, which at that age was a historical necessity. At the same time Barani also realized the possibility of an increase in terror and oppression as a result of the deployment of excessive force. Coupled with this was the increasing power and authority of the Sultan. Such a situation for Barani would be tragic for the future of the Sultanate. In his analysis of the reigns of Alauddin Khilji and Muhammad bin Tughluq, Barani repeatedly emphasized on this use of force and terror as an instrument of administration, and a mark of the increased power and authority of the Sultan. At one point of time it even came to characterize the political ideology of the Sultanate and defined the medieval State in the eyes of its contemporaries.

However for Barani the use of force must not compromise the dispensation of justice in the Sultanate. Since the proper functioning of any political order depends on the ability of rulers to provide justice impartially between litigants, together with an equal treatment irrespective of their social position. Barani sees justice as protecting the weak and oppressed, while curbing the strong, which can only be ensured through a proper application of the faculty of reason. Such a deliverance of justice, for Barani, is possible through the hands of a strong and pious *Sharia*-oriented Muslim ruler. The enforcement of justice leads to the defeat and punishment of those who bring disgrace to the faith, and disobey the *Sharia*. It is only when justice is delivered and punishment meted to the oppressor that the banner of Islam is held higher and the discipline of the Sultan is established in his domain.[30] This is irrespective of time and space.

Barani divides justice into two categories: one that guarantees universal equality, and that which ensures special or limited equality. The former implies a situation where the ruler obliterates the distinction between the ruler and the ruled. Here justice is delivered by combining them as one. The latter is a situation in which a king by the authority of his royal status delivers justice to the people. This is carried out from the portals of his royal court, ensuring equality among litigants. For Barani the first form of justice though came to an end with the first four Caliphs of Islam, is an ideal that needs to be pursued by every pious Muslim ruler. Its emulation and application is to be sought after if proper rule is to be established and the truth of the faith upheld within the Sultanate.[31]

During the execution of justice the actions of the Sultan, for Barani, is determined by the aims intended to achieve. The latter should primarily be tuned towards achieving the interests and well-being of the Muslim subjects in a Sultanate, even if it brings harm to other communities. Since royal action should be guided by the interests of Islam and its peaceful career in the domain of the Sultan, even if that action is deemed despotic in the eyes of law. Any law and its resultant action are considered tyrannical if it overlooks the interests of Islam for securing the good of other communities.[32]

Barani's political theory though influenced by the classical thinkers of the Islamic world, builds itself on the Indian context. In doing so he takes into consideration the political environment in which Muslim rule came to establish itself in the subcontinent. Though he repeatedly emphasized on adherence to *Sharia* and the establishment of an ideal Muslim State, he was well aware that most Sultans of his age ruled on political pragmatism. In him we see a combination of secular laws with the principles of *Sharia*—a possible outcome of political expediency which conditioned his thought to a great extent while he was formulating his political ideals.

Endnotes

1. Iqtidar Husain Siddiqui, *Medieval India: Essays in Diplomacy and Culture*, Adam Publishers and Distributors, New Delhi, 2009, pp. 223-24.
2. K.A. Nizami, *On History and Historians of Medieval India*, MunshiRammanoharlal Publishers Pvt. Ltd., New Delhi, 1983, p. 130.
3. *Ibid.*, p. 129.
4. *Ibid.*, p. 131.
5. Iqtidar Husain Siddiqui, *Perso-Arabic Sources of Information on the Life and Conditions in the Sultanate of Delhi*, MunshiRammanoharlal Publishers Pvt. Ltd., New Delhi, 1992, p. 107.
6. Nizami, *On History and Historians*, p. 131.
7. Muzaffar Alam, *The Languages of Political Islam in India*, Permanent Black, Delhi, 2004, pp. 41-42.
8. Nizami, *On History and Historians*, p. 131.
9. *Ibid.*, p. 133.
10. *Ibid.*

11. *Ibid.*, p. 132.
12. Peter Hardy, *Historians of Medieval India: Studies in Indo-Muslim Historical Writing*, MunshiRammanoharlal Publishers Pvt. Ltd., New Delhi, 1997, pp. 124-25.
13. Nizami, *On History and Historians*, p. 128.
14. Hardy, *Historians of Medieval India*, pp. 37-38.
15. Siddiqui, *Medieval India*, p. 224.
16. Hardy, *Historians of Medieval India*, pp. 25-26.
17. Alam, *The Languages of Political Islam*, p. 37.
18. Hardy, *Historians of Medieval India*, pp. 26-27.
19. Nizami, *On History and Historians*, pp. 13, 136.
20. Alam, *The Languages of Political Islam*, p. 40.
21. Siddiqui, *Medieval India*, p. 225.
22. *Ibid.*, p. 227.
23. Hardy, *Historians of Medieval India*, p. 27.
24. *Ibid.*
25. Siddiqui, *Medieval India*, p. 225.
26. Hardy, *Historians of Medieval India*, p. 29.
27. *Ibid.*, p. 116.
28. *Ibid.*, pp. 33-34.
29. Alam, *The Languages of Political Islam*, p. 36.
30. Siddiqui, *Medieval India*, p. 290.
31. Alam, *The Languages of Political Islam*, pp. 38-39.
32. *Ibid.*, pp. 37-38.

Suggested Readings

Habib, Irfan, "Barani's Theory of the History of the Delhi Sultanate". *Indian Historical Review* 7 (1981): 99-115.

Habib, Mohammad and Afsar Umar Salim Khan, *The Political Theory of the Delhi Sultanate*, Delhi, 1961.

6

Abu'l Fazl and the Politics of *Wahdat al-Wujud* (1551-1603)

Kingshuk Chatterjee

INTRODUCTION

The concept of "Islamic polity" has by default quite often been understood to be limited to the enforcement of the Shari'ah. The primary responsibility of the ruler/ruling establishment has mostly thus been identified as upholding the "Islamic order." From such depictions, it would not be unreasonable to conclude that "Islam" and "Shari'ah" are one and the same thing—such a conclusion would, however, be wrong. There was far greater complexity in the conceptualisation of an Islamic order in medieval India, as much as in other parts of the Islamic world, that serve to undermine the widely held view about Islamic intellectual tradition. The Mughal Empire that was put together in the 16th century was remarkably different from the stereotype of Islamic political dispensations, and witnessed one of the most vigorously contested intellectual debates on the nature and contours of Islamic order. The architect of that inclusive, multi-ethnic political experiment within an Islamic body-politic was the Emperor Jalal al-din Muhammad Akbar; the principal ideologue of that experiment was his close associate, Abu'l Fazl Allami, who laid down the intellectual parameters of the theory of sovereignty inspired by the doctrine of *Wahdat al-Wujud*.

I
LIFE AND TIME OF ABU'L FAZL

Abu'l Fazl (1551-1603) was the second son of Shaikh Mubarak Nagauri, a highly reputed Islamic scholar, and the younger brother of the poet Faizi, whom Emperor Akbar was later to look upon as a friend. Between the three of them Shaikh Mubarak and his two sons exercised considerable intellectual influence on Akbar, and were instrumental in the shaping of the expansive and inclusive political discourse that posterity has come to associate with him. Of the three, though, Abu'l Fazl is the most renowned, not least because he provides one of the most authoritative accounts of Akbar's reign, the *A'in-i Akbari*.

Abu'l Fazl was born in Agra at a time when the Mughal Empire was yet to be reestablished by Humayun, a decade and a half after having been driven out by Sher Shah. Trained principally by his father, Abu'l Fazl could read and write Arabic by the time he was five years of age, and had committed to memory most of the conventional learning that was typical of the times well before he was ten. Noted for his erudition by the time he turned twenty, he developed a rare capacity of providing new interpretation to old problems. His reputation for forming his independent judgement based upon his own reading was subjected to much disdain from many his peers who were accustomed to *taqlid* (blind emulation). His refusal to be cowed down by authority prompted him to publicly refute a very powerful *'alim* in the Mughal court, which enraged the *'alim* so much that he embarked on a personal vendetta against both Shaikh Mubarak and Abu'l Fazl. This attracted the attention of Emperor Akbar himself, who was then trying to break the stranglehold the Sunni *'ulema* enjoyed over the Mughal establishment. By 1573, Shaikh Mubarak made his entry into the Mughal court; Abu'l Fazl followed in 1574-75.[1]

Abu'l Fazl rose rapidly in Akbar's favour, and in his court, in course of the theological debates that took place at the *'Ibadatkhaneh* at Fatehpur Sikri during 1576-78. Championing a more liberal reading of Islam, Abu'l Fazl worsted virtually all of the established *'ulema* in the court. Soon after, a noticeable change began in the nature of Mughal polity, culminating in a veritable transformation of the nature of the body-politic in a manner that came to define Mughal political culture for more than a century. In a major break from the past practices of Muslim rulers in India, in 1579 Akbar read the *Khutba* (sermons after Friday prayers) himself, rather than in the name of the *Khalifah*; in the same year he abolished the *jizyah*, to the great chagrin of the *'ulema*. He followed this up with the *Mahzarnama*, which authorised him to reason out the legal position in any matter by himself on which the 'ulema were not unanimous. Since there was hardly any matter on which the *'ulema* were ever in complete agreement, it virtually freed him from the shackles of *'ulemaic* opinion altogether. This was followed by Akbar's promulgation of the *Sulh-i Kul*, a doctrine generally attributed to Abu'l Fazl rather than the Emperor as being the author.

Abu'l Fazl was pivotal not merely to the theological but also the intellectual dynamics in Akbar's court. Apart from being the author of the *Akbarnama* (of which the third volume is the *'Ain-i Akbari*), he also translated the Bible and the *Panchatantra* (*Iyar Danish*, lit. Pillars of wisdom) in Persian and wrote the introduction to Persian translation of the *Mahabharata*. He became one of the closest of Akbar's friends in course of the 1580s and '90s, handling many delicate diplomatic and political missions. Largely on account of the proximity he had with the Emperor, and of the influence he was believed to enjoy over the latter, Abu'l Fazl fell foul of the crown prince Salim, who had him assassinated in 1603.

II
THE POLITICS OF *WAHDAT AL-WUJUD*

Abu'l Fazl worked out his political ideas at a time when the foundations of the Mughal Empire were being laid. Crowned as the successor to the Timurid throne in Delhi in 1555 at the age of twelve, Akbar's realms stretched across the Punjab and the Doab regions of North India, stretching as far as Kabul to the west and most of the middle Gangetic valley in North India. The Mughal military machine, drawn from and dominated by warriors from Turan and Iran, proved formidable enough to establish Mughal overlordship with relative ease. Yet, the Mughal Emperor was not secure himself due to factional tussle among the nobles of the dominant Irani and Turani groups in the Timurid court. Akbar needed to create a balance in the ranks of nobility by inducting new groups of people, which would make the Empire more durable than a blind dependence on the Iranis and Turanis would allow. In the 1560s, Akbar found precisely such a group (other than the Muslim nobility domiciled in the subcontinent for several generations) in the Rajputs, who became the sword-arm of the Mughal Empire in return for access to the Empire's resources. The rapid rise of the Rajputs, and following them other Hindu rajahs of the countryside, was treated with considerable misgiving not only by the Turani and Irani nobility but also the 'ulema. They feared that such ascendancy of non-Muslims in the Mughal apparatus would compromise the Islamic character of the polity in Hindustan, which had come into being from the 13th century. In grappling with such scepticism towards his policy, Akbar was trying to negotiate a way out of the impasse without alienating the Irani-Turani axis in the 1570s, when Shaikh Mubarak, Faizi and Abu'l Fazl came to his court and helped him fashion the Mughal paradigm.

Many of Abu'l Fazl's contemporaries as much as colonial historians held him in some disdain, because Abu'l Fazl single-mindedly projected his master, Akbar, in a larger than life manner—magnifying his slightest success, deftly justifying anything that warranted criticism. Most importantly, Abu'l Fazl downplayed the role anyone (including himself, his father and his brother) may have played in the formulation of any aspect of imperial policy, always making it out as though all the positive developments were the doing of one man only.

Indeed, Abu'l Fazl was not much of an original thinker, nor did he claim himself to be such. And yet, in the theological debates held at the *'Ibadatkhaneh*, Abu'l Fazl stood out as perhaps the most erudite scholar in Islamic philosophy after Shaikh Mubarak, completely pulverising the votaries of more traditionalist readings of Islam. His distinctiveness was not the originality of his formulations, rather the originality in blending traditions as diverse as the peripatetic philosophy of Ibn Sina (980-1037),[2] the *Ishraqi* thinking of Nasir al-din Tusi (1207-74),[3] with the phenomenally expansive ideas of Ibn al-'Arabi (1165-1240)[4] which was championed in India by Shaikh Mubarak. In the hands of Abu'l Fazl ideas of such diverse vintage were woven into the tapestry of a line of political thinking that served to vindicate the actual experience of politics during the reign of Akbar, and presented a political paradigm that dominated the political imagination in India till the advent of the British Raj.[5]

In the three centuries before the coming of the Mughals, a discourse had developed on Islamic order in the subcontinent around the vortex of Turko-Afghan rule.[6] From the days of the Mamluk dynasty in Delhi, political legitimacy stemmed essentially from upholding the Islamic order, which was taken to mean that Islamic laws constituted the bedrock of the jurisprudence in the Sultanate. The Sultan located himself in the hierarchy of authority in the Muslim world as a representative of the Khalifah in his own realm, and thus was entitled to the allegiance of all good Muslims. As the representative of the Khalifah, the Sultan was required to institute the laws of Islam, i.e. the Shari'ah, as the law of the land. In practice, however, as the overwhelming majority of their subjects were non-Muslims, the Shari'ah could not be easily applied where they did not involve Muslims without risking rebellion. As the position of the Sultans strengthened over time, courtesy of rulers like Balban, Ala al-din Khilji and Muhammad bin Tughluq, they were able to negotiate a degree of freedom from any harsh and literal interpretation of the Shari'ah either in the name of exigencies of the state, or in his capacity of being *Zill-i Ilahi* (Shadow of God, thus unlikely to commit any mistakes). However, regardless of how strong the position of a Sultan might become, it paid to be mindful of the sensitivities of the *'ulema*, whose allegiance as the custodians of the Shari'ah (functioning as jurists of the realm) was pivotal to any continued enjoyment of legitimacy. Muslim rulers before Akbar generally addressed this by giving Muslims a disproportionately preferential treatment in the body-politic, allowing them a monopoly of high office and substantive authority.

In his quest for a more inclusive order, including Muslims as well as non-Muslims, Akbar needed to toe a fine line so that he did not transgress the limits of Islamic order, and yet bring to an end the monopoly of power enjoyed by the incumbent elite, who happened to be Muslims. The greatest contribution of Abu'l Fazl and his father was to formulate a political theory that allowed just that.

Abu'l Fazl opened up the question as to what constitutes the Islamic order. As indicated, the principal benchmark of Islamic order was enforcement of the laws of Islam. There was however no rigid consensus on any matter pertaining to Islamic law. The principal source of laws in Islam, the Qur'an, was open to multiple readings; the various *mazahib* (schools of law) subscribed to different *ahadith* (traditions of the Prophet)—there was, thus, no monolithic Shari'ah that need be upheld everywhere. Laws were meant to regulate human behaviour in such a manner that man remains on the *Sirat al-Mustaqim* (the Straight Path [which leads to God], i.e. Islam). Hence, whether an order was Islamic or not could not be judged in terms of enforcement of any individual law or not; its principal benchmark had to be whether it conforms to the essence of Islam or not.

Abu'l Fazl's understanding of Islamic order flowed directly out of the transcendentalist theory of *Wahdat al-Wujud* (Unity of Being). Devised by the 12th century Andalusian philosopher, Ibn al-'Arabi, the theory argues that the *Khaliq* (Creator) and His *Khalq* (Creation) were not distinct entities; the divine element pervades in all of Creation, and there is no "being" that is not a part of the higher "Being". Abu'l Fazl laced this theory, however, with the theory of *Wajib al-Wujud* (Necessary Being),[7] which argues that *Khair-i Mahaz* (Pure Good) is the essence of Divine Majesty, and thus absolute goodness permeates all that He created. Anything that deviates from this goodness is not an indication of the existence of evil, but the result of man's confusion in the material world, where he confuses the material with the Real world. The purpose of faith (in this context, Islam) is to keep man on the *Sirat al-Mustaqim* by keeping him abreast of the elusive nature of the material world and the Reality behind it. An Islamic order, in other words, would promote the well-being of all who were a part of it, and would elevate them in the direction of *Khair-i Mahaz* so that they could subsume their "beings" in Him—a concept that the Sufis speak of as *Fanah*.

The foundational principle of Ibn al-'Arabi's theory of *Wahdat al-Wujud* was to reinterpret the cardinal formula in Islam—*La Illaha Illa'llah* (lit. There is no God except Allah) as reading "there is no God that is not Allah." Since the plurality of existence is God's Will, the multiplicity of beliefs is also God's will; all that exists do so in God. Abu'l Fazl applied this theory to man's relations with his fellow men, that all that emanates from God must be good. He maintains, accordingly, that there can be only two possible attitude towards men: a minimalist attitude requires man to be "at peace with all" (*Sulh-i Kul*), and the ideal was to be loving towards all.[8]

Hence, to Abu'l Fazl a good life does not consist of prayer and invocation alone, but demands an attitude of *Sulh-i Kul*, and service to the whole of mankind rising above religious and sectarian differences is the highest service to the Creator.

The significance of political application of this theological formulation was nothing short of revolutionary. Abu'l Fazl's formulation of *Sulh-i Kul* as a religious duty legitimised the dispensation that Akbar considered a political necessity. Confronted with the challenge that promotion of non-Muslims jeopardised the Islamic character of the Mughal polity, it was possible to counterpose the very opposite. If non-Muslims accepted and served the Islamic order, fulfilling all the obligations that are incumbent on a Muslim, then it was un-Islamic to not treat them equally.[9]

The language of sectarian tolerance theorised by Abu'l Fazl remained the hallmark of the Timurids till the second half of the Aurungzeb's reign. Although it was subjected to major challenges all through, and not always practised overtly, the theory of sovereignty and the idea of body-politic that emerged from this language had a more durable shelf-life. To this we turn next.

III
THEORY OF SOVEREIGNTY AND THE BODY-POLITIC IN ABU'L FAZL

Abu'l Fazl's theory of sovereignty, and indeed his entire political thinking, was closely imbricated with his approach to the theory of *Wahdat al-Wujud*. If the Creator pervades every bit of the Creation, then the divine element is present in everyone. Thus, mankind has the right to a peaceful and orderly life, and to seek happiness that feeds into the goodness that stems from the divine element. Virtually taking a leaf out of Ibn Sina's views on politics, Abu'l Fazl seems to argue religion to be a life dedicated to God, and therefore service to mankind. Necessarily because of the functions a ruler discharges, Abu'l Fazl implied, the sovereign is the greatest among such servants of God, a veritable giant among men.

Determined to place Akbar's authority head and shoulders above the various Sultans who came before him, Abu'l Fazl derived his theory of sovereignty from the Sassanid theory of Kingship. The most powerful of the Sultans had always claimed themselves as being *Zill-i Ilahi* (Shadow of God), to ensure unflinching loyalty from the faithful. Abu'l Fazl argued instead that rightful rulers were endowed with *farr-i izidi* (divine effulgence).[10] This differed considerably from the Sultani theory of kingship (viz. as in Barani) where the authority was exercised in the ruler's capacity of an intermediate authority between the Rasul al-lah (Messenger of God, i.e. Prophet Muhammad) and Khalifat al-Rasul (Deputy of the Prophet, i.e. the Caliph) on the one hand, and the umrah (nobility) on the other hand. The authority wielded by the Sultan was conditional upon his satisfactory performance as the amir al-mominin (leader of the faithful) in defence and promotion of the faith; allegiance was not automatic and eminently retractable. Abu'l Fazl, however, is categorical. A ruler endowed with the *farr-i izidi* "does not need the intermediate assistance of anyone; and men in its presence, bend...[in] submission."[11]

Abu'l Fazl does not imply that all rulers necessarily are endowed with *farr-i izidi* by the mere fact of their holding authority. Political power, which is enjoyed by both rightful and selfish rulers, is characterised by a large treasury, a considerable military force, wise counsellors, loyal followers, and skillful workmen. But—he points out—selfish rulers enjoy their control over these only temporarily, while rightful rulers enjoy these all through. The latter dedicate themselves to the essence of rulership by suppressing cruelty and promoting well-being of their people; the selfish ruler, by contrast, remains fixated with the external forms of power that feed his vanity, and thus contributes to rising insecurity, strife and oppression.[12]

In arguing that the ideal ruler is one who works only for the highest perfection of happiness, Abu'l Fazl follows the footstep of al-Farabi, but unlike al-Farabi he does not speak of the perfection and happiness of Sunni Muslims alone; instead, he includes all people regardless of their confessional affiliations within its scope. In Abu'l Fazl's reckoning the ideal ruler is not merely one who adheres to the Shari'ah to be on the right path, rather he is an *Insan al-Kamil* (Perfect Man), capable of observing "the connection between spiritual and temporal things and preserving both of these high matters" in their proper place.[13] He does not totally ignore the Shari'ah, but if implementing its rules jeopardises the welfare and happiness of his subjects, he feels at liberty to disregard it.[14]

Abu'l Fazl argues that kingship is a gift of God, neither mere lineage, nor access to resources, nor support of the people makes a sovereign. The true king must possess a number of essential qualities—viz. magnanimity, benevolence, endurance, exalted understanding, innate graciousness, natural courage, rectitude, justice, proper conduct, thoughtfulness, willingness to overlook the trivial and acceptance of excuses. Most importantly, if over and above all these, the monarch is not in possession of "sufficient wisdom to overpower improper desires and unbecoming anger, he is not fit for the lofty office."[15]

Such attributes of the sovereign are essential to Abu'l Fazl's theory of sovereignty, because he maintains that the function of *jahanbani* (world-rule) is in the nature of guardianship on behalf of the Creator (who bestows that sovereign authority), whom the ideal ruler worships by maintaining or restoring peace and stability.[16] A true ruler always prevails over any force that challenges peace and stability of the realm. "A great fire cannot be put out by a little water."[17] Evil-doers and mischief-makers are undone by their own evil deeds.[18] He considers military action and expansion as inevitable for uprooting of dissension and "repose of the mortals," which he compares to "cleaning the weeds and rubbish" from a garden.[19]

At the vortex of Abu'l Fazl's scheme of sovereignty lies the concept of justice. Unlike most of the Muslim commentators on the notion, though, Abu'l Fazl does not define the scope of justice in terms of Islam. Following the paradigm propagated by *Akhlaq-i Nasiri*, he advocates the notion of universal justice. He considered foresight, reason and forbearance as essential attributes of a broad-based justice. Rulers endowed with such attributes cannot be swayed by narrow personal considerations, and do not discriminate between friends and strangers in matters of justice.

It is a requisite of the high office of sovereignty that justice be administered to the oppressed without distinction between friend or foe, relative and stranger, and that it place retribution of tyranny on the shoulder of the tyrant, so that those connected with the sovereign, and those attached with the court may not make their relationship a means of oppression, and that if, ... any such even occur out of infatuation, right-acting men...may boldly bring it forward.[20]

Abu'l Fazl was quite categorical in stressing on this as the central attribute, saying that if the sovereign does not uphold *Sulh-i Kul* (universal peace), and if he does not regard all conditions of humanity, and all sects of religion in the same light, he is not worthy of the exalted dignity of kingship.[21]

While he recommends that the ruler should view all his subjects with equal favour, though, Abu'l Fazl is not naive enough to argue that the subjects are intrinsically all the same. He classifies subjects in any realm under five heads. First, is the commendable man who does only what is proper and necessary, and is the most suitable person to be consulted in state affairs. Second, is the man of good intentions who is himself of good conduct but is less reliable in advising what is right conduct for other people. Third comes the man who is neither good nor evil; he should be allowed to live a life of ease, and be encouraged to do good. The fourth sort is the inconsiderate man who is himself evil, but does not harm others. Such men are to be made to do good by good counsel and severe rebukes when warranted. Lastly comes the vicious man, whose evil spreads like a contagion, harming others. Such people should be effectively sequestered from the rest; if that does not work, he should be banished from his dwellings; if he does not respond even to that than he should either be blinded, or have any of his limbs amputated more as deterrent than retribution.[22]

It follows from his idea of justice that Abu'l Fazl thought justice should be corrective, and not retributive. Just as a gardener, Abu'l Fazl argues, adorns the garden by moving some trees, and reject many, extirpate bad trees and lop off rotten branches, and graft some others, "so do just and farsighted kings light the lamp of wisdom by regulating and instructing their servants."[23]

Such treatment applies as much to rebel leaders as religious leaders opposed to imperial policy, refractory officials as much as ordinary subjects. He further maintains harsh disciplinary measures should be meted out in case of serious offences, but advocates capital punishment in very rare circumstances alone, for the human form is "an edifice made by God and should not be destroyed easily."[24]

The Body-Politic in Abu'l Fazl

Quite typical of Islamic thinkers inspired by generations of Platonist approach to the body-politic, Abu'l Fazl too compares the body-politic to a living organism. Drawing upon medical terminology prevalent in the middle ages, he argued that just as the equilibrium in any animal constitution depends on the balance between the four elements of fire, water, air and earth, similarly equilibrium in the body-politic is maintained by a judicious division of ranks. Each rank contributes to the prosperity of the whole, and if any rank transgresses its limits or functions, it results in a disbalance in the equilibrium.

Abu'l Fazl classifies the body-politic into four components. Contrary to most other Muslim (and Hindu) political thinkers, he considers the warriors to be the first class, akin in nature to fire. These *ahl al-saif* (men of the sword) comprised of all those who bear arms as a profession, and helps maintenance of peace and order by consuming "the straw and rubbish of rebellion and fire." The second are the manufacturers and merchants, without whose cooperation daily life of the species would be impossible, resembling the element of air—"the breeze of contentment [that] nourishes the rose-tree of life." Third in Abu'l Fazl's order are the *ahl al-qalam* (men of the pen), i.e. men of learning, who resemble water, irrigating the body-politic. Unlike Nasir al-din Tusi and other Muslim thinkers, Abu'l Fazl did not consider the *'ulema* and the *fuqaha* (jurists) as among the ahl al-qalam at all, or at least, deliberately does not mention them. Last come the husbandmen, corresponding to the element of earth, who by their exertion bring strength and happiness.[25] Unlike other Muslim thinkers before him, Abu'l Fazl does not stresses on the combination between the "men of the pen" and the "men of the sword." By deliberately downplaying the role of the "men of the pen" Abu'l Fazl emphasised the need for legislation based on the principles of sulh-i kul and not on the Shari'ah alone.

Having thus identified the structure of the body-politic, he compared the administrative structure also to the animal constitution, working on the basis of equilibrium between its four elements.[26] At the top were the *nuwinan-i dawlat* (the highest nobility), whose "devotion illuminates the battlefield," making up the element of fire. Second in line were the *auliya-i nusrat* (the revenue officials, lit. "fathers of assistance") who resemble the wind, in providing the wherewithals required for administration, allowing it to "breathe" (or not). Third were the *ashab-i suhbat* (advisors of the king), who represent the element of water in the body-politic. Perceptive, experienced and informed about human nature, if they are moderate in their views "irrigate" the body-politic, contributing to peace and prosperity; if not, they "inundate" the world with deluge and calamity. In the fourth category were the king's personal attendants, resembling earth. If free from chaff and dross, they are like an elixir for the body; otherwise they were like dust in the face of success. According to Abu'l Fazl, the benchmark of a good administrative structure was a proper coordination among these four elements. He maintained "Whatever can be done by words should not be done by the sword, and whatever can be done by...officers of middle or lower rank should not be done by great ministers."[27]

The cardinal principle in Abu'l Fazl's schema was, however, the emphasis on selfless loyalty to the ruler, which was integral to the idea of Akbar's Din-e Ilahi. Abu'l Fazl's *iklas-e chahrgana* (fourfold loyalty) involved the willingness on the part of those in state service to sacrifice the four things—*jaan* (life), *maal* (property), *din* (faith), *maan* (honour)—that could prompt defiance to authority. Abu'l Fazl was convinced that if the ruler was moderate and displayed forbearance, the people would also be able to profess absolute loyalty, and peace and stability would ensue. Conflict and discord arises when either the one or the other is found wanting in a system.

IV
THE SIGNIFICANCE OF ABU'L FAZL AS A THINKER

In the realm of political thinking, a major shift had taken place in the Indian subcontinent with the foundation of the Delhi Sultanate in the early 13th century. The largely-Hindu political culture that characterised Indian polity during the first millennium of the Common Era was gradually overturned by the incoming Islamic political order. Necessarily, the dynamics of imposition of one political culture atop another proved exclusive towards the earlier order, as the Perso-Islamic political culture acquired its unique character in the hands of thinkers like Nasir al-din Tusi and Zia al-din Barani. The Islamic political culture that emerged as a result was characterised by its emphasis on the centrality of the Shari'ah, even as allowances continued to be made towards the non-Muslim majority who lived beyond the pale of the Shari'ah.

The political thought of Abu'l Fazl was devised as an inclusive theory for the integration of Muslims and non-Muslims alike in Akbar's empire. In formulating the imperial ideology, Abu'l Fazl successfully transcended the parameters set by Muslim political thinkers who came before him, liberating the polity from the narrow confines of the Shari'ah, without compromising its essentially Islamic nature. Providing an Islamic justification for the creation of a polity where non-Muslims were given equal stakes and entitlements, Abu'l Fazl laid the foundations of a political imagination where the religious affiliation of the subject was secondary to his political allegiance. The political culture thus envisaged by Abu'l Fazl was durable enough to survive even the turbulent era of Aurungzeb well into the British Raj.

While admittedly the Mughal state did not treat all its citizens equally qua citizens, Abu'l Fazl inaugurated in India a line of political thinking that refrained from discriminating between the subjects on the basis of their sectarian identity. The emphasis he laid on sovereignty as a trust from God, the objective of which was to promote the well-being of the people, was definitively Islamic in its inspiration. And yet the manner in which he formulated the theory was non-sectarian enough to make it seem analogous to the Hindu concept of Rajdharma. Even more interestingly, it was remarkably similar to the developments in the Western intellectual tradition—both in terms of sovereignty as a trust from God (as in the 17th century English thinker John Locke, inter alia) and in terms of an emergent non-sectarian view of politics (as in the 17th century Dutch thinker, Baruch de Spinoza). In thus transcending not only the time but also the space of its origin, Abu'l Fazl's political theory continues to be of lasting interest.

Notes

1. For a brief biographical treatment of Abu'l Fazl, see S.A.A. Rizvi, *Religious and Intellectual History of the Muslims in Akbar's Reign* (New Delhi: MunshiRammanoharlal Publishers, 1975), pp. 90-93.
2. For a brief treatment of the philosophy of Ibn Sina, see Shams Inati "Ibn Sina" in Seyyed Hossein Nasr and Oliver Leaman (eds.) *History of Islamic Philosophy,* part I, (Tehran: Ansariyan Publications, 1993), pp. 231-46.
3. See Hamid Dabashi, "Khwajah Nasir al-Din Tusi: the Philosopher/vizier and the Intellectual Climate of his Times" in *Ibid.*, pp. 527-84.
4. William Chittick, "Ibn 'Arabi", in *Ibid.*, pp. 497-509.
5. The essentials of Abu'l Fazl's political (and religious) thought can be gleaned from his magnum opus, the *Akbarnama*, and in particular its third part which we know of as the masterpiece

'*Ain-i Akbari*. Additionally, there is the seldom used, but no less important work, the *Mukatabat-e Allami*.

6. See K.A. Nizami, *Religion and Politics in India During the Thirteenth Century* (New Delhi: Oxford University Press, 2002).
7. The theory was derived from the Ishraqiya tradition of Shaikh Shihab al-din Suhrawardi. For a brief treatment of the Ishraqiyas, see Hossein Ziai, "Shihab al-din Shuhrawardi: founder of the Illuminationist School", in Hossein and Leaman, pp. 434-64.
8. Rizvi, op. cit., p. 351.
9. This argument was deployed most spectacularly in 1579 to argue that, since non-Muslims went to war in defence of Islam, i.e. waged jihad (which is obligatory only for Muslims), they need not pay the *jizya*, which was incumbent on *zimmis* (lit. the protected people, non-Muslims who accept Islamic order and enjoy protection of the state).
10. Abu'l Fazl 'Allami, *Akbarnama*, (translated by H. Beveridge), (Calcutta: Royal Asiatic Society, 1897), Vol. I, p. 3.
11. *Ibid.*
12. *Ibid.*
13. *Ibid.*, Vol. III, p. 274.
14. Rizvi, op. cit., p. 356.
15. *Akbarnama*, Vol. II, p. 289.
16. *Ibid.*
17. Cited in Rizvi, op. cit., p. 362.
18. *Akbarnama*, Vol. II, p. 217.
19. *Ibid.*, Vol. III, p. 122.
20. *Ibid.*
21. Abu'l Fazl, Cited in Rizvi, op. cit., p. 364.
22. *Akbarnama* I, p. 5.
23. *Ibid.*, Vol. II, p. 323.
24. Abu'l Fazl, *Mukatabat-i Allami*, cited in Rizvi, p. 365.
25. Abu'l Fazl Allami, *A'in-i Akbari*, Vol. 1 [translated by H. Blochmann] (Calcutta: Royal Asiatic Society of Bengal, 1897), p. 4.
26. *Ibid.*, pp. 5-9.
27. *Ibid.*, p. 9.

SECTION III

Social and Political Ideas of Reformist Thinkers

7

Political Thought of Rammohun Roy (1772-1833)

Partha Pratim Basu

I
INTRODUCTION

Rammohun Roy, India's first consciously modern political thinker was born in a Hindu Brahmin family of Bengal in 1772, i.e., seven years after the British East India Company (henceforth "Company") had established its rule in India. He went through an early phase of personal religious inquiry, and wrote a rational critique of Hindu idolatrous practices at the age of 16 which led to a breach with his family. Later in life he amassed some landed property, also worked for the Company for some years between 1803 and 1813, and simultaneously sharpened his knowledge of English as well as Western science and philosophy. He finally gave up his job to settle in Calcutta in 1815 which brought him in close contact with European free traders who were ardent critics of the monopoly of Indian trade enjoyed by the Company. More importantly, it ushered in the most eventful phase of his public career as a champion of monotheism, protagonist of Western liberal and scientific education, progenitor of modern Bengali prose and journalism, propagator of women's rights and advocate of administrative, judicial and political reforms. In 1830, he sailed to England ostensibly as the accredited emissary of the then Mughal emperor (who gave him the title "Raja") though his real object was to explicate before the British public the atrocities as well as potentialities of British rule in India, and the submission he made before the Select Committee of the

House of Commons on the revenue and judicial systems of India remained an invaluable historical document. During his sojourn in England, he met eminent members of the British intelligentsia including William Roscoe, Jeremy Bentham and Robert Owen and attracted their respect and admiration for his ingrained spirit of rationality and passionate love of freedom. Following a brief illness, however, Rammohun passed away at Bristol in 1833 when he was contemplating a visit to the United States at the behest of his Bostonian Unitarian friends.

Ideologically speaking, Rammohun was the champion of constitutional liberalism of the classical variety with an accent on the rights of the individual. However, as will be argued below, his political position also contained elements of "social" or "positive" liberalism which conceived the state also as an active promoter of the rights of the people. Of course his political ideas were not systematically spelt out in any political treatise; rather they evolved in the context of the critique he developed of the despotic tendencies the Company's rule in India was increasingly betraying since the departure of Lord Hastings as Governor General in 1818. This critique in turn was largely —though not entirely as will be shown below—a product of his persistent engagement with European and American debates about constitutional government raging in the early decades of the nineteenth century.

Again, Rammohun's social, religious and political thoughts were seamlessly woven together which makes a clarification of these interconnections a precondition for grasping his political ideas (Biswas 1983). Rammohun's agenda of social reform was instigated by the all-round degeneration that gripped the society in Bengal—and India in general—in the final days of the Mughal Empire. However, his vision for rejuvenating this crippled social edifice was impregnated by the profound awareness of a global social makeover: the collapse of the feudal order and control of the means of production passing into the hands of the bourgeoisie, the Renaissance in Europe which encouraged rationalist thinking and dissemination of modern scientific knowledge, the simultaneous transformation in religious thought, practices and organization known as Reformation, and the growing clamour for the Republican Government in the aftermath of the American War of Independence (1776-83) and the French Revolution (1789). He was convinced, moreover, that the new middle class that was raising its head slowly but surely in India as well subsequent to the introduction of new property relations under the British rule was going to become the driving force of the future Indian society and polity. At the same time he realized that these promises could never be fulfilled under the then claustrophobic social and intellectual ambience, a realization which propelled him towards the goal of undertaking a thorough revamp of the social order. It is in this backdrop that a study of his religious and political thought needs to be situated.

Rammohun's programme of religious reform had two major aspects to rid Hinduism of orthodoxy, superstition, and hollow customs and rituals, and to propagate the ideal of Unitarianism, drawn from a comparative study of religions and embodied in the Brahmo Samaj founded by him in 1828. However, more important in the present connection is the fact that for him, religious reform did not merely pertain to the realm of private beliefs and practices of the individual; rather the acknowledgement of its *political* implications was the hallmark of his religious agenda. Thus in a letter dated 18 January 1828, he maintained that "It is, I think, necessary that some change should take place in their (i.e., of the Hindus) religion, *at least for the sake of their political advantage and social comfort*" (emphasis ours) (Roy 1977, 296). This remarkable statement had various ramifications (Basu 2009, 39-40) but in the present context its most pertinent implication consisted in liberation of the individual mind from the age-old conventions and habitual submission to the authority of the clergy which he saw as a critical step towards extension of individual liberty which, it may be recalled was the bedrock of constitutional government. Rammohun's move to translate the *Vedantic* literature in vernacular language—one of his major religious projects under which he published between 1815 and 1823 *Translation of an Abridgement of the Vedanta* and translation of several *Upanishads* in Bengali, Hindi and English—needs to be viewed in this light. Its primary object was to do away with the monopoly of Orthodox Brahmins over the interpretation of the sacred texts, allow the ordinary people to understand and interpret the religious books on their own, and also to evaluate the place of these teachings in their day-to-day lives (Dasgupta 2001, 6). This emphasis on enlarging the domain of individual liberty underlying his agenda of religious reform provides us a convenient entry point into the world of his political thought.

II
RAMMOHUN ROY'S POLITICAL THOUGHT: CONSTITUTIONAL GOVERNMENT AND RIGHTS OF THE PEOPLE

Rammohun's earnest admiration for constitutional government based on separation of powers was well-known and well-documented—in fact he always took a live interest in the various struggles between the forces of tyranny and liberty taking place all over the globe (Majumdar 1967, 27-28). No wonder his presence was noted by the local newspapers in the meeting held at Calcutta's Hooghly riverbank in August 1822 and attended by "the children of Lusitania" along with "those of Britain and India" (Bayly 2007, 26) to celebrate the second anniversary of the proclamation of constitutional government in Portugal. In the previous year, the news of the fall of the Neapolitan republic had come as a rude shock to him while he threw a gala dinner and treated 60 European friends in the city to commemorate the liberation of some American colonies from Spanish subjugation. The same commitment to the spirit of liberty goaded him to take an active interest in the "Reform Bill" debate in Britain in the 1820s and state in 1832 that if it failed in the Parliament, he would sever all connections with that country. Similarly, he was greatly delighted by the overthrow of the Bourbons in France in 1830 and visited Louis Philippe more than once during his trip to Europe in 1832-33 (Roy 1947, 80, 89; Collet 1962, 91).

Rammohun was enamoured of the British system of rule because the British monarchy was neither despotic nor tyrannical but represented a constitutional monarchy fully respectful of individual rights. Similarly, while he was not oblivious of the downside of the British rule in India (Basu, 11-12) the highlight of this regime, he believed, was that it had nevertheless released his countrymen from the tyrannical excesses of their previous rulers. In his *Appeal to the King in Council against the Press Ordinance* in 1823, he wrote that though under Muhammadan rule Muslims and Hindus enjoyed similar political rights, intervention in personal beliefs, plunder of property or mindless killings were routine affairs. Hence under British rule, Indians were not so discontented to lose the previous political entitlements because in their daily lives, in the areas of property, religion and personal security, they enjoyed much wider autonomy and freedom (Roy 1988, 508-09). At the same time, he regarded himself as equivalent to the *British* subjects of the British government entitled to the same genre of rights and civil liberties and raised a voice of protest whenever any act of the government deviated from this principle of equality before the law. This spirit was revealed first in 1809 when questioning the misbehaviour of the Bhagalpur Collector he wrote to Governor-General Lord Minto: "Your petitioner is aware that the spirit of British laws would not tolerate an act of arbitrary aggression even against lowest classes of individuals" (Roy 1988, 508-09).

Indeed Rammohun was convinced that establishment of rule of law was the key to maintaining the structure of a constitutional government, and realization of the rights of the ordinary people called for their protection by a general and impartial legal arrangement. Hence during the representation before the Select Committee of the House of Commons he underscored the necessity of codification of the customary civil and criminal laws prevalent in the then India. His logic was that while before the advent of British rule, India was governed by Islamic laws promulgated during the Muslim period, the regulations introduced by the British government since 1793 had brought about extensive modifications in Muslim laws. He felt that these laws should be codified in such a way as to leave no scope for any ambiguity and confusion or any need for interpretation with reference to any other legal principle.

According to some scholars, this proposal was inspired by British political philosopher Bentham's ideas, but it needs to be borne in mind that the practice of developing codes of law in India remained quite old of which Manu *Sambita* and *Fatwa e Alamgiri* provided well-known instances. Rammohun presumably was no less influenced by these examples though Bentham's arguments may have helped to refine, enrich and update the traditional Indian notions. Besides, his views diverged with Bentham's in at least one major respect. The universal legal code contemplated by Bentham rested on some abstract legal principles which he insisted were equally applicable in Britain, India and elsewhere. But Rammohun believed that the legal system of a country must have organic connections with its traditions and ways of life; otherwise the needs of the people could never be appropriately addressed (Majumdar 1996, 105; Biswas 1983, 362-63).

Again, to reinforce "rule of law", Rammohun stressed the importance of separation of powers, i.e., legislative and executive powers should not rest in one hand, and hence opposed the proposal for setting up a separate legislature for India (Biswas 1983, 324). He demanded that India should be ruled through the laws made by the British Parliament itself for he clearly understood that the legislature if set up in India would be dominated by the Governor-General and his Council; the principle of separation of powers would be flouted and the possibilities of despotic government opened up. Also, he had great faith in and respect for the impartiality and public spiritedness of the members of the British Parliament and he did not want the Indian people to be deprived of its benefits. Rammohun's concern with separation of powers may be perceived as yet another instance of Western influence upon him going back to Montesquieu's thesis and the structures of American governments as its practical embodiment. But interestingly he argued that ancient India did have a constitution which reflected a system of division of powers and it was the decline of this constitution and the attendant checks and balances that had sunk the country into backwardness. He recounted that in ancient times, the Brahmins had the legislative authority and the

Rajputs or the Warrior Castes exercised the executive authority which produced peace and harmony for many centuries. After that unfortunately an absolutist government came to prevail as the Brahmins abandoned their legislative role and began to take offices in the political department thus becoming dependent on the Rajputs and later Maratha rulers which ultimately paved the way for India yielding to Muslim invasions from abroad. Yet he equally believed that if the Indian mind had once managed to conceive of the notion of constitutional balance and separation of powers, it was very much capable of restoring the same in future. Meanwhile, the Parliament was supposed to assume the role of the Brahmin legislators while the Company government that of the Rajput protectors (Bayly 2007, 30). Simultaneously, he was fully cognizant of the pitfalls of enacting laws for India from far away England which led him to extend three suggestions: first, freedom of the press to ensure reflection of public opinion in legislation; second, appointment of commissions from time to time to make detailed assessment of governance in India; and third, ascertaining the views of the educated and affluent Indians before the passage of any law. While the third proposition exhibited an elitist bias, it needs to be conceded that in those days, the meaning of democracy even in the advanced countries was yet to encompass the views of the common people. Rammohun's awareness of the level of education of the average Indian too may have precluded him from demanding complete democracy in the matter of legislation (Biswas, 324).

Personal experience also taught him that fair and effective implementation of laws was impossible without thorough reform of the judicial system. In his representation before the Select Committee of the British House of Commons, he severely criticized the incompetence of the judges appointed in India before proceeding to analyze the flaws of the Indian judicial system. These, he felt, stemmed from three sources: "In the want of sufficient number of judges and magistrates, in the want of adequate qualifications in many of them to discharge the duty in foreign languages, and in the want of a proper code of laws by which they might be easily guided" (Roy 1947 [Part III],

11). While addressing the third issue, as we have seen above, he suggested introduction of a regular code by the government, pending which he was in favour of continuing with the existing set of laws since these were already in general familiar to the natives (Roy 1947 [Part III], 32). With regard to the crucial role of language in the judicial process, he initially wanted English to replace Persian as the language of courts. But there must have been a shift in this position as he later asserted during his stay in England that the Englishmen living in India should adopt Bengali as their mother tongue. As to the eligibility of the judges, he demanded that quality and knowledge of law would remain the sole criteria for their recruitment, and civilians of the Company could not be entrusted judicial responsibilities unless they had some acquaintance with the British law. Rammohun also pleaded for separating administrative and judicial offices and dividing the duties between the magistrates and the judges, and 'double the jurisdiction of each'. He reasoned that "(B)y this arrangement each gentleman discharging one class of duties would find them more easy and simple, though the field embraced was more extensive, and the expense would be the same as under the present system" (Roy 1947 [Part III], 25).

On top of it, despite being a staunch adherent of judicial independence, he called for popular supervision of the judicial process for promoting cost-effective, corruption-free, speedy trials, and welcomed the trial of jury. Here again Bentham's influence on his views has been contemplated but the relevance of India's time-tested *panchayat* (literally "a body of five men") system too cannot be ruled out. Of course, he stressed the differences between the modern jury system and the traditional *panchayats* but also argued in clear and detailed terms that this traditional arrangement, adopted with requisite modification and modernization, could very well act as an antidote to forgery, false witnessing and other forms of malpractices. The British Juries Act (1825) gave jurymen wide power to judge points of law as well as fact but the debarment of Indians from selection for grand juries under the Indian Juries Act (1927) rested on several grounds. First, being non-Christians, they were incapable of taking a meaningful oath; second, they would not send their own people to punishment particularly if they were Brahmins; and third, they suffered from moral depravation as a race having been long subjected to despotic rule (Bayly 2007, 34). Rammohun organized a strong movement against the blatantly anti-Indian Act and petitioned the British Parliament through his British friend J. Crawford which could lay a strong claim to being the first political movement of India. While answering the above points, Rammohun and his associates contended that (a) respectable Indians were morally fully capable of taking oaths as Hindu religion abominated lying; (b) they were long accustomed to the ancient system of jury the *panchayat* system had enshrined; and (c) by taking part in judgement Hindus and Muslims would be contributing their essential local knowledge to the proceedings (Bayly 2007, 35). Finally, shortly before his death, the new Juries Bill, shorn of its discriminatory provisions, was enacted in 1832.

Again, the sustenance of constitutional government called for acknowledgement of the right to freedom of expression on the part of the ruled; hence no wonder Rammohun was drawn to the world of newspapers widely regarded in liberal thought as *vox populi* and became an ardent champion of free press in colonial India. Of course his association with the press was occasioned by his polemical engagement with the Christian missionaries of Serampore and he published two papers—*Brahmanical Magazine* (in English) and *Brahman Sebadhi* (in Bengali)—in 1821 to answer their calumnies against Hinduism. These papers however were brought out with this specific object in view—since the missionaries were not prepared to accommodate his responses in their mouthpiece—and were closed down once they had served their immediate purpose. Yet this brief experience impressed on him the immense possibilities opened up by the advances in print technology for deliberations on various policy-related issues and mobilization of public opinion around them forging thereby a crucial link between the rulers and the ruled (Dasgupta 2001, 42). With this perspective in view, he became associated with the publication of *Sambad Koumudi* in 1821—which in effect marked the beginning of Indian journalism—and though it was formally published by Tarachand Datta under the editorship of Bhabani Charan Bandyopadhyay, the moving spirit behind this paper was undoubtedly Rammohun Roy. In its first issue, it was declared that the paper would publish discussions on religious principles and the state's affairs and letters pertaining to important domestic developments and foreign events; in a word, promotion of popular welfare would be its motto (Bera 1996). Unfortunately, no files of this paper could be retrieved, but it was learnt from indirect sources such as the contemporary English papers (e.g. *Calcutta Journal* or *Asiatic Journal*) that several socio-political issues—some addressed to the government and some to the people in general, but all focusing on public good widely defined—figured among its reports and features. Curiously enough, all these issues ranging from solicitation of trial by jury to the Mofasil, Zillah and Provincial courts through pleas for setting up schools and hospitals for the poorer members of the native community to exhortations to the wealthy Babus to curtail expenditure on social functions and devote funds to the cause of education remained close to Rammohun's heart (Das n.d. 101-05). He was also the co-proprietor, along with James Silk Buckingham, of the *Calcutta Journal*, a short-lived radical journal which printed both translations of articles in Rammohun's Bengali newspapers and also supplied material to them. For a series of explosive issues he took up in his *Journal*, which included parliamentary reform, anti-slavery (he claimed that the Company was running a clandestine slave trade) and improvement of the conditions of the British and Indian sea-men ("lascars"), Buckingham was deported from India by Lord Amherst in 1823 (Bayly 2007, 36). However, the paper Rammohun brought out in 1822 under his own name was in Persian, titled *Mirat-ul-Akhbar*. Persian remained the language of the royal court and the judiciary in India till 1835, and probably this led him to believe that a paper published in Persian would be accessible to the entire learned community in India (Bera 1996). Incidentally, Rammohun and his associates maintained that like the separation of powers and the jury system, the press too had indigenous antecedents in the news-writers (*akhbarnaviss*) of Mughal India who informed officials of breaches of justice and upheld the rule of law (Bayly

2007, 37). However, the publication of *Mirat* was stopped by him within a year in protest against the new press curbs and this valiant struggle called for separate discussion in its own right.

In 1823, the infamous Press Ordinance enforced by the new Governor-General Lord Adam made obtaining governmental clearance mandatory for the launch of periodicals, a measure doubtless prompted by the Company authorities who regarded a free press as an impediment to administration and incompatible with colonial interests. They argued, a free press was needed only in a democratic set up which was absent in India and so was the necessity of press freedom. Moreover, the Government of India, they maintained, exercised only a delegated authority derived from the Court of Directors and Board of Control of the Company, and therefore effectively resided in England. Hence if the British officials had any accountability, it was to the British Parliament and the English public, and issues arising out of their conduct could be discussed in England alone. Finally, unchecked criticism of the government would be harmful to its image precipitating loss of popular confidence in it; and ultimately it might spark off a revolt among the *sepoys,* a risk no regime based on brute force could afford to take (Majumdar 1965, 231).

To protest this illiberal step, publication of *Mirat* ceased and Rammohun (along with his friends Chandra Coomar Tagore, Dwarakanath Tagore, Prasanna Coomar Tagore, Hara Chandra Ghose and Gauri Charan Banerji) sent a memorandum to the Supreme Court in Calcutta and ultimately petitioned to the King-in-Council in England in which he furnished a point by point rejoinder to the Company's contentions. He asserted that it was the absence of a democratic structure of rule in India that made the functioning of a free press all the more necessary because it provided the only avenue for the common people to convey their grievances to the government and seek remedial measures. It was only through the press that they could appeal to the good sense of the British nation against the arbitrary and unjust acts of the Indian government, or the Directors of the Company could ascertain whether the laws enacted for the welfare of the local people were really serving their purpose. The acts of the government officials, their attitude and disposition towards the ordinary people should unfailingly remain subject of public scrutiny for this had close bearing on governance. India had a sizable chunk of educated population who, given the freedom of discussion could also highlight the positive sides of British rule. In fact, unless their motives remained questionable, governments need not fear a free press; indeed it might be conducive to enhancing the government's image and popularity as well. On the other hand, if the people are allowed to grumble with their complaints going unattended, it might precipitate a rebellious outburst (Roy 1988, 508-09). He also drew attention to the contribution made to popular welfare by the newspapers which "by introducing free discussion among the Natives and inducing them to reflect and inquire after knowledge, have already served greatly to improve their minds and ameliorate their condition" (Roy 1947 [Part IV], 6). It may be noted that many of these arguments put forward by him in defence of a free press later found their way into the works of John Stuart Mill, the apostle of British liberalism in the second half of the 19th century (Dasgupta 2001, 48-52) though, regrettably, Rammohun's plea in favour of a free press went unheeded altogether. The Press Ordinance was withdrawn only after Charles Metcalfe became the Governor-General in 1938 who was felicitated by Calcutta's literati in a public meeting for this move. Dwarakanath Tagore took this opportunity to recall the epic battle fought by Rammohun years ago in support of the freedom of the press even at the risk of exposing himself to the charge of sedition and peril of imprisonment (Dasgupta 2001, 47).

Rammohun, the defender of individual rights, was equally vocal however in demanding state activism in the interest of public welfare and social security. In classical liberal thought, the state was supposed to uphold a single general and neutral framework of law within which all members of the society could, according to their capabilities, try to pursue their economic interests and attain prosperity which many felt was the surest way to promote common good. But later, this narrow conception of pursuit of common good gave way to the notion of "social" justice which gave rise to the demand for the state actively working for ameliorating social iniquities and discrimination and foster the well-being of all. Reverberations of this concept of achieving social justice through state intervention were found in Rammohun's thought through his demand for women's rights, his plea for right to education, and his proposals for improving the lot of the peasants of Bengal (Majumdar 1967, 42-43).

As to women's liberation, Rammohun's role in the anti-*Sati* movement is primarily highlighted, though he was not the first to take up the cudgels against this social evil primarily prevalent among the upper caste Hindus. But what singled out his engagement was that he did not stop at simply demonstrating, sometimes through scriptural references, sometimes in the role of a grammarian, that widow burning was nothing short of cold-blooded women-slaughter under the garb of religious pretext. He asserted in his later works that burning of widows often brought about material gain for some male members of the widow's family, an argument amounting to an assault on patriarchal interests which explained why his struggle for putting an end to this evil practice entailed such fierce resistance as to reportedly invite attempts on his life as well. Thus, ending this wicked practice remained in his eyes only a phase in the wider struggle for restoring women's liberty and autonomy which ultimately aimed at confirming their economic rights. Towards this end, Rammohun laid bare in a pamphlet titled *The Modern Encroachment on the Ancient Rights of Female* the extent of property rights enjoyed by women in ancient India and made a strong case for restoration of these rights. He argued that according to ancient Hindu laws, widows following the death of their husbands were entitled to an equal share of the familial property but the right was later taken away by Jimutvahana, the author of *Dayabhaga* School of law. True, Rammohun in this work did not seek to directly link the demand for restoration of this ancient right of the women with the practice of widow-burning but the logical connection between the two is not at all difficult to discern (Dasgupta 2001, 30-34).

Simultaneously, he realized that a modern society could not be ushered in by quoting scriptures alone; without the lashes of modern education, India could not emerge out of its medieval bondage. Hence, he wrote a forceful letter to the Governor-General Lord Amherst in 1823 protesting against the proposal to set up a Sanskrit College under the auspices of the Company for the promotion of traditional and classical knowledge (Roy 1947 [Part IV], 108). He not only demanded instead the introduction of a liberal and scientific system of education free from the influences of religion, customs and tradition but at the same time accused the government of a plot to deprive the Indian people from acquiring the knowledge of truth. He was himself well-versed in Sanskrit and deeply respectful of its rich heritage; yet, in his view this kind of learning was clearly anachronistic and unequal to the needs of the hour. Thus, he admonished the authorities in the following language:

> ...the Sangscrit system of education would be best calculated to keep this country in darkness if such had been the policy of the British legislature. But as the improvement of the native population is the object of the Government, it will consequently promote a more liberal and enlightened system of instruction, embracing mathematics, natural philosophy, chemistry and anatomy with other useful sciences which may be accomplished with the sum proposed by employing a few gentlemen of talents and learning educated in Europe, and providing a college furnished with the necessary books, instruments and other apparatus. (Roy 1947 [Part IV], 108)

In fact, though he suggested an alternative list of subjects—described by him as 'Post-Baconian'—that needed to be included in the new syllabi, it is interesting to note that that some of these advanced disciplines were yet to be introduced in England itself (Dasgupta 2001, 39)!

Finally, to his proposals before the Select Committee of the House of Commons for rectifying the miserable conditions of the Bengal peasants which rested on an incisive analysis of their the then predicament. Lord Cornwallis's Permanent Settlement instituted private property in land relations which gave birth to a new landed class in Bengal who were to regularly collect the rent from tenants and hand over to the Company, and the dues of these *zamindars* were permanently fixed. It was expected that this new dispensation would incentivize the new landlords to introduce improved agricultural practices, bring fallow and uncultivable land under cultivation and thereby contribute towards the overall development of agriculture. In practice however the quantum of agricultural land increased no doubt but there was hardly any improvement in agricultural practices or production; and the sufferings of the peasants, the actual tillers of land, became progressively unbearable. Since the *zamindars'* dues remained unchanged, they resorted to all kinds of repression including confiscation of the tenants' movable and immovable property in order to extract the maximum from the hapless peasants. Rammohun, presented a graphic description of the plight of these peasants before the Select Committee of the British House of Commons and stressed that the Permanent Settlement, though beneficial for the British government and the *zamindars,* deprived the peasants most because while the settlement was arrived at between the first two parties, the peasants were not made a party to this arrangement. He enunciated a set of proposals for the alleviation of the peasants' distress and demanded that the dues of the peasants should also be permanently fixed; *zamindars* would have to give *a patta* (legal land-ownership document) to each peasant; a list of the tillers working under each landlord would have to be submitted to the Collector's office; the peasants would enjoy their rights to land on an inter-generational basis and could not be summarily evicted; and the *zamindar* could not demand any additional money on any pretext, otherwise they would have to pay fines or face jail term. It was in connection with this permanent determination of the tenants' rent that Roy suggested reduction in the rent payable by the landlords and also advised the government to meet the shortfall in revenue through taxing luxury goods. His proposals were predictably rejected both by the government and the *zamindars* but his fervent plea to the government for assuaging the miseries of the peasants through these distinctively modern recommendations firmly set his political thought within the tradition of social or positive liberalism (Datta 1989, 134-36).

III
RELEVANCE OF RAMMOHUN THOUGHTS

Rammohun Roy's political vision had a trans-national context as he earnestly believed that political reforms in India were critically dependent on the success of constitutional revolutions throughout the world. Hence, he wholeheartedly sided with the forces which were bent on reforming the British Parliament for he hoped that a liberal rule in Westminster would ensure closer parliamentary oversight with regard to Indian legislation and divide judicial from executive powers across the subcontinent. Any successful rebellion against autocracy across the world was for him a cause for rejoicing, and he hosted several celebrations in Calcutta Town Hall for Spanish, Portuguese and Latin American revolutions between 1820 and 1823.[1] According to C.A. Bayly, Rammohun belonged to the 'small international public sphere' that emerged in the 1810s and 1820s unified by the 'global imagining of constitutional liberty' and made possible by the great expansion of the press and idea of association at world level since the 1780s (Bayly 2007, 28). The international range of Roy's imagined political community, Bayly continued, made him in effect India's first indigenous "public man" (Bayly 2007, 29).

But while Western influences undoubtedly underpinned his scheme of constitutional government based on rule of law and separation of powers, the indigenous elements with reference to which he often justified the workability of such a governmental framework in the Indian setting could hardly be overlooked. His allusions to the separation of legislative and executive powers existing between the Brahmins and Rajputs in ancient times, the unmistakable shadow of the legal codes prevalent in ancient or medieval India that crept into his plea for codification of law under the colonial regime or his contention that long familiarity with the *panchayati* system of justice would make it easier for the Indians to effectively participate in the trial of Jury have already been taken note of. As Bayly observed, Rammohun's identification of these home-grown components of a future Indian constitution which rested on a 'melding of *itihasa*, divine legends and a particular "Hindu" reading of the medieval Indian history', sought to underscore the fact that this constitution depended on *Indian* agency. This was necessary to combat the early British constructs of a "Hindoo constitution" which presented an essentially static picture of Indian history and implied that it was the British who would re-establish ancient India's "constitution" (Bayly 2007, 31).

It may further be noted that in Rammohun's perception, individual liberty was prioritized over and above the right to self-determination or political independence. The end of British rule, he believed, would happen only some long time in future; meanwhile, he hoped that the imperial Parliament would act as the legislative guardian of India and other colonial dependencies. In fact he regarded British rule in India as a period of political apprenticeship for Indians which would in course of time impart to them the skills of sharing political power and legislative authority. He was fully conscious of the limitations of his countrymen—their lack of education, their unquestioning subjugation to social customs and clerical diktats, and the lack of public spirit in their conduct which was the sine qua non for running a responsible government. Hence, he regarded the liberation of the minds and intellect of the people which would render them capable of exercising independent political power and legislative authority as the first and foremost task of the day. From this standpoint, moreover, he regarded British rule in India both in the sense of a legal system as well as a knowledge system as a period of political apprenticeship which would allow the people of India to attain the requisite intellectual, cultural and political maturity. It was in this context that he made his profound yet much misunderstood statement made in a letter written to the French journalist Jacquemont: 'India requires many more years of English domination so that shc may not have many things to lose while she is reclaiming her political independence' (Sen 1989 [Appendix], 78). For him, declaration of political independence without attainment of individual liberty in the above sense was like putting the cart before the horse which virtually amounted to self-deception.

But while the question of India's independence remained for him a deferred agenda, what he wholeheartedly concentrated on in the interim was to tame the despotic power of the Company and prevent its rule from being totally indifferent to the social and cultural needs of the native community. He persistently wielded his pen, sought to mobilize popular opinion and, within limits, strove to organize movements in order to ensure the recognition and expansion of individual rights in British-dominated India. It may be recalled that initially British colonialism in India was guided by the conservative philosophy of engagement in routine economic exploitation, political oppression and non-interference with the native society. But with the passage of time the British government had to experiment with a carefully devised statecraft in order at least to appear to be responsive to the myriad pressures generated from various social strata. And the credit for forcing this reversal of the earlier stance of the rulers went largely to the way Rammohun along with his followers chose to bombard the government with a host of demands whether for introducing Western education, upholding a free press, acknowledging the role of the natives in the judicial system or giving a better deal to the Indian peasants. This activism was rooted in his perception, if not conviction, that the political authority, even if alien, had to be responsive to the needs of society. He wanted to ensure that whoever ruled the country must have the necessary legitimacy which was hardly furnished by the flimsy title of territorial conquest. With this object in view he sought to fashion and nurture a civil society in India to combat the worst excesses of foreign rule by disseminating political education and stirring up political movements.

Rammohun, for reasons cited above, could not perhaps be called a nationalist in the conventional sense and the movements he organized undeniably aimed at making the British rule in India more bearable or sufferable. But the technique he employed to this end, i.e., directly petitioning the Governor-General or even the King-in-Council, clearly bore the mark of defiance towards the rules and regulations of the Company's regime. Again, his plea for introduction of Western liberal and scientific education contained in the letter to Lord Amherst (1823), when compared with his protests against the Press Ordinance (1823) and the Juries Act (1827), brought out a fundamental change in his perception of the subjects' rights. While in the first case he stressed the people's right to voice opinion and criticise in matters pertaining to governance, in the latter instance the crux of his contention was that the rulers would *have* to rule in consonance with the opinion of the people (Dasgupta 2001, 8). In other words, here we find an attempt to circumvent the despotism of the rulers by the doctrine of people's rights. Of course, he never pressed for "revolutionary" change; appeal to reason and good sense whether of the government or the entrenched interests in the Indian society was for him the key to progress and prosperity. He did not believe in application of force and initially he did not even support Lord Bentinck's attempt to put an end to the practice of widow-burning through legislative intervention lest it antagonized the vested interests so bitterly that the laudable move would become a non-starter altogether. Still Rammohun undoubtedly remained the pioneer of constitutional agitations in India, the technique faithfully pursued by the first generation leaders of the Indian National Congress formed more than half a century after his death. His political arguments were re-appropriated and reconstructed by later Indian thinkers and politicians from Dadabhai Naoroji to Jawaharlal Nehru who embraced the ideal of secular and progressive republicanism.[2] On top of it, the constitution adopted by free India in 1950 incorporating separation of powers, fundamental rights and provision for affirmative action constituted a glowing tribute to the canons of Rammohun Roy's political thought.

Notes

1. It is interesting to note that the active interest Rammohun and his ilk showed in European and American concepts and movements for freedom and constitutional government did not go without reciprocation. Thus when Spanish reformers reissued the original 1812 Cadiz constitution, it was dedicated as follows: "Al liberalismo del noble, sabio, y virtuoso Brahma Ram-Mohan Roy" (See Bayly 2007, 28). Similarly, a leader of the anti-slavery campaign in USA signed a pamphlet addressed to the members of the Congress under the pseudonym of Rammohun Roy! (See Collett 1962).
2. S.S.O 'Malley paid homage to Rammohun's spirited defence of freedom of the press during the Round Table Conference

held in London in 1931, almost a century after his demise, in the following words: 'A Round Table Conference to discuss India's future, with Indians taking a full share in the discussions, would have been a preposterous and incredible suggestion to Englishmen of the Company's days. It might never have come about had the great Rammohun Roy not taken the lead and the three Tagores, a Ghose and a Banerji not joined him in the process that led to it'. See Majumdar 1965, 231, cited in Dasgupta.

References

Basu, Partha Pratim. 2009. *Revisiting Rammohun Roy's Political Agenda: Implications for the Post-colonial Indian Polity*, Calcutta: Raja Rammohun Roy Memorial Museum.

Bayly, C.A. 2007. "Rammohan Roy and the Advent of Constitutional Liberalism in India 1800-30", *Modern Intellectual History*, Vol. 4, Issue 1, April.

Bera, Anjan. 1996. "Rammohun Roy o Sangbadikata", *Pashchim Banga,* Rammohun Number, (in Bengali), Calcutta: Govt. of West Bengal.

Biswas, Dilip Kumar. 1998. *Rammohun Sameeksha*, (in Bengali), Calcutta: Saraswat Library.

Collet, S.D. 1962. *The Life and Letters of Raja Rammohun Roy*, (eds. Dilip Kumar Biswas and Prabhat Chandra Ganguli), Calcutta: Sadharan Brahmo Samaj.

Datta, Bhabatosh. 1989. "Raja Rammohun Roy o Bharatiya Arthaniti" in Pulin Bihari Sen et al. (eds), *Rammohun Smaran*, (in Bengali) Calcutta: Raja Rammohun Roy Smritiraksha Samiti.

Das, Jogananda. n.d. *Rammohun o Brahmo Andolan* (in Bengali), Calcutta: Sadharan Brahmo Samaj.

Dasgupta, Surajit. 2001. *Rammohun o Byakti Swadhinata* (in Bengali) Calcutta: Progressive Publishers.

Majumdar, B.B. 1967. *History of Indian Social and Political Ideas*, Calcutta: Bookland.

Majumdar, Durga Prasad. 1996. "Rammohun Rayer Rajnoitik Chinta o Karjokolap Prosonge" in *Paschim Banga*, Rammohun Number, (in Bengali), Calcutta: Govt. of West Bengal.

Majumdar, R.C. ed. 1965. *British Paramountcy and Indian Renaissance*, (Part II), Bombay: Bhartya Vidya Bhaban.

Roy, Rammohun. 1947. *The English Works of Rammohun Roy* (eds. Kalidas Nag and Debajyoti Burman), Calcutta: Sadharan Brahmo Samaj.

———. 1977. *Selected Works of Raja Rammohun Roy*, New Delhi: Govt. of India.

———. 1988. *Rammohun Rachanavali*. Calcutta: Haraf Prakashani.

Sen, Pulin Bihari et al. (eds). 1989. *Rammohun Smaran*, (in Bengali) Calcutta: Raja Rammohun Roy Smritiraksha Samiti.

8

Syed Ahmed Khan: Views on Colonial Rule and Modernisation (1817-1898)

Nandini Bhattacharya

I
INTRODUCTION

Colonial India experienced the rise of a number of distinguished thinkers who were creations of their own historic context and at the same time, with their vision and insights, they challenged their milieu and initiated new historic epochs. Sir Syed Ahmed Khan was one such epoch maker. He was the pioneer of the modernisation process of the Muslim community in colonial India. His contribution towards the Muslims of India can be marked in three pillars, his institutional drive towards educating his Mohammedan brethren in the viable Western knowledge, his political awareness to situate his coreligionists in a favourable position in the complex colonial context and his deep introspection into the Islamic philosophy and knowledge to justify the eternal essence of rationality and humanity embedded in Islam. The first two aspects would fall under the purview of this essay and would be discussed in details for understanding him as a colonial reformer. It would be attempted to bring out the essence of his thoughts and deeds which inspired his people to revive self-confidence and enabled them to face the changed political reality of 19th century India. However, in spite of all good intensions, like all other social reformers of the colonial India, Syed Ahmed's reform projects also carried some crucial fault lines. While making an effort to understand and analyze his ideas and their ramification in the contemporary historic context, the present essay would attempt to provide a rational understanding of this particular leader with all his positive contributions and obvious shortcomings.

Colonial rule brought a baggage of knowledge and mindset conveniently clubbed under the umbrella term 'modernism' that challenged the pre-colonial Indian life and thought. The set of qualities enlisted under modernism were elusive as it spoke of rule of law, civil justice, democracy and liberalism, practically unachievable under the colonial constraints. But at the same time, this set of lofty ideals created an image of an advanced West as against the dwindled Orient. The rationale behind the rise of the West had been carefully portrayed as a celebration of advanced knowledge, scientific, reasonable and modern as against the backward, degenerated and stagnant hoard of Eastern knowledge. Many of the first generation intellectuals of India had been trapped by this logical fallacy, whereby they wanted to upgrade the Indian knowledge, reform social discipline and learn from the Western masters, the method of disciplined governance. Raja Rammohun Roy of Bengal pioneered this process of reforms and revival at the early phase of 19th century. Syed Ahmed who was born in 1817, toed the same line about half a century later, when the political scenario of colonial India turned much more complex. Understanding Syed Ahmed, therefore, demands a very careful study of his historic context and also the community he represented.

The colonial inroad did not have the same impact on the different Indian communities because they shared various power equations in the pre-colonial political scenario. A large section of the aristocratic Muslims, directly linked or remotely attached to the ruling aristocracy found the British ascendancy, a direct assault on their dignity and prowess and abstained from contact with the ruling race for a longer period of time. Meanwhile, other communities, who were less prominent, but subtly ambitious, took advantage of the colonial structure and markedly advanced in the socio-economic ladder in the early colonial days. The patriotic Muslims abhorred this category of collaborators and refrained from the set of values and qualities they inculcated to settle themselves in an advantageous position in the new power equation. Sir Syed Ahmed belonged to this genre, being a part of the Mughal *durbar* (aristocracy), he empathized strongly to this vanquished lot of the forgotten era. The moment of take off for his public image is marked by the aftermath of the Great rise of 1857. The Muslims taking recourse to avenge the newly founded Western political authority by their medieval weapons and strategies collapsed miserably in the rise of 1857, although it was no exclusive a revolt of the Muslims, rather an exemplary event of a combined Hindu-Muslim upheaval against the British Raj. 1857 remained a watershed in the history of colonial India, for both the ruler and the ruled. The British empire of hundred years were shaken to its core by the combined challenge of the army and civil rebels. However, once the rebellion was curbed down, the British took recourse to ruthless destruction in order to avenge their loss. Since the old Mughal Emperor was made the symbolic head of the movement, the Muslims of Upper India made a spontaneous participation in the rise. Hence, the colonial vengeance was lashed out largely on them. The city of Delhi, especially the area inhabited by the erstwhile Mughal court people were ravaged and the Muslims of this old *gharana* (milieu) were the victims of severe atrocities. Syed Ahmed, who already held a public office of *munsif* (a local level administrative post) under the colonial government, now felt the ardent need to remove the misunderstanding between the rulers and his own community. At the aftermath of British carnage on the Muslim enclaves of Delhi, he returned home from Bijanur, his place of work to salvage his family and witnessed the seamless deaths and destructions. His own mother died as an after effect of this suffering and trauma. Syed Ahmed decided his plan of action. Interestingly, unlike the common medieval chivalrous reaction, he took a rational course to elevate his fellow people from this tragic fate. He took the course of collaboration, so far abhorred and rejected by his fellowmen. He realized that fighting the British power had been a foolhardy effort that brought nothing but misfortune and ruins to his community. He tried to reprimand his fellowmen from the wrath of the ruling race. According to his biographer, K.A. Nizami, "Syed Ahmad's appraisal of the situation was realistic and once he had considered the problem in all its aspects, he threw himself headlong in the breach without hesitation. He thought that the situation could be well utilized by the Indians for accelerating the process of change from the medieval to the modern pattern of life. Resistance to British would be futile because it would be a fight of ignorance against knowledge and would ultimately ruin and defeat."[1] Hence, his effort began to reorient the image of his fellowmen in the eyes of the alien anguished masters. His essay titled "The Loyal Mohammadans of India" written in 1860, intended to reorient the Muslim image as loyal subjects to the British Raj. To quote some of his significant arguments, "Be it known however that I am no advocate of those Mohammadans who behaved undutifully, and joined in the Rebellion; on the contrary I hold their conduct in utter abhorrence, as being in the highest degree criminal, and wholly inexcusable." He further argued, "Verily, such unworthy Mohammadans have well deserved the righteous indignation of all right thinking men; but at the same time, I must deprecate that wholesale denunciation against the entire class of Mohammadans, in which the newspapers are wont to indulge, and which stains the pages of those who have written upon the events of 1857."[2] He then went into detailed discussion regarding the scope of Muslim-Christian interaction according to traditional religious teachings on both sides and justified the subjugation and subservience on part of the Muslims towards the benevolent mastery of the Christian rulers. He tried to establish from various standpoints as to how, the rise of 1857 cannot be considered a *jihad* (a holy war) and why the Mohammadans would not consent to rise in a *jihad* against the British Raj.

II
SYED AHMED—A HARBINGER OF MODERNITY

Syed Ahmed Khan decided to upgrade the condition of the Muslims in India by a series of constructive efforts, of which Western education served as the fulcrum, therefore, instead of fighting the authorities, he furthered his amiable understanding with his British superiors. Thus, there began the process of modernisation among the Mohammadans, who mostly rejected the ruling race and their baggage of knowledge and power so far. As a visionary, he realised that to get over this stagnation, one must master the knowledge of the ruling race. It was a mammoth task and needed multidimensional inputs. Positive propaganda among backward Muslims and the British authorities was one of the basic theoretical premise for him to begin with. Being a prolific writer he embarked on changing the mindset of both his fellow Muslims as well as the colonial masters by replacing hatred and skepticism with honour and trust. *Asbab-E-Bhagwat-E-Hind* (Causes of the Indian revolt) and *The Loyal Mohammadans of India, Mohammadans Eating Food With Christians, Islam and Tolerance*[3] are some such essays which tried to remove the tainted image of the Muslims in the rulers' gaze. But , in *Review on Hunter's Indian Mussalmans* he was upright in his critic of Mr. Hunter for his biased approach towards the Muslim subjects (especially the Wahabis) of the British India, as he lamented "It is unfortunate for Dr. Hunter that he has, throughout his work, relied upon very weak authorities when treating of Mohammadan creeds. The learned Doctor has shown little discretion in not sifting more carefully the chaff from the wheat."[4] He was determined to remove all misnomers on the Indian Muslims and did not hesitate to combat the version of government representative Hunter, that endorsed his commitment to the cause.

But a more difficult combat for him was to convince his own community to come out of their centuries old inertia to embrace Western knowledge. It took him much pain to assure them that there remained no other choice for them if they wished to survive and prosper in the changed world. At the same time, he understood that people of his community would feel skeptical to enroll their wards in the alien ambience of existing educational institutions for the fear of losing attachment to religion and tradition. Thus began his preparation for the creation of an institution where they could pursue Western education without compromising their faith and culture. As one of his oft quoted golden saying goes, "Call me by whatever names you like. I will not ask you for my salvation. But please take pity of your children. Do something for them (send them to the school), lest you should have to repent (by not sending them)."[5]

In his process of persuasion towards Western education, much after the creation of his own institution at Aligarh, in a speech titled, "On Education", he enumerated the reason behind the Muslim backwardness in colonial context and showed education as the only process to get over this stagnation. "Government in its generosity has made colleges in every place; but Mussalmans have reaped very little benefit from them.... The real reason of the backwardness of Mohammadans in English education is that from their non-acquaintance with modern learning they had no respect for it, and considered it mean and degraded in comparison with their own learning, which they got from the Greeks. This feeling was strengthened by false religious superstitions. And the result of it was that they did not pay the least attention towards the acquisition of modern learning, while other nations did, and have thus advanced far ahead, so that now it is very difficult for our nation to get abreast of them."[6]

His acquaintance with the British superiors came of use when he began to contemplate an institutionalised version of his dream. In his critical appreciation of Sir Syed Ahmed and his historic context, Dr. Nazir Ahmed made an interesting enumeration in the Encyclopedia of Islam, "In the dialectic between Europe and the Muslim world, Syed Ahmed Khan of India occupies a unique position. He was perhaps the first Muslim leader to contemplate the *possibility* of coexistence between the two global civilizations. Muslim reformers before him had either totally disregarded the European challenge or were hostile to any accommodation with Europe. The initiatives taken by Sir Syed had far reaching consequences for the Muslims. He demonstrated the possibility of coexistence and cooperation between the European and Islamic civilizations, although in his own lifetime, with the British firmly entrenched in India, he could achieve no more than a supportive role for Indian Muslims."[7] Syed Ahmed's desperate drive to recover the degenerating community was based on a simple realisation that, "since the fall of Bengal in 1757, all of the higher positions in civilian, military and judiciary service were reserved for the British. The more educated Hindus filled the lower positions that were open to Indians. The Muslims were practically shut out."[8] And obviously, so long the mutual suspicion and hostility persisted between the Muslims and the British, the Muslim isolation and degeneration would continue.

Syed Ahmed Khan as an Educationist

Syed Ahmed's alternative for his downtrodden, depressed and tormented fellowmen was to acquire the potential for understanding this new system of a state and then participate in it, as men of many other communities were already doing, in order to recover their lost position and prestige. Instead of confrontation he brought the mantra of collaboration among the common Mohammadan mindset towards the alien authorities. He not only accepted the alien rule as a fait accompli but justified it as a God's will.[9] And in order to equip them in the current context, his primary task was to initiate the process of Western education among his fellow men. After a few experiments with the creation of Scientific Societies and schools at Gazipur (his place of work) he changed the centre for educational reforms to Aligarh where he envisaged an institution for higher education, suitable for Muslim candidates. From his careful survey, he realized that the miniscule participation of the Muslims in Western schools and colleges were because of the fear of clash of faith and culture. In order to increase their numbers in Western education one must provide them with a favourable environment to pursue their own faith and practices. It was with this conscious motto to cater the need of his own community he had conceived the idea of an institution of his own paradigm. And hence, the inception of his "Mohammadan Anglo-Oriental College" in Aligarh near Delhi in 1875. The creation of this college remained a high water mark in his career which survived the test of time and still continues with it glorious legacy with an enhanced status of a university in the same location. K.A. Nizami defined the motto of this college in a simple yet comprehensive manner, "Sayyid Ahmad wanted this college to act as a bridge between the old and the new, the East and the West. While he fully appreciated the need and urgency of imparting instructions in Western learning, he was not oblivious of the value of oriental learning and wanted to preserve and transmit to posterity the rich legacy of the past."[10] Therefore, along with Western knowledge in English, the college imparted lessons in Arabic, Persian as well as Sanskrit. From the very inception this institute was based on some very significant guiding principles. Primarily, this was created with the patronization of the colonial Govt., with the lofty ideal of Oxford and Cambridge in mind, but it was distinctly apparent that the management would never be conferred to the alien British hands. This was on principle focused on the advancement of Muslim youth and envisaged their progress in a familiar Islamic ambience. However, this did not make it an exclusivist institute for Muslim students alone, both for students and teachers its door was open to talents, irrespective of religion. Thus, Sir Syed Ahmed had envisaged quite a unique platform for education in this which, he could combine in a delicate balance a number of apparently incompatible features of his contemporary context. In fact, the very essence of Anglo-Oriental College was supposed to flourish on the proportionate use of each feature to produce English educated Muslim youth holding respectable positions in the colonial public service, confident and capable of facing their contenders from Hindu community. But in spite of such a communitarian focus, Syed Ahmed did not make his institute exclusively for the Muslims, Hindu students were not debarred from getting admission in this college. Undoubtedly, the focus was to upgrade the standard of education among the Muslims, so that they could soon equip themselves in necessary knowledge and accomplishment in order to be at par with their already advanced Indian counterparts, namely the high caste Hindus. Although the Mohammadan Anglo Oriental college, had its main focus on higher education in modern Western model for the Muslim community, yet its door was kept open for pupils of all religions. Syed Ahmed clarified this himself whereby, he was proved to be non-communal in his values although highly communitarian by his faith and perspective. In Nizami's apt articulation, "He envisaged a community institution and not a communal one."[11] In fact, Syed Ahmed's appeal for the college had attracted generous funding from a number of Hindu patrons, which endorsed the non-communal nature of the college from other way round. As a visionary he continued to uphold his lofty ideals for the steady development of this institution that would have opened a new arena for the depressed and directionless Muslim community of that time. Progressive Muslim scholars like Nizami[12] and K.M. Ashraf had compared his educational drive with the pioneering efforts of Raja Rammohun Roy in case of Bengali society. "His diagnosis led him to the same path that Raja Rammohun Roy had followed half-a-century earlier. Like the Raja again, he was fanatically convinced that unless Muslims take to new learning and rear up a middle-class, they are doomed."[13] This comparison with the first modern educationist of Bengal as well as India, was not only a lofty epithet but it carried a number of nuanced implications. Raja Rammohun, as a first generation Indian did not realize the subtle mode of exploitation embedded in the colonial rule, but rather welcomed the rule of law and advent of modernity as a blessing for the chaotic and indecisive Indian states. Fifty years later, when the rest of India, who got the exposure to Western education under colonial rule and also many of them received respectable jobs under the regime began to get disillusioned with the colonial Raj, Syed Ahmed toed the line initiated by Rammohun. This was not only out dated by then, but highly contradictory to the rising tide of anti-colonial movement. Thus his ideas on education also carried a kind of ambivalence. However, in spite of his complex time frame and difficult fellow Indian citizens, Syed Ahmed received support from a large number of Hindus, in his initiative for an educational institution.

But, in spite of all his sense of progress in balance, there remained a shortcoming in his notion of community development through education. He was evasive and reluctant on the question of women's education. He refused to admit the ignorance prevailing in the domestic abode and discouraged the government to initiate the process of introducing school education for Muslim girls. Although he was not opposed to the idea of imparting education for women at home within their given structure, he refused to devote much energy to institutionalize the process as such. He might have feared that breaking the enclave would be a grave challenge for the community and that may hinder the progress of men as well. Thus, in his progressive discourse there was no space for institutionalization of women's education. Not that he was against it, but he preferred female education within the family enclave, following the practiced norm of Pardah (veil). This lopsidedness was nothing unusual of his time and context, but this had its ramification as time moved on and women of other communities (mainly caste Hindus, Parsis, etc.) began to make public appearances equipped in Western knowledge which increased the distance between Hindu and Muslim women of affluent communities.

However, Mohammadan Anglo-Oriental College remained a landmark, not only in Syed Ahmed's life and career, but for the entire community as it served the purpose to combine the scope of Western education along with the innate religious faith and practice of the Muslims. According to the estimate given by K.M. Ashraf, his initiative really bore fruit in the direction he had envisaged, "It was estimated on the death of Syed Ahmed Khan in 1898 that Aligarh had until then produced 126 graduates and secured honourable employment for 334 of its boys including 31 barristers and 37 other practicing lawyers."[14] The tireless effort of Syed Ahmed in the direction of education and progress centering round the institution received the sympathy and involvement of the students, teachers and other members and patrons and soon this process took shape of a movement and became popular as Aligarh Movement. The dynamism of the movement acted as a moral inspiration for the Muslims of India, so far disoriented and directionless. In Ashraf's analysis, "For once, a section of Muslim intelligentsia overcame the old sense of frustration and felt the necessary urge to line up with their fellow countrymen on the necessary progress. For the first time, Aligarh movement had given them a sense of unity and solidarity which transcended all barriers of provincial and sectional loyalties."[15]

His views on politics, somehow, represents certain ambivalence. He, on the one hand wished his fellowmen to revive the lost prestige and position in society by acquiring Western knowledge, but on the other he had vehemently forbidden them to participate in the rising tide of Indian nationalism. He openly preferred to accept subservience to the ruling authorities and advised the followers not to commit the same mistake of challenging the British Raj as had been done in 1857. He anticipated further onslaught of the colonial authorities would completely destroy the already downtrodden and dwindling Muslims of India. Therefore, he pioneered a new path of reforms and progress which was not possible without the benevolent support of the colonial authorities.

Two Nation Theories of Khan

Syed Ahmed was convinced that education would provide the key to overcome the backwardness of his community, and bring them at par with those advanced section of Indians who already accomplished Western education and achieved professional success under the colonial regime. Although a venerated visionary of all time, Syed Ahmed's view was constricted by two short-term considerations, first, to elevate the position of the Muslims in unconditional collaboration with the colonial masters and second, to set a goal to get at par with those handful elites, mainly belonging to high caste Hindu community. He desperately wanted his Muslim fellowmen to progress faster and for that they needed to concentrate solely on their education while politics was looked upon as a harmful distraction. Syed Ahmed had carefully evolved his political opinion that justified a temporary bifurcation of the two communities (Hindus and Muslims) without rupturing the harmony and cohesion of the whole nation for ever. The much publicized 'two-nation theory' was formulated in this context. This theory has served as the very basis of his political ideas about India and the Indians in the colonial context. To quote his own expression, from the address titled, "*Reply to Address Presented by The Indian Association, Lahore*," in 1883, "Friends, in India there live two prominent nations which are distinguished by the names of Hindus and Mussalmans. Just as man has some principal organs, similarly these two nations are like the principal limbs of India. Both of us being common inhabitants of India, actually constitute one nation; and the progress of this country and that of both of us is possible through mutual cooperation, sympathy and love."[16]

Here he used the term nation with two different connotations, one to mean the distinctive identity of the two major religious communities of India and then to imply the Indian nation as a whole. And to his philosophy there was no contradiction in this very thought as he took the distinction as irremovable part of the harmonious whole: "By the word Qaum I mean Hindu and Mussalman both, and this is the meaning I attach to the word nation (Qaum)."[17] In the same speech Syed Ahmed made that famous statement which became an all time quote for communal harmony of this land, "My friends, I have repeatedly said and say it again that India is like a bride which has got two beautiful and lustrous eyes—Hindus and Mussalmans. If they quarrel against each other that beautiful bride will become ugly and if one destroys the other, she will lose one eye."[18] The same notion of co-operation and cohesion continued in his speeches and letters in other occasions, such as the reply to the address of the Indian Association, Lahore Session in 1883. Here he made honest admission in favour of the advancement of the Bengalis as a race, "I confess that in our country only Bengalis are such a nation of whom we can be proud and the enlightenment we have had in the field of education, liberty and patriotism has been due to them. I can honestly say that they occupy the topmost position among all people of India."[19] And then while narrating the motto of the foundation of his institution in Aligarh he had placed a subtle appeal to this already advanced nation (community), "Suppose there are two brothers, one of them is quite healthy while the other is ill and in delicate health. It will be the duty of the other brother to help him towards his recovery."[20] Syed Ahmed's drive towards Western education was neither new, nor too out of place, as this trend was set half a century ago in Bengal, by Raja Rammohun Roy, Iswar Chandra Vidyasagar and so on, soon replicated in other parts of India. But when Syed Ahmed had fixed his bull's eye in the recovery of his nation or community keeping aside all other possible issues, Indian politics of the mainstream was brewing to surface. Therefore, when Syed Ahmed brought the call for reformation, it coincided and clashed with the rising tide of early Indian Nationalism. While, Western educated Indians realized the hoax in the promise of British 'rule of law' and began to question and challenge the authorities through various regional political platforms that ultimately joined together to form the Indian National Congress in 1885, Syed Ahmed and his followers took up a diametrically opposite approach not to disturb the colonial power-structure at that moment. For the advancement of their own community, the protective umbrella of the colonial authorities seemed indispensable. Hereafter, the 'two-nation theory' took a sharper contour as manifested in his speeches and writings although never ever did it pronounce the ultimatum of complete schism, yet the possibility of a disjuncture imbedded in his position became more and more visible.

His open critique of the Indian National Congress acted as a perpetual deterrent towards Muslim participation in this all-India platform for freedom struggle. Therefore, his speeches during the early days of Congress was full of strong critic of its members and their scheme of plans on the one and the warning towards the people of his own community not to be a party to their movement on the other. Syed Ahmed vehemently opposed any political mission against the colonial authorities at that historic moment. And when the Congress began to thrive in its full swing, he earnestly requested his Muslim brethren not to participate in its activities, lest, his mission for enlightenment in a protective colonial atmosphere would fizzle out. He made fiery critic of the Congress programmes of the initial days in his speeches, some of which attest his emotional out bursts against those advanced races who were in the forefront of the platform, like the Bengalis. It is unbelievable to accept such vituperation coming from a sane person as Syed Ahmed. Two years before the foundation of the Congress he had praised the Bengali initiative towards advancement and at the platform of Indian Association where he took them as a trendsetter in the process of modernization and progress. But just two years after the foundation of Congress, in December, 1887, he addressed his own people in Lucknow and developed a highly sectarian thesis to dissuade the Muslims to join the movement initiated by the Congress. One of the primary agendum of the INC was to introduce more job opportunities for the Indians on the basis of competitive examinations. Syed Ahmed was uncomfortable with such an apparently fair play because, given the historic context of India, there were not many candidates to fill up such posts in the colonial administration from each and every community. Bengali elites, being markedly advanced in Western education had more potentials to succeed in the competitive examinations to acquire important legislative and administrative posts. Syed Ahmed's dormant prowess of medieval chivalry came out in vengeance against this very remote possibility of a Bengali dominated India. He tired to induce a definite anti-Bengali sentiment among the gathering as he said, "Think for a moment what would be the result if all appointments were given to competitive examinations. Over all races, not only over Mohammadans but over Rajas of high position and the brave Rajputs who have not forgotten the swords of their ancestors, would be placed as rulers a Bengali who at the sight of a table knife would crawl under his chair. There would remain no part of the country in which we should see at the tables of justice and authority any face except those of Bengalis."[21] In fact, his entire speech on this occasion was replete with many such anti-Bengali outbursts. Interestingly, if seen beyond the sectarian bias against the apparently obscure Bengalis, this statement carries a much more fallacious proposition within it. Syed Ahmed, who remained the harbinger of modernism for the Mohammadan people of India, who realized the blunder in the rise of 1857 and took up the challenge of introducing Western education among his own people in order to break their obsession with the lost past, was himself still a prisoner of the same bygone memory of the bravery of the battlefield. This comment went not only against the Bengalis as a race but also against the goal set by Syed Ahmed himself in the Aligarh Movement where he replaced the force of sword with that of pen. If seen from other way round, this very derogatory comment on the Bengalis also carried a hidden compliment that they were way ahead of any other community in acquiring Western education and political awareness under the British rule. Never the less, one should be cautious before putting such comments under the category of communal outbursts (i.e., religious communal apathy). For here while comparing the obscure background of the Bengalis as against the glorious legacy of the Mohammedans he had mentioned the gallantry of the Rajputs and other Hindu Rajas at par. His attitude showed the helpless complexes of a social reformer who began late and lagged behind. He tried by all means to prevent the rising tide of nationalism jeopardize his scheme of educational reforms in collaboration with the colonial empire. Expression of racial arrogance against the leading nationality (Bengalis) came as a useful means of propaganda for the time being. But this had also created a disjuncture between the Muslims of the Aligarh movement and the leaders of the Congress that remained a perpetual weakness of India's struggle for freedom. It was his strong conviction that the Congress led by the Bengalis and other Hindu elites of the country would try to dominate and displace the Muslims and other ruling races of the pre-colonial era. In clarification of his speech in Lucknow he had given a press release soon afterwards where he had even stated that the Congress was a civil war without arms![22] He knew for sure that even if the Muslims joined whole heartedly in Congress programme they would be perpetual losers, remaining at the rank and file while the more educated layer, without any legacy of political authority would dominate them. So it was his vendetta to prevent his fellowmen from entering the Congress movement. However, his attempt for keeping away the Muslims from Congress politics was not fully successful. The highly progressive Bombay Muslims like Badruddin Tyabji remained a glaring example against Syed Ahmed's appeal. Syed Ahmed was strongly critical of the Muslim leaders like Tyabji for going against his mission. His disgruntled voice resonated heavily against Tyabji's shifted allegiance, "So we are not such fools as to put boys in our laps and let them pull out our beards. Our respected master Badruddin Tyabji's beard must be strong one which cannot be pulled out; but my beard is not so strong."[23] In fact, he initiated a new forum against Indian National Congress, named The United Indian Patriotic Association in 1888 with the support of his close associate and the Principal of M.A.O. college, Mr. Theodore Beck. The motto of this organization was to communicate with the British Parliament about the views of those Hindus and Muslims who were opposed to the National Congress. Interestingly, this was not a communal platform as it allowed people from both communities although Beck intended to transform it into a pro-British forum and tried to "prevent the Hindus and Muslims from coming together."[24] However, this forum had little political significance for Beck did not allow public meetings and local branches under its banner.

III
RELEVANCE OF AHMED KHAN IN MODERN WORLD MAKING

Actually speaking, Sir Syed Ahmed's drive for social reforms and educational upliftment in Western model coincided with and collided against the early phase of the mainstream Indian nationalism, initiated by the elites (mainly caste Hindus) in the three Presidencies of Calcutta, Madras and Bombay culminating in the creation of a common political platform of Indian National Congress. The issue of Muslim backwardness vis-à-vis their Hindu counterparts portrayed by Syed Ahmed was not a uniform feature all over India. It had a two-layer fallacy imbued in it. Primarily, his view was restricted to the elite society of both Hindus and Muslims, for other wise, in terms of rural India and even for Urban poor, English education and advent of Western knowledge remained as alien to a Hindu as his/her Muslim counterpart. Secondly, neither could the Hindu-Muslim distinction even among the elites be claimed in absolute terms. In fact, the Bombay Muslims, who were not so closely attached to the previous sovereign authorities of the Mughals, and had more scope to commercial interactions with various European communities, also remained substantially larger period under the British governance as a presidency gave rise to many urban Muslims who nurtured a much more cosmopolitan mindset and found nothing wrong in the participation of National Congress. Such was the case of Tyabji who stood on the reverse side of Syed Ahmed. Last but not the least, one must mention that the presence of an overwhelming number of Bengali Muslims had been ignored by Syed Ahmed while slandering at the Bengalis as an alien race.

Thus, Syed Ahmed's lofty ideals had limitation even within the heterogeneous Muslim community. His milieu consisted of a handful of English educated elite carrying a legacy of being part of the ruling race in the pre-colonial days. Yet, a large number of urban Muslims of upper India, who so far remained confined to their abode of a lost milieu, were inspired by Syed Ahmed, joined his drive for educational upliftment and made his mission a success story.

It is interesting to observe the binary between and amongst various strands of leadership at the formative phase of national awakening. In spite of the distinctive differences of their strands, each of them were somehow or other affected by the advent of colonialism and were trying to negotiate with the challenges posed and transformation brought forth by the new regime. It is also very interesting to note that what Syed Ahmed began to think around 1857-60 onwards, were identical with the thoughts and ideas of the social reformers of the previous generation of Bengal-Bombay and Madras Presidency. Apparently in the history of human civilization fifty years lag is no irrecoverable break. But for colonial India, within that time period, a crucial change took place in the mindset towards the ruling class as well as the goal of the educated intelligentsia. While Rammohun, the first modern man of India lived and died with the illusion that the British rule was a blessing for India, his lack of awareness about the colonial evil was justified in terms of historicity. If seen minutely, Syed Ahmed had a strange similarity in his thoughts and visions for the revival and progress of his fellow brethren, who so far refused to make this compromise and as a result suffered from various quarters. But Syed Ahmed's demand stood mismatched against the mainstream politics which by then began to consolidate under the banner of Indian National Congress, and started bargaining with the colonial authorities on a number of issues.

Syed Ahmed and his apparently self-contradictory policy, can thus be understood only in terms of its own historicity. It was the call of the hour that made him conscious of his community and the imperative need to revive it by special concessions, be that go contrary to the mainstream national will of the moment. But at the same time, he was highly conscious of the possible schism his ideas may carry and how in the long run it was dangerous for a state like India (undivided). As his articulate demand went on and on harping the same point:

> If Hindus and Mussalmans build their buildings of two bricks and one-and-a-half bricks separately, nothing will be achieved. They should first of all complete one one work and unitedly and when it is complete they should start the other…it is not advisable that one work should be left unfinished and the other started.[25]

Jawaharlal Nehru in his Autobiography made a critical appreciation of the position taken by Syed Ahmed from his own perspective, as he commented, "So, to this education he turned all his energy trying to win over his community to his way of thinking. He wanted no diversions or distractions from other directions" and further added, "The beginnings of a new nationalism, sponsored by the Hindu bourgeoisie, seemed to him to offer such a distraction, and he opposed it."[26]

However, his analysis did incorporate the obvious limitation of this great mind with due respect to his historic milieu.

> …. Sir Syed's message was appropriate and necessary when it came, but it could not be the final ideal of a progressive community. It is possible had he lived a generation later, he would himself have given another orientation to that message.[27]

That his name continues to be a living force among the educated Muslims of India, even today, not for his skepticism against the Hindus, not for his allegiance towards the British colonial authorities, but for his steadfast commitment for regenerating the power of knowledge and rationalism among his fellowmen, seems to be a reassuring fact. The lasting impact of his thoughts and deeds had been reassessed by one of the veteran alumnus of the AMU in a very recent article:

> If we take up his political views, they are as rational and practical as other views. He did not support Indian National Congress but that was not due to any ill-feeling or grudge.

> Education was his primary concern and he did not want to destabilize it by any action. Hence, he advised, students not to take part in politics and concentrate only on education. Even Pt. Jawaharlal Nehru has pointed out that, "He was deeply committed to the national cause, though education was his first priority and love as far as the Muslims were concerned". Sir Syed was aware that Muslims can be a party in nation building only if they get quality education at par with Hindus.[28]

His main target was to impart education and bring progress to his Muslim brethren. To attain this goal he could sacrifice any other agenda, even if that be a call for Pan-Islamic movement. Nizami had rightly pointed out that Syed Ahmed Khan had completely rejected the idea of Maulana Jamaluddin Afghani's pan-Islamic movement for the condition of India was entirely different from those prevailing in other parts of the Muslim world.[29] He abhorred the idea of internationalization of Islamic politics as much as the participation in the national agitation under the banner of Indian National Congress. Thus, he stood far from being branded as a communal leader in spite of remaining committed for community service throughout his life. His stand was made so clear by his words and deeds, that he can never be blamed as the harbinger of Hindu-Muslim communalism. But the ambivalence imbued in his thoughts could have taken a communal turn with a little twist in its perspective. That was what happened in the next historic epoch when the students of MAO college were turned *en masse* into cadets of communal politics. Never the less, the creation of the binary between the Hindus and the Muslims under the colonial umbrella remained a negative force that justified the sectarianism on both sides, and allowed the growth of the British design of divide and rule. Syed Ahmed did not consciously act as a harbinger of communal disharmony. His lofty words on the unity of two nations, remain the most oft quoted statements among the Muslim intellectuals of India, especially to those belonging to AMU (MAO college) alumni. His living legacy till date is this institution and the special focus it continues to carry forward ever since its inception. Anyway, Syed Ahmed expected in his hypothesis that the need for this special attention would come to an end sometime, when the Muslims would be able to fight in the mainstream for gaining power and position. However, his vision on his own community was rather restricted to the elites, which was incomplete and therefore could not be effective on his over generalisation. On the other hand, politicisation of the Muslims could not be restricted for long, yet they refrained from the mainstream political banner of the National Congress. As a result, the Muslims of India who were patriotic by nature tried to participate in other alternative political ideologies, some into communist politics, some into communal politics, often those in the communist movement had converted themselves to communal cadets in a frenzy. Indian politics in the late 19th and early 20th century had turned extremely complicated due to communal issue. The demand of concession and British collaboration was consciously taken up by the communal and rightist branch of the Muslim leaders. Though unconsciously, Syed Ahmed's notion for separation had a tall shadow on the political direction later taken by his fellow people. However, one cannot be made responsible for the eventualities one did not experience. So, neither should Syed Ahmed be blamed of the extension of his Two Nation theory into a theoretical premise for the intensification of communal politics in the final phase of colonial rule—it had much more complex dynamism involved in it. Yet in the cumulative effect of this tendency that ultimately had dangerous outcome through communal carnages and Partition, can Syed Ahmed be left aside without any contribution to the development of such sinister end.

Though a visionary of rare magnitude his vision remained restricted to the cause of that community whose misfortune he could identify himself with. Though a modernizer per excellence, his zeal for progress remained confined to his dream of resurrecting the lost glory of the same segment of Indian society. Without his historic context he could be grossly misunderstood and misinterpreted in the transformed and further complicated communal question during the mature phase of Indian nationalism and even afterwards in a post-independence, post-colonial India. However, considering his complex historic backdrop, one must balance between his broader vision of national harmony and temporary focus on the communitarian development for a rational, impartial and complete image of this great thinker of modern India.

References

Books

Ashraf, K.M., *Hindu-Muslim Question and Our Freedom Struggle (1857-1935)*, Vol. I, Sunrise Publications, 2005.

Amir Safia, *Muslim Nationhood in India, Perceptions of Seven Eminent Thinkers,* Kanishka Publishers and Distributors, New Delhi, 2000.

Mohammad Shan, *Writings and Speeches of Sir Syed Ahmed Khan,* Nachiketa Publications Limited, Bombay, 1972.

Nehru, J.L., *An Autobiography*, Oxford University Press, 1981.

Nizami, K.A., *Sayyid Ahmad Khan*, Publications Division, Ministry of Information and Broadcasting, Government of India, 1965.

Journals

C.M. Naim, "Syed Ahmad and His Two Books Called 'Asar-Ul-Sanadid'", *Modern Asian Studies,* 2010.

Shakeel Samdani, "Sir Syed Ahmad Khan: A Global Phenomenon", *Indian Mirror*, Special Issue, February 2014.

Encyclopaedia

Nazeer Ahmed, "Sir Syed Ahmed Khan", An encyclopaedia of Islamic History, http://historyofislam.com/contents/resistance-and -reform/sir-syed-ahmed-khan/History of Islam, 29th August, 2014.

Azhar Mohammed K., "Sir Syed Ahmed Khan: His Life And Contribution", Tuesday, October 20, 2009 04:48:12 PM, http://www.ummid.com/news/October/20.10.2009/sir_sayyad_life_and_vision.htm).

Notes

1. Shan Mohammad and S.A. Khan, 1972, 36-37.
2. Mohammad, 1972: 15-64.
3. *Ibid.*
4. *Ibid.*, 78.
5. Mohammed K. Azhar, 2009.

6. Mohammad, 1972, 199.
7. Nazir Ahmed, 2014.
8. *Ibid.*
9. Mohammad, 1972, 194.
10. Nizami, 1966, 84.
11. *Ibid.*, 85.
12. *Ibid.*, 69.
13. K.M. Ashraf, 2005, 40.
14. *Ibid.*, 42.
15. *Ibid.*
16. Mohammad, 1972, 159.
17. *Ibid.*, 163.
18. *Ibid.*, 160.
19. *Ibid.*, 162.
20. *Ibid.*
21. *Ibid.*, 209.
22. *Ibid.*, 219.
23. *Ibid.*
24. Nizami, 1966, 146.
25. Mohammad, 1972, 176.
26. J.L. Nehru, 1981, 461-62.
27. *Ibid.*, 463-64.
28. Shakeel Samdan, 2014.
29. Nizami, 1966, 139.

9

Ishwar Chandra Vidyasagar (1820-1891): A Social Reformer and a Humanitarian Activist

Lopamudra Sengupta

> And there was the great European, who was a Brahmin pandit—Vidyasagar—who translated from Sanskrit as well as from Shakespeare.[1]
>
> —*Bishnu Dey*

I
INTRODUCTION

A book on Indian Political Thought and its Contemporary Relevance is incomplete without paying homage to the great legendary persona of the nineteenth century Bengal Renaissance, Ishwar Chandra Vidyasagar. If Rammohun Roy is considered to be the 'First Modern Man of India'[2] to light the torch of scientific knowledge to liberate his countrymen from darkness to light, it was Ishwar Chandra Vidyasagar who was the most able lineal descendant who had carried forward the movement of championing right to equality and social justice in a society that was torn by the vile and vicious customs of the moribund Hindu Society and religious orthodoxy.

His Early Life

Ishwar Chandra Vidyasagar, who is popularly known to all his countrymen as *'Pandit' 'Karunasagar'* and *'Dayarsagar'* was born on 26, September 1820 in the village of *Birsingha* in the Hooghly district of Bengal which later on had been incorporated in the Midnapore district since 1872. His father was Thakurdas, and mother Bhagwati Devi, the daughter of a logician Ramkanta

Tarkabagish. The forefather of Ishwar Chandra originally belonged to a village named Banamalipur situated in the district of Hooghly. They were pundits by profession who used to earn a living for running *tol* to impart education in Sanskrit literature. Ishwar was the eldest among the children—seven boys and three girls.[3] At the age of five, Ishwar Chandra was placed in charge of Kalikanta Chatterjee, who used to run the local village school. It was probably due to the genetic ability of being born into a family of pundits, that Vidyasagar's diligence towards learning was exposed from early childhood. He mustered all the learning within three years in the village school for which his father in November 1828 decided to take him to Calcutta for higher education and in 1829 he was admitted to Sanskrit College as a student of Third Class of the Grammar Branch, which provided opportunities of learning English and Sanskrit.

An incident which showed Vidyasagar's eagerness towards learning since early childhood was reflected when on his way to Calcutta from his native village he is said to have picked up the English numerals by looking at the milestones. Thus even within great economic adversities in life, Ishwar Chandra emerged as one of the most illuminating scholar that Bengal had ever produced.[4]

However, in consonance with the rules of those times, Vidyasagar himself was married at an early age of fourteen to Srimati Dinamoyee Devi, who was chosen for him by his father.

Vidyasagar's apparent simplistic look in a traditional Bengali outfit of a *dhoti*, along with a *chaddar* and wooden sandals fails to define the strong man behind it. His masterful, masculine type of personality made him an utopia for centuries. Vidyasagar recultivated in himself the qualities of wisdom not ritualistic proficiency, *Sila* (conduct), not *Kula* (lineage often concocted); self imposed poverty, righteous indignation against moral wrong not timid or selfish temporization generosity and charity as the material of mind and rule of life, not social sadism born of complex. He reinforced some of the qualities of the archetypal; protestant of the West—rationality, individuality, enterprise, devotion to worthy causes, capacity for leadership in critical situations, obstinacy of principle and courage of conviction, innate sense of justice that put the public over the private interest, hatred for solemn cant and preference for work to words, and, finally, a concern for life.[5]

Vidyasagar has been aptly summarized in the words of Rabindranath Tagore, as a man of *"invincible manliness"* and *"indelible humanity"* (*ajeya paurasha O akshaya manushyatva*).[6]

Vidyasagar's range of perception and empathy which led him to repudiate customs oppressive to women can be traced to the influence of his mother, an influence that had unending inspiration for Vidyasagar throughout his life, and to the unforgettable personality of *Raimani*, the widowed daughter of Jagaddurlab Choudhuri, in whose house Vidyasagar stayed long, after he had first come to Calcutta at the age of eight. He was however shocked at the plight of early widowhood of the girl who had been an intimate play mate in his childhood. In his autobiographical note, there is a sketch of Raimani:

> The image of this noble woman is indelibly engraved in my mind. She was a goddess to me, I cannot help shedding grateful tears at the recollection of her amiable appearance and noble qualities.... Many people hint at my showing of special favour for womankind. I believe they are not wrong.[7]

II
VIDYASAGAR: AN ARDENT SOCIAL REFORMER AND AN ACTIVIST

It is difficult to categorize Vidyasagar, as a political thinker if by politics we strictly mean the practice or profession of conducting political affairs, or seeking power in the governmental or public affairs of a State, or pertaining to the State and its government.[8] He is understood more in terms of a social reformer and an activist, a pioneer in bringing burning social issues in the eyes of the vast ignorant mass on the one hand and the perpetrators of the misdeeds on the other. For redressal of these social maladies he relied heavily on the British Government. He had firm faith on the Western values and had conviction that changes from the darkness, ugly, evil and ignorance is possible only with the 'intervention' of the Britishers. This in fact is a crucial link of seeing Vidyasagar not just as a social reformer but as a social and political activist who brought positive changes in the society by actually taking help of the State Arm,—the Law.

Vidyasagar's attitude of reliance on the British Government for bringing necessary welfare measures in the society is also reflected in a book *An Indian Pilgrim* by Subhas Chandra Bose. In this book Subhas Bose observed that though Keshab Chandra Sen and Vidyasagar were men of highest moral stature, they were by no means anti-government or anti-British. While Keshab Chandra Sen openly stated that he regarded the advent of the British as Divine Dispensation, Vidyasagar also was not eager to shun himself away from the contact of the British.[9]

However, Vidyasagar had never compromised on the issue of self prestige and dignity. His fitting reply to Mr. Clarke's haughtiness by welcoming him imperiously stretching his feet over the table, proved beyond doubt that only an erudite scholar with great strength of mind and sense of dignity could possibly guard himself against all kinds of indignities and humiliations.[10]

A man of astute pragmatism Vidyasagar realised that he had to free his countrymen from two types of bondages. On the one hand, it was the British rule that had enslaved the countrymen and on the other was the orthodoxy of Hindu religious practices which had reduced men (especially women) to mere objects of non-entity. They were simply treated as mechanistic individuals devoid of any thinking and feeling and were treated as slaves of the mere "dictates" of Hindu religion.

It was Vidyasagar, a vast scholar of Sanskrit, who could decipher the *slokas* of various *Sastras* and bring into focus, the deviations made by those who upholded the religion. Thus, he declared war with not social institutions but social aberrations.[11] He not only started campaigning against vicious atrocities like evils of *Kulinism*, *Kulin* Polygamy, child widows, child marriage but ensured that the Acts were translated into reality. All these Vidyasagar did firmly by remaining within his own religion. For this attempt to do away with age long practices, Vidyasagar was socially ostracised in many circles.

As Brian Hatcher pointed out that Vidyasagar, Bengal's most learned Sanskrit scholar, was the most successful social reformer; he was an ardent rationalist, but spent most of his time justifying that rationalism from Hindu text; and he considered himself a good Hindu—dressed, ate and acted accordingly—yet was known to be a dedicated humanist and professed atheist.[12]

Thus his zeal for social reforms was directed against the Hindu custom prohibiting re-marriage of the widows, practice of child marriage and opposed polygamy among the upper caste Hindus. Vidyasagar's first essay on social reform titled *Balyobibaher Dosh* was addressed against the (Evils of Child Marriage, 1850) and it held that

> Unfortunately bound by the constraints of customs and Shastras, we are forever suffering from the endless misery and irredeemable predicament of child marriage.

His argument turned on considerations of 'health' and 'education' of future mothers. He emphasised the danger of early widowhood and above all, the need for a mature mind and body to fulfill the conditions of true marital love. It is because of the ills of child marriage.

> that sincere marital love is so rare in our country; it is merely living out one's life in hazards of household routine—the male as housekeeper and the female as housemaid.[13]

Thus, Vidyasagar wrote against child marriage without invoking the authority of the *Shastras*; on the contrary, senseless customs and outmoded *Shastras* were together held responsible for the evil of child marriage.[14]

Vidyasagar's first tract on the re-marriage of widows was published in 1855. It provoked great agitation among the upper caste Hindu gentry. A large number of pamphlets were published in severe criticism of his analysis and conclusions. Towards the end of the same year in October 1855, Vidyasagar brought out a second tract ('Whether Widows Ought To be Married or Not') to answer the objections, most of them by renowned Sanskrit scholars of traditional learning. His arguments were derived from ancient and accepted Sanskrit authorities and endowed with an immense learning and unremitting logic to prove the accuracy of his sources and the validity of his scriptural interpretation.

However at this point he became conscious of the fact that it was not *Sastras* but *Desachar* that was responsible for inhuman practices against the women.

Vidyasagar exposed and renounced the utter inhumanity of the existing custom as opposed to the true teaching of the *Shastras*.

> A total disregard of the Shastras and a careful observation of mere usages and external forms is the source of the irreversible stream of vice which overflows the country....[15]

However, as Ashok Sen observes, that reforms envisaged by Vidyasagar had no need to abide by the principle of equality of sexes; on his interpretation the scriptural maxims were taken to affirm the legitimacy of re-marriage to save widows from their sufferings and the contingent social vices of adultery and foeticide.

Vidyasagar sent to government a petition with nearly a thousand signature requesting a suitable enactment. A Bill was very soon moved in the Legislative Council. Numerous memorials were received by the Council from all over India, both for and against the provisions of the Bill. The number of opponents were much larger, about 56,000 as against a few more than 5,000 who supported the Bill. Raja Radhakanta Dev of Calcutta organized a petition of about 37,000 persons against the Bill.[16] Amidst various oppositions and incessant campaigns against Vidyasagar, critical reports in periodicals and news papers that were full of filthy satires, Vidyasagar carried on with what he characterised as 'the most important work of his life'. A number of widow—marriage took place not only in Calcutta and other leading towns, but also in some villages. Vidyasagar had to bear a large part of their expenses and also supported several families who were victimized in many ways for their participation in widow re-marriages.

On the 17th November 1855, a draft Bill of An act to remove all legal obstacles to the marriage of Hindoo widows was introduced into the Legislative Council to the Government of India by the Hon'ble Mr. J.P. Grant one of the members of the Council. The Bill was read for the second time on 19th January 1856, and finally on the 19th July 1856, the Bill was read for the third time and passed into Act XV of 1856, which received the assent of the Governor-General a week later and became a Law of the country. The act, which was thus passed, was Act No. XV of 1856, which received the Governor-General's Assent on 26th July 1856.[17]

Contemporaneously with the Widow Re-Marriage Movement, Vidyasagar had set foot on an agitation on another subject of social reform namely, the prevention of the practice of polygamy among the Hindus particularly the *Kulin Brahamanas* of Bengal.

Vidyasagar fought vehemently against *Kulinism*, a peculiar custom prevalent specially in Bengal. According to the caste system in Hinduism, *Kulins* belong to the highest grade of the *Brahamanas*. According to the *Kulinism* system, it was obligatory on the part of a high caste *Brahmana* parent to marry his daughters into *Kulin* families, and the *Kulin* bridegrooms were very much in demand in the marriage market. This became a profitable trade, and paved way for polygamy where marriage took place in exchange of money and properties. As it was considered auspicious of getting married to a *Kulin*, girls of tender age were forced to marry bridegroom as old as their father. Thus, they were sacrificed at the altar of the so-called *Kulin* marriage. In many cases as the old bridegroom died after marrying girls of tender age, they were left to life long suffering, an observance of celibacy and other strict social commitments.[18]

On 27th December 1855, he submitted a petition to the government subscribed by 25000 persons, some of whom were member of influential and leading personages. But even after the attempts the petitioners failed, Vidyasagar a man of great strength of mind, fixed purpose and perseverance did not lose heart and after nine years, on 1st February 1866, he again submitted a petition for the prevention of polygamy.

In July 1871, he again published a paper on polygamy, the subject of discussion whether polygamy was consonant to the

Hindu *Sastras* and issued his second paper against polygamy in March 1872.

He based his arguments from the works of *Manu*, and attempted to demonstrate that under any other circumstances, the taking of more wives than one was uncannonical according to the Hindu *Sastras*.

In this pamphlet Vidyasagar pointed out that it is due to the evil customs of the society the female sex being comparatively weaker depend on male sex, and this weakness and dependence lead them to a life of degradation and humiliation.[19]

For Vidyasagar, polygamy was the most pernicious of all evil social custom and this inhuman practice has caused incalculable sufferings to the woman kind.[20]

Vidyasagar: An Inspiration behind Mass Education

As an erudite scholar Vidyasagar, could sense the pulse of his countrymen. He realised that a few changes in the social arena is like touching the tip of an iceberg.

For a complete reformation changes should occur within the society. For this he aimed at the growth of education amongst the masses and especially of women, who were submerged into the darkness of ignorance for a long time.

Mr. John Drinkwater Bethune who was an enthusiast for female education in India had established in 1851 the *Hindu Valika Vidyalaya*, of which Vidyasagar became the first Secretary.

After the death of Mr. Bethune, the school was renamed after him as Bethune Girls' School. Since then Vidyasagar made ceaseless efforts to spread education among Indian women.[21] His work as the principal of Sanskrit college and initiation of the Metropolitan College for higher education for women deserves special mention.

Vidyasagar's first attempt at spreading primary education through the medium of Bengali under the British rule took place during the Governor—Generalship of Sir Henry Hardinge. In 1855, Vidyasagar founded a free school in *Birsingha*, his native village, at his own expense. In 1854, he became a member of the Board of Examiners and in 1855, he was appointed as additional inspector of schools for four districts of Bengal: *Nadia, Hooghly, Burdwan* and *Midnapore*. In 1856, Vidyasagar became the special inspector of schools, during which period he took the initiative for setting up a number schools for girls. Within one year, the number of girls schools reached thirty-five mainly in these districts with the admission of about thirteen hundred girls.[22]

Vidyasagar was a man of strict discipline and enforced it in both the students and the teachers. It was with his initiative that Miss Kadambini Bose from Bethune School was sent up for the first time to sit for the Entrance Examination of Calcutta University in 1878, and came out successful being placed in the second division. It was, no doubt, a great event in the annals of the Women's Education in India. She later on took the B.A. Degree in January 1883. She was followed by Chandramukhi Bose who took the M.A. Degree with 'Honours' in English and was appointed as a teacher to take classes in the collegiate section of the Bethune School.[23]

Vidyasagar had sincerely believed that if the benefits of education were to reach the common man and the modern truths of science to be imbibed in the minds of people, it was imperative that printed standard books containing useful information should be made available to all. With this aim in mind he started writing and publishing books relentlessly. Not only did he write the class books in Bengali but he also brought out into the vernacular language the wealth of Sanskrit and English vocabulary. His first book was *Vetal Panchavinsati* which was printed from an outside press. The next book was *Annada Mangal*. In 1848, he brought out *Banglar Itihas,* a free translation from *Marshmen*. In 1849, he wrote *Jiban Charita*, and in 1851 *Bodhodaya* (Dawn of Knowledge) for the young boys, and *Sakuntala* an adaptation from *Kalidas* in 1854. But the best evidence of his efforts for the development of Bengali language was *Varna-Parichaya*, (published in 1855) or an acquaintance with Bengali letters, which was the suitable book to new learners. It was through this *Varna-Parichaya* that the Bengali alphabet received for the first time an uniform mould and an scientific arrangement. Later on he also wrote *Kathamala* (published in 1860) that is stories from "Aesop's Fables" in Bengali and in 1869 he wrote *Bhranti—Vilas* a transcreation in Bengali of Shakespear's "Comedy of Errors". Vidyasagar's contribution to Bengali language and literature was immense. As an erudite educationist Vidyasagar tried to uphold moral values which were to be instilled in a man from childhood. His stories on *Rakhal* and *Bhuban* in *Varna-Parichaya* bear testimony to this evidence and his school texts are full of warnings about the immortality of theft.[24]

Vidyasagar on Nationalism

Vidyasagar's endeavours for the spread of education within common masses, reflects his spirit of Nationalism. It was his objective to use as a weapon the enlightenment and knowledge for modernisation of the social mind. In his efforts to pursue this objective he rejected a British Civilian and Academician Dr. Ballantyne's recommendation of introducing Bishop Berkley's "Inquiry" into a class book. Vidyasagar had firmly pointed out that Berkley's book had similar or identical conclusions with the *Vedanta* or *Sankhya* and which is no more considered in Europe as a sound system of philosophy.

On the question of reading both in Sanskrit and English, Vidyasagar firmly kept rooted on infusing the spirit of a new consciousness to his already existing old and traditional structure. He knew vernacular language is the only medium of instruction that can percolate the benefits of education even to the lowest stratum of the society including the working class and tribal people.

Vidyasagar could more easily agree with the words of the Bengali Christian Rev. Lal Behari De, when he said that, "The vernacular language of a country is the guardian of its improvement, and the foster parent of its genius".[25]

Moreover, Vidyasagar's national pride was deep in his heart which appeared prominently even in his simple dress of a *dhoti,* a *chadder* and a pair of *choti.*[26] He wore his *chappals* and *chadder* much as *Bharata* bore his brother *Rama's* wooden footwear on his head. They were his silent weapons,—the careless armour that returned with a dull dazzle the missiles and barbs of arrogance of the British *Sahibs*.[27]

Vidyasagar's pride was the obverse of his love for his Motherland. His age and times was the peak of the British Colonial rule in India. Our own people were 'natives'—though a harmless word by its origin and etymology it had a distinct contempt. Vidyasagar could not help the Political Domination of the British but zealously guarded the 'human dignity' of his countrymen.

Vidyasagar: His Ideas of Liberalism and Humanism

Vidyasagar had never travelled to the West. But he was exposed throughout his life to ideas of individualism, rationalism, scientific temperament and objective reality. The dynamics of Vidyasagar's world view is captured by the Bengali poet Bishnu Dey, when he says that Vidyasagar was "the best and purest of our Europeans or humanist because (he was the) most deeply rooted in the best of the native culture." Dey's evocation of Vidyasagar's attempt to create 'a new and literary language' with help of 'Sanskrit', together with his 'European virtues', is a good epitome of the cultural convergence.[28] His attempt was to fuse 'oriental' and the 'western' for the improvement of India, but never its conversion. Vidyasagar possessed a deep burning sympathy for the helpless and poor. His life was full of activities loaded with instances helping men in distress. Vidyasagar was the living practitioner of the highest lore of the *Geeta*—one is all and all is one; there is no mean or noble; high or low; the sinner or the saint. All creatures, all human beings were equal to Vidyasagar as beloved as they are beloved of Lord God himself.[29] His natural instinct made him look after the ill and ailing women suffering from infectious diseases (Cholera) in those days forgetting his own food and bath and his own household and work.

Vidyasagar's life is full of instances of the service to humanity. Devi Prasanna Roy Choudhury observed in his writings that Vidyasagar the poor godly man would give away, shower charity as a perennial fountain whenever a turn or opportunity should present itself. There were times when he was prepared to mortgage his own dwelling house for the sake of some good work.[30] It is for this greatness of heart that he was coined by the Bengali poet Michael Madhusudan Dutta as *Karunasagar.* The poet wrote that the first man among us; above flattering any man, the genius and wisdom of an ancient sage, the energy of an Englishman and the heart of a Bengali mother; not only Vidyasagar but *Karunasagar.*[31]

III
RELEVANCE OF VIDYASAGAR AND HIS IDEAS IN CONTEMPORARY INDIAN POLITICAL THOUGHT

Vidyasagar's contribution to the Indian Political thought and society should be assessed in the shadow of some of the limitations, that challenged his work both during his life time and afterwards.

First, there has been a major tendency on part of the critics to estimate Vidyasagar's movement of widow remarriage in terms of number. It is pointed out that inspite of his relentless effort in to legalize widow remarriage, he had failed to see many widows remarried at is was not socially acceptable neither was it possible to enforce it with the help of the police force. So Vidyasagar had to ultimately depend on social consent, and not on the power of the state, and it was here that his defeat was manifest.[32]

Secondly, the legitimisation about widow remarriage had taken only among the educated sections of the community and was not widespread.[33] It was also strictly forbidden among the upper castes and most of the middle-ranking castes in the nineteenth century.[34]

Thirdly, Recent Feminists have sharply criticized Vidyasagar's paternalistic bias and his patriarchal control over the private spheres of life, over female sexuality and family discipline. He is accused for the concern of increasing social tendency towards adultery and foeticide, all due to the unsatiated sexual appetite of widowed women who had put to shame all the three lineages of their husband, father and mother. According to the feminists this reform was undertaken to provide a legitimate channel i.e.

marriage for these widows thus re-inforcing social discipline and patriarchic control over women's bodies and desires.[35]

Though Vidyasagar was conscious of the ideology of hierarchy he did not offer any radically different ideological alternative. Moreover he had put in great faith on the colonial rule. Even Vidyasagar's own personal life was not spared from criticism. What he did when his own daughter returned home as a widow, or why Dinamoyee Devi, his wife remained virtually illiterate, are questions that remain mostly unanswered. His policy of educating the masses too has been put to question.

The limits of Vidyasagar's ideas and reform activities do not lessen the 'exemplary' role he had played in the Indian society. As eminent scholar, Sumit Sarkar has pointed out that the spread of women's education combined with the questioning of norms that Vidyasagar had provoked, led on towards the beginning of a female literary public sphere in the decade that immediately followed the peak of his educational and reform initiative.[36]

The *Bambodhini Patrika* which was founded in 1863, provided a platform for great stimulating writings by women. In the same year Kailashbashini Devi's *Hindu Mahilaganer Heenabastha* was published, and then in 1868, Rashshundari Devi's *Amar Jivan* was published.[37] As Professor Rinita Mazumdar points out that in India 'the First Wave' of feminist movement happened simultaneously with the Bengal Renaissance during the British rule in the late nineteenth and early twentieth centuries with events such as the introduction of female education, Vidyasagar's widow-remarriage movement, 'the coming out' of women into public was made possible.[38]

A silent revolution giving birth to new ideas, consciousness, identity formation took place in the nineteenth century Bengal which has been referred to as the period of Bengal Renaissance (Re-awakening).

Of late there is a tendency on the part of the scholars to equate feminism with the Western feminist movement and get attached to their ideas and themes of interest which emerge and re-emerge in their understanding of the women and about their problems in the society.

If we look at some of the seminal works of the west, like 'A Vindication of the Rights of Woman', written in 1792 by Mary Wollstonecraft, or works of Olympia De Gouges who had proclaimed 'The Rights of Women and the Female Citizen', in 1789, or the activities of Lucria Mott and Elizabeth Cady Stanton's, we will see that most of these works revolved around the crucial question of women's right to equality.[39] The nature of feminism in India that was initiated during this nineteenth century Bengal by the reformers had a vastly different character than that of the west and it is because of this that relevance of the ideas of Vidyasagar is strikingly appealing even today. It tried to restore the basic rights of a human being from which the women were largely denied in the name of local customs practices, etc. For example, the practice of *Sati* (often spelt as Suttee) which practiced the ritual of throwing young widows in the funeral pyre of their deceased husbands (thereby denying them the right to life) and also right to live with dignity (when the young widows were made to undergo all sorts of humiliating rituals like tonsuring of head, observance of fast, isolation from other social commitments). There was also least concern about a woman 'health' or even 'education'.

It was at the initiative of these reformers, that feminism, or *Stri Swadhinata* (Freedom of Women) in India was born out of the 'womb of a greater humanist movement' which later on became crystallized and paved the way for women's rights in post-independent India.[40]

In an era of globalization where traditional values are replaced by consumerist culture, where 'dignity' of women are denigrated and 'bodies' dehumanized and exploited at every opportune moment, and the perpetrators of violence are mostly men (like committing rape, wife beating, molestation) we realize that women are still vulnerable both in their nature and bodies.

Therefore a need to instill and re-instill the values which were advocated by reformers like Vidyasagar had to be realized in order to usher justice in the society. He was a *Karmayogin*, and fought for women's right throughout his life. He had realized that people were made 'slaves of local customs', or *desachar*, which can be removed only with the right type of social consciousness.[41] Vidyasagar wanted the young students of India to become modern men who would be able to come out of the old prejudices and proceed to the path of the new generation of young men of the world. He had also appealed to men for bringing in change in their attitudes, and act not just as a part of the 'system' but as a rational individual. Vidyasagar truly recognized that without a change in the attitude of men who have remained captive within the narrow boundary of patriarchal domination for centuries, it is difficult for women to realize their freedom unless there is a transcendence from 'we' to 'them' and to the benefit of mankind in general. We conclude with the words of Vidyasagar himself, written in his first book on Widow Remarriage.

> But unfortunately you are so much under the domination of long established prejudice, so slavishly attached to custom and the usages and forms of society, that I am afraid you will not soon be able to assert your dignity and follow the path of rectitude. Habit has so darkened your feelings that it is impossible for you to have compassion for your helpless widows....
>
> .... You perhaps imagine that with the loss of their husbands your female lose their nature as human beings and are subject no longer to the influence of passions....
>
> Where men are void of pity and compassion, of a perception of right and wrong, of good and evil, and where men consider the observance of mere forms as the highest of duties and the greatest of virtues, in such a country would that women were never born *Woman! In India thy lot is cast in misery.*[42]

Notes and References

1. Originally published In the Sun and the Rain (New Delhi; People's Publishing House, 1972, p. 14) quoted in Hatcher, Brian A., 1992. *Yatna Dharma: The Religious World—View of Pandit Ishwar Chandra Vidyāsagār,* Ph.D. Dissertation unpublished Manuscript, UMI, Dissertation Information Service, USA, p. 34.
2. Rammohun Roy, known as 'Father of Modern India' quoted in Hatcher, Brian A., *Yatna Dharma: The Religious World—View*

of Pandit Ishwar Chandra Vidyāsagār (Doctoral Dissertation) unpublished Manuscript, UMI, Dissertation Information Service, USA, p. 252.

3. Tripathi, Amalesh, 1974, *Vidyāsagār: The Traditional Moderniser,* New Delhi, Orient Longman Limited, p. 7.
4. *Ibid.*, p. 8.
5. *Ibid.*, p. 3.
6. *Ibid.*, p. 4.
7. Sen, Ashok, 1977, *Ishwar Chandra Vidyāsagār and Elusive Milestones,* Calcutta Published by Shri Shyamal Bhattacharya on behalf of Riddhi, p. 77.
8. *Webster's Encyclopedic Unabridged Dictionary of the English Language*, 1983. New Revised Edition, 1996, Gramercy Books,
9. Mukherjee, Sumit, 1994, "*Vidyāsagār and Netaji*", In the context of India's Freedom Struggle, New Delhi, *Bharat Pathik.*
10. *Ibid.*
11. Tripathi, Amalesh, 1974, *Vidyāsagār—The Traditional Moderniser,* New Delhi, Orient Longman Limited, p. 62.
12. Hatcher, Brian A., 1992, *Yatna Dharma: The Religious World—View of Pandit Ishwar Chandra Vidyāsagār,* Ph.D Dissertation unpublished Manuscript, UMI, Dissertation Information Service, USA, p. 23.
13. Sen, Ashok, op. cit., p. 53.
14. *Ibid.*, p. 54.
15. *Ibid.*
16. *Ibid.*
17. Mitra, Subal Chandra, 2008, *Ishwar Chandra Vidyāsagār: Story of His Life and Work,* Kolkata, p. 191.
18. Bandyopadhyay, Pranab, 1988, Reprinted in 1989, *Pandit Ishwar Chandra Vidyāsagār: The Compassionate Educationist,* Calcutta Anglia Books, p. 30.
19. Mitra, Subal Chandra, op. cit., p. 371.
20. *Ibid.*, p. 372.
21. Bandyopadhyay Pranab, op. cit., p. 18.
22. *Ibid.*, p. 20.
23. *Ibid.*

24. Adhikari, Santosh Kumar, 1995, *Vidyāsagār Educator, Reformer, Humanist,* Calcutta: Sahityika, pp. 29-30.
25. Hatcher, Brian, A., op. cit., p. 349.
26. Bandyopadhyay, Pranab, op. cit., p. 71.
27. Banerjee, Shyamal, 2002. Translated And Rendered in English based on Bengali title *Karunasagar Vidyāsagār* by Indramitra, Sri Hara Kasturi Memorial Trust, Kolkata, Preface.
28. Hatcher, Brian A., op. cit., p. 347.
29. Banerjee, Shyamal, op. cit.
30. *Ibid.*, p. 33.
31. Bandyopadhyay, Pranab, op. cit., p. 64.
32. Bandyopadhyay, Shekhar, 2007, "Caste, Widow Re-marriage and the Reform of Popular Culture in Colonial Bengal", in *Women and Social Reform in Modern India,* Vol. I, ed. Sumit Sarkar, Tanika Sarkar, Ranikhet Permanent Black, p. 146.
33. *Ibid.*
34. *Ibid.*, p. 147.
35. *Ibid.*, p. 161.
36. Sarkar, Sumit, 2007, "*Vidyāsagār* and Brahmanical Society", ed. by Sumit Sarkar, Tanika Sarkar in *Women and Social Reform in Modern India,* Vol. I, Ranikhet, p. 201.
37. *Ibid.*, p. 202.
38. Mazumdar, Rinita, 2001, A Short Introduction To Feminist Theory, quoted in "Bharater Rajnaitik Prekshapate Nari Andolan" by Gauri Shankar Nag in Mukhopadhyay Apurbamohan and Nandi Debashish ed. *Bharatiya Rajneeti*, Kolkata: Jay Durga Library, p. 141.
39. Bhaduri, Arun Kumar, 1998, "Position of Indian Women", A Brief Study, *Humane* Quarterly Magazine February 1998—July 1998, Society for Participatory Action and Reflection, Calcutta.
40. Sengupta, Lopamudra, 2012, Talk on *Nari Swadhinata* aired in Prasar Bharati All India Radio, Kolkata—A, Programme Sameeksha (on Nari Saptaha) in Bengali on 06.03.2012 in the event of celebrating International Womens' Day.
41. Bandyopadhyay, Shekhar, op. cit., p. 155.
42. Extracts from the book 'Marriage of Hindu Widows' by Pandit Ishwar Chandra Vidyasagar quoted in Adhikari Santosh Kumar

1995, *Vidyāsagār, Educator, Reformer and Humanist,* Sahityika, Calcutta, Appendix J.

Further Readings

Binoy Ghosh, *Vidyāsagār O Bangali Samaj.*

Rabindranath Tagore, *Vidyāsagār Charit.*

Hironmoy Banerjee, *Ishwar Chandra Vidyāsagār.*

Vidyāsagār Rachana Samgraha, writings of *Vidyāsagār* Volume 2: Social Writings.

Unpublished letters of *Vidyāsagār* edited by Aurobinda Guha, Editor of Revised Edition Biswanath Maji.

Ashok Sen, 2011, *Itihaser Upakule,* Ashin Dasgupta Smarak Baktrita Samkalan 1999-2010.

Brian A. Hatcher, *Vidyāsagār: The Idiom of Improvement.*

Brian A. Hatcher, *The Life and after Life of an Eminent Indian.*

Glossary

Vidyasagar (The Ocean of Learning)—A name obtained due to vast knowledge (Vidya) compared with the depth of Sagara (Ocean).

Karunasagar, Dayarsagar—Karuna and *Daya* in Bengali means pity and compassion. A man who has noble qualities like pity and compassion as vast as that of *Sagar*. Term coined by the Bengali poet *Michael Madhusudhan Dutta.*

Bidhaba Bibaha—Widow Re-marriage.

Mahilagan—Women Folk.

Heenabasthya—Heen in Bengali means low, poor and heenabasthya indicates the low, poor condition in which those women lived.

Amar Jiban—Autobiography of One's Life, Here that of Rasshundari Devis.

Pandit—Certificate of Merit, suggesting well-versed in Sanskrit.

Banglar Itihas—History of Bengal.

Bambodhini—A Journal for Women.

Desachar—Local customs, practices.

Karmayogin—A person who believes in Karma, Work.

10

Social Reforms and Gender Justice: Thoughts of Phule, Ranade, Tilak and Gokhale

Mahasweta Das Sharma

INTRODUCTION

Maharashtra, "the great country", the legacy of Shivaji, became the cradle of great movements that would leave an indelible imprint on the course of Indian history. By the early decades of the nineteenth century the British had effectively suppressed the warlike activities of the Marathas. They were sought to be won over through Western education. It was this liberal education that left deep impression on the minds of Maratha intellectuals who became pioneers of social reforms. While Mahatma Phule, Justice Ranade and Gokhale regarded British rule as godsend, Tilak openly challenged British rule and demanded *Swaraj* or self-rule. The thoughts of these eminent personalities played a significant role in shaping Indian history and continues to be relevant in the post-Independence Indian context.

I
JOTIRAO GOVINDRAO PHULE (1827-1890)

Jotiba was born in Poona in 1827 in a *Kshatriya Mali* caste. As his father Govindrao followed the trade of florists, their family came to be known as 'Phule'. Phules belonged to the *Shudra* caste.

Jotiba was sent to a local Marathi school and was taught by a traditional teacher called 'Pantoji'. He was temporarily removed from school but was later on admitted to a Scottish mission school. Missionary education left a lasting imprint on the young

Phule. While in college, he met some brilliant students such as Sadeshiv Ballal Govande, Moro Vithal Walvekar and Sakharam Yeshwant Paranjpye who remained great supporters in all his ventures. In 1848, Jotiba came to read Thomas Paine's Rights of Man and became convinced early in life that as children of the same god, all must enjoy equal rights irrespective of caste and creed.

About this time a stray incident took place which changed his whole outlook towards life. During the marriage procession of one of his Brahman friends he was insulted in public. This rankled in the young Phule's mind and led to his anti-Brahman stance.

From this time onwards Phule dedicated his life to the cause of uplift of women and the downtrodden classes through education. In 1848, a girls' school was opened for the lower castes in Budhwar Peth. It was difficult to secure services of women teachers and so he trained his wife, Savitribai to become a teacher in this school.

The opening of the girls' school created quite a stir in society and Jotiba and his wife were asked to quit the ancestral home. He also was forced to shut the school due to social ostracism but was able to reopen the school with support from European and Indian friends. Soon, other schools were established where untouchable Mahars and Mangs came to study. He founded a Native Library for low caste people. In 1855, a Night School was started for adults at his house, where he and his wife imparted free education to farmers and their wives for two hours. In 1860, he founded a home for widows. Women belonging to the Brahman caste often went astray. They could take shelter and even deliver babies at this home. Jotiba and his wife adopted a child born of a Brahman widow.

Mahadev Govind Ranade (1842-1901)

Mahadev Govind Ranade was born in 1842 in a middle class Chitpavan Brahman family of Nasik district. His education began at Kolhapur. In 1858, he joined Elphinstone College and in 1859 he passed his Matriculation examination. In 1862, he graduated with first class honours in History and Economics and passed the M.A. examination in 1864 with a gold medal for proficiency in History and Economics. In the same year he passed the L.L.B. examination with first class honours. Ranade was a brilliant student and he became a tutor during his college career. As fellow he taught a variety of subjects to junior classes: History, Geography, Mathematics, Economics, Logic and English literature. He was assistant professor of History and English at the Elphinstone College between 1868 and 1871.

Beginning his public life in the Education Department, he held several posts in the judiciary and was a Judge of the Bombay High Court between 1893 and 1901. During his official career he had to perform an unusual variety of duties and was held in great esteem.

Bal Gangadhar Tilak (1856-1920)

Balwantrao Gangadhar Tilak was born in the village of Chikalgaon on July 24, 1856. His father, Gangadharpant, a Chitpavan Brahman was a teacher of a Marathi elementary school. Before he turned sixteen he was orphaned. Before the death of his father, he was married to Tapibai who was only ten years old.

After his matriculation, Tilak was enrolled in the Deccan College. He was drawn to the study of the *Vedas*. He collected data on astronomy from the Vedic hymns. The results were published in his book, *The Orion* (1893). He completed his B.A. at Elphinstone College. Sanskrit was his forte. However, Tilak failed to qualify in M.A.

In these years the country was recovering from the impact of the Revolt of 1857. Basudev Balwant Phadke had raised the standard of revolt. An unprecedented famine had the country in its grip. In such circumstances Tilak welcomed the path of patriotic endeavours. In 1880, Tilak founded the New English School. For the spread of education, Deccan Education Society and Fergusson College were founded. But in 1890 due to differences with Agarkar and Gokhale, Tilak resigned from the Deccan Education Society.

Soon after, his public life began. He started writing in two newspapers, the *Kesari* and the Mahratta. The columns of the *Kesari* and Mahratta were thrown open to reports of famine, plague, exaction and injustices committed upon the people.

In 1890, Tilak joined the Congress. He was a member of the Municipal Council of Pune, the Bombay Legislature and elected fellow of the Bombay University.

Gopal Krishna Gokhale (1866-1915)

Gopal Krishna was born on 9 May 1866 in Chiplun Taluka of Ratnagiri district in a poor Chitpavan Brahman family. His father's name of Krishnarao Sridhar and his mother's name was Satyabhama. Gokhale was a sincere student and his elder brother had to sacrifice his own education so that the younger sibling could continue his studies (Sen, II: 73).

After passing his Matriculation in 1881, he went on to study at Rajaram College (Kolhapur), Deccan College (Pune) and the Elphinstone College (Bombay). He acquired his B.A. degree but failed to complete LLB. At his young age, he was influenced by such stalwarts as M.G. Ranade, G.V. Joshi and Dadabhai Naoroji.

He joined the Deccan Education Society as a Life Member. When the Fergusson College was opened in 1885, he was invited to lecture on English Literature and Mathematics. He retired in 1902 specifically to devote himself to public life.

In 1889, Gokhale became a member of Congress and in 1890 he was elected Honorary Secretary to the *Poona Sarvajanik Sabha*. In 1896, he became a member of the Deccan Sabha, founded by Ranade. In 1897, he was appointed a member of the Royal Commission or the Welby Commission. In 1899, he was elected as a member of the Bombay Legislature Council and in 1902 he was elected to the Imperial Legislature Council. Through such multi-farious public activities, Gokhale emerged as a prominent nationalist leader. He fought all his life to obtain greater representation and power for Indians in public affairs.

II
JOTIRAO GOVINDRAO PHULE

Critique of Caste System

Phule has been hailed "as the father of Indian Social revolution" by his biographer Dhananjay Keer. Beginning his life as a social reformer Phule turned to the reform of the traditional Hindu *Varna*-based society. He argued that the Brahmans were responsible for the degradation of the *Shudra* castes. The Brahmans, who were descendants of Aryan invaders, had usurped the rightful property of the original inhabitants (O'Hanlon, 2010: 141). They used the Brahmanical religion to impose their authority over the *Shudras*. In order to strengthen his anti-Brahman stance he re-interpreted the stories, symbols and figures in popular Hinduism from a radical perspective. Between the years 1869 and 1873, Phule constructed his critique of orthodox religion which became the framework for his anti-Brahman movement. His work *A Ballad of the Raja Chhatrapati Shivaji Bhosale* put forward a new anti-Brahman interpretation of Maratha history. He represented the *Shudras* and *ati-Shudras* as the forgotten descendants of *Kshatriyas* of ancient India, led by the mythical ruler, Bali. In the Priestcraft Exposed and Slavery, he traced the Aryan invasion and subsequent history of Brahmanical oppression. He appealed to the British government to check the power of the Brahmans.

After establishing his anti-Brahman stance ideologically, he moved on to direct rejection of the religious authority of the Brahman priests. In Priest-craft Exposed he proclaimed that no intermediary was necessary between man and god. Though the decision of dispensing with the service of Brahman was undertaken, it was rather difficult to establish a fragile basis of coordination between a range of caste groups. There was also the question of defining the exact status of the non-Brahman in relation to the broader Hindu community.

Satyasodhak Samaj and Emancipation of Shudras

In 1873, the *Satyasodhak Samaj* was established. The members of the society which included *Kunbi, Mali,* potter, carpenter and other *Shudra* castes launched a movement to make themselves independent in religious matters. They refused to call Brahmans in social and religious ceremonies, like marriage. The *Samaj* aimed at freeing the *Shudras* from slavery to Brahman, Bhats, priests and others. The society aimed at spreading education and removal of vices and harmful social practices among the *Shudras*.

On Education

The greatest weapon of the non-Brahman movement was education. Education came to be regarded as the panacea for almost every social and religious evil. It would serve three purposes. It would provide the *Shudras* the required occupational skills which was required for obtaining jobs. Second, Western education would emancipate them from the doctrines of Brahmanical Hinduism. Finally, education would provide them with the means of reforming themselves. A set of harmful practices such a child marriage' reluctance to educate women, addiction to drinking and habitual indebtedness were responsible for their backwardness (O'Hanlon, 2010: 234). The *Satyasodhak Samaj* thus paved the way for a great social movement aiming at the uplift of the down-trodden classes.

Understanding British Rule

Phule had a favourable opinion about British rule in India from the point of view of introduction of modern notions of justice and equality in Indian society. But in economic terms, Phule was highly critical of British rule as it had increased the sufferings of the cultivators (O'Hanlon, 2010: 269). He also criticised the top-heavy administrative super-structure composed of European and Brahman officials who enjoyed comfortable salaries while the peasants staggered under a great burden. In 1888, at a reception held in honour of the Duke of Connaught, Phule proclaimed that the real people of India lived in the villages and the duty of the British was to protect them.

The greatest contribution of Phule in Indian history was his constant tirade against male patriarchy and brahmanical patriarchy. By supporting women's education, widow remarriage, opposing child marriage, Phule emerged as one of the earliest advocates of gender justice. He came to be associated with such eminent reformers as Pandita Ramabai and Tarabai Shinde. Mahatma Phule's life and work served as a source of inspiration for Bhimrao Ambedkar.

MAHADEV GOVIND RANADE

Ranade and Social Reforms

Ranade expressed his social ideas from the forum, The Association for the Spread of Knowledge (Dnyanprasarak Sabha).

In Maharashtra social reform movements had been initiated by such leaders as Atmaram Pandurang, Gopalhari Deshmukh and Jotiba Phule. Under their influence Ranade was drawn into social reform movements. Ranade joined the Vidhava-Vivaha Uttejaka Mandal which encouraged widow re-marriage. In 1869, a widow remarriage was organised. There was a great reaction and the orthodox section organised a boycott. They pronounced their verdict against the widow remarriage and Ranade was asked to do penance. But Ranade was prepared to face excommunication and refused to do penance.

Ranade was one of the prime movers of the Deccan Education Society whose object was to facilitate and cheapen education and establish schools and colleges under native management. Under its auspices the Fergusson College was founded. All the professors of the Fergusson College were Indians.

In 1887, Ranade founded the National Social Conference. The National Social Conference became to social reformers what the Indian National Congress was to Indian politicians (Wolpert: 38). Soon there were differences between Ranade and Tilak. Tilak was not in favour of any outright changes in the social system.

Ranade supported the *Sharadasadan,* an institution founded by Pandita Ramabai. This was a home that aimed at providing a home and a school for widows. Ramabai also founded another association called the Arya Mahila Samaj. Ranade's wife, Ramabai Ranade was one of its leading members. Ranade had educated his wife and coached her on the rudiments of social service. She became a political activist and even held public meetings.

In his social thinking, Ranade believed in the eternal law of justice, compassion and love. For him social progress was equivalent to moral progress and social reform implied abolition of inhuman customs (Jagirdar: 97).

Ranade's Political Ideas

Ranade was a prolific writer. We can form an idea of his political views from his writings. Ranade's political ideas may be traced in the prevailing condition of national life in India which was in a state of political subjection. But he did not agree that foreign rule is in itself an avowed evil. The British rule had led to improvement as far as social and economic conditions were concerned. The English educated class to which he belonged would be largely responsible in mediating the desired change.

Ranade believed that India's progress was related to Western liberalism. The essential ideas of liberal traditions that Ranade upheld were individual freedom, supremacy of the law of reason, constitutional government and participation in political life. Though individual freedom was the goal of liberalism, he believed that individuals must recognise some authority. The only authority consistent with freedom is the authority of law. Law as supreme authority was conceived as rational, universal and eternal (Jagirdar: 82). The political expression of liberalism is the constitutional government. This would provide the means of control through which the rule of law would be enforced. Ranade believed that for the realisation of freedom there was the necessity of participation in organised political life.

Ranade's views on freedom were based on his views on religion and Metaphysics Like Idealist thinkers, he believed that a spiritual force acts as an unseen force leading to ultimate good of all. To Ranade this faculty may be regarded as "Viveka and Vijnana" (Jagirdar: 84) or the conscience. This moral concept of liberty is applicable to both the society and the state. The state and society are spheres in which individual freedom can be attained.

Ranade defines state "as the collective humanity", The State in its collective capacity represented the power, the wisdom, the mercy and charity of its best citizens (Ranade, *Misc. Writings*: 78). The basis of the State is not force but will. That the Indian state was ruled by foreigners did not prevent Ranade from applying this concept of state to his ideas. As an administrator of justice and as an active public man, Ranade had noticed the wisdom and spirit of service of Indian citizens. These citizens were part and parcel of the government in day-to-day administration and played a significant role in the functioning of the state.

Ranade's Economic Ideas

Ranade has been regarded as the father of Indian economy. By the end of the 19th century, the nationalist leaders had begun to question the efficacy of British rule in India. Dadabhai Naoroji's path breaking work poverty and un-British rule in India had shown how British rule had ushered in famines, impoverishment and exhaustion of the people. In the Quarterly journal of the *Poona Sarvajanik Sabha*, Ranade practically dissected every aspect of the Indian economy for nearly two decades. His *Essays on Indian Political Economy* was published in 1898.

Ranade had a deep regard for India's past and employed the historical method for economic analysis of the problems of colonial India.

Ranade wrote in 1890 that the poverty of this land is phenomenal and went on to elaborate the reasons for such poverty. The establishment of British supremacy in India led to the disruption of the centuries' old union between agriculture and manufacturing industry. This resulted in the decline of handicrafts which deprived millions of workers of their traditional occupations. They were forced to turn to land which resulted in increasing ruralisation. Ranade felt that the progress of ruralisation in modern India also meant "its rustication, i.e., loss of power and intelligence and self-defence" (Ranade: *Essays*: 27). New industries were not introduced and the result was that the country's economic life came more and more under foreign economic domination.

The solution to this evil was industrial development with a through going revitalization of the Indian economy. He may be regarded as an 'apostle' of industrialisation. He believed that the Indians possessed in abundance many of the qualities such as providence, intelligence, skills, self-reliance and capacity to labour hard to transform India into an industrial state. For the industrial development of the country, of utmost importance is the vigorous activity of the state. Ranade urged the government to take up a positive role in this respect. By protecting home industries and by providing capital large-scale industrial development could take place. For such development Ranade felt that the most appropriate financial organisation was the joint stock company. Ranade also advised importing of foreign technicians and training of Indians in technical institutes in India and abroad. In 1890, he pioneered the Industrial Association of Western India and the Industrial Conference first met at Poona with the aim of promoting industry.

As far as agriculture was concerned, Ranade favoured reduction in the burden of land revenue, and remissions in cases of crop failure. He also held the British government responsible for increasing rural indebtedness. He also pressed for easier and cheaper credit facilities for the ryots.

However, the major limitation of his economic idea was his failure to realise that the colonial state was incapable of promoting development in any basic manner or in ending of economic drain or providing tariff protection against imports from Britain.

BAL GANGADHAR TILAK

Tilak and Social Reforms

Born in a Chitpavan Brahman family of Ratnagiri, he had imbibed a love of Sanskrit and Mathematics form his father. Tilak had a deep regard for Hindu religion and culture. The impact of Western knowledge had dazzled the Indians of his times but Tilak did not forsake his deep regard for ancient learning.

Tilak was an ardent believer of political reform but during his early career he was drawn into contentious issues which earned him the oppobrium of a revivalist. The two cases were that of Rakhmabai and the Age of Consent Bill. In the Rakhmabai Case, the husband pleaded for restitution of conjugal rights. Rakhmabai refused to live with her husband as she argued that the marriage had occurred without her consent. In this sensational issue, while Ranade supported Rakhmabai's claim to her freedom, Tilak defended the husband's position. Tilak's argument was that a case of this kind should be tried according to the Hindu *shastra*. The other was the Age of

Consent controversy. Malabari and his friends proposed in the Imperial Legislature Council that intercourse with a wife under twelve years of age should be made penal and in cases of infant marriage the bride should be entitled to repudiate the marriage on attaining maturity.

In both cases Tilak took a stand which was regarded as reactionary. Just as he failed to support Rakhmabai, in the same way he expressed himself against the Age of Consent Bill. His defence was that "the government should not interfere with customs which have been carried on our society from time immemorial" (Kesari, VII, 23, June 7, 1887).

Tilak was not against social reforms as such, but he believed that social reconstruction should not be undertaken prior to political emancipation. He wrote in the Bombay Chronicle a year before his death.... "I did not think...that a legislature which is not wholly responsible to the public, is competent to deal with social questions."

Tilak had enlightened views on women's education and widow remarriage. He was also against the evil of untouchability. But Tilak was not merely a 'platform reformer' (Jog: 35). He practised what he preached. Though Tilak was not a revivalist in the strict sense of the term, he "allied himself with the forces of reaction" (Chandra: 371).

Nationalism and Tilak

Lokmanya Tilak lived in a dynamic period in Indian history and was regarded as "the Maker of Modern India" by no less a person than Mahatma Gandhi. Patriotism was his passion and he knew no other religion, but love of his country.

Tilak realised very early that the secret of British power was not physical but moral. The mission of his life was to break this spell and make Indians aware of their basic strength. Through his writings in the Kesari and the Mahratta and the "Tenets of the New Party" he tried to enthuse the masses. The Ganapati and Shivaji festivals ensured involvement of the people in the freedom movement. Aptly regarded as the "Father of Indian Unrest" Tilak made of their rights and imparted them with moral courage to exert themselves to secure them.

Tilak had limitless faith in the people and their political action. Instead of approaching the princes or landlords for support, he went to the masses and organised them into a national movement. It was for this reason that Tilak was branded a rebel and a rabble-rouser. However his understanding of the masses was inadequate as he believed in a generalized concept of the masses (Chandra: 370). He failed to understand the economic issues and relied on religious and cultural sentiments to organise a mass national movement.

Yet his ideas on *Swaraj* were refreshing different from what the Moderate had been propagating. In 1916, at Belgaum Tilak demanded self-government. He proclaimed: "The essence of *Swaraj* is that we should manage our domestic affairs to our wishes...." Tilak claimed India's right to independence not only for the material well-being but also for moral well-being. The liberty of the spirit was the basis of his Home Rule agitation (Tahmankar: 236).

Tilak and the Four-Fold Programme

On 16 October 1905, the partition of Bengal was put into effect. Bengal rose as a man to fight the partition. Tilak heartily welcomed the upsurge and regarded it as a blessing is disguise. On this occasion Tilak propagated his four-fold programme of Boycott, *Swadeshi*, National Education and *Swaraj*.

Boycott of British goods had great scope both in economic and political terms. The principle of boycott could be applied not only against the Partition of Bengal but also on a national scale for the attainment of *Swarajya*. Closely connected to the boycott programme was his idea of *Swadeshi*. Ranade and G.V. Joshi had already exhorted the people to use *Swadeshi* articles. Tilak realised that *Swadeshi* could become a powerful tool of economic salvation and liberation of the people.

Swadeshi enterprises and exhibitions were organised to popularise the idea. In "Tenets of the New Party" Tilak expanded the idea of passive resistance which was built up around *Swadeshi* and boycott. He explained "If you have not the power of active resistance, have you not the power of self-abstinence so as not to assist the foreign Government to rule over you? This is boycott and this is what is meant when we say boycott is a political weapon. "By proposing not to cooperate with the Government in collecting revenue, in the administration of justice and in providing the British with armed forces, Tilak was anticipating the non-cooperation movement of Gandhi by fourteen years (Jog: 101).

One of the great pillars of Tilak's philosophy was education. As a founder of Deccan Education Society Tilak's first love was education. He strongly protested government control of educational institutions and urged them to maintain their independence even at the risk of forfeiting grants-in-aid. In 1906, Tilak helped to established the Maharashtra Vidya Prasarak Mandal and organised a lecture tour to collect funds. To Tilak, national education enabled one to know the nation and that was what the British system had failed to do. Tilak also advocated technical and industrial education. He proposed mother-tongue as the medium of instruction. In 1905, Tilak took the lead in proposing Hindi in the Devanagari script as the national language of India.

The crowning glory of Tilak's political career was the idea of *Swaraj*. He explained that the "essence of *Swaraj* is that we should manage our domestic affairs according to our wishes..." (Tahmankar: 234). He believed that liberty is the birth right of every man.

Servants of India Society

In 1905, Gokhale founded the Servants of India Society with the object of training men to devote themselves to the service of India as national missionaries and to promote through constitutional means the national interests of the Indian people. True political changes would be possible when a new generation of Indians became educated as to their civil and patriotic duty to their country and to each other. The society took up the task of promoting Indian education in earnest and among its projects were mobile libraries, schools and night schools for factory workers. However, the members of the society accepted the British connection as ordained, as it was a divine dispensation. Their goal was self-government within the empire (Wolpert, 1989: 160).

GOPAL KRISHNA GOKHALE

Gokhale on Liberalism

Gokhale was influenced by the humanitarianism and liberalism of Western thought which he had imbibed in life through the writings of Edmund Burke, John Stuart Mill and in the writings of Ranade (Wolpert 1989: 296). To Gokhale, the liberalising influence of Western education was a great blessing. He felt that mass education was a prerequisite of political consciousness. It was through the spread of education that people could be trained in techniques of administration, in the rudiments of public health and sanitation and in the basic principles of communal harmony and social equality (Wolpert: 298).

Understanding of British Rule

Gokhale had an overriding faith in the integrity and beneficence of British rule (Wolpert: 299). He was an optimist and an idealist and believed in an evolutionary approach as far as politics was concerned (Wolpert: 300). He believed that reforms could be obtained through constitutional means. But though conscious of the Providential nature of British rule, he strove to fulfil his responsibility of presenting the 'un-British' nature of British rule. As editor of *Poona Sarvajanik Sabha* Journal, as Congress leader, as founder of Servants of India Society and as official delegate to England. Gokhale lost no opportunity in demanding reforms that would improve the condition of Indians. He was gifted with a unique command of the English language. This enabled him to fashion his protests, petitions and pleas in the Legislative Council and in the public platform. But unlike Tilak who upheld *Swaraj* Gokhale appealed for a self-governing status in the empire. For this reason Gokhale was regarded as a Moderate.

But inspite of appreciating the benefits of British rule, Gokhale never failed to criticise the high-handed actions of the government. He strongly criticised Curzon's scheme of Partition of Bengal. He severely criticised the oppression of Indian labour in South Africa.

Gokhale's Economic Ideas

Gokhale was extremely critical of the economic effects of British rule. Like Ranade, Gokhale believed that British rule had remitted in the impoverishment of the country. The Free Trade Policy had resulted in the destruction of cottage industries. He pleaded for higher scientific and technical education and demanded that Indian students should be sent abroad to acquire scientific and technical education. Like Ranade and Tilak, Gokhale too, upheld the cause of *Swadeshi.*

In agriculture Gokhale expressed the need to introduce agricultural science and improved agricultural implements. He strongly criticised the chronic indebtedness of the Indian peasant. He felt that establishment of cooperative credit societies could alter the condition of peasants.

Gokhale acknowledged that the handloom industry was doing good work but he felt that the textile industry could improve with mechanisation. Thus, like Ranade-Gokhale strongly supported industrialisation as the solution for economic problems. As for capital, Gokhale favoured joint stock enterprise.

Gokhale was one of the earliest nationalists to ask for reduction of Home Charges. He criticised the expenditure incurred in connection with the India Office and in connection with the Indian Army in England. He pointed out that "the interests of Indian taxpayers were subordinated to the interests of British commerce" (Wolpert: 110). His Budget speeches were memorable. In these speeches he advocated reduction of Salt Duty and Indianisation of services. For his incisive criticism of the colonial government he was characterised as the leader of the Opposition (Sen, II: 76).

III
RELEVANCE OF THEIR THOUGHT IN POST-INDEPENDENT INDIA

The thinkers of Western India were responsible for initiating some of the greatest movements of their times. Their thoughts on society, economy and polity played a significant role in delineating the role India was to play in the post-Independence period.

Their greatest contribution was in the field of education. All the thinkers virtually agreed that education was the panacea of all evils. For Phule, education was the instrument of social revolution. It was through education alone that social equality and social justice could be attained. The idea of universalisation of education irrespective of caste, creed, sex, religion and physical disability as propounded by Mahatma Phule found its place in the Indian Constitution. Promotion of Hindi in the Devnagari script has proved to be a bond of unity. The special emphasis on science and technical education taken up in post-Independence India was no doubt a brainchild of early thinkers such as Ranade and Gokhale. They even underlined the notion of collaboration between India and foreign countries in science and technical education.

In the social sphere, their thoughts on gender justice went a long way in amelioration of condition of women. Though women's emancipation gradually occurred during Gandhian movements of the 20th century, the first stirrings took place in the 19th century. A strong stand against child marriage and encouragement given to marriage of widows marked a definite change in the attitude towards women. In attempting to remove injustices against women and by pointing out the inequalities, they paved the way for gender justice.

Phule was probably the earliest thinker to propagate the idea of emancipation of *Shudras* and *ati-Shudras* from Brahmanical oppression. The movement against untouchability begun by Phule and later on taken up by Gandhi in his movement for upliftment of *Harijans* played an eminent role in the establishment of social justice. Movements aimed at curbing drinking and habitual indebtedness among lower classes played a vital role in removing the disabilities of the *Shudra* and *ati-Shudra* castes. These issues are still to be addressed in post-Independence India.

As far as economic ideas, Gokhale and Ranade initiated ideas of industrialisation. They believed that industry and agriculture together could bring about economic development. The notion of *Swadeshi* advocated by Ranade, Tilak and Gokhale showed the direction in which India industry could revitalise itself through motivation to cottage industries. The improvement of the condition of the farmer through development of agricultural cooperation banks showed the way for improvement of farmers.

Their ideas, thus, came to influence farmers of our Constitution such as Bhimrao Ambedkar and many of their ideas have found their place in the Indian Constitution. They still continue to inspire us and encourage us to build a society on the basis of social justice.

References

Chandra, Bipan, *Ranade's Economic Writings*, Gian Publishing House, New Delhi, 1990.

———. *Rise and Growth of Economic Nationalism in India*, Peoples' Publishing House, New Delhi, 1966.

———. *Nationalism and Colonialism in Modern India*, Orient Longman, New Delhi, 1979.

Jagirdar, P.J., *Studies in the Social Thought of M.G. Ranade*, Asia Publishing House, Bombay, 1963.

Jog, N.G., *Lokmanya Bal Gangadhar Tilak*, Publications Division, New Delhi, 1959.

O'Hanlon, Rosalind, *Caste, Conflict and Ideology Permanent Black*, 2010.

Ranade, M.G., *Miscellaneous Writings of the Late Hon'ble Mr. Justice M.G. Ranade*, Sahitya Akademi, New Delhi, 1992.

———. *Essays on Indian Economics: A Collection of Essays and Speeches*, G.A. Nateson and Co., Madras, 1920.

Sen, S.P., *Dictionary of National Biography*, Vol. II, Institute of Historical Studies, 1973.

———. *Dictionary of National Biography*, Vol. III, Institute of Historical Studies, 1974.

———. *Dictionary of National Biography*, Vol. IV, Institute of Historical Studies, 1974.

Tahmankar, D.V., *Lokmanya Tilak: Father of Indian Unrest and Maker of Modern India*, John Murray, 1956.

Wolpert, Stanley A., *Tilak and Gokhale: Revolution and Reform in the Making of Modern India,* Oxford University Press, Delhi, 1989.

11

Bankimchandra Chattopadhyay (1838-1894): The Linguistic Nationalist

Sarbani Guha Ghosal

I
INTRODUCTION

Literature in Bengal made the greatest contribution to the development of nationalistic and patriotic feelings during the freedom movement. Bankimchandra Chattopadhyay (1838-1894), the master litterateur, can be considered as the greatest figure in this category and the pioneer of the second phase of the Bengal renaissance, as Raja Rammohun Roy was that of the first. He rescued the Bengali language and literature from the "thralldom of religious verbosity" (Banerjee, 1985: 110). Bankim, a bright luminary in the firmament of the nineteenth century Bengal was the herald of a new spirit markedly bolder than one introduced by Rammohun. His exposure to the European philosophy and modern science was much advanced than most of his contemporaries. His thought in the real sense marked a watershed between the moderate nationalism of Rammohun and the articulate and vigorous nationalism of S.N. Banerjea, Bipin Chandra Pal, Aurobindo Ghosh and ultimately Vivekananda in the later phase. His broad humanism was combined with his rational spirit of enquiry and bold espousal of the cause of social and political regeneration. This great "novelist, satirist and easily the most acclaimed man of letters in the Calcutta of his day, was one of the first systematic expounders in India of the principles of nationalism" (Chatterjee, 1999: 54). The concept of nationalism as propagated by Bankimchandra can never be understood properly without hurling some light to his formative influence which includes the sociopolitical and economic environment of his time as well as the different stages of development in his thought. In other words, Bankim has to be understood in the context of the contradictions, presuppositions and possibilities of his own time.

Early Life

Bankimchandra Chattopadhyay, the third son of a Deputy Collector Jadavchandra Chattopadhyay was born at Kanthalpara, Hoogly on 26 June 1836. He hailed from a family where both the oriental and occidental cultural influences were quite strong. His government official father was quite conversant in Arabic, Persian and English language. The British government awarded him with the *Raibahadur* title. Several of his family members were also on coveted governmental services. Still the family played a crucial role in carrying forward the Hindu *Brahminical* tradition with deep sincerity. Sanskrit education, *Vaishnavite* devotionalism and the ideal of *Bhagawat Geeta's* principle of work were the domineering forces of the family. In the later part of this article we will find that on many occasions Bankim was able to critique and transcend the religious impact of his family while on some occasions he preferred to abide by those.

A talented and brilliant student of Hoogly Mohsin College Bankim later was admitted to the Law Department of the Presidency College. He passed the Entrance Examination in 1857 and the B.A. Examination in 1858. He enjoyed the reputation of being one of the only two graduates passing out in 1858 from the first batch of the University of Calcutta. Bankim had to discontinue his law studies as he was appointed as the Deputy Magistrate and Deputy Collector at Jessore in 1858. He retired from the government service on 14 September 1891. His experiences in the administrative services and his tremendous learning helped him to have an in-depth understanding about the situations of the Indian society, the cause of its bondage. He realized well that a total overhauling was needed to overcome the plight of the countrymen.

II
INFLUENCES ON BANKIM

The nineteenth century Indian intelligentsia predominantly was influenced by three major streams of thought: the impact of English liberal thought; the influence of German philosophical ideas, particularly of Schelling, Fichte, Kant and Hegel; and finally the traditional Indian thought deriving mainly from the *Vedic*, *Vedantist* and the *Puranic* traditions. Bankim imbibed influences from all these three sources.

His introduction to Western education, particularly during his days in Presidency College, drove him towards the then dominant philosophies of the west; especially Auguste Comte's Positivism had a lot of influence on him. The influence of Raja Rammohun Roy was also noticeable in him. However, Bankim was "highly selective when dealing with Positivist philosophy". He and his friends like Bhudev Chandra Mukherjee and Satish Chandra Mukherjee all lacked clarity regarding the Positivist thought and often mixed Positivist and metaphysical ideas. They were more "interested in the religious and sociological doctrines and almost completely ignored the scientific basis of the whole structure. When they expressed an interest in science, it was more in the discoveries of science than in the scientific method". Bankim believed that the Indians should learn Western science but maintaining the true Hindu identity is the key to their development. Thus, he could not accept the "essential atheism of Comte's doctrine even though he was fully aware that Comte did not deny the supernatural but instead ignored it as something which was beyond understanding" (Forbes, 1975: 129-31).

Besides Comte's Positivism, the rationalism of John Stuart Mill, Herbert Spencer's agnosticism and Jeremy Bentham's utilitarianism have fair share in developing the mental world of Bankim. Like J.S. Mill he favored the rule of the intellectually superior people. Following him he strongly recommended a stricter restraint on birth and social control of the ownership of property. Bankim agreed with Spencer on the necessity for each to take due care of him. He had high regard for Bentham though did not accept utilitarianism as the whole truth or a substitute for religion. The Western ideas of justice and equality influenced him a lot. Particularly in the early stage he tried much to connect the idea of the regeneration of the nation with the principle of equality. The overwhelming influence of equality was so much evident in his works that some later scholars have often identified him as the "trumpeter of the socialist ideas" (Mehta, 1992: 161). In his different essays he favoured equality in terms of synthesis of Hinduism and socialism.

As a reaction against the British raj and more specifically as retaliation against the severe colonial exploitation a group of Indian intelligentsia of the nineteenth century was increasingly attracted towards the German ideas. Bankim also developed a natural inclination towards the German philosophical tradition as a sensitive and modern educated Indian with direct knowledge about the British discriminatory policies owing to his administrative position. The British ideas of individualism, materialism and laissez-faire faced direct challenge in the Indian minds which by then was also equipped with German ideas of *volk*, community and duty. The cultural exchange between India and Germany also influenced scholars like Goethe, Schelling to get influenced by the *Upanishadic* tradition of idealism. The British influence in the Indian social life antagonized Bankim, furthermore in his professional life he became a victim of the British discriminatory policy regarding the promotion of the government officials. He swiftly scaled the ladder as high as Deputy Collector, but there stopped for eighteen years (Seal, 1971: 118). This disenchanted him towards the British. So, in the latter part of his life he was precisely influenced by the German ideas while developing his philosophy of nationalism in particular.

Bankim very often criticized the timidity and meekness of Hindu religion and had not shown much sympathy for the *Vedic* and *Vedantist* philosophies, perhaps because of their quietest and reflective modes which were incompatible with militant and heroic agenda and also because the *Brahmos* of his time used this tradition mostly. He was also in relentless polemic against the dominant form of *Bhakti* tradition, particularly expressed in the *Vaishnava* cult of worshipping Krishna as a figure of love or erotic excess (Sarkar, 1994: 2555). Nonetheless, he never had done away with religion. He had profound admiration for Hinduism for its capacity to adjusting changing conditions. In his essays in *Samya* he considered it as the best religion. He chose the *Puranic* tradition by drawing the figure of Krishna as a heroic, vindictive, willy and violent savior. In his opinion Hinduism was "the most perfect of all religions and went far beyond even the most valuable ideas found in the Positive Philosophy" (Forbes, 1975: 137).

Bankim firmly believed that religion and society are inseparable; both are parts of the process towards liberation. He was very much against atheism. For the liberation of India he preferred Hinduism as to him it had the potential for ensuring all round progress of the Indian people. He was very much aware of the problematic features of Hindu society, but was not in favour of abandoning its structure. He strongly believed that amendments in Hinduism had to be done from inside. Bankim's attraction towards Hinduism was mostly a reaction against *Brahmo Samaj* movement and British interference in the Indian social structure and custom.

Political Ideas of Bankim as a Social Critic

Bankim was neither a political practitioner nor he was a political theorist in the real sense of the term. His association with the government service as well as his creative mind both prohibited him to be in active politics. However, he was a patriot of the highest order. A ring of patriotic fervour and urge for social regeneration of the country were found in all his writings. He was intensely disturbed by the alienation of the educated section of his time with the common masses. He thus asked them to change their orientation and to seek mass support in their efforts at social reformation by communicating their thoughts and ideas through vernacular languages. He felt this would help in creating a social sentiment that in turn would be conducive to the cause of reform. Predominantly with this objective he launched the *Bangadarshan Patrika*, the pioneering Bengali language magazine in 1872 and in the long run this magazine played an immense role in transmitting patriotic and nationalistic feeling among the middle-class Bengalees. Bankim was utterly frustrated at the degeneration of the Indian society and culture under the British rule which resulted in the crisis of the Indian middle-class. He saw the new middle class as a class that was "born retarded"; its excessive dependence on colonial legislation for initiating social change appeared as "basic moral flaw" to him as it intensified "the lack of a will to freedom and nationhood" (Sarkar, 1994: 2554). He considered that in order to inculcate nationalistic feeling among the masses we have had to "de anglicise ourselves to a certain extent, and to speak to the masses in the language they understand" (Sinha, 1991: 307).

Thus, to Bankim, mass education and not government legislation was the panacea to the prevalent social evils like early marriage, caste system, polygamy, oppression of women and mass poverty. To him, early marriage was responsible for much of the poverty and miseries of the Indians. In his articles on *Samya* he emphasized that female education should precede women's emancipation. He considered that proper women's education as a means would enable women to earn their livelihood and strive for equality with men in the society. Bankim was a staunch supporter of women's rights and pleaded for their equal right to inheritance. He justified the wife's right to sever connections with her husband if betrayed by the latter.

Bankim was against the caste system of the Hindu society as it was against the principle of equality. To him, caste as a determinant of social stratification had given importance to the unnatural difference by incorporating heredity and tradition and so it must be given up. He made a subtle difference between *varna* and caste. To him *varna* is not unjust as it recognizes diversity. *Varna* is a mechanism to cope with the natural differences of men. By making this distinction between the two Bankim became the forerunner of many other social reformers including Mahatma Gandhi. Yet, he failed to recognize that "the Indian society required a surgical operation, almost a total revolution in relation to caste" (Mehta, 1992: 169). He criticized the inequalities of caste but did not sufficiently appreciate the inequalities as a result of land and capital imbalances, or the class dimension of the problem. He was also not sure of the role which the state would play in such a system and pinned his hopes in a messiah who would come and purge the society of this evil.

According to him, with the spread of popular education among the masses, including women, social inequality would gradually disappear. Social equality was a necessity in national regeneration as it formed the basis of civil and political and economic equality. Indian society was divided both on caste and class lines. So, in absence of social equality the poor and the lower caste people would be continuously denied civil equality. To speed up the process of social equality the poor people must be assured of economic equality, i.e., the right to earn a livelihood, which was the minimum requirement of a moral life.

The concept of equality had a special connotation in Bankim's thought. By equality he did not refer to equality of circumstances, but equality in terms of equal rights or equality of opportunity. He considered that all kinds of social diversities are not of equal importance. He rejected the importance of family and caste and regarded the diversity of circumstances as natural as it was the basis of human progress. He quoted Aristotle in defining equality as "the same treatment to similar persons". Bankim wedded the principle of equality of circumstances to the *varna* system with a subtle principle of substitution. He argued that in any society some are required for production and some others for the pursuit of knowledge. The conditions required for both the purposes are of course different. Following Aristotle he regarded "leisure" as essential for those who are in the pursuit of knowledge. However, he did not accept the hereditary basis of any profession. Bankim was also against monopolistic tendency in all walks of life, including education, bureaucracy, politics and economy. Lack of education and privilege broadened the gap between the rich and the poor, strong and the weaker sections of the society. Bankim modified the European doctrine of equality of opportunity by adding "right to achieve excellence" to it. This flowed directly from his recognition of the diversity of human life. Each person has a special temperament which he identified as *swavab* and consequently each is entitled to a different *anusheelana* or cultivation of excellence in consonance with his *swavab*. That is why he made a distinction between caste and *varna* and tended to justify the latter at the theoretical level. Bankim knew well that equality would be impossible unless it was based on the concept of fraternity and liberty. Thus, he interlinked the doctrine of equality to the development of integrated personality in which different parts of one's nature—physical, moral and spiritual converge in the achievement of a common purpose.

He was very much disturbed with the anguish of country's peasantry, and Bengal peasants in particular. He tried to explain the poverty of the peasants in terms of profits and wages and even used the doctrine of surplus value. He used terms like *samajik dhana sanchaya* (social accumulation of wealth) and *adim dhana sanchaya* (primitive accumulation of wealth) to interpret agricultural relations. However, while using the concept of class conflict he did not think the existence of permanent class conflict between the landlord and the tenants. He differentiated between the rural exploiter landlords and the urban educated landlords. To him, the latter spent a lot in peasant's welfare. Critics saw it as an attempt to defend his class. He mainly accused the subordinate staff of the zaminders for exploitation and oppression of the peasantry. Bankim also blamed the tenants for non-payment of their rents unless coerced to do so. He never favoured any peasant revolt to terminate feudalism. Contrarily, through British Indian Association, of which he was a member, he pleaded the enlightened landed interest to end the oppression of the uncultured landlords. According to Partha Chatterjee, "Bankim's devotion to what he regarded as the fundamental principles of a rational science of economics makes it impossible for him to arrive at a critique of the political economy of the colonial rule" (Chatterjee, 1999: 63).

Bankim was aware about the existence of inequality in different countries and the unending political initiatives to end it. Ancient Rome had tried to establish equality through different kinds of political compromises. France chose the revolutionary path to eradicate inequality. It was always either through dialogues or through the use of force attempts had been made to establish social equality. According to Bankim, historically speaking Gautama Buddha, Jesus Christ and Rousseau had left indelible marks in the journey towards equality. Buddha had tried to overcome inequality basically in the caste-divided society of India. Jesus was another prophet of equality on class lines by attempting to free the bondage of slavery and to establish universal fraternity. Rousseau considered equality as a natural phenomenon and became the father of the modern concept of equality and socialism. Later on St. Simon, J.S. Mill, Charles Fourier also contributed and expanded the idea of equality as propounded by Rousseau. However, Bankim lacked enough clarity regarding the establishment of equality in a basically unequal society. Thus, often his theory turned into utopia, which was revealed in his idea of nationalism very much.

He did not find much contradiction between self-rule and alien-rule as long as it was a just-rule, meaning thereby good governance. The rule of the alien forces not necessarily made a country dependent. On the other hand, non-deliverance of liberty and independence could be found under native rule also. The British rule over India, to Bankim, should not be condemned for just because it was an alien rule. On many occasions he praised the role of Western science, philosophy and literature in the development of the Indian community. To Bankim, the real criterion of liberty was that whether in a particular country there was exploitation and discrimination against the subject race. British rule would be condemned in India as it was not giving adequate attention to the problems of the colony, the Indians were not getting due status befitting their talent, education and other attainments. The British rulers were practicing discriminatory policies by denying the Indians of political education and training in modern techniques of defense and administration. Bankim watched the British administration closely, carefully in an objective and dispassionate manner. The racial prejudice in the official and personal level aggrieved him. He derived the causes for humiliation of the Indians and realized that unless India became a nation it would not be freed with the rights of its people. It was of utmost importance to establish a separate and united identity for the Indians. He understood clearly the value of freedom and nationality.

Bankim's Concept of Nationalism

Emergence of nationalism was one of the key features of the history of the nineteenth century Bengal. There were some historians who found the roots of this development in the thought and actions of Raja Rammohun Roy while some others sourced its origin in the radical thought of the Derozians. A remaining group found the beginning of Indian nationalism in the discriminatory civil, political and economic policies of the colonial rulers. The last perturbed Bankim most though the influence of other two was also prevalent in him. Concept of nationalism gradually became most important phenomenon in Bankim study both during the colonial period and in our contemporary time.

Prof. T.W. Clarke like historians charged him of imparting communal strain in the extremist thought of the Indian freedom movement. It was also said that, "Bankim blazed the trail for the Extremists in contemptuous criticism of the moderates." His *Anandamath* (1882) profoundly moved the generation of Aurobindo, the pioneer of extremism. It provided an example and served as an inspiration for selfless, fearless struggle; for the freedom of the motherland from tyranny and oppression. He translated and interpreted *Geeta* in the light of the Western knowledge to make it acceptable before the Western educated intelligentsia and it became very popular among the extremist youths. It was for this Bankim was often identified as "social reactionary, an implacable enemy of liberal reforms and a blatant spokesperson of the orthodox and obscurantist who opposed progress". This labeling was omnipresent in the 1990s when the Hindu fundamentalist discourse of the country drew frequent paradigms from Bankim. Scholars like Amales Tripathy, however considered that this kind of view "portrays ignorance or deliberate misinterpretation" of his thought. Bankim never loved tradition blindly and patriotism was never a substitute of religion for him as it was for the extremists. He also showed utter futility of parochial nationalism and his target was not the Muslims but the decadent tyrants of both communities (Tripathy, 1967: 6-17). Modern historians like Tapan Raychaudhuri or Tanika Sarkar argued that Bankim's complex "mediation of

Western colonial and Indian indigenous discourses reveal the author's fascination with, yet resistance to British colonial discourse on Bengal/India" (Chakraborty, 2011: 39).

Bankim's nationalism bore his concern for national solidarity and on it depend his dream of Hindu society. But communal tag could not be attached to him just for this. Several positive Muslim characters had place in his creations. In reality Bankim was confused in finding out the ways for salvation of the Indians. The idea of Indians as a community was non-existent in his time and it was an extremely fragmented and custom ridden society. Bankim again could not launch any all-out attack against the Britishers because firstly, he was in government service and naturally was bound by its written and unwritten obligations. Secondly, from the core of his heart he favoured several English philosophical and scientific traditions which were instrumental in reorienting the consciousness of the native people. Actually national solidarity was his key concern and in order to procure it he took recourse to certain elements of Hinduism. But he remained a harsh critic of the social evils of Hinduism and never blindly followed any of its ideas. Bankim was much against the politics of verbosity. The "politics of droning", the major techniques of the moderates was strongly rebuked by him (Ray, 2005). He was in favour of strong, determined and action-oriented programmes and realized that this could be attained only by generating a new sense of nationalism in which the new *mantra* would be of "identity, unity and strength". However, European kind of nationalism was difficult to develop in India because of the diversities regarding race, religion, language, tradition, heritage and culture. The people did not have any "sense of cultural oneness". The commoners in India were not bothered about who were the rulers as long as they were ruled properly. A sense of deep fatalism was all pervasive. In this context Bankim took recourse to *karmavad* to ensure unity among his countrymen.

In this turbulent situation of 1882, Reverend Hastie of General Assembly wrote a nasty tract severely criticizing Hinduism. Bankim prepared a long, careful and angry reply. Thereafter "in *Samya* in his prose's he became exclusively preoccupied with the theme of a reconstructed Hindu form of knowledge and leadership" (Sarkar, 1994: 2555). His anger was probably fueled by the changing political environment since the mid-1870s. The Bengali middle-class was entirely loyal to the British during the Sepoy Mutiny of 1857. But the end of Mutiny did not fetch anything good and contrarily, the subsequent discriminatory racist policies like the Act XI of 1860 related to indigo cultivation, the Vernacular Press Act of 1878, the anti-Ilbert agitation among the Britishers in 1883, the Rent Acts of 1859 and 1885 angered the middle class. The anti-colonial critiques and organizations developed both in liberal and Hindu-revivalist lines. In Bankim, the caste, class and gender references suddenly disappeared and his concern centred on "what constitutes authentic Hinduism, what possibilities exist in early Hinduism and can be used for future nation building.... Bankim looks for an ethico-religious site for the Hindu people whose dominant priority is not social justice any more, but what is truly indigenous, i.e., Hindu" (*ibid.*). His task then was to imbue a sense of nationalism among the Indians in the aspects of both identification and differentiation and to develop themselves as a nation vis-à-vis other nations predominantly under a Hindu umbrella. Bankim did not make any distinction between abstract God and concrete humanity and preferred to combine both by stating that "God was the inmost essence of all human beings and that worship of one was the worship of other as well". Thus, God and humanity are one and the *dharma* or religion of man was laid in his attainment of full humanity (*purna manushattwa*) through the cultivation and harmonious development of all his physical and mental faculties and through the performance of dutiful actions in a selfless spirit. Bankim termed it *anusheelan*. Through this idea Bankim simultaneously tried to impart knowledge of what was good for the community and one was supposed to do under specific circumstances. *Anusheelan* meant complete devotion to God with progressive extension of one's love for oneself and one's family to one's community to one's country and finally to whole of humanity. This was very difficult to practice. Bankim suggested his countrymen to take the love for their country as the highest form of religion (*dharma*) of their time. He thus deserved the credit of raising nationalism to the dignity of religion. Bankim became the founding father of Indian nationalism by channelizing religious discourses in political direction and ensuring a fusion of religion and politics which inspired a number of Hindu youth of his time. In this way he provided an intellectual foundation to Indian nationalism.

Bankim contested the British identification of the Indians, particularly the Bengalees, as a weak community and attempted to rupture the colonial binary of "manly British" and "effeminate Bengalee". He initiated the construction of a masculinised Hindu identity in the Indian nationalist literature. In *Anandamath* (1882) and *Devi Chowdhurani* (1884) he reversed the colonial critique of Hinduism to present martial Hindu ascetics from the past as models of nationalist emulation. To him "...Revolutionary violence as nationalist praxis entails recovering the 'lost' or 'forgotten' masculinity, from which displays of national prowess in battle with the British and the Muslims" (Chakraborty, 2011: 35). Bankim tried to create a collective masculine identity rather than an individualized one through the retrieval and reinscription of a fragmented past. His concept of nationalism developed in the context of the crisis of the masculinity in the late nineteenth century Bengal. For him religion lied at the public domain and reformed Hinduism emerged as the basis for ethical and political actions in his works. He creatively merged the traditional archetypes of warriors (*Kshyatriya*) with the priestly (*Brahman*) caste and transgressed "traditional scriptural prescriptions to construct ascetic martiality as normative Hindu masculinity." His essays delineated "how ascetic practices, such as celibacy, meditation, devotion to a deity, and physical culture –when reframed as work for the nation-constitute Hindu martiality" (Chakraborty, 2011: 45-48). He went to the extent of developing a band of Hindu militia, namely the *santans*. Bankim hoped to build self-esteem through self-criticism; to masculinise the politically conscious Bengali he initiated a "self-ironising tradition" that positions Bengali male differently from the colonial representation.

As the high priest of Indian nationalism Bankim interpreted subordination of Indians to Britishers in several ways. In order to combat the British allegation of effeminacy he found certain flaws in the Bengali character which required immediate amendment. It was the lack of physical strength and courage or the absence of the nationalistic vibes that was the main cause of India's subordination. He interpreted the dependent status of the Bengalees in two ways. First is their lack of desire for liberty. Very few people nursed "a vague feeling that independence is better than subjection, but never has this feeling become a compelling desire; never have the majority of Indians fought for their liberty...the second great reason for the of India: the lack of solidarity in Hindu society" (Chatterjee, 1999: 54-55). According to Bankim, Indian subjection to Britain was more cultural than material or physical. The dominant Hindu philosophy and Buddhism emphasized too much on fatalism and other worldliness i.e., *niyotibad* and *vairagya*. This encouraged a lackadaisical attitude among the people. Bankim asserted that Hindus and Indians at large failed to develop a sense of political nationalism and resistance against foreign invaders for their other-worldly asceticism. Against this negativity his positive doctrine "naturally was to look for a principle of this worldly asceticism, particularly an asceticism of action.... It was because the world is real, and its order must be improved and made less unjust, that people must undertake energetic but unselfish action. Unselfish here meant in the interest of a collectivity of an extended self, a sense of a community which was still half-spelt, and thus half-seen in Bankim's times, which would later be called the nation. Thus, there was a strong ineradicable link between the coming of the nation and people acting in a particular way. The nation, nationalism was not a mode of being, but of acting" (Kaviraj, 1995: 151-52).

The corporeality of colonial discourse was produced in *Bangalir Bahubal* (The Physical Valor of the Bengalees), 1874. Bankim stated that physical strength and force or power were not equal. Power as well as lack of power was a social phenomenon resulting from the application on physical strength of four elements: enterprise, solidarity, courage and perseverance. The

Bengalees as a group always lacked these elements and became powerless. Here he mentioned that the cultural attributes of power can be acquired if the Bengalees acquire a compelling desire for some national good and if this compulsion became too great that people were prepared to stake their lives for it, if this desire became permanent then only they would be powerful race (Chatterjee, 1999: 57). Thus, for him moral, mental and physical developments are simultaneously required for nationalism.

III
RELEVANCE OF BANKIM

Bankimchandra was often identified as spiritual nationalist. However, neither his spiritualism nor his nationalism was ever devoid from the practicalities of his time. For me he was more a linguistic nationalist as it was his language which contributed most in flaring up the idea of nationalism among common masses. His several historical novels climaxed by *Anandamath* with the clarion call of *Vande Mataram* "sought to evoke a new interest in the history of the country, striking a note typical of nationalism the world over" (Sarkar, 1983: 83). Bankim left specific and permanent contribution by stating that our country, having little history of her own must hunt up material from the forgotten or neglected indigenous sources to revive a spirit of constructive national service. This has initiated a new trend in the process of nationalistic development in the country. Complaints have been made on his over-enthusiasm for Hindu revivalism and his rather unfair treatment of the Muslims. In *Bharater Lajja* (Disgrace of India) 1872, he categorically described his understanding of nationalism. In this article he identified himself as a staunch Hindu and never hesitated to say that what was good for the Hindus must be good for all. Again, this same Bankim while analyzing the lot of the common people observed in *Bangadesher Krishak* (Peasants of Bengal) that India could not develop truly as a nation so long as there was not equal and simultaneous improvement in the conditions of Hashim Sheikhs and Rama Kaibartas, i.e., the commoners of the country. Thus, it could be said with conviction that the conscious communal intention in Bankim was definitely a matter of big debate. He should not be blamed for the use of his writings by the communalists of his time and afterwards by any means. One thing which was consistent in Bankim was his emphasis on human endeavor (*karmavad*) with underlying spirit of social service and philanthropy. His dispassionate critiques of Western intellectual tradition and Indian religio-cultural tradition together were quite uncommon. In reality we find several swings in Bankim's thought between traditionalism and modernity. This was however, nothing unique but very much a part of the nineteenth century intellectual tradition of India. It was definitely a watershed; the time of a great leap from pre-colonial to colonial phase loaded with conditions for further transition. Other thinkers of the period like Rabindranath Tagore or Swami Vivekananda also displayed contradictions in their thought which was very much inherent in that specific time. As a student of social studies we have to contextualize Bankim with all his contradictions and conjectures. Thus, despite his conservatism and inconsistencies Bankim, the greatest linguistic nationalist of the country continuously made us conscious about our glorious past as well as he emphasized on the innovations of survival in the future. The ultimate aim of his social and political thinking was to end social suffering and promotion of interpersonal goodwill.

References

Banerjee, Bholanath. 1985. "Bankim Chandra Chatterjee" in *Bengalee Intellectual Tradition*, ed. Amal Kumar Mukhopadhyay, 110-26. Kolkata: K.P. Bagchi.

Chakraborty, Chandana. 2011. *Masculinity, Asceticism and Hinduism*. New Delhi: Permanent Black.

Chakarabarty, Radharaman. 2008. *Aspects of Political Thinking in India: Nationalism, Civil Society and Internationalism*. Kolkata: Progotishil Prokashak.

Chattopadhyay, Bankimchandra. 1983. *Rachanaboli*. Kolkata: Mousumi Prokashani. (in Bengali)

Chatterjee, Partha. 1999. "The Moment of Departure: Culture and Power in the Thought of Bankimchandra" in *The Partha Chatterjee Omnibus*. New Delhi: Oxford University Press.

Forbes, G.H. 1975. *Positivism in Bengal*. Kolkata: Minerva Associates Publications.

Kaviraj, Sudipta. 1995. *The Unhappy Consciousness—Bankimchandra Chattopadhyay and the Formation of Nationalist Discourse in India*. New Delhi: Oxford University Press.

Mehta, V.R. 1992. *Foundations of Indian Political Thought—An Interpretation*. New Delhi: Manohar.

Ray, Anil Baran. 2005. "Bankimchandra: Development of Nationalism and National Identity" in *Prabuddha Bharat*, August 2005.

Sarkar, Sumit. 1983. *Modern India: 1885-1947*. New Delhi: Macmillan.

Sarkar, Tanika. 1994. "Imagining a Hindu Nation: Hindu and Muslims in Bankimchandra's Later Writing" in *Economic & Political Weekly*, September 24, 1994. Vol. 29(29).

Seal, Anil. 1971. *The Emergence of Indian Nationalism-Competition and Collaboration in the Later Nineteenth Century*. New Delhi: S. Chand & Company.

Sen, Amiya P. 1993. *Hindu Revivalism in Bengal 1872-1905: Some Essays in Interpretation*. New Delhi: Oxford University Press.

Sinha, Nirmal. 1991. *Freedom Movement in Bengal 1881-1904*. Kolkata: Academic Publishers.

Tripathy, Amales. 1967. *The Extremist Challenge*. Kolkata: Orient Longman.

12

Three Faces of Indian Feminist Thought: Tarabai Shinde, Pandita Ramabai Saraswati, and Sarala Devi Chaudhurani

Karabi Mitra

I
INTRODUCTION

Late nineteenth century India experienced a widespread cultural turmoil with the spread of Western education. In the indigenous society social agendas emerged with multiple ends and the central point of debate was the status of the women. The development of indigenous feminist thought centered around the modernisation of the women and assertion of their rights. In this context the three educated women we have selected represented Maharashtra and Bengal, being the hot bed of the interaction of Western impact and indigenous response. They belonged to the high caste, enlightened families and argued in favour of womens' rights in general. The areas of their action were different from each other. Tarabai Shinde was a strong antagonist of patriarchal hegemony while Pandita Ramabai Saraswati wrote and worked for the upliftment as well as the empowerment of the high caste widows. Later on her project included lower caste women too. Sarala Devi Chaudhurani wrote and worked for the national regeneration. She made efforts to regenerate strength among the people irrespective of gender, class and caste though she is well-known as the foremost feminist activist of twentieth century.

II
LIFE AND THOUGHTS OF THREE FACES

Tarabai Shinde (1850-1910)

Tarabai Shinde was born in Buldhana, Berar. Her father was Bapuji Hari Shinde, a member of the Satyasodhak Samaj. The *Samaj* was founded by Jotirao Phule. He was a renowned social reformer and denounced Brahmanic hegemony. She hailed from a traditional family where the system of seclusion or *Maratha mola* was strictly observed. The word meant "the true old Maratha custom...whereby the women of...Marathas have to wear the burqa" (quoted by O'Hanlon from a Maratha dictionary of 1829, 1994, 21). She was influenced by Phule and her bitter experience of the traditional norms of keeping women at check was articulated in her writings.

Pandita Ramabai Saraswati (1858-1922)

By birth Pandita Ramabai Saraswati (1858-1922) belonged to the Chitpavan Brahmana caste, a traditionally eminent community of Maharashtra. Her upbringing in an adverse situation trained her up to face challenges throughout her life. She learnt Sanskrit from Lakshmibai, her mother. Gifted with excellent memory she memorized *Bhagabat Gita* and *Bhagabat Purana* at an early age. Her father Anant Shastri Dongre, a Sanskrit Pandit lived as outcaste due to his non-conformity with the Brahminical society and 'democratisation of Sanskrit learning' in the forest of Gangamul, Andhra Pradesh. The Chitpavans were included among the 'new Brahmanas' due to their acceptance of the Western learning however Ramabai and her brother were well conversed only in traditional learning. She lost her parents at an early age.

In 1878, she arrived at Calcutta with her brother Srinivas. Her eloquence in Sanskrit earned great fame and she was hailed as Pandita and Saraswati. Henceforth she was known as Pandita Ramabai Saraswati. Keshab Chandra Sen advised her to study the *Upanishads*, the *Vedanta* and the *Vedas*. In order to lecture on the duties of women she also studied the *Dharmashastras*.

A new Ramabai was born at this juncture who defied Shastric injunctions by marrying Bepin Bihari Medhabi, a non-

Brahmin by Civil Marriage Act. Her married life lasted for two years only and her husband died leaving a baby girl. She came to Mumbai and with the support of the liberal nationalist friends from the Prarthana Samaj founded Arya Mahila Sabha (1882). In front of the Hunter Commission she spoke in favour of womens' education since lady teachers and doctors were urgently needed by the society. She felt the need of medical education and decided to leave for England (1883). There she was converted to Christianity along with her daughter (1883).

Collection of fund for the widows' home was the main objective of Ramabai's venture to the Western world. She visited America, made extensive tours and delivered lectures in hundreds of meetings for this cause. Her renowned publication *The High Caste Hindu Woman* (1888) won the heart of the people of America. The American Ramabai Association was formed to raise fund for the proposed widows' home in India. The Sharada Sadan was founded (1889) in Mumbai virtually without any opposition from the conservative section and the liberal nationalists also supported her.

The famine of Kathiwar (1900) vividly exposed the vulnerabilities of the womens' life in front of her. Numerous women were dragged by the flesh traders. She volunteered for the rehabilitation of the distressed women and chalked out a project for their vocational training. Most of them belonged to the downtrodden milieu and imparting of vocational training was necessary for their livelihood. She inaugurated Mukti Mission at Kedgaon far away from Poona and despite opposition from the conservative section tried to ensure self-sufficiency for around nineteen hundred women. They were enriched in a variety of vocational training. Her project of empowerment of women irrespective of class and caste remains a memorable aspect of her contribution towards the development of Feminism in India.

Sarala Devi Chaudhurani (1872-1954)

The status of women presents a problematised space in the studies on Colonial Bengal. Being born to Swarnakumari Devi and Janakinath Ghoshal in the Tagore house in Jorasanko Sarala Devi's maternal family was the primary center of social regeneration. She graduated with Honours in English and mastered in French, Persian and Sanskrit. Besides she learnt music, composed songs and contributed to *Bharati*, a journal edited by her mother. She joined Maharani Girls' School as a teacher in Mysore.

Sarala Devi Chaudhurani introduced *Veerasthami* (1902). *Pratapaditya Utsav* (1903) and propagated the cult of physical culture among the Bengali youth. Professor Murtaza, a "travelling acrobat and a professional strong man" (Chaudhury, 2001, 152) was engaged to train the boys up in fencing. She opened an outlet of indigenous products known as *Lakshmir Bhandar* and it was meant for the women only. She played a pioneering role in the popularization of patriotic songs and her memorable recital of '*Atito gauraba bahini momo bani*' in the Calcutta Congress (1901) earned her great fame. Rabindranath Tagore requested her to tune *Vande Mataram* for the Benaras Congress (1905).

She was married (1905) to Rambhaja Dutt Chaudhury, an Advocate by profession from the Punjab and editor of *Hindusthan*, an Urdu journal published from Lahore. He was also an *Aryasamajist* leader. This relation helped her to spread the programme of womens' regeneration in northern India. Following her husband's imprisonment she shouldered the responsibility of editorship of the journal and published an English version. She founded the *Bharatstrimahamandal* (1910), an all-India organization for womens' regeneration.

With the passage of time she became more involved in the nationwide programme of regeneration of women and editorship of the journal. At this stage she became a believer of non-violent politics and follower of Gandhiji. She was the first Indian lady to congratulate Gandhiji for his decision of non-cooperation with the colonial government and published the writings of Gandhiji and Mahadev Govind Ranade in *Bharati*.

Sarala Devi was the spokesperson for women's franchise in the Thirty-third session of the Indian National Congress held in Delhi (1918). She again came in the forefront of women's movement for rights in the 1930's. In view of the disinterested attitude of the Congress leaders in matters of their rights the female members decided to form a party of their own. Restoration of the national honour was the aim of her life. Editorship of a journal, propagation of cultural unity, introduction of hero worship and culture of physical exercise, establishment of the first National level women's organization, campaign for women's suffrage, support of Gandhian movement, demand for legal, economic, social and educational equality for women were some landmarks in her active political career.

III
RELEVANCE OF THE THINKERS IN CONTEMPORARY INDIAN POLITICAL THOUGHT

The word 'feminism' has multiple connotations. The Dictionary explains the term as "the belief and aim that women should have the same rights, power, and opportunities as men". Veena Oldenburg defined the term from the non-specific gender point of view "as a person (and not necessarily a woman) whose analytical perspective is informed by an understanding of the relationship between power and gender in any historical, social, or cultural context" (quoted by Forbes, 1999, 8-9). Assertion of the rights of women in a genderised social system may be described as one of the objectives of the activists of the feminist movement. In contemporary India the word 'Feminism' denotes a concept imported from the West. However, it is evident that, several Indian women asserted their rights to empower the women and give a voice to them.

Truly no feminist movement in the strict sense of the term was organized during the period under discussion though the women suffered from numerous discriminations. An era of social reforms was initiated during the early decades of the nineteenth century with a declared objective to the betterment of womens' condition. Rammohun Roy and Ishwar Chandra Vidyasagar were the foremost champions for the cause of the women in Bengal. While Rammohun Roy cooperated with the colonial government in the passage of the Anti-Sati Act (1829) Ishwar Chandra Vidyasagar dedicated his life for the introduction of the widows' remarriage (1856).

The anti-Sati enactment (1829) assured the Hindu widows' right to live however their social honour and means of livelihood were left in the oblivion. The problems were acute for the high-caste Hindu widows who faced acute politicization of their social status. Indian nationalism was 'feminized' and upheld the agenda of *Swadeshi* womanhood being a reassertion of the Shastric injunctions regarding women. Problematisation of the women's rights commensurated with other contemporary issues namely, clamour for social reforms from the Western educated milieu in the first half of the century while the nationalists equated the womens' issue with *Swadeshi* ethos during the next half of the century. The 'Victorian' ideal of womanhood was mixed up with the indigenous ideal of *Swadeshi* womanhood.

As a result of modernization of the social status of women the issue became a hotbed of controversy among the conservative and liberal nationalists. The Christian missionaries' criticism of the social status of the Hindu women, the enactments of 1829, 1856, 1873, 1891 for their better livelihood i.e., emancipation from the customs of Sati, child marriage, polygamy, right to remarriage and restitution of conjugal rights created a clear difference of opinion within the nationalist circle. The conservatives opposed the interference of the colonial government within the Hindu Shastric domain because with the emergence of Hindu nationalism *Sanatana* Shastric principles were accepted as synonymous to nationalism. The inner compartment of the Hindu household was supposed to be free of colonial intervention and the women were considered as the repositories of traditional norms and customs. These were the means to tighten the patriarchal control especially on the erulite women. The main focal point was how the modernisation of the indigenous women will be tailored to suit the nationalist need.

Virasalingam Pantulu, Jyotiba Phule, Mahadev Govind Ranade and other social thinkers considered the progress of the women as one of the pre-conditions of nationalism. However, they did not pay heed to the actual demand of the women. Therefore the reforming acts necessarily did not become fruitful because they could not feel the womens' actual necessities. The Widow Remarriage Act may be an appropriate example. The objective was noble however education and empowerment of the widows were practical options than their remarriage. The Age of Consent Act 'degenerated into a battle for control of Indian women's sexuality (Forbes, 1999, 31). The scheme of reforms was programmed in conformity with the preference of the male reformers however the womans' question did not ask 'what does the woman want'.

The colonial government was 'unconcerned' with the education of the women therefore the projects of their modernization were bound to be half-hearted. The missionaries' efforts aimed at facilitating the process of conversion. Therefore their education largely depended on private initiatives. Geraldine Forbes presented a graphic picture of their education. According to her, around 1854 'there were approximately 626 girls' schools...with a total of 21,755 students' which definitely pointed at the 'shift of attitude towards female education' (Forbes, 1999, 41). Towards the end of the century the number of girl students in Secondary schools increased from 2,054 to 41,582 (Forbes, 1999, 45). However, the training did not aim at developing the women as individual beings rather making them suitable life-partners of the educated male.

Towards the end of the century with the foundation of the Indian National Congress (1885) most of the male reformers busied themselves in nationalist politics. The Congress was to act as a 'purely political organization' (O'Hanlon, 1994, 17) and deliberately put the social issues outside. Ranade and others founded National Social Conference (1887) for the discussion of social issues. Besides with the emergence of the 'Sita-Sati-Savitri' model the agenda of modernist reforms for the Indian women were 'no longer compatible' any more (O'Hanlon, referred to Uma Chakravarty, 1994, 60-61). The mantle of the movement was laid on a new milieu. The period witnessed the emergence of the 'new women' (the term is borrowed from Forbes) who were educated and keen to forward the cause of the women. In the words of Geraldine Forbes they 'were part of a modernizing movement which sought to modify gender relations in the direction of greater equality between men and women' (Forbes, 1999, 28). The nationalist-cum-colonial control over some women produced an exclusive effect. First they identified the agents of exploitation on the women and next they tried to show the ways and means to overcome the bondage and in effect clamoured in support of the womens' empowerment. The modus operandi varied however the point of unity in their approach was that, they considered the women as *the individual being* and capable to assert herself in a patriarchal order. They were precursors of the womens' multifarious roles in the freedom movement of the following century though the idealized images of Indian women continued to influence the thinking of leaders like Gandhiji (quoted by O'Hanlon from the articles by Madhu Kiswar and Sujata Patel, 1994, 60-61).

During the 1880s Maharashtra became the principal site of controversies around women. The leading nationalist leaders like Bal Gangadhar Tilak and Gopal Ganesh Agarkar stood on the opposite camps regarding the issues like women's education, restitution of conjugal life, etc. The refusal of Rukhmabai to live with her much older husband who sued against her and demanded her return as his 'lawful property' infuriated both the camps. However the protesting tone of the Maharashtrian women could be heard from the memorable letters of Rukhmabai to the *Times of India* (May, September, 1885) under the pseudo name 'Hindu lady'. She criticised the 'loss of power' (mental and physical freedom) of the child bride who was enforced to enter the cycle of reproduction at the age of fourteen (Chakravarty, 1998, 254-55).

Hindu Shastric injunction of the Hindu widows' 'chaste and pure celibate life' and it's confirmation by the colonial government was a much debated issue and this brings Tarabai Shinde's single contribution to the discussion. Her *Stri Purush Tulana* (1882) was written in "reaction of a criminal case involving Vijayalakshmi, a young Brahmin widow who was charged with murdering her 'illegitimate' infant at birth". She was sentenced for death on the ground of immorality however the higher courts sentenced her for transportation for life (Chakravarty, 1998, 250-51). Regarding the purpose of writing the book Tarabai disclosed that, she intended 'to defend the honour of all my sister countrywomen. I am not looking at particular castes or families here. It's just a comparison between women and men' (quoted by O'Hanlon, 1994, 9).

In this context one of her quotation from Bhartrihari's *Satakatrayam* may be pertinent:

> Woman is only the axe, that cuts down trees of virtue
>
> Hindrance to creatures through thousands of births
>
> Know her to be the temptress, embodiment of pains in this world....

She commented "So this is what you do—you heap all of your contempt on women's heads, so it's you who become the very image of virtue!" (O'Hanlon, 1994, 100). She exposed the wickedness of the male which adversely affected the social status of the women in a vehement language. Jotirao Phule referred to Tarabai as *Chiranjivi* and credited her for writing the book "to express the anger that many women felt at their ill-treatment by menfolk, and to spell out to men what they needed to do to recover their women's affection and loyalty" (O'Hanlon quoted from Jotirao Phule's *Satsar* (1885), 1994, 19). Though the book lacked 'internal structure' yet the fiery criticism of patriarchal society is clearly understood.

The question of the miserable social condition of Hindu widows haunted Pandita Ramabai Saraswati too. To the nationalist circle she emerged as the modern embodiment of the ladies belonging to the *Vedic* times and a suitable idol for the imagined *Swadeshi* womanhood. Paradoxically these learnings convinced her regarding the negative social projection of the women in the Hindu *Shastras*. She used her profound knowledge of Sanskrit *Shastras* as a tool to coup with the gender-biased Sanatana tradition. As a result she became 'potentially a dangerous figure' with her extensive knowledge of the Sanskrit scriptures and 'the most controversial Indian woman of her times' due to her conversion to Christianity and allegations of conversion of Hindu widows in her Home.

Following the prohibition of the *Sati* (1829) the social status of the high caste Hindu widows problematised the nationalist discourse on them. The anxiety to control the chastity of the young Hindu widows found expression in reinstating the principle of *pativratya* or wifely devotion towards the husband. According to the Hindu Shastric norms the widow becomes a living *Sati* and by means of leading a celibate and austere life she tries her best to wipe away her sins and gain heaven for her deceased husband (Chakravarty, 1995). Ramabai visited Benaras, Vrindaban—the abode of the widows and acquired a first hand experience of their exploited condition. She wrote "...that women of the high and low caste, as a class were all bad, very bad, worse than demons, as unholy as untruth and they could not get *moksha* [like]men. The only hope of their getting this much desired liberation from Karma and its results...was the worship of their husbands..." (*A Testimony of Our Inexhaustible Treasure* by Pandita Ramabai, 1998, 18-20). The inner paradox of the Hindu *Shastras* promoting worship of numerous goddesses were clear to her. Therefore she decided to set up a home for the high caste Hindu widows in face of immense social opposition.

Her vehement speeches portrayed the social torture of the women irrespective of their caste and marital status. Her nationalist associates gradually withdrew from her because she could easily point at the patriarchal agenda of woman-centric social reforms. She viewed the society from the standpoint of a woman and aimed to undertake projects for the betterment of their position with a view to empower them. Therefore remarriage of the widows was not a solution to her because she wanted a complete regeneration of a widowed lady who apart from marriage might opt for serving the society in numerous ways.

Her first book *Stri Dharmaniti* or the morals of women earned great popularity. Prof. Uma Chakravarty described the book as "less about the companionate wife and more about her self-cultivation even as they performed the roles of wife and mother" and "she was probably one of the first woman who wrote and lectured for a living in the nineteenth century". It also indicated her close link with the moderate reformers and reflected the reformist approach towards Hindu womanhood (Chakravarty, 1998, 316).

The Anglican church was not ready to see a protest from Ramabai against it's decisions to not allow her to teach the young English men and women. On the contrary, she was used to the environment of teaching since her childhood where no discrimination on the ground of gender was made. Despite conversion she never, "became a pliant tool in the hands of the missionaries" (Chakravarty, 1998, 320-21) and realized that, no religion allows free voice to the women and the hold of tradition is identical in every religious system. She wrote:

> ...I have a conscience and a mind of *my own*...I have with great effort freed myself from the yoke of the Indian priestly tribe so I am not at present willing to place myself under another similar yoke by accepting everything that comes from the priests as authorized command of the Most High.... (quoted from the *Letters and Correspondences*, Chakravarty, 1998, 322)

One may hear the voice of feminist activist in these writings. She also questioned the miraculous birth of Christ and the concept of the Holy Trinity. Her conversion to Christianity did not bring her the peace of mind because as a woman she was too self-reliant for any institutional religion. Her austere lifestyle like a Hindu widow was also criticised by the church authority. The attitude of the church voiced the arrogance and racialism of the colonial state. The press hailed her and wrote that, the 'race' that had produced her had nothing to despair' (quoted from the *Bombay Educational Record*, Chakravarty, 1998, 326). For the time being her role as the 'champion of women's issues' received social acceptance and she participated in the Annual Congress meeting (1889). Prof. Uma Chakravarty pointed at the significance of her participation being "at a time when the liberal Ranade considered it undesirable that women should take part in politics" (Chakravarty, 1998, 326). In front of the participants comprised of several woman delegates she commented "It is not strange, my countrymen, that my voice is small, for you have never given a woman the chance to make her voice strong" (quoted by Chakravarty, 1998, 326).

She protested against tonsuring of widows against their wish in the third National Social Conference on the humiliation of child widows. Her another significant demand was to ensure the right to free speech and the right to decide for themselves to the women. She criticised the 'tokenist display of loyalty to the Queen' and "redefined loyalty and patriotism in terms of the worship of mothers" (Chakravarty, 1998, 327). Towards the solution of the problem of national language she supported the use of Hindi as "the most effective language for the nation" (Chakravarty, 1998, 327).

On a close analysis of her activities the Pandita may be described as a born-rebel against injustice—namely, as a converted Hindu woman she was a caustic critic of the conservative Hindu ways of life, as a Congressite lady her social welfare projects were financed by the West however she exposed the weakness of the British colonial educational policy in front of the Hunter Commission. She criticised the anomalies of the colonial administration and pointed at the mismanagement of the Plague hospitals in Maharashtra. She supported Rukhmabai since it 'revealed' the secret ploy "between the colonial government and Indian men in questions involving Indian women" (O'Hanlon, 1994, 17). Her plan to teach the men, opening of the doors of *Mukti Sadan* to the distressed famine-stricken girls did not match with the gendered view of the Anglican church. Similarly the charges of conversion of the Hindu Brahmin widows against her led the nationalist liberals to cut off contact with her. The projection of the tragedies of the high caste Hindu women in the pages of her monograph bearing identical title deconstructed the myth of the glorified inner compartment of the Hindu household in front of the West. Besides acceptance of foreign donations for the betterment of the condition of the widows led to her denunciation by some 'liberal' Hindus also.

Celebration of motherhood aiming to glorify the women serving patriarchal needs was the essence of the nationalist discourse on Indian womanhood. Sarala Devi Chaudhurani was not prepared to conform to these patriarchal norms. Long before the emergence of feminist movement in the West she placed the women's agenda in front of the people and the ruling authority.

Her mother's *Sakhi Samiti* was a renowned organization for the development of the women. Her father's close association with Indian National Congress and her mother's participation in Congress activities influenced her since young age.

The period coincided with the discriminative political practice by the colonial authority. Application of the colonial policy of 'Divide and Rule' isolated the educated high caste Hindus who gradually became critic of the colonial policies. The nation was to be regenerated on all aspects. Rajnarain Bose, Nabagopal Mitra and their associates propagated cultural regeneration and introduced Hindu *Mela*. Sarala Devi carried out their mission and through her bold writings in the pages of *Bharati* appealed to the readers to metamorphose themselves into a physically and mentally strong nation.

The Martial race theory categorized Indian nations into martial and non-martial races. While the Sikhs, the Marathas, the Rajputs fell into the first category the Bengalis fell into the second and were described as 'effeminate'. In fact terminal attacks of Malaria, other diseases and early marriages were the chief reasons behind the physical weakness of the Bengali youth. Swami Vivekananda was the first to address this issue and stressed on the building up of a strong generation of youth. His appeal had a strong influence on the Bengali psyche and several physical culture clubs emerged.

Sarala Devi told in a gathering—

> How proud are the Marathas of Shivaji...so we did during the reign of Pratap. Let the Bengalee boy remember this and hold his head as high up as his Marathi brother. (quoted by Chaudhury, 2001, 151)
>
> She tried to restore the heroic glory of Bengal during the medieval period. She wrote in *Bharati* '...a race that has a past—must also have a future'. (quoted by Chaudhury, 2001, 152)

A series of monographs for the children were published under the title of *Banger Bir*. Indira Chaudhury described how these celebrations of heroism fostered unity among the Indian nations. Besides these festivals 'provided a symbolic space' for the assertion of aggressive 'Hindu' politics compared to the 'annual, institutionalised politics of the Congress' (Chaudhury, 2001, 152).

Behind the foundation of Bharatstreemahamandal her aim was "to bring together women of every race, creed, class and party...on the basis of their common interest in the moral and material progress of the women of India" (Forbes, 1999, 70). Her political ideology underwent several twists. In the beginning of her career she was a strong supporter of the cult of strength and made effort to infuse heroism among the youth of Bengal. She applauded the mothers of Bengal as mothers of heroic sons who dared to sacrifice their life for the cause of the motherland. With this aim she introduced Veerasthami and exhibition of martial skill of the youth. A number of akhadas or schools of physical culture were founded in all corners of Bengal which carried out clandestine revolutionary activities. Despite her family tradition of Congressite political involvement she criticised the weak points in the moderate plans of action and pointed at the possible ways of success.

She presented the resolution and declared in clear language that, women 'had as much right to chart their own destinies as men for this was the age of human rights, justice, freedom, and self-determination.' She criticised the "fanciful division of intellect and emotion being the respective spheres of men and women" and asserted that, the 'sphere of women' included "comradeship with men in the rough and tumble of life and to being the fellow workers of men in politics and other spheres". Geraldine Forbes described her as "grandmother of politics and feminism" (Forbes, 1999, 142) who clearly pointed out the spheres of deprivation experienced by an woman since her childhood. She criticised the gendered outlook of the leaders who never offered any post to the woman members in the party. The women, in her language were "assigned to...the position of law-breakers only and not law-makers". Forbes described her speech as the "most forceful feminist speech of the 1930s with a call for legal, economic, social and educational equality" (Forbes, 1999, 142-43).

Long before the emergence of feminist movement she placed the women's agenda in front of the people and the ruling authority. Forbes described her as "an unusual woman for her time" (Forbes, 1999, 30). Autobiography mirrors the interplay of forces of a specific time and her account *Jeevaner Jharapata* sheds light on the emergence of the 'new woman' who challenged the colonial ruler and dared to propagate the message of overcoming physical and mental weakness among the colonized people of India. She developed independent perception of nationalism which was not linked to discrimination of gender, language, province, caste.

The modern women of India are vocal regarding their rights and despite challenges from the established order tries to modify the surrounding environment. They challenge the gender biased role of the patriarchal social system. In this context reference may be made to the earlier expositions of the patriarchal exploitation by Begam Rokeiya Sakhawat Hossain, Rasasundari Devi and others. They also looked into the paradox of the patriarchal social systems prevailing in both Hindu and Muslim tradition and articulated their thoughts in their writings.

The women under discussion perceived the male-dominated world not with disdain but with a firm resolution to stand on a strong footing independently. While Tarabai presented the story of enslavement of the women the Pandita forwarded a plan of self-dependence and Sarala Devi presented the portrait of a politically conscious lady. They had first hand experience of the sufferings of the women under the "dual oppression of colonialism and patriarchy" (Forbes, 1999, 3). The account proves that despite the absence of labelled feminist movement the Indian "women began asking for their rights before they were brought into the nationalist agitation". They could bring the womens' question in the public forum and formed individual projects for their empowerment. They were not necessarily successful always yet kindled the fire for the posterity.

References

Bandyopadhyay, Sunita, *March towards Modernity: Bengali Women*, Kolkata: Dolphin, 2006.

Chakravarty, Dr. Shankarprasad, *Sarala Devi Chaudhurani Rachana Sankalan*, Kolkata: Dey's Publishing, 2011.

Chakravarty, Uma, *Rewriting History, Life and Times of Pandita Ramabai*, New Delhi, Kali for women in association with the Book review literary trust & quotations from *A Testimony of Our Inexhaustible Treasure* by Pandita Ramabai, 1998.

———, "Gender, Caste and Labour: Ideological and Material Structure of Widowhood," *Economic & Political Weekly*, September, 9, 1995.

Chandra, Sudhir, *The Oppressive Present: Literature and Social Consciousness in Colonial India*, New Delhi: Oxford University Press, 1999.

Chowdhury, Indira, *The Frail Hero and Virile History: Gender and the Politics of Culture in Colonial Bengal*, New Delhi: Oxford University Press, 2001.

Chaudhury, Prasenjit, *Maharastriya Nabojagaran, o Nari Jagaraner ek Adhyay*, trans. Das Basudev, Kolkata, Setu, 2014.

Forbes, Geraldine, *The New Cambridge History of India IV:2 Women in Modern India*, New Delhi: Cambridge University Press, 1999.

Ghoshal, Sarala Devi, "The Heritage of the Bengalee", translated and reprinted in *The Bengalee*, 5th June, 1903, p. 3: "Senapati Kali", *Bharati*, Jan-Feb. 1904, p. 851.

Kosambi, Meera, *Pandita Ramabai Through Own Words: Selected Works*, New Delhi: O.U.P., 2000.

Mitra, Karabi, "Experiencing the wind of changes: case study of the Maharashtrian women of the 19th century", *The Social Ion*, Vol. 1, No. 1 & 2, January-December, 2012.

O'Hanlon, Rosalind, *A comparison between women and men: Tarabai Shinde and the critique of gender relations in colonial India*, Madras: O.U.P., 1994.

Sarkar, Tanika, *Hindu Nation Hindu Wife: Community, Religion and Cultural Nationalism*, New Delhi: Permanent Black, 2001.

Sengupta, Subodhchandra and Anjali Basu, *Sansad Bangali Charitavidhan*, Calcutta: Sahitya Sansad, 2002.

The Partha Chatterjee Omnibus, New Delhi: O.U.P., 1997.

13

Rabindranath Tagore (1861-1941): Concept of Nationalism in the Socio-Political Discourse

Kumkum Chattopadhyay

I
INTRODUCTION

Rabindranath Tagore was born in 1861 at Jorasanko, Kolkata, in a very renowned family of scholars, social reformers and entrepreneurs. He was the fourteenth and youngest child of *Maharshi* Devendranath Tagore. As Rabindranath Tagore was against any sort of formal education through school and college, he was educated at home and through his travels. He showed his talent as a poet from his boyhood and in 1913 won Nobel Prize for his book *Gitanjali* (Song offerings). He was a prolific writer, a successful music composer, a painter, an actor, a drama director and what not. Besides these talents, he was also a social activist and contributed a lot to Indian Social and Political Thought, although this area has not been very much explored till now. Yet, we can argue, "...Rabindranath Tagore the thinker and prophet is by no means out of place in an anthology of Indian political writing."[1] In this context, his views on nationalism can draw our attention for their originality and uniqueness.

II
DIFFERENT PERSPECTIVES OF TAGORE'S OUTLOOK

Concept of Nationalism

Rabindranath Tagore could feel that the contemporary Indian Nationalist Movement had it's root in European culture and civilization due to the long drawn colonial rule. In fact, the Indian society had lost its original character under the domination of the British. The educated Indians were influenced by the brand of Western nationalism and began to consider that as the only way out.

Tagore treated the concept of nationalism in a way which was completely different from the contemporary version. A thorough study of his works shows that his earnest attempt was nation-building which, he thought, was a pre-condition for developing a society. The mission all through his life was to enlighten the Indian people by introducing the true spirit of Indian integrity among them. His basic motto was to build up a confident and powerful nation in India. But his concept of nation was original in the sense that instead of imitating the European brand of nationalism he was interested in developing Indian nationalism which would be exclusively indigenous in the strict sense of the term. According to him, possibility of success of any society is inherent within it and so it is necessary to make a search in that sphere to find out the potentials and to proceed accordingly.

Nation-building

As has been previously mentioned, the concept of nation-building by Tagore was completely different from its Western counterpart. According to him, the feeling of unity or attachment to one's own country cannot have a static model which can be imposed from outside. To him, humanism should be the ultimate ideal and each and every country should interpret nationalism according to her own context. That might delay the whole process but that would be the only way out.

Tagore considered that nation-building was a necessary pre-condition in the path of progress. But so far as India was concerned, it was necessary to look at the problem from a different angle. He felt that the Western concept of nation was applicable to a Western society only. That model should not be meant for any eastern/non-Western society. In fact, after a rational consideration, it becomes evident that the Western societies due to their cultural and religious similarities could be integrated easily which was not possible in case of the non-Western countries. So, in these regions nation-building in one society would be bound to become different from the other. Thus, the process of nation-building or national integration in India would be exclusively Indian in character. This process would not follow the Western model. To quote Tagore, "We speak of eastern civilization, but that is a negative term, merely implying that it is not European. There is no concord between the minds of China and Arabia; in many respects they are even contrary. The Hindus of India and the Semitic races of Western Asia are quite dissimilar in their culture. The absence of co-operation in the learning of the Asian nations has led to their ancient history being split into different sections. Under the compulsions of history some areas may have had cultural exchanges but the mind of Asia never became a unified entity. So, it is that, when we speak of eastern civilization, we are thinking only of our own national civilization. That is why Asia, unlike Europe, has been unable to make a strong impact on the modern age."[2]

In order to clarify the concept of nation, Tagore tries to trace the origin of this concept. According to him both 'nation' and 'national' are Western concepts and while we are trying to use these two concepts in any Bengali discussion, it is better to use these terms in English. The translation of these words into Bengali might create confusion. Moreover, as these concepts had been borrowed from the British, it is logical to use them in English which would convey the original meaning of these concepts.[3]

Nation always gives emphasis upon unity. Any civilization tries to glorify the spirit of unity and it is this unity which develops a nation. A nation, if properly organised, never advances towards disunity or separation. The nature of this unity differs according to time and place. The feeling of unity in any part of Europe is definitely different from Hindu unity. For in Europe, the emergence of nation was closely related to state while this sort of unity was totally absent in India before the advent of the British.[4]

The very concept 'Hindu' is unique according to Tagore for it had integrated so many diversities—lingual, racial, religious and so on. This 'Hindu' had sacrificed a lot and had been deprived in various ways. In spite of that, it had accepted and integrated all the variations and refused none. Here lies its greatness. While European nationalism had been characterized by conflict, Indian nationalism had emphasized upon union through historical evolution. Interestingly, Tagore treated Hinduism not as a religion but as a way of life. He identified the concept of 'Hindu' with the concept of 'Indian'.[5]

Tagore very carefully observed that European nationalism was a living entity. It was being transmitted from one generation to the other and there the people were protecting that spirit very actively and enthusiastically. As they used to develop this spirit from amongst themselves they could enjoy freedom of thought in this sphere. The case of India was just the reverse. The Indians, as Tagore felt, used to imitate the apparent gestures of the Europeans. Thus, on the one hand, they were loosing the glorified tradition of their predecessors and on the other hand, they failed to realise the proper spirit of European character. The British did never accept or imitate anything blindly and indolently. So, when the Indians were engaging themselves in acquainting with a state-based European civilization, they were basically damaging their social identity. In fact, Tagore was of the opinion that excessive dependence upon state, a habit the contemporary Indian society borrowed from the west, was the other name of loss of freedom. So, it was necessary to make the society self-sufficient. This social freedom, to him, was precious to any other freedom.[6] One should free himself from any sort of parochialism and should come forward to uphold the interests of all. This was basically the message of Tagore to the society.

Hindu-Muslim communal conflict was a very hot issue during that period which is still a black spot in Indian history. Tagore tried to treat the issue very rationally, intelligently and sympathetically. He went deep into the problem and realised the basic sentiment lying behind this problem. As a very sincere thinker, he treated Hindu-Muslim unity as an essential condition for developing nationhood. In order to develop that sentiment he gave a very attractive interpretation of this concept. To him, Hindu was not a religion but a way of life, while Islam was a religion. So, the Indian Muslims were Hindu Muslims while the Indian Christians were Hindu Christians. The Hindu Muslims were Hindu by nation and Muslim by religion while the Hindu Christians were Hindu by nation and Christian by religion. Thus, he tried to fight out all sorts of religious fanaticisms by incorporating all the religious nationalities within the confines of 'Hindu' by which he actually meant Indian. But, here confusion is very likely to arise because in this context he did not address the majority of the Indian people, who were Hindu by religion. While Hindus were treated as a religious sect by the society, Tagore wanted to use it to mean nation as he conceived the term. For example, he liked to call Krishna Mohan Bandyopadhyay or Gyanendranath Tagore Hindu Christians. He argued that whatever was precious in the Hindu society used to belong not to any individual or group but to the society as a whole. If the society members thought to expel any one from the Hindu society it would not be necessarily true. His basic nature which he had inherited from the Indian (Hindu) tradition would always remain inherent within his soul. Here naturally one question arises as to what would be the status of an Indian who is known as Hindu by religion. The answer is not there in Tagore's texts.[7]

The Indian national leaders tried to introduce the Western brand of nationalism in India during the *Swadeshi* movement. Initially, Tagore very honestly accepted and followed that trend. But very soon he could realise the situation. He was disillusioned by the nationalist leaders and their deceptive characters as he perceived. So, instead of demagoguism, he preferred to come out of political movement and to prepare practical programmes for the benefit of the common men.

Ram Chandra Guha commented "Tagore was a patriot without quite being a nationalist."[8] Tagore did never want to become a violent nationalist in the Western sense, rather he preferred to become a patriot in the indigenous way. So, he never supported frantic nationalism.

Rabindranath Tagore was born in 1861. The great outbreak of 1857 occurred just four years before his birth. Again at his young age of twenty-four he observed the formation of Indian National Congress (1885) which was an expression of growing Indian nationalism. These incidents and the contemporary situation had a deep impact upon him and naturally he joined the *Swadeshi* Movement very enthusiastically which emerged as a protest against the proposed partition of Bengal by Lord Curzon in 1905. But with the growing experience and with the developing intuition, he could feel that political freedom was not the only freedom to cherish. It was the basic necessity to make the people aspire for basic social freedom which would ultimately bring political freedom. He felt that the Indian society was not ready during that period to enjoy political freedom. So, before acquiring political freedom it was necessary to build up the selves of the people. The deceit and duplicity inherent in the ongoing political movements shocked him. One of his famous novels *Ghare Baire*[9] (Home and the World) was a brave and bold revelation of this sentiment. The nature of the dishonest leaders, their greed for wealth and political leadership, their false promises and communal politics not only cleared his vision but also hurt him a lot. He became aware of opportunism and demagoguism which were then prevalent in the arena of national freedom struggle. With such experiences and with the emergence of terrorist movements he withdrew himself from active participation in politics.

Disillusioned by his contemporary situation, Tagore tried to look back to Indian tradition in order to find out proper India. He studied Indian history thoroughly and tried to follow the sequence according to that tradition. During his time the Indian students used to study British history as a colonial legacy. Tagore realised that the study of Indian history was essential for each and every Indian in order to find out one's own identity. Thus, very sincerely and efficiently he tried to prepare the background of political freedom.

Nation-Building vis-à-vis Society Building

Tagore could truly comprehend that in order to establish a united India it was necessary to build up a powerful social structure. But to his utter disappointment, he failed to convince his contemporary nationalist leaders about his comprehension. Ultimately, besides his extensive literary works, he himself came forward to carry on the programme of social development.

Swadeshi Samaj[10] is a well-known essay by Tagore which was published in 1904. This paper was his first comprehensive statement of his strong patriotic feeling. Here his suggestions are expressing his views about indigenous nationalism or *Swadeshi*. Here, the role of the leader has been specifically emphasised. The leader, as the essay opined, should function as the centre of unity under whose supervision a required number of subordinates should operate. Tagore was very hopeful to bring harmony among the masses in this manner which is the precondition of developing nationalist/*Swadeshi* feeling among his countrymen. He felt that the people should be made conscious about their own power, which would make them confident. He was also very eager to bring communal harmony among the Hindus and the Muslims. Politics or political leaders could make no appeal to Tagore for a number of reasons. Tagore had a feeling that politics was something like a wall between the political leaders and the masses. Besides, the political assemblies preferred English which failed to make any communication with the masses. Moreover, politics used to give undue emphasis upon preparation rather than actual necessities. So, Tagore tried to turn the political movement into an effective mechanism of nation-building activities. To him, this nation-building was the other name of *Swadeshi*. In his perspective, a social leader was more effective than a political leader. He very sincerely tried to define and find out that social leader.[11] Tagore had in mind, as can be anticipated, a fascination for charisma and excellence, besides other qualities such as responsibility, kindness and honesty.

This venture initiated by him might be referred to as society building which was actually a method of awakening the people so that they would be able to recognise their identity. His attempt, in this respect, was multi-dimensional. We can broadly classify all his ventures for nation-building into three categories: (i) Rural Reconstruction; (ii) Education; and (iii) Culture.

Rural Reconstruction

Tagore came into direct contact with the rural Bengal after he took the charge of their *Zamindari* estate at East Bengal according to his father's order. That incident can be described as a landmark in his life for it was during that period the idea of rural reconstruction came to his mind. Being disillusioned by the role of the political leaders, he made up his mind to assume the responsibility by himself. That was the first phase of his venture for rural reconstruction. He was then about thirty years of age. His estate included mainly three districts. Birahimpur—headquarter Shelaidaha, Kaligram—headquarter Potisar and Sahajadpur where the headquarter was named after the district.

That was the beginning of his rural reconstruction programme. But even from that very moment, he had a holistic vision and he was very sincere, honest and determined to achieve his goal even in the formative phase. His programme included health, education, cottage industries, agriculture, fisheries, weaving, etc. In a word, an all-round development of a village was his ultimate objective which to his mind was necessary for making a self-sufficient and self-confident society. He introduced the experiment of tractor for cultivation, furnace for potteries and ceramics, a husking machine for paddies which proves his scientific bent of mind.[12] The most remarkable innovation in this phase was the introduction of *Mandali Pratha* at Birahimpur which was basically a Hindu dominated area. Here, he had to face resistance from all sides organised especially by the Hindus.[13] He concentrated on the Muslim dominated Kaligram.[14]

His experience during his *Zamindari* at Birahimpur and Kaligram benefited him during the rural reconstruction phase at Sriniketan. He was very scientific in his approach when he thought of applying Western strategies and tactics in the exclusively native method of social development. He considered this rural reconstruction programme to be the most important dimension in the attempt of nation-building. In this programme of reconstruction he incorporated development of agriculture and cottage industries, introduction of cooperative principles, medical help, spread of education, etc. In this reconstruction programme he was encouraged by many among whom Leonard Knight Elmhirst and Kalimohan Ghosh need special mention.

(ii) Education

Besides, this practical programme of rural reconstruction he established *Santiniketan Brahmacharyashram* and *Visva-Bharati* in order to spread education. He had a completely different vision about the method and purpose of education although he had to compromise to some extent under the compelling situation. "Father's faith in the creative nationalism of India steadily grew and developed into the larger ideal of a cultural cooperation among the peoples of the East and the West, which he chose to call the ideal of *Visva-Bharati*."[15]

Tagore believed that systematic and disciplined organisation was the key to any sort of development. So, he wanted to introduce the concept of organisation from the very beginning, a practice which was being followed from the first phase of *Santiniketan Brahmacharyashram*. The system which was being followed in the residential hostel amply proves it. This system tells about the necessity of organised effort in any sphere of life.

The system of *Chhatraswaraj* (self rule by the students) was a very important aspect of Tagore's constructive programme. By introducing the concept of *Chhatraswaraj*, he wanted to teach discipline and self-dependence along with the concept of active participation. This idea of *Chhatraswaraj* was not only an exceptional but also a revolutionary one which then roused much criticism. In fact, how far the students would be able to properly utilize freedom was a debatable issue. Some of the teachers, the guardians and even some of the students were against the concept of freedom of the students. Tagore also had to face strong opposition on the question of discipline because he transferred the responsibility of maintaining discipline to the students. He was proclaimed to be unpractical guided by poetic whim.[16]

Ashram Sammilani was a committee of the students to carry on their programmes. That committee was treated as the Parliament of the students. All the students were the members of that Parliament. This Parliament elected an Executive Committee which actually used to hold power. Each *Sammilani* had one secretary and even the captains also used to obey him. The *Sammilani* or the Parliament had the power to set rules and the Executive Committee supervised the implementation of rules. One Court of Justice was formed to give judgment on serious crimes. The secretary and the captains were the judges. The court used to operate after dinner maintaining its confidential nature.[17] The crimes used to vary from violation of rules to mimicry. But any sort of physical assault was not allowed as punishment. The maximum punishment was to bring out the boy from the queue of the students or eat separately instead of sitting in a row with the other boys. Again, cleaning of extra rooms in addition to allotted ones, prohibition on playing were also other types of punishment. This students' union might be known as a Junior Republic.[18]

Tagore had a vision, the vision of properly upbringing every child in order to develop a complete man, because, the success or failure of any society is virtually dependent upon its members. Tagore was an educationist and his innovations and contributions have indeed enriched the indigenous culture. "At a time when English education attempted completely to de-nationalize the educated citizens of this country, when Indian art was dying for want of encouragement by the state, when Indian life was looked down upon as backward and inferior, there arose this great poet who brought pride in their culture to the hearts of the educated and hope to the hearts of the so-called uneducated."[19]

As a very sensitive social thinker, Tagore realised that the spread of education is the first step for developing the culture of a society. With that view he was eager to establish an educational institution which would contribute to develop citizens with proper culture and free mind. He himself was a very successful teacher for he knew the art of attracting the students. Apart from the form of teaching he was very sincere about the contents of the lesson to be taught. He used to think that open air teaching would attract the students, would develop their love for nature and would make them free and liberal in their pursuits. Initially, this school as a hermitage was established at

Bolpur *Santiniketan* which later on developed as the University of *Visva-Bharati*. His major contribution was to popularize the mother tongue and to introduce it as the medium of instruction. This love for mother tongue expresses his genuine love for the country.

> His Visva-Bharati is an international university, where the whole world has become a single nest.... In this institution, he tried to impart the background of internationalism and help the students to realise 'the true character of interlinked humanity and deeper unities of our civilization in the West and the East'.[20]

Culture

Tagore realised that the culture of the colonies was different from that of the colonial powers. And it was a fact that the original culture of any colony was changed, modified and sometimes shattered by the colonial powers during the period of their prolonged colonial exploitation. So, the primary task of these colonies was to find out their lost tradition and culture which could develop their proper feeling of freedom and identity.

The contributions of Tagore in the spheres of music, dance, drama, painting and literature are commendable. Tagore was a superb musician as well as a singer. His songs brought a new trend in the sphere of Bengali songs. Most of these songs possess a deep philosophy, while some of them have close inclination to nature and some are, again, national songs. His songs usually known as *Rabindra Sangeet* or *Rabindranather Gaan* are unique in the sense that here diversities from various corners of India as well as the world have been integrated, thus upholding the glory of Indian culture and at the same time representing some sort of universal appeal. These lyrics fetched him the 'Nobel' award and his '*Geetanjali*'[21] has not only enriched the Indian culture but is considered as an asset of India.

Rabindranath Tagore popularised dance. During his time there was a social ban on dance. He tried to fight out all the oppositions, gave dance a new form and dimension and used to organise dance programmes and dance dramas occasionally. Today '*Rabindra Nritya*' has become a branded form of dance.

By this, he tried to develop our culture aesthetically and also transferred various social messages with universal appeal. His *Chandalika*[22] is such a dance drama. *Tasher Desh*[23] is another one which is a revolt against all sorts of mechanical discipline. Both are excellent declarations of the triumph of freedom. He has also written a number of other dance dramas which are very popular till now.

Tagore was a good painter having a new dimension and introduced a new art form. Last, but not the least he was a writer. Basically, he is famous as a poet and titled as '*Kabiguru*'. His poems are inspiring in many ways and they have also tried to unfold the nature of freedom. He has written a number of novels among which *Gora*[24] and *Ghare Baire* need special mention here. In '*Gora*' his pen revealed the nature of supreme freedom. In '*Ghare Baire*' he tried to point out the limitations of the *Swadeshi* Movement. His short stories are the narratives about the joys and sorrows of the countrymen and reflect the true culture of India. His essays on various topics have established him as a social thinker as well as a philosopher. All his writings encourage us to free ourselves from all sorts of bondage and to feel the eternal universal at our heart.

Tagore's contribution to the sphere of folk culture was immense. He tried to revive folk art, folk song and folk dance by collecting them from different corners of India and by giving them a national character.

III
SOCIO-POLITICAL CONTEXT IN TAGORE'S CONCEPT AND ITS RELEVANCE

Tagore recognised the true character of our interlinked humanity and deeper unities of our civilization in the west and the east. "Rabindranath asks us to preserve the old attitude of keeping firm our own framework and receiving and adapting outer influences."[25] Then and then only Indian culture would be able to preserve its identity and carry the society on to the development of true Indian nationalism.

It is really interesting to find out Tagore as a social and political thinker. He was a true Indian with a liberal approach and so he could accept any positive thing which was in consonance with the true Indian spirit. His initiative for developing folk art along with cottage industries was an attempt to develop our indigenous art, on the one hand, and to create an alternative occupation for the agriculturists. The introduction of *Mandali Pratha* in Kaligram proves his faith on local self-government. On the whole, his programme of rural reconstruction reflects his vision about decentralisation, popular participation and administrative training.

The same concept of administrative training is also predominant in the concept of *Chhatraswaraj*. The model introduced in the form of *Ashram Sammilani* was a training ground for imparting the art of governance among the students. Through this system, the students became aware about legislation, execution and adjudication. They, also, learnt about the methods of identifying the collective problems with finding out their solutions. He did not want to introduce the practice of active politics among the students, although, active politics undoubtedly make the students politically experienced. Yet we cannot ignore the fact that administrative training is the pre-condition of political independence of any country. Here lies his originality and here he departed from the Western influence.

Besides, his initiative for cultural uplift was equally important in unfolding the spirit of patriotism among his countrymen. He is a poet whose two compositions have been accepted as national anthems *Janaganamana* in India and *Amar Sonar Bangla* in Bangladesh. His patriotic songs have roused the spirit of nationalism among the people in various ways. He traveled in every cultural sphere in order to bring unity among the people.

Tagore and Protection of Environment

Tagore, himself, was always very careful about maintaining the environmental balance. So, besides his contributions in other spheres, his role as a conscious protector of environment is no less important especially when this area has come to the limelight for the last thirty years in order to secure our planet earth from rapid decay. In his venture, he always tried to avoid too much of mechanization, application of chemicals and technology.

Modern age cannot avoid these and accordingly problems and sufferings are also unavoidable. In order to save and protect this planet earth, it is necessary to become eco-friendly about which Tagore gave a warning long ago. The introduction of *Halakarshana* and *Vriksharopana* festivals prove him as an environmental activist.

Tagore was definitely different from his contemporary leaders. Naturally, he had been misunderstood, misinterpreted and criticised in various ways. Of course, some of his attempts were utopian, some were a bit conservative and some were detached from technology or active politics. In spite of all these limitations, we cannot deny the fact that Tagore was a social thinker as well as a social activist.

Finally, it may be said that the conventional rod of measuring success or failure has only a limited applicability here. The real value of the efforts made by Tagore during his lifetime lies in the fact that they bear a poignant witness to the depth of his feeling and reveal more effectively than anything else could, how near he held the cause to his heart.[26] Moreover, sometimes attempts to realise any goal transcend in importance all immediate results. Judged in this sense, efforts were bigger than achievement.

Notes

1. Guha, Ramchandra. 2012. *Makers of Modern India*, New Delhi, Penguin Viking, p. 187.
2. Tagore, Rabindranath. 1929. *The Cooperative Principle*, Calcutta, Visva-Bharati, (The English version). 1963, p. 35.
3. Tagore, Rabindranath. 1308. B.S. 'Nation Ki' in *Rabindra Rachanabali, Centenary,* Volume-XII, Kolkata, Government of West Bengal, Kolkata, p. 675.
4. Tagore, Rabindranath, 1308 B.S. 'Bharatvarshiyo Samaj' in *Rabindra Rachanabali Centenary,* Volume-XII, Kolkata, Government of West Bengal, p. 679.
5. Tagore, Rabindranath. 1319 B.S. 'Atmaparichiaya' in *Rabindra Rachanabali Centenary*, Volume-XIII, Kolkata, Government of West Bengal, pp. 174-75.
6. Tagore, Rabindranath. 1308 B.S. 'Bharatvarshiyo Samaj' in *Rabindra Rachanabali, Centenary*, Volume-XII, Kolkata, Government of West Bengal, p. 681.

7. Tagore's Atmaparichaya, loc. cit.
8. Guha, Ramchandra, op. cit., p. 186.
9. Tagore, Rabindranath. 1323 B.S. 'Ghare Baire' in *Rabindra Rachanabali, Centenary,* Volume-IX, Kolkata, Government of West Bengal.
10. Tagore, Rabindranath. 1311 B.S. 'Swadeshi Samaj', *Rabindra Rachanabali, Centenary*, Volume-XII, Kolkata, Government of West Bengal, p. 683.
11. Tagore, Rabindranath. 1311 B.S. 'Swadeshi Samaj', *Rabindra Rachanabali, Centenary*, Volume-XII, Kolkata, Government of West Bengal, 694-98.
12. Bandyopadhyay, Arunendu. 2007. 'Santi-Sri Avenue' in *Paschimbanga, Special Rabindra Sankhya*, May, 2007, Kolkata, Government of West Bengal, p. 37.
13. Tagore, Rabindranath. 1908. *Chithipatra*, Volume 13, Kolkata, Visva-Bharati, 1992, p. 71.
14. Paul, Prasanta Kumar. 2004. *Rabijibani*, Volume-VI, Kolkata, Ananda Publishers Pvt. Ltd., p. 20.
15. Tagore, Rathindranath. 2003. *On the Edges of Time*, Kolkata, Visva-Bharati, p. 63.
16. Bisi, Pramathanath, 1335 B.S., *Gurudev o Santiniketan*, Kolkata, Viswa Bharati Granthalaya, pp. 42-44.
17. *Ibid.*, p. 44.
18. Mukhopadhyay, Prabhat Kumar. 1406 B.S., *Rabindrajibani*, Volume-II, Kolkata, Visva-Bharati, p. 49.
19. Arundale, Rukmini Devi, 'Tagore and Indian Culture', *Rabindranath Tagore: A Centenary*, Volume-1861-1961, Radhakrishnan, Sarvepalli et al. (ed.) 1992. New Delhi, Sahitya Academy, p. 74.
20. Radhakrishnan, Sarvepalli, 'Most Dear to the Muses', *Rabindranath Tagore: A Centenary*, Volume-1861-1961, Radhakrishnan, Sarvepalli et al. (ed.) (1992). New Delhi, Sahitya Academy, p. xxiii.
21. Tagore, Rabindranath. 1401 B.S., *Gitanjali*, Kolkata, Visva-Bharati.
22. Tagore, Rabindranath. 1933. 'Chandalika' in *Rabindra Rachanabali, Centenary*, Volume-VI, Kolkata, Government of West Bengal.

23. Tagore, Rabindranath. 1933. 'Tasher Desh' in *Rabindra Rachanabali, Centenary,* Volume-VI, Kolkata, Government of West Bengal.
24. Tagore, Rabindranath. 1316. 'Gora' in *Rabindra Rachanabali Centenary*, Volume-IX, Kolkata, Government of West Bengal.
25. Radhakrishnan, Sarvepalli, 'Most Dear to the Muses', *Rabindranath Tagore: A Centenary*, Volume-1861-1961, Radhakrishnan, Sarvepalli et al. (ed.) (1992). New Delhi, Sahitya Academy, p. xxiii.
26. Sen, Sudhir. 1943. *Rabindranath Tagore on Rural Reconstruction*, Kolkata, Visva-Bharati, p. 113.

Glossary of non-English Words

1. *Maharshi* – The honoured title of Devendranath Tagore.
2. *Gitanjali* – Song Offerings.
3. *Swadeshi* – Indigenous.
4. *Swadeshi Samaj* – Indigenous Society.
5. *Zamindar* – Landlord.
6. *Mandali Pratha* – A System of Local Self-rule.
7. *Brahmacharyashram* – A hermitage school.
8. *Visva-Bharati* – A University established by Tagore.
9. *Chhatraswaraj* – Self rule by the students.
10. *Sammilani* – Assemblage.
11. *Rabindrasangeet* – Song of Tagore.
12. *Rabindranather Gaan* – Song of Tagore.
13. *Rabindra Nritya* – Dance with Tagore's Song.
14. *Chandalika* – A Dance drama by Tagore.
15. *Tasher Desh* – A Dance drama by Tagore.
16. *Kabiguru* – Master of all Poets.
17. *Ghare Baire* – Home and the World (a novel by Tagore).
18. *Gora* – A novel by Tagore.
19. *Janaganamana* – National Anthem of India.
20. *Amar Sonar Bangla* – National Anthem of Bangladesh.
21. *Vriksharopana* – Festival of tree plantation.
22. *Halakarshana* – Festival of cultivation.

14

Political Thought of Swami Vivekananda (1863-1902)

Sibranjan Chatterjee

I
INTRODUCTION

Narendra Nath Datta, the future Swami Vivekananda, was born on January 12, 1863, in the famous Datta family of Simla, in Calcutta. His father Viswanath Datta, endowed with versatile qualities, proficient in English and Persian, a man of deep compassion and great sympathy, was a successful attorney-at-law in the Calcutta High Court. His mother Bhubaneswari Devi was exceptionally intelligent, noted for her unusual memory and possessed royal dignity and fire. Since his childhood the extraordinary qualities of Narendra Nath—courage, leadership capacity, prodigious memory, truthfulness, love for the poor, rare intelligence, etc.—were visible. After passing the Entrance Examination Narendra Nath first studied at Presidency College and then at the General Assembly's Institution (subsequently renamed as Scottish Church College). In College, he attracted the attention of both Indian and British professors, who were astounded by his brilliant intellect. During the youth of Narendra Nath the influence of the Brahmo leader Keshab Chandra Sen over the young intellectuals of Bengal was very strong. Narendra Nath was impressed by the writings and lectures of Keshab Chandra. He became a member of the Sadharan Brahmo Samaj. But this did not satisfy his spiritual appetite. At this stage he came in touch with Sri Ramakrishna and this meeting between the two at Dakshineswar, four miles to the north of Calcutta, was a historical event not merely in the life of Narendra Nath, but in the life of the entire nation too. Narendra Nath soon recognized Sri Ramakrishna as a great spiritual personality, but his mind was not fully prepared to accept him as a Guru (master). He did not accept any word of Sri Ramakrishna without testing it by his own experience or reason. But he was ultimately conquered by the love, purity and selflessness of Sri Ramakrishna. It was the abiding confidence of Sri Ramakrishna in the integrity of Naren's character as also the Master's selfless love for him that conquered his powerful heart. After the passing away of the Master in August 1886, Narendra Nath organized his brother-disciples (all young) into a monastic brotherhood. They performed the sacred Viraja Ceremony and formally accepted the monastery life. The old names were changed for new ones to complete their severance from their earlier life and its associations. Narendra Nath became Swami Vivekananda who in 1888 left his home-town and began his historic wandering of two years throughout India. Vivekananda, in the course of his pilgrimage around India, came into close contact with all sorts of people. He found himself today a despised beggar sheltered by 'pariahs' identifying himself with their misery, and tomorrow a guest of the princes, discussing on equal terms with them, inspiring them to work for the masses, particularly the poor and downtrodden people. On tremendous enthusiasm of a group of dedicated young men of Madras, his ardent adherents, Vivekananda decided to attend the Parliament of Religions at Chicago. These young men took active steps to raise necessary funds for this purpose. On May 31, 1893, he sailed from Bombay. In 1893 September 11, the session of the Parliament of Religions began. Vivekananda emerged as the most celebrated personality of Parliament. The American press unanimously described him as the greatest figure in the Parliament of Religions. The news of Vivekananda's unparalleled success reached India and created unlimited enthusiasm among the masses, particularly the youth community. The unknown monk blossomed into a world-figure and became the man of the hour. After his return to India in 1897, under his initiative Ramakrishna Mission was set up on May 1, 1897, to translate the idea of Sri Ramakrishna that service to the God through selfless service to the mankind. The foundation of Ramakrishna Mission is a great event in the history of modern India. Only at the age of thirty-nine this great spiritual and revolutionary son of India breathed his last on July 4, 1902.[1]

II
POLITICAL IDEAS

Swami Vivekananda was not a politician nor had he any connection with any political party or political movement. Swamiji himself said: "I am no politician or political agitator." Ramakrishna Mission has no link with politics. In a letter to one of his disciples in September 1894, Swamiji said: "God and truth are the only politics in the world, everything else is trash."[2] But at the same time he was the source of inspiration of thousands of young men and women who laid down their lives for the liberation of our motherland. According to Subhas Chandra Bose, though Swamiji never gave any political message, every one who came into contact with him or his writings developed a spirit of patriotism and a political mentality.[3] Vivekananda was not a monk in the traditional sense. He was an outstanding spiritual master in all history and the first great social revolutionary of India. Swamiji did not consciously develop any political idea, and that was not his mission. He wanted the all-comprehensive development of human being and society—physical, intellectual, moral and spiritual. In this process of balanced development he did not rule out the role of politics. He had no negative approach to politics. At the same time he realized that the real disease of our body politic could not be cured simply through politics, whose role is rather inconsequential and supplementary. Swamiji developed a deep political insight by his historical pilgrimage throughout the length and breadth of Hindusthan, his contact and interaction with cross-sections of people in our country and abroad, and his extraordinary capacity of observation into the behavioural pattern of the people of different countries. For the convenience of systematic discussion we may classify the subject under several heads.

Concept of 'mass'

Confidence in and respect for the mass or common people constitute an important component of the thought-process of

Swamiji having political bearing. During Swamiji's life-time the prevailing social viewpoint was that the educated community or the elite represented the brain and conscience of the country and was, therefore, the natural custodian of the interests of the common people. Vivekananda changed this trend of idea. He categorically said that the masses were the backbone of the nation in all countries and "the reservoir of all powers."[4] In "Modern India" Swamiji explained the nature of mass strength. According to him, the leadership of society might be in the hands of the learned people or wealthy class or of those who wielded the power of arms. But the source of its power was always the subject masses. To the extent the governing class distanced itself from this source, the base of its authority was sure to be weakened. But such was the irony of fate, Swamiji lamented. The masses, from whom the power of governing society was directly or indirectly drawn, were soon forgotten by the ruling class. What were the methods of capturing state power? These, to Swamiji, were deceit, stratagem, force or voluntary gift; in other words, fair means or foul. Here Swami Vivekananda, with the mind of a scientific historian, looked at the history of India. To his analysis, when in course of time, the priestly power totally estranged itself from the masses, it was overthrown by the then kingly power which took its stand on the strength of the mass support. In course of time the kingly power considered itself to be perfectly independent and a gap was created between itself and the subject people. The inevitable consequence was that either the monarchy was fully destroyed or it became a mere puppet in the hands of the Vaishyas, or as we term it, commercial or capitalist class. By this time, this commercial class started commanding the confidence of the masses. Lastly, Swamiji warned that as the *Vaishya* class had also dissociated itself from the people and no longer cared to count on their support, its destruction or fall was only a matter of time.

In this connection it may not be irrelevant to refer to the discussion that Aswini Kumar Datta had with Swami Vivekananda at Almora in May or June 1897. Aswini Kumar was a prominent leader of the Indian National Congress at that time. During Swamiji's stay at Almora Aswini Kumar met him and held, among others, discussion about Indian National Congress. In that meeting Swamiji impressed upon Aswini Kumar the urgency of involving the masses in the activities of the Congress. Attempts must be made to involve the common people in its activities and to awaken the masses. Otherwise, the passage of a few resolutions cannot bring freedom.[5] Only a few months later in December 1897 at Amraoti Congress, people heard Aswini Kumar criticizing the Congress role as being confined to three days' 'annual tamasa' and urging its leaders to make it an effective mass-based organization.[6]

Socialist Idea

From the concept of 'masses' follows Swamiji's socialist idea. Several basic aspects of Swami Vivekananda's socialist idea are as follows:

> Vivekananda was the first to draw the attention of the Indian leaders to the social implication of the curse of mass poverty. Before him many great people attempted in their individual ways to feed the starving. But no person before Vivekananda had categorically pointed out that freedom of the people from want of daily bread was the first condition of national regeneration of India. Hence, an organized, time-bound programme was essential to contain poverty.

In our country Vivekananda for the first time realized the urgency of involving the farmers and the workers in any movement, social or political. The mission of any national organization should be, in Swamiji's view, for the destitute, the poor, the illiterate peasantry and the labouring classes, and if after everything has been done for them first, there is spare time, then only the gentry.[7] In his writings and speeches in various contexts he has paid high tribute to the working class of the country.

Swamiji firmly stood for land to the tillers, that is, land should be owned by the actual cultivators of land. He wanted technology-based farming, in other words, reorganization of agriculture on scientific lines.

Swami Vivekananda was confident about the inevitability of the rise of the *Shudras* or downtrodden section of the community. The rule of the *Shudras* would be established after the completion of the cycle of castes, and initiative in this regard would be taken by the country where the *Shudras* were most oppressed and exploited. In Swamiji's analysis, in the beginning, society was a theocracy under the rule of the Brahmin or priestly caste. This was followed by the military caste, the *Kshatriya*. Now we are under the sway of the *Vaishya*, and commercial interest rules the world. This phase is nearing its end, and would be followed by the ascendancy of the *Shudra*, the labourer. Sister Christine writes: "Sometimes he [Vivekananda] was in a prophetic mood, as on the day when he startled us by saying, the next great upheaval which is to bring about a new epoch will come from Russia or China. I can't quite see which, but it will be either Russia or China." Sister wondered: "This he said thirty-two years ago, when China was still under the autocratic rule of the Manchu Emperors, from which there was no prospect of release for centuries to come, and when Czarist Russia was sending the noblest of her people to the Siberian mines. To the ordinary thinker those two countries seemed the most unlikely nations in the world to usher in a new era."[8] Although Swamiji was certain that the social development would ultimately result in the establishment of the *Shudra* rule, he found the driving force in the innate tendency of human beings to manifest their inherent spirituality and not in economic motive alone. Swamiji, however, did not rule out altogether the role of economic force in history. It may incidentally be mentioned that Subhas Chandra Bose rejected the Materialistic Interpretation of history, one of the fundamental postulates of Marxism-Leninism.

Swamiji was not in favour of annihilating and crushing the upper class. His approach was not negative. He wanted to improve the lot of the lower strata of society through proper education and all types of necessary assistance. He sought to raise the lower classes without bringing down anybody. To quote Swamiji, "You must take care not to set up class-strife between the poor peasants, the labouring people and wealthy classes."[9]

Likewise, Subhas Chandra rejected the theory of class strife or class struggle and described it as a crime against nationalism.

Vivekananda's socialism was not in conflict with religion. By contrast, Lenin in his "The State and Revolution" described religion as the "opium of the people." To the contrary, religion is the basis of human life. To Swamiji, the vitality, the life-principle, the soul of India is *Dharma* which is wider in connotation than religion, as is understood in the West.

Defects of Socialism

Socialism has an inherent defect. Swamiji himself pointed out that in socialism individuality would be checked, in other words, identity of the individual would be destroyed. But Swamiji was against any form of bondage.

Secondly, Swamiji apprehended that the *Shudra* rule might result in the lowering of culture. As he observed, its advantages would be the distribution of physical comforts, its disadvantages perhaps the lowering of culture. There would be a great distribution of ordinary education, but extraordinary geniuses would be less and less.

Swamiji described himself a socialist not because he considered it a perfect system, but half a loaf was better than no bread. The other systems had been tried and found wanting. Let this one be tried—if for nothing else, for the novelty of the thing. A redistribution of pain and pleasure, to him, was better than always the same persons having pains and pleasures. Then, like Plato, Swamiji depicted his ideal state: "If it is possible to form a state in which the knowledge of the priest period, the culture of the military, the distributive spirit of the commercial, and the ideal of equality of the last can all be kept intact, minus their evils, it will be an ideal state. But is it possible?"[10]

Idea of Freedom or Liberty

Swamiji accorded top priority to freedom or liberty. Freedom, according to Swamiji, is the first condition of growth. There cannot be any growth without liberty. There is a general impression that one can make others grow, can direct and guide others retaining the freedom of the teacher. Such notion, to

Swamiji, "is nonsense, a dangerous lie which has retarded the growth of millions and millions of human beings in this world."[11] Swamiji emphasized liberty of thought, speech and action. He also stressed liberty in food, dress and even marriage.[12] He said: "even the best work loses its charm if one is forced to do it by another. Without the idea of personal responsibility, no one can achieve anything great.... A slave suffers the miseries of hell both here and hereafter."[13] What is required is "a free body, a free mind, and free soul."[14] To quote Swamiji, "Liberty, Mukti, is all my religion."[15] "I would rather be doing evil freely than be doing good under bondage."[16] Recalling the past history, Swamiji noted that our ancestors freed religious thought, and hence we had a wonderful religion. But they put a heavy chain on the feet of society, and our society is, therefore, "horrid (and) diabolical."[17]

Swamiji's stress upon the need for political freedom of India emanates from his concept of freedom in its totality. The people of a subject nation cannot be free physically, psychologically and spiritually. Swamiji repeatedly and in various contexts noted that India must be freed politically first, because that was pre-requisite for her cultural as well as economic freedom.

Swamiji was very much aware of the fact that there could not be any absolute or uncontrolled individual liberty, because that would lead to social chaos. He admitted individual freedom of thought and action so long as it did not injure or affect others.[18] Since the mid-nineteenth century the traditional concept of liberalism in Europe began to be modified by the political thinkers like J.S. Mill, Herbert Spencer and T.H. Green. These philosophers pleaded for regulation of individual liberty in the greater interest of the society. Swamiji was very much conversant with the contemporary political literature of Europe. He realized the need for limiting individual liberty for the greater social welfare.

Idea of Self-governance or Democracy

By democracy we generally mean elections to the national legislature and provincial legislatures, elections of the President, Prime Minister of the country, etc. Swamiji went to the root of the system. The basis of democracy is individual—recognition of the dignity of the individual. Swamiji repeatedly asserted that the illiterate, poor and exploited people had to be given back their lost individuality.[19] For this what is essential is mass education. Only through education can the people be given back their lost individuality and be made aware of their individual dignity. Here Swamiji raised a practical problem. We may open schools all over the country. But will the poor and illiterate people come to the schools to receive education? The poor boys would rather go to help their fathers in the fields or otherwise try to earn their livelihood, than to attend the schools. Swamiji asserted: "if the poor boy could not come to education, education must go to him."[20] For this purpose he devised realistic schemes also. As noted by Swamiji, suppose the villagers after their day's work have assembled at a particular place. They are sitting under a tree, smoking and gossiping. At that time one may go to them and with the help of camera throw astronomical or other pictures, scenes from different nations, histories, etc. The villagers, through conversation and stories, can be given the preliminary knowledge of geography, history, astronomy, science, etc.[21] Swamiji said: "The ears are the best educators."[22]

The second significant component of self-governance is initiative and involvement of the common people in any matter of public interest at the grass-root level. Swamiji accorded priority to this component. He wanted the villagers to be actively involved in any programme of the village development. He wanted them to decide for themselves what was good and beneficial for them and then to act accordingly. Thus, the people will not be mere beneficiaries. They will be participants both at the stage of choice of their priorities and at the stage of implementation of the scheme. Our public leaders and administrators realized this at a much later stage.

Thirdly, Swamiji stood for social justice and strongly protested against the practice of untouchability and the evils of casteism. He wanted equality of rights. To Vivekananda, ignorance and inequality are the principal causes of human misery, and each follows the other in inevitable union.[23] Inequality is the source of all bondage, physical, mental and spiritual.[24] In the words of Swamiji, "No man and no nation can attempt to gain physical freedom without physical equality, nor mental freedom without mental equality."[25] Without social justice and equality and with the evils of casteism there can be no democracy. Besides, Swamiji championed the cause of equal rights and equal status of man and woman. He did not tolerate any discrimination in the social and economic spheres on the ground of gender. It may incidentally be noted that during the last part of the nineteenth century the concept of equal socio-economic status of man and woman was unthinkable even in dream in India and in entire Asia. Even in Europe this concept was not more than a mere theoretical exercise. It was yet to take practical shape there.

Fourthly, by equality Swamiji did not mean absolute or arithmetical equality. He realized the need for discriminatory treatment to help the have-nots and underprivileged section of the society. According to Swamiji, if the Brahmin has more aptitude for learning on the ground of heredity than the pariah, then no more money should be spent on the Brahmin's education, but all be spent on the pariah. To quote Swamiji: "Give [more] to the weak, for there all the gift is needed.... This is justice and reason as I understand it."[26] The essence of the idea is that more rights and facilities for the weaker people are essential to enable them to have a healthy competition with others who are already in a more advantageous position socially and culturally. Following this line of thought, in our Constitution there are special arrangements for the benefit of the Scheduled Caste, Scheduled Tribe and other backward classes. There is, however, scope for controversy regarding the questions: for how many days this special arrangement shall continue and for how many generations the special facilities shall be extended. But this is a different issue.

Nationalism and International Brotherhood

Swamiji realized the urgency of the development of the feeling of mutual love, confidence and brotherhood among various nations of the world as a step towards the promotion of world peace. He felt that the problems which appeared to be national could hardly be solved absolutely on national ground, because even a so-called national problem had the tendency to assume international dimension. In his own words:

> Even in politics and sociology, problems that were only national twenty years ago can no more be solved on national grounds only. They are assuming huge proportions, gigantic shapes. They can only be solved when looked at in the broader light of international grounds. International organizations, international combinations, international laws are the cry of the day. That shows the solidarity.[27]

III
RELEVANCE

Swami Vivekananda, a great visionary, was much in advance of his age.

Swamiji's emphasis upon mass power as the backbone of the society seems to be more relevant in the present context. He rightly stated that the masses, not the elite, represented the brain and conscience of the society.

Reference to the socialist ideas of Vivekananda may be made. In India, he for the first time, felt the urgency of involving the farmers and the workers in any social or political movement. The peasant discontent against established authority was a familiar feature of the nineteenth century. But the necessity of associating the peasants with the political movement and the freedom struggle could not be conceived before the 1930s. Likewise, the modern industrial worker made his appearance in India in the second half of the nineteenth century with the slow beginning of modern industry and the growth of utilities like the railways and the post and the telegraph network. Towards the end of the nineteenth century there were several agitations including strikes by the workers in the textile mills of Bombay, Calcutta, Ahmedabad, Madras, etc. But these agitations were mostly unorganized and had hardly any wider political implications. Since the end of the First World War in 1918 attempt was made to involve the working class in the mainstream of nationalist politics and the freedom movement. In this respect also, Swamiji was much in advance of his time.

As has already been noted, Swamiji was in favour of making a harmony between the individual liberty and the greater interest of the society. This balanced idea of liberty was unthinkable in the whole of Asia including India during Swamiji's life-time. In Europe this idea was just in the rudimentary stage. Today we are, in fact, following the idea of Swamiji. In Article 19(1) of Part III of our Constitution six freedoms have been guaranteed to the citizens of India. Simultaneously the state has been empowered to impose reasonable restrictions on the exercise of these freedoms on a number of grounds as mentioned in clauses 2 to 6 of the same Article. The purpose is to strike a balance between the liberty of the individual and the collective interest of the society.

Today we are conversant with such sophisticated terms as informal education, adult education, audio-visual method, etc. Swamiji much earlier gave considered thought about these methods of imparting education. Swami Vivekananda rightly emphasized that through education the qualities like self-consciousness, self-dignity, etc. are developed, and without the development of these qualities among the vast majority of people there cannot be any self-governance or democracy.

Till recently our planning process travelled from top to bottom and the people at the bottom level were just beneficiaries and spectators. They had no role to play. The requirements of the villagers were finalized from the air-conditioned chamber at the national capital or at the State capital and by those most of whom had hardly any direct acquaintance with the problems and requirements of the rural people. Gandhiji developed an alternative approach to development—his ideal of village republic or self-sufficient village. But at the time of framing of our Constitution no constitutional mechanism was devised for the development of local self-government institutions. Just to satisfy Gandhiji, only one Article in the Non-Justiciable Part, that is, Directive Principles of State Policy, was inserted: The state shall take steps to organize village panchayats.

Subsequently, however, institutions at the base level have been steadily strengthened and vested with effective powers and responsibilities, and particularly after the 73rd and 74th constitutional amendments the panchayats have been associated in several States including West Bengal with the formulation of plans at the block level, taluka level and district level. We may recall the observation of Vivekananda—even if the wealth of the whole world was invested in a small village of India, there would be no development unless the residents of the village came forward, took initiative and stood on their own feet. This is called grass-root democracy. It is true that our panchayat institutions are suffering from lack of administrative experience and training. There are also allegations of too much politicisation and financial irregularity. But at the initial stage of any constructive work with long-term positive effect the existence of obstacles is a natural phenomenon. Nevertheless, this experiment is a good beginning and the reflection of Swamiji's idea of mass participation and involvement in the developmental process at the grass-root level as an indispensable pre-requisite of meaningful self-governance.

Swamiji felt the need of International Organization and International Law in the 1890's. The first International Organization, the League of Nations, was established in 1919 after the end of the First World War. But the League did not attach much emphasis to the aspect of cultivation of the spirit of mutual love, trust and confidence among the sovereign nations. The United Nations, set up in 1945 after the Second World War, for the first time dealt, in detail, with this aspect of International Relations. The concept of development of International Law was not in the agenda of the European nations during the life-time of Swamiji. The United Nations, again for the first time, has accorded priority to the codification of International Law. Thus, this great spiritual leader and the first social revolutionary of India visualized the crying need of the human society that could be comprehended by the European statesmen four decades after the death of Swamiji. Vivekananda did not find any contradiction between the national aspirations of a people and the spirit of international brotherhood. He looked at Bharat

(India) as a national entity when the concept of administrative and political integration of this country was in the rudimentary stage of its development. Swamiji may rightly be described as the father of modern Indian nationalism.

In conclusion, reference to the observations of Dr. R.C. Majumdar and Sardar K.M. Panikkar may be made. In the words of the eminent historian Dr. R.C. Majumdar, "Vivekananda vitalized the nationalism of India by putting it on a spiritual level, and making a clarion call to the Hindus to realize the value of their spiritual heritage which it was their mission to spread to the West."[28] While analysing the background of Indian national movement Sardar K.M. Panikkar observed: "What gave Indian nationalism its dynamism and ultimately enabled it to weld at least the major part of India into one state was the creation of a sense of community among the Hindus to which the credit should, to a very large extent, go to Swami Vivekananda."[29] The term 'Hindu' used here does not refer to a particular religious sect, but the entire population, irrespective of religion and nationality, of Hindusthan. Thus, an integrated approach to national aspiration vis-à-vis internationalism is another significant aspect of Swamiji's political thinking.

Notes

1. For a short biography of Swami Vivekananda, see Swami Tejasananda, *A Short Life of Swami Vivekananda* (Kolkata: Advaita Ashrama, 2013).
2. Quoted in Das Gupta, R.K., "Vivekananda's Message of Freedom", as published in *The Statesman* (Calcutta), December 23, 1984.
3. Bose, Subhas Chandra, *The Indian Struggle, 1920-1942*. Bombay: Asia Publishing House, 1964, p. 21.
4. *The Complete Works of Swami Vivekananda*, Vol. IV (Mayavati Memorial Edition, Advaita Ashrama, Calcutta, reprinted in January 1989), p. 471 (Hereinafter referred to as 'C.W.').
5. *The Life of Swami Vivekananda by his Eastern and Western Disciples*, Vol. 2 (Calcutta: Advaita Ashrama, 1981, 5th Edition), p. 354.
6. Sen, Amit, *Notes on the Bengal Renaissance* (Calcutta: National Book Agency Private Ltd., 1957, 2nd Edition), p. 62.

7. *C.W.*, Vol. VI, p. 427.
8. Sister Christine, "Swami Vivekananda as I saw him", *Reminiscences of Swami Vivekananda* (Calcutta: Advaita Ashrama, 1961, 1st Edition), pp. 203-04.
9. *C.W.*, Vol. VI, p. 428.
10. *Ibid.*, p. 381.
11. *Ibid.*, Vol. II, p. 115.
12. *Ibid.*, Vol. IV, pp. 367-68.
13. *Ibid.*, Vol. VII, p. 392.
14. *Ibid.*, Vol. III, pp. 515-16.
15. *Ibid.*, Vol. V, p. 72.
16. *Ibid.*, Vol. III, p. 516.
17. *Ibid.*, Vol. IV, p. 367.
18. *Ibid.*, Vol. V, p. 29 and Vol. IV, p. 368.
19. *Ibid.*, Vol. VIII, p. 307.
20. *Ibid.*, Vol. IV, p. 363.
21. *Ibid.*, Vol. VIII, p. 308.
22. *Ibid.*, p. 89.
23. *Ibid.*, Vol. IV, p. 328.
24. *Ibid.*, p. 329.
25. *Ibid.*, p. 328.
26. *Ibid.*, Vol. III, p. 193.
27. *Ibid.*, pp. 240-41.
28. Majumdar, R.C., *Three Phases of India's Struggle for Freedom* (Bombay: Bharatiya Vidya Bhavan, 1967, 2nd Edition), p. 21.
29. Panikkar, K.M., *The Determining Periods of Indian History* (Bombay: Bharatiya Vidya Bhavan, 1st Edition, 1962), p. 53.

SECTION IV

Social and Political Ideas of the Thinkers of Modern Period

15

Mohandas Karamchand Gandhi (1869-1948) The Father of Nation

Chittabrata Palit

> Generations to come will scarcely believe that such a one as this ever in flesh and blood walked upon this Earth.
>
> —Albert Einstein on Mahatma Gandhi in 1944

> "...SOFT dark eyes, a small frail man, with a thin face and rather large protruding eyes, his head covered with a little white cap, his body clothed in coarse white cloth, barefooted. He lives one rice and fruit, and drinks only water. He sleeps on the floor-sleeps very little, and works incessantly. His body does not seem to count at all. There is nothing striking about him—except his whole expression of "infinite patience and infinite love." W.W. Pearson, who met him in South Africa, observed that there is an almost childlike simplicity about him.[1] His manner is gentle and courteous even when dealing with adversaries and he is of immaculate sincerity.

This is the description of Mahatma Gandhi, cited by famous French novelist Romain Rolland in his book *Mahatma Gandhi, The Man Who Become One with The Universal Being*. Romain Rolland who was himself largely influenced by Mahatma Gandhi, writes, this is the man who has stirred three hundred million people to revolt, who has shaken the foundation of the British empire and who has introduced into human politics the strongest religious impetus of the last two hundred years.[2]

I
INTRODUCTION

Mohandas Karamchand Gandhi fondly remembered as Bapu or the *maha atma* (great soul) was born in a little semi-independent state in the north-western part of India, at Porbander, Gujarat on October 2, 1869.

Gandhiji's family was well-to-do and belong to a cultivated class of society, but it was not of superior caste. His parents were followers of the Jain school of Hinduism, which regard *ahimsa,* the doctrine of non-injury to any form of life as one of its basic principles. This was the doctrine which Gandhi proclaimed victoriously throughout the world. Gandhiji's father cared little for wealth and material values, and left scarcely any to his family, having given almost everything away to charity. Gandhiji's mother was a very devout woman, who kept fasts and gave alms to the poor. In Gandhiji's family the *Ramayana* was read regularly. His first teacher was a Brahman who taught him to memories the texts of *Vishnu.*[3] In later years Gandhi regreted at not being better *Sanskrit* scholar, and one of his grievances against English education in India is that it makes the natives lose the treasures of their own language. Later on Gandhi became a profound student of Hindu scriptures, although he read the *Vedas* and the *Upanishads* in translation only. Gandhiji was engaged at the age of eight and married at the age of twelve. At nineteen he was sent to England to complete his studies at the University of London and at the law school.[4]

He passed Bar at Law from England in 1891, returned to India and began practising law. He went to Natal in South Africa in 1892 and his political life began there. About 10,000 Indian labourers and businessman lived in South Africa in those days that had no rights of citizenship. They were under the oppressive rule of the white people from which Gandhi didn't find himself to be an exception. Gandhi united the Indians there to stop the atrocities in a total non-violent way and became successful at the end. His non-violence came to be recognized as strong political weapon in those days and the movement thus conducted by him became known as *Satyagraha*.

Gandhi was deeply influenced by the books namely *Kingdom of God* by Tolstoy and writings of Thoreau, Tolstoy and Emerson and found his ideas of *Satyagraha*, the main base of which was non-violence and truth and conducted against injustice. *Satyagraha* according to him was the force of soul that of love. The important features of the *Satyagraha* organized by Gandhi in South Africa were.

1. He united all the Indians of South Africa irrespective of religious caste and creed and got them to struggle which was an evidence of his organizing capability. According to Judith Brown, the historian, most of the Indians of South Africa belonged to the Muslim business community. Because of his struggle on their account he was able to earn the respect and sympathy of the Muslims of India.
2. The procedure of non-violent movement successfully tested against South Africa was employed in India in later years.
3. His international reputation began to spread with his victory against South Africa. The effect of his leadership was felt in India as well and on the basis of the experience of the movement over there; he became the leader of the Indian struggle for freedom. The historian S.R. Mehrotra felt that Gandhi himself was the best present from South Africa for the struggle for freedom in India.

He returned to India during the First World War where India too became involved as a part of the British Empire. In those days he was quite a believer of the English justice, civilization and culture and he was in favour of the Indian connection with the English. So he gave total support to the English in the war without any conditions and felt that it was not the right time to press for a better and more responsible government. He received a gold medal 'Kaiser-e Hind' from the government for his valuable work.

During 1917-18, he led three regional struggles and became famous all over the India.

1. Was the poor peasants of the Champaran district of Bihar.
2. There was another case of oppression of the poor peasants of the district of Khera in Gujarat.
3. He also stood by the mill workers of Ahmedabad who were asking for rise in wages since a long time.

II
GANDHIAN MOVEMENTS

Non-Cooperation Movement

The year 1920 was an important one in the Indian history as Gandhiji was established as a leader of the Indian National Congress and led them to believe in non-violent and non-cooperation movement against the English Government to forsake. The old practice of 'political mendicancy' appeals and submissions etc. and go for direct struggle and against the government was no doubt an epoch making decision in the Indian political history of struggle for freedom. The days of prayer, petition and protest was over. The people looked forward eagerly to positive and fearless collective direct action against the foreign government.

Civil Disobedience Movement

There were certain reasons behind the beginning of the movement by Gandhiji—

> The worldwide economic depression resulted in great dissatisfaction among the peasants, laborer and middle class. The prices of raw cotton, jute, rice and other raw trading items came down considerably causing severe problems for the peasants of Bengal, Bihar and Uttar Pradesh. The Peasants got involved in violent movement in many places, due to the retrenchment of factory employees and reduction of wages, the workers had no other alternative but to go on strike. The situation became serious as the government chose the path of repression.

During the time, the import of Socialistic ideas and the up rise and collective movements of the communist and other socialist groups and various repressions against the Communist leaders created a fearful situation in the country. The Indian revolutionists were quite active at this time Association of Sanduarsh, bomb blast at Legislative Council, Lahore Conspiracy Case, Death of Jatin Das excited the youth of the country. The Indian capitalists were affected as a result of the unjust trading policy of the government they too, realized the fact that without *Swaraj*, it would become impossible for them to compete with the English traders congress and all its associates realized that only a big mass movement could force the government to submit to the Indian demands. In the Lahore Session in 1929, while speaking for the Civil Disobedience Movement Gandhiji said that in order to protect the country from violent politics, anarchism and terrorism there was no other alternative but to initiate the Civil Disobedience Movement.

Gandhiji placed before the government the proposals (11 items) for the reformation of the administration through 'Young India' newspaper on 30th January 1930 namely boycotting of liquor, release of the prisoners, reduction of land tax and that of the pay of the high ranked officer, salt tax abolition and the others. If the proposals were accepted he would withdraw the plan for the Civil Disobedience, he promised. This was totally ignored by the government. In the Executive Committee meeting of the Congress at Sabarmati Ashram from 14th to 16th February, 1930 the decision of non-violent Civil Disobedience Movement was taken on 2nd March, Gandhiji intimated the Viceroy of his intension of openly breaking the salt act at the place called Dandi situated at the coastal plains of Gujarat to initiate Civil Disobedience Movement. The movement would be postponed if the government agreed to the earlier 11 point proposal. The viceroy in reply warned Gandhiji not to go for any kind of movement. An agitated and disappointed Gandhiji wrote to the Viceroy "on bended knees, I asked for bread and have received a stone instead", the comment of Gandhiji was criticized by many as one couldn't sacrifice total independence for reformation of a few administrative matters.

Quit India Movement

The International situation underwent unexpected changes with the outbreak of World War II. The Indian National Congress unequivocally condemned fascism and the fascist powers for their violation of human rights. But the congress at the same time condemned British Imperialism and declared that India would not join the British in this war because the latter was an imperialist power. If British Government really wanted India's support then the British Government must give a promise to grant freedom to India.

Gandhiji's Idea of State, Trusteeship and *Ram Rajya*

We have already discussed the historical context of Mahatma Gandhi's life and work which explained the evolution of political ideas. It is now time to sum up the main currents of his political thought. Throughout of his life his, main concern was human freedom. He spent 18 years of his life as a lawyer for the Indian in South Africa against the Draconic laws of apartheid enforced by the British rulers of South Africa. As an activist, he saw its practice of segregation in public place forbidding the blacks in schools, clubs and hospitals. He was convinced that it was the basic concept of individual freedom prevailing in England. From this experience of experimentally with truth, he formulated his basic concept of ethical truth as outlined in Erikson's book. His thrust with truth led him to take the plunge into the anti apartheid movement to secure the individual freedom and equality before law. He took part in the mass agitation and carried the issue to local court. The coercive state could not suppress this mass movement by use of arms. Ultimately the government gave up the policy of repression and after negotiation with Gandhi lifted the hated laws of apartheid. From this encounter, Gandhi enunciated his basic principles of truth and the power of non-violence. He was convinced that truth only triumphs and non-violence can be effective weapons of the weak.

Back in India, he utilized this experience in cases of Champaran, Khera, Ahmedabad, Bardoli, Warli and Vikok. In each case his instruments of non violence, succeeded against state and social operation of course, these were mass issues and he was already the President of Indian National Congress.

From this Indian scenario he evolved his idea of the state as coercive machinery. He was therefore in favour of minimum government as remover of obstacles and promoter of welfare.

He would allow maximum autonomy to the individual and the community. He therefore challenged the supremacy of the state, sovereignty, which was against individual freedom. This sovereignty was generated by the ruling classes and not from the masses over whom they ruled.

Gandhi had his first hand experience of rural poverty and believed in the purity of the poor drawn from his reading of John Ruskin's *Unto this Last*. He therefore worked for the empowerment of the poor man and women in India. Charka was the symbol for his purpose as an instrument of self help for those who could not even afford even to buy mill make clothings. But he was not against big business. He was afraid of Birla, Puroshottam Das, Thakur Das and others and considered them nation builder as well as only if they acted as trustees of the people and invested their surplus profit for their welfare. Obviously against the, Marxist Doctrine of class struggle, revolution and dictatorship of the proletariat. Gandhi has been variously described as an anarchist trying to enforce the rules of the coercive state, but he was not a Hobbesian, instead he was a follower of Rousseau in his outlook.

His trusteeship idea was not an advocacy of plutocracy. He only appealed to the moral conscience of big businessman.

As Nelson Mandela observes that from Gandhiji's understanding of wealth and poverty came his understanding of labour and capital, which led him to the solution of trusteeship based on the believe that there is no private ownership of capital; it is given in trust for redistribution and equalization. Similarly, while recognizing differential aptitudes and talents, he holds that these are gifts from god to be used for the collective good. He seeks an economic order, alternative to the capitalist and communist, and finds this in *sarvodaya* based on non-violence (*ahimsa*).

He rejected Darwin's survival of the fittest, Adam Smith's laissez-faire and Karl Marx's thesis of a natural antagonism between capital and labour, and focuses on the interdependence between the two.

He believed in the human capacity to change and wage *Satyagraha* against the oppressor, not to destroy him but to transform him, that he cease his oppression and join the oppressed in the pursuit of truth.[5]

Gandhi's concept of *Ram Rajya* and the song *Ramdhun* has been misconstrued as a Hindu State with a Hindu refrain. But one must not equate *Ram Rajya* with the hindu theocracy. For Gandhi the name Ram stands for morality. In fact he is speaking of a moral state of social Justice. This is clear from the tune *Ramdhun* where both *Ishwar* and *Allah* are hailed as personified in Rama. Rama had even forsaken Sita and consigned her to the ordeal of fire to prove her chastity to satisfy his subjects. *Ram Rajya* therefore as a concept is far from the idea of Hinduttva ascribed to him.

Last but not the least, Gandhi was known for his high thinking and plain living. He therefore prescribed an austere menu for his followers for food and shelter. He also advised naturopathy for treatment at the cheapest cost. Now there is a crusade for both vegetarianism and nature healing. Gandhi can be regarded as one of the early crusaders for both.

Gandhiji's Concept of Ethics and *Satyagraha*

In his autobiography Gandhiji says that he did not belong to any particular religion. He had an ethical God. Truth was for him the goal. All his life he made various experiments with truth. He sought truth in politics, in economics and in environment.

Gandhiji spent twenty-one years of his life in South Africa as a lawyer and political leader of the Indian immigrants who brought him from India and hired him to fight a legal battle for their right of citizenship. During this long tenure, he developed his concept and practice of *Satyagraha*.[6]

Gandhiji's *Satyagraha* had for its goal the establishment of truth in the end. His method was to make a case study of the issue on the spot. He studied both sides of the case with reference to existing unequal laws. He was convinced that the authorities were guilty of denial of justice. His next course of action was to petition the government for redress of the grievance and to ascertain government's attitude to the question. Truth could only be established by hearing both sides and weighing evidence. When the government's attitude proved negative and stubborn, the only course left was exposing injustice.[7]

He began his discovery of India by locating a few storm-centres of protest to do his field work. One such area was Champaran in North Bihar. Here a peasant agitation had been going on for a long time against the oppression of indigo planters who had reduced the peasants to bonded labour and forced them to cultivate indigo against their will. In his search for the truth in the matter, Gandhiji chose a Harijan village in which to do social work in order to gain their confidence. He came to know the nature of their grievance, and his sage-like appearance and beneficial activities made him their spokesman. Gandhiji's way of arriving at the truth was to explore the point of view of the adversary which could also contain some grain of truth. In this case he sought appointments with government officials and planters to elicit their views. On weighing the evidence, he was convinced the planters were the unjustifiable oppressors. Once he found out this truth, he decided to take up the cause of the peasants and asked them not to sow indigo or any other crop dictated by the planter. This is known as the 'Champaran Satyagraha'.[8]

Economy

Gandhiji's experiments with truth were extended to economic issues as well. His propagation of the *charka* (spinning wheel) came out of his experience in rural Champaran. He found village women here in shabby and dirty clothes and held their dirty habits responsible for it. He enquired through his wife why they wore such clothes. They were surprised that Gandhiji being a Mahatma did not know the cause. They were so poor that they could not afford a pair of *sarees*, and they did not have any facility to wash their dirty clothes. Gandhiji shuddered at the thought and as he deeply pondered over the matter, the idea of charka came to his mind as the only solution. As they could not afford buying another mill-made *saree*, they could weave one themselves by resorting to the *charka*. This would make them self-reliant and if they could weave more, they could sell the extra produce in the market and earn a few rupees. This would lead to overall improvement of their living conditions.[9]

He therefore decided to propagate the message of *charka* wherever he went in his later wanderings among the rural poor.

He urged his followers and congressmen, in particular, to buy homespun cotton from these poor folks so that they could become solvent, 'Buy *Khadi*' became the new slogan of the Gandhi-led Congress.[10]

Giving priority to the *charka* over modern industries in search of the indigenous and the pure was not a backward-looking idiosyncrasy. It was born out of his experiments with truth and concern for the poor. He was not basically against big industries. As is well known, he was very close to Indian business magnates such as Lalbhai Kasturbhai, Purushottamdas Thakurdas, Jamunalal Bajaj, G.D. Birla and others. He urged the people to solve all labour disputes amicably. He pleaded them to work for the welfare of the nation as a whole.[11]

Gandhi remains today the only complete critic of advanced industrial society. Others have criticized its totalitarianism but not its productive apparatus. Gandhiji was not against science and technology but he placed priority on the right to work and opposed mechanization to the extent that it usurps this right. Large-scale machinery, according to him concentrated wealth in the hands of one man and tyrannizes the rest. He favours the small machine which kept the individual in control of his tools, to maintain, as Nelson Mandela observes and interdependent love relation between the two, as a cricketer with his bat or Krishna with his flute. Above all he seeks to liberate the individual from his alienation to the machine and restore morality to the productive process. As Nelson Mandela observes that in the era of globalization where we increasingly find ourselves in job-less economies, societies in which small minorities consume while masses starve, we are forced to rethink and ponder over the Gandhian alternative.[12]

Environment

He had a penchant for cleanliness. He befriended the untouchables and called them 'Harijans' (God's people). On one occasion during his tour in rural districts, he remarked that the 'Mehtar' (sweeper) was like one mother. The mother keeps the baby clean and beautiful, the Mehtar keeps the public clean and civilized.

All his life, he struggled for a better deal for this community. His whole idea of rural reconstruction was based on primary education health care and economic self-reliance which were most needed by the poor. To him, small was beautiful, and plain living was divine. After meeting the necessities, one should not strive to satisfy unnecessary desires; that breeds unhappiness.[13]

Gandhiji like Tagore was against consumerism and overexploitation of nature. For an enduring civilization, he thought, a serene environment was desirable. This could only be achieved by limiting wants and rendering service to mankind. In this age of global warming and environmental pollution, Gandhiji is becoming more and more relevant for his message of plain living and high thinking.[14]

Gandhiji's concern with environment began in the ambience of South Africa where he went to set up his legal practice among the Indian community at the turn of the 20th century. The house in which he put up in Durban was built after the Western model of the time and the rooms had no outlets for dirty water. Each room had chamber pots. Young Mohandas and Kasturba did not engage any sweeper or servant but used to clean them themselves. This was the common practice with the clerks who lived there. Gandhi supervised the work, Mohandas insisted on doing his bedroom. Kasturba feel out but ultimately yielded to his cajoling. Gandhiji writes in his autobiography, "I regarded myself as her teacher and so harassed her out of my blind love for her". He calls it his sacred recollection and penance. This is how he practised cleanliness as godliness and moralized the issue.[15] This environment pollution and Gandhiji's concern mounted when he became familiar with coolie locations orghettoes in Johannesburg. The team 'coolie' ordinarily meant a porter in India, but in South Africa it meant a pariah or untouchable. The location was like a labour concentration camp and the coolies were sardine-packed in their hutments. The municipality did not provide for even the minimum sanitary facilities, much less good roads or lights. The bulk of the Indians who went to South Africa were ignorant pauper peasants who needed care and protection. "The criminal negligence of the Municipality and ignorance of the Indian settlers made the location thoroughly insanitary", writes Gandhiji. This unbearable condition was made the excuse to destroy the location without rehabilitation of the settlers when he arrived in Johannesburg. He took up their case against the authorities. This was his first *Satyagraha*. The location was soon visited by the dreaded black plague. As the location was to be destroyed, all semblance of municipal care was withdrawn and the settlers, as tenants now neglected their hygiene so much that as the number of tenants increased, the squalor and disorder spread accordingly. There was a sudden outbreak of the black plague or the pneumonic plague, more terrible and fatal than the bubonic. It spread from the nearby gold-mine and twenty-one infected Indians returned to the location causing the epidemic. This was Gandhiji's first major experience of health care. With Dr. Godfrey by his side, he began nursing the sick. He characteristically says, "There was not much nursing required. To give them their doses of medicine, to attend to their wants, to keep them and their beds clean and tidy and to cheer them up was all that we had to do."[16]

Gandhiji was a votary of nature cure. He was unsparing in his criticism of practitioners of Western medicine: "Hospitals are institutions for propagating sin. Men take less care of their bodies and immorality increases. European doctors are the worst of all. For the sake of a mistaken case of the human body, they kill annually thousands of animals. They practice vivisection. No religion sanctions this.... Most of their medical preparations contain either animal fat or spirituous liquors.... To study European medicine is to deepen our slavery. Doctors make a show of their knowledge and charge exorbitant fees. Their preparations which are intrinsically worth a few pence, cost shillings."

That is not Gandhiji's obscurantism. The noted demographer Mckeown in his work makes the same observations.[16] The passage above also reflects his concern for the cruelty to animals which would later form his anti-cowslaughter plank back in India.[17]

His supreme concern was for Khadi even beyond satyagraha for freedom, which was a passing phase in his whole career of service to humanity.

Gandhiji says that in *Hindi Sawaraj*, he described it as the panacea for the growing pauperism of India without having seen a handloom or a spinning wheel. In that book, the took it as understood that "anything that helped India to get rid of the grinding poverty of her masses would in the same process also establish *swaraj*.

Now we turn to his crusade for the untouchables which was inspired by both his humanism and concern for sanitation. During his visit to a Namasudra school in a Bengal district, Gandhiji said; "I am very happy to be here. I am confident the blot of untouchability is being erased. All life is one. It is the Hindu Dharma to give up regarding the so-called 'untouchables' as untouchables. Indian villages suffer from horrible insanitation. We must keep our water supply pure. Not attending to sanitation makes our bodies diseased and impure. Mental sanitation too is necessary and in order to keep our minds pure, we must keep them engaged in some healthy activity."[18]

Gandhiji's penchant for cow protection can be related to his concern for flora and fauna. In *Hind Sawaraj,* he had strongly censured the killing of thousands of animals in the name of guinea pig experiment for drugs. The rule of not killing venomous reptiles had been practised for the most part at Phoenix, Tolstoy Farm and Sabarmati. Gandhiji writes: "At each of these places, we had to settle on waste lands. We have had, however, no loss of life occasioned by snakebite. I see with the eye of faith in this circumstance the hand of the God of Mercy. Even if it be a superstition to believe that complete immunity from harm for twenty- five years in spite of a fairly regular practice of non-killing is not a fortuitous accident but a grace of God, I shall still hug that superstition." The so-called funny story of his switching over to goat's milk has to be interpreted in this light. Gandhiji himself describes the incident: "Whilst I was engaged on the recruiting campaign in Kheda, an error in diet laid me low and I was at death's door. I tried in vain to rebuild a shattered constitution without milk.... I might not take cow's or buffalo's milk as I was bound by a vow. The vow, of course, meant giving up of all milk, but as I had mother cow's and mother buffalo's only in mind when I took the vow and as I wanted to live, I somehow beguiled myself into emphasizing the letter of the vow and decided to take goat's milk. I was fully conscious when I started taking mother goat's milk that the spirit of my vow was destroyed."[19]

This vow was, however, kept in another more lasting form, his crusade for cow protection. This had its origin during his tours in North Bihar. Gandhiji narrates: "I had seen in the course of my travels that cow protection and Hindi propaganda had become the exclusive concern of the Marwadis. A Marwadi friend had sheltered me in his *dharmashala* whilst at Bettiah. Other Marwadis of the place had interested me in their *goshala* (dairy). My ideas about cow protection had been definitely formed then and my conception of the work was the same as it is today. Cow protection in my opinion included cattle-breeding, improvement of the stock, humane treatment of the bullocks, formation of model dairies, etc. The Marwadi friends had promised full co-operation in this work but as I could not fix myself up in Champaran, the scheme could not be carried out. The *goshala* in Bettiah is still there but it has not beyond his capacity and the so-called Hindu still cruelly be labours the poor animal and disgraces his religion." The cruelty to animals pained him more than ill-management of a animal husbandry. In another context, he bewailed: "Raw hides worth 90 million rupees are exported. There are 1500 *pinjrapoles* (houses for animals) in the country at present and still you are unable to have a single slaughter house closed."[20]

In the same context he says, "All the activities—*khadi*, removal of untouchability, cow protection—all of them are equal in my eyes. Don't mix up *shuddhi* and *sangathan* (activities of conversion to and organisation of Hinduism) with the *khadi* work of mine.... I cannot understand the *shuddhi* and the *tabligh* (conversion to Islam) as they are carried on at present. This attempt to make people change their religion is beyond my ken."[21]

Indeed his whole range of activities centered round humanism and natural harmony. Last but not the least is a small incident reported by Louis Fischer. "He did the same with floral garlands thrown around his neck. 'Why kill flowers unnecessarily', he asked, 'when they could garland him with a ring of yarn'. Yarn garlands became an Indian custom."[22] It was an Indian custom of the poor. It has now become the raging fashion of the rich and the poor alike.

Contemporary Relevance of Gandhiji Today

Relevance of Mahatma Gandhi in contemporary Indian Political Thought cannot be summed up without referring to the debate that ensued between Gandhi and Ambedkar during the colonial and even in post colonial period. The political and intellectual legacy of Mahatma Gandhi have become the focus of intense political engagement in recent times.

The two were involved in a debate regarding the issue of representation of the depressed classes; the removal of untouchability and the caste question that continued even after the departure of both.[23] The significance of Ambedkar as a historical figure and of his continuing legacy has been examined largely within the context of dalit emancipation. Scholars have studied his role as a leader and advocate of Maharastra's dalits as well as a support of constitutional safeguard for Indian's dalit community and his central role in drafting India's constitution and the Hindu Court Bill. Ambedkar wrote extensively about the institution of caste and its effect on Indian society, particularly its negative impact on the possibility and conditions for creating democracy and a shared sense of national belonging. Though B.R. Ambedkar's *Annihilation of Caste*, was published in 1936, his clash with M.K. Gandhi over separate electorates for untouchables began from 1932 which led to his disagreements with the Congress and ultimately his support for conversion to Buddhism as a way to escape caste hierarchy.[24]

Gandhiji has been repeatedly accused of not openly attacking the 'caste' system as such, and was not keen on abolishing untouchability. Gandhi did not have a theory of caste system. He argued that caste is a distortion of the *Varna* system, the latter is a pure form and the former is a degeneration.

According to Mahatma Gandhi untouchability as it is practised in present day is a sin against God and man and is, therefore like a poison slowly eating into the very vitals of Hinduism. In Gandhiji's opinion, it has no sanction whatsoever in the Hindu *Shastras* taken as a whole.[25]

Gandhiji therefore did not have believe in the caste system though he had firm faith in the *Varnashrama Dharma*. He believed that every man is born in the world with certain natural tendencies. Every person is born with certain definite limitations which he cannot overcome. It established certain spheres of for certain people with certain tendencies. Gandhiji believed that this law of *varna* admitted no distinction of high and low; on the other hand, it guaranteed to each the fruits of his labours; Gandhiji believed that *Varnashrama Dharma* has its limitations and that an ideal social order will only be evolved when the implications of this law are fully understood and given effect to.[26]

Gandhiji did realize that an overemphasis on caste system and formation of separate electorates might lead to further division in the society, while Ambedkar claimed that caste and untouchability caused a deep breach in the Indian social order and is a hindrance for claiming unity in the political realm Gandhi, on the other hand, prefereed to believe (a) in the feasibility of political unity despite social inequality; and (b) in simultaneous efforts for uniting society politically and socially.[27] It is true that Gandhi could not provide a agenda to get rid of the prejudices that were prevalent in Hindu practices but it is also true that along with maladies of the caste system dalit politics too has seemingly plagued the Indian society till today.

In the context of global pollution, ecological imbalance and mounting lethal diseases, in other words, the crisis of civilisation, Gandhiji appears to be the prophet of environmentalism with his panacea of naturopathy, vegetarianism, a simple and austere life in fresh air away from sooty factories and concrete jungles in communion with nature with its flora and fauna. One has to breathe into this idyllic setting his deep concern for the dignity of man. This is the alternative he was posing to materialistic civilization in his *Hind Swaraj* in his younger days. This again makes him the prophet of the 21st century.

Gandhiji's relevance to Indian Politics cannot be summed up in two or three words. Gandhiji was a champion of non violence and truth for which he is regarded all over the world. One must not forget that he is regarded all over the world as the messiah of peace in the background of global conflict and targeted warfare. One has to recall the tribute given by Albert Einstein that a century later such a person an ever work for the face of the earth. In India we should learn to respect the father of the nation instead of washing dirty linen in public. Though Ganhiji's role in Indian politics had ended before his death but his doctrine of non violence as a solution for political issues earned his martyrdom.

Mosley, pays high tribute to Gandhi in his final analysis

> In many ways, Gandhi was a saint. The three great aims of his life
>
> was Indian Freedom, the unity of his people. Hindus and Muslims,
>
> And the betterment of the lot of the untouchables for these goals, he
>
> was willing to suffer and die.[28]
>
> In this broader sense he remains the Father of the Nation.

Notes and References

1. Rolland, R. (2013). *Mahatma Gandhi: The Man Who Become One with The Universal Being*, New Delhi: Srishti Publishers & Distributors, p. 1.
2. *Ibid.*, p. 2.
3. *Ibid.*, p. 3.
4. *Ibid.*, p. 4.
5. Mandela, N. (1999). "The Sacred Warrior". *TIME*, vol. 154, no. 26, pp. 74-75.
6. Palit, C. (2013). *Authentic Gandhi*, New Delhi: Kunal Books, p. 7.
7. *Ibid.*, p. 8.
8. *Ibid.*, p. 9.
9. *Ibid.*, pp. 10-11.
10. *Ibid.*, p. 11.
11. *Ibid.*
12. Mandela, N. (1999). "The Sacred Warrior". *TIME*, vol. 154, no. 26, p. 75.
13. Palit, C. (2013). *Authentic Gandhi*, New Delhi: Kunal Books, p. 12.
14. *Ibid.*, p. 12.

15. *Ibid.*, p. 13.
16. *Ibid.*, pp. 14-15.
17. *Ibid.*, pp. 20-21.
18. *Ibid.*, p. 29.
19. *Ibid.*, p. 33.
20. *Ibid.*, p. 34.
21. *Ibid.*
22. Fischer, Louis. *The Life of Mahatma Gandhi*, Jonathan Cape, London, 1962, p. 252.
23. Palshikar, S. (2015). "Ambedkar and Gandhi, limits of divergence and possibilities of conversation". *Economic & Political Weekly*, Vol L. no. 15. April 11, 2015, pp. 45-50.
24. Tejani, S. (2013). "The Necessary Conditions for Democracy, B.R. Ambedkar on Nationalism, Minorities and Pakistan". *Economic & Political Weekly*, vol. XLVIII, no. 50. December 14, 2013: pp. 111-19.
25. Gandhi, M. (2014). *India of My Dreams*, Delhi: Rajpal & Sons, p. 235.
26. *Ibid.*, p. 232.
27. Palshikar, S. (2015). "Ambedkar and Gandhi: limits of divergence and possibilities of conversation". *Economic & Political Weekly*, Vol. L. no. 15. April 11, 2015, p. 49.
28. Palit, C. (2013). *Authentic Gandhi*, New Delhi: Kunal Books, p. 91.

Suggested Readings

1. Bhattacharya, B. (1969). *Evolution of the Political Philosophy of Gandhi*, Calcutta: Calcutta Book House.
2. Mukherjee, R. (ed.) (2014). GANDHI READER, New Delhi: Penguin.
3. Guha, R. ed & introduced (2012). *Makers of Modern India*, New Delhi: Penguin.
4. Fischer, L. (1951). *The Life of Mahatma Gandhi*, Noida: Vintage publications.
5. Gandhi, M. (2014). *India of My Dreams*, Delhi: Rajpal & Sons.
6. Rolland, R. (2013). *Mahatma Gandhi*, New Delhi: Srishti Publishers and Distributors.

16

Nationalism and Democracy in the Light of Sri Aurobindo (1872-1950)

Anurag Banerjee

I
INTRODUCTION

> ...long after this controversy is hushed in silence, long after this turmoil, this agitation ceases, long after he is dead and gone, he will be looked upon as the poet of patriotism, as the prophet of nationalism and the lover of humanity. Long after he is dead and gone, his words will be echoed and re-echoed not only in India but across distant seas and lands.

Thus was Sri Aurobindo described by Chittaranjan Das, the famous barrister and political leader who had defended Sri Aurobindo when he was convicted in the Alipore Bomb Trial. C.R. Das's utterance turned out to be prophetic for during Sri Aurobindo's lifetime as well as sixty years after his physical departure, he is revered across the globe as one of the greatest seers and philosophers of the bygone century whom Rabindranath Tagore had described as the voice incarnate of India's soul.

Sri Aurobindo was born on 15 August 1872 in Calcutta. His father Dr. Krishnadhan Ghose was a renowned but anglicised physician who despised everything that was Indian. With the view of providing his sons (Benoy Bhushan, Manmohan and Sri Aurobindo) with a complete Westernized education and to remove all probable Indian influences on their outlooks and personalities he sent them first to Loreto Convent School in

Darjeeling and later to England in 1879 where Sri Aurobindo and his two elder brothers lived for fourteen years. After spending his early years in Manchester, Sri Aurobindo was taken to London where he studied at St. Paul's School from 1884 to 1889. He turned out to be one of the brightest students of the school and won the Butterworth Second Prize and Bedford Prize for proficiency in Literature and History respectively in 1889. Afterwards he joined the King's College at Cambridge where he won a number of college prizes including the Rawley Prize for Greek Iambics. He passed the First Part of Classical Tripos in 1892 in the first class. He also qualified for the Indian Civil Service examination but deliberately got himself disqualified by remaining absent from the riding test as he had no desire to serve the British Crown. He returned to India in February 1893 after securing a job in the administration of Maharaja Sayaji Rao Gaekwad, the ruler of Baroda. For the next few years he worked in various departments under the Baroda State Service. Later he joined the Baroda College as a lecturer of French and Professor of English and went on to become its Vice Principal as well as the Acting Principal for a brief period. In 1906 during the agitation against the partition of Bengal which took place a year earlier he resigned from his services at Baroda, went to Calcutta where he joined the newly established National College as its Principal on a meagre salary. He became the editor-in-chief of the nationalist journal *Bande Mataram* started by Bipin Chandra Pal. Under his leadership the journal became the mouthpiece of the nationalist workers. In July 1907, he was arrested for publishing certain seditious articles in *Bande Mataram* but was eventually acquitted. Within a very short span of time he became one of the foremost leaders of the Nationalist wing of the Indian National Congress. It was Sri Aurobindo who had played a decisive role in splitting the Congress during its Surat session in December 1907. In May 1908, he was arrested in connection with the Alipore Bomb Case and after a year-long trial he was acquitted due to lack of evidence. After his release he started two weeklies—the *Karmayogin* in English and *Dharma* in Bengali—where his articles on philosophy, yoga, education and literary criticisms were published. Following an inner command, he went first to Chandernagore and then to Pondicherry in April 1910 to devote his time to yoga the practise of which he had started in 1905. From 1914 to 1921 he published a monthly philosophical journal titled the *Arya* in which most of his major prose works like *The Life Divine*, *The Synthesis of Yoga*, *The Secret of the Veda*, *Essays on the Gita*, *The Human Cycle*, *The Ideal of Human Unity* and *The Future Poetry* were serialised. During the 1920s, a small group of spiritual seekers had gathered around Sri Aurobindo. This small group led to the formation of Sri Aurobindo Ashram in 1926 the charge of which Sri Aurobindo handed over to his spiritual collaborator Mirra Alfassa—better known as the Mother—and retired to complete seclusion to devote his time to intensive sadhana. He worked to realise and bring on earth the higher consciousness which is required for the next step in evolution—the Supermind. He would appear before his devotees and disciples four times a year in the months of February, April, August and November on certain specific dates which came to be known as the Darshan Days in Sri Aurobindo Ashram. Following a brief illness Sri Aurobindo passed away on 5 December 1950.

II
SRI AUROBINDO'S POLITICAL PHILOSOPHY: AN ANALYSIS

Sri Aurobindo's predecessors and most of his contemporaries who were members of the Indian National Congress were 'Moderates'. They were satisfied to present before the British Government a list of petitions for small concessions. When Sri Aurobindo returned to India in 1893 at the age of twenty-two, he did not fail to notice the shortcomings of the policies adopted by the Congress leaders. Even at that early age he did not hesitate to express his disgust over the inadequacies of the Congress party and its plans and programmes adopted by its leaders. In a series of nine articles titled *New Lamps for Old* which were serialised in a weekly newspaper *Indu Prakash* Sri Aurobindo wrote that the aims of the Congress were mistaken, the spirit in which it proceeded towards the accomplishment of the aims was not in a spirit of 'whole-heartedness' and 'sincerity' and that the methods chosen were wrong and the leaders who were trusted were not the right sort of individuals to be leaders. To quote Sri Aurobindo's own words: "...we are at present the blind led, if not by the blind, at any rate by the one-eyed."[1] He had also pointed out that the Congress party represented a single and limited class of individuals. Through his articles in the *New Lamps for Old* he strongly criticised the policies of pray, petitions and protest of the Congress and asked for a dynamic leadership based on self-help and fearlessness.

From 1893 to 1905, Sri Aurobindo was a keen observer of the political scenario of the country. Since he was employed in the Baroda State Service he could not openly participate in politics. However, he began to prepare himself for his future political work silently. He had established contacts with nationalist politicians, organised a secret revolutionary society around 1900 and joined another secret society in 1902 with the view to explore an armed rebellion to oust the British. He got a Bengali revolutionary named Jatindranath Banerjee (the future Niralamba Swami) enrolled in the Baroda army to obtain training in the art and science of warfare.

Following the partition of Bengal in 1905, Sri Aurobindo resolved to join active politics to secure political freedom of India. Around that time he prepared the plan for 'Bhavani Mandir' where a community based on spiritual lines would be formed, trained and sent to various places within India to serve its inhabitants. The political freedom of India was undoubtedly the chief aim but for its attainment it was necessary for Indians to unite strength and devotion, that is, *Shakti* and *Bhakti*, to liberate India from the clutches of British domination and restore her economic and spiritual health.

It is generally assumed that politics and spirituality cannot proceed side-by-side. However, Sri Aurobindo not only tried to spiritualise politics but also sought to govern politics by high spiritual ideas. In fact he started practising yoga to attain spiritual strength which would enable him to fight for the liberation of India. "For Sri Aurobindo, politics was but service to the motherland in the spirit of religious devotion."[2] In one of his speeches too, he has proclaimed nationalism to be a religion which has come from God. But it is essential to remember that

Sri Aurobindo did not use the word 'religion' to imply a set of rituals or beliefs but a "high and noble calling under the direction of a higher power." To Sri Aurobindo, nationalism itself was a religion made up of faith, courage and selflessness. He never believed in infusing formal religious spirit in politics.

Swaraj, Swadeshi, Boycott and National Education

As the leader of the Nationalist Party, Sri Aurobindo put forward the proposals of *Swaraj*, *Swadeshi*, Boycott and National Education. Through these proposals he aimed to bring not only political but economic and cultural independence for India. While the Moderates looked upon *Swaraj* as colonial self-rule within the British empire, Sri Aurobindo demanded absolute *Swaraj*—that is, complete political freedom from British rule. It is essential to remember that Sri Aurobindo was the first political leader in India to demand complete independence in public. In a thought-provoking article titled *Nationalism Not Extremism* (published on 26 April 1907 in the *Bande Mataram*), Sri Aurobindo explained the philosophy of nationalism. According to him, nationalism was a constructive impulse towards the creation of a modern India through the attainment of national self-realisation and that it was a gospel of national faith and hope. Hence, we observe that *Swaraj*—according to Sri Aurobindo—did not merely imply political freedom but spiritual freedom as well. In another article published in the *Bande Mataram* on 18 February 1908 Sri Aurobindo has remarked that spiritual freedom would be recovered by political freedom because "God has not set apart India as the eternal fountain-head of holy spirituality, and He will never suffer that fountain to run dry" so he prophesised: "Once more in the land of the saints and sages will burn up the fire of the ancient Yoga and the hearts of her people will be lifted up into the neighbourhood of the Eternal."[3] Sri Aurobindo also realised that *Swaraj* was necessary for the fulfillment of India's actual role in the comity of nations because according to him: "India is the *guru* of the nations, the physician of the human soul in its profounder maladies; she is destined once more to new-mould the life of the world and restore the peace of the human spirit.

But *Swaraj* is the necessary condition of her work and before she can do the work, she must fulfil the condition."[4]

Low priced products manufactured by British industries had ousted the local Indian manufacturers from the market. To support the indigenous manufacturers Sri Aurobindo propagated the principle of *Swadeshi* and boycott of foreign goods not only in Bengal but in other provinces as well. Like Bal Gangadhar Tilak, he wanted Boycott to be a political weapon instead of being a mere aid to Swadeshi. He propagated self-sufficiency in key industries and as well as in the manufacture of all basic necessities in which India's natural resources could be utilised.

Sri Aurobindo also advocated moves to boycott British-run academic institutions and to replace them with national colleges and schools. He was well aware of the shortcomings of the British system of education which tended to impoverish and spoil the productivity and rationality of the Indian brain. To illustrate the gospel of national education, he penned a series of articles titled "A System of National Education" in the journal *Karmayogin* between 12 February and 2 April 1910. According to Sri Aurobindo, national education can be described as the education which starts with the past and makes full use of the present and builds a great nation. He considered the system of Western education to be faulty due to its "calculated poverty and insufficiency, its anti-national character, its subordination to the Government and the use of that subordination for the discouragement of patriotism and the inculcation of loyalty."[5]

Sri Aurobindo's concept of national education consisted of three significant elements. (1) A proper place has to be provided to study the noble heritage of our motherland and that one should fit himself for existence under actual situations and that he must keep himself abreast with the march of true knowledge. The system of education also must be up-to-date in the form of substance and modern in life and spirit. (2) Modern truth and knowledge should not be ignored and that our foundations should be established on our own being, mind and spirit. (3) It should underline that since the most brilliant minds of the West are turning to Asia with the expectation of a new and more spiritual civilisation it would be an error to cast away our own self and potentialities and entrust ourselves in the fading past of Europe.

Sri Aurobindo and Passive Resistance

Along with the principles of *Swaraj*, *Swadeshi*, Boycott and National Education, Sri Aurobindo also preached the doctrine of Passive Resistance in a series of articles published in the *Bande Mataram* from 11 April to 23 April 1907. To achieve freedom, an organised national resistance in the form of passive resistance was required. According to Sri Aurobindo:

> The present circumstances in India seem to point to passive resistance as our most natural and suitable weapon.... Under certain circumstances a civil struggle becomes in reality a battle and the morality of war is different from the morality of peace.... But where the oppression is legal and subtle in its methods and respects life, liberty and property and there is still breathing time, the circumstances demand that we should make the experiment of a method of resolute but peaceful resistance which while less bold and aggressive than other methods, calls for perhaps as much heroism of a kind and certainly more universal endurance and suffering. In other methods, a daring minority purchase with their blood the freedom of the millions; but for passive resistance it is necessary that all should share in the struggle and the privation.[6]

Sri Aurobindo's political programme consisted of three strategies. The first one was to start a secret revolutionary propaganda and organisation the central objective of which was the preparation of an armed insurrection. The second strategy was to convert the whole of India to the ideal of independence. The third strategy was the organisation of the people of the country to carry on a public and unified opposition and undermining of the British rule through an increasing non-cooperation and passive resistance. A thorough reading of Sri Aurobindo's *The Doctrine of Passive Resistance* would reveal that Sri Aurobindo did prefer spiritual strength (*brahmatej*) to physical strength (*kshatratej*), that is, violence. However, it should also be remembered that the possibility of an armed revolution was not ruled out by him in case there was no other way of gaining independence. Therefore he prepared the nation for both peaceful passive resistance and violent revolutionary actions simultaneously.

Sri Aurobindo's concept of passive resistance included an 'organised' and 'relentless boycott' of British goods, British-run academic institutions, justice and executive administration supplemented by the development of national education, arbitration courts and leagues of mutual defence. It also included a programme of social boycott of betrayers and civil disobedience of unjust laws. Sri Aurobindo had also—in 1907—suggested mass courting of arrest through violation of unjust laws. Thus, we observe that Mahatma Gandhi's theory of passive resistance (with the exception of non-violent methods) was quite similar to that of Sri Aurobindo's. The only differences were that Sri Aurobindo's doctrine was formulated before Gandhi's and that his concept of non-violence differed from Gandhi's. Sri Aurobindo has pointed out in his *Essays on the Gita* that there would be no construction without destruction, no harmony "except by a poise of contending forces won out of many actual and potential discords, but also no continued existence of life except by a constant self-feeding and devouring of other life."[7] Therefore violence—if properly guided—could lead to welfare of mankind as such conflicts originate new life and ushers in a new age. Though Sri Aurobindo recognised the principles of harmlessness and soul-force and that non-violent measures could be the highest and best form of conduct but in case violent forces become too powerful and annihilative, soul-force would be an impotent instrument against it. Therefore, he advocated the destruction of such destructive forces since: "Evil cannot perish without the destruction of much that lives by the evil."[8]

To Sri Aurobindo, passive resistance was not an article of faith as it was to Gandhi for he was well aware of its limitations. He writes about it:

> So long as the action of the executive is peaceful and within rules of the fight, the passive resister scrupulously

> maintains his attitude of passivity, but he is not bound to do so a moment beyond. To submit to illegal or violent methods or coercion, to accept outrage and hooliganism as part of the legal procedure of the country is to be guilty of cowardice, and, by dwarfing national manhood, to sin against the divinity within ourselves and the divinity in our motherland.... Passive resistance cannot build up a strong and great nation unless it is masculine, bold and ardent in its spirit and ready at any moment and at the slightest notice supplement itself with active resistance. We do not want to develop a nation of women who know only how to suffer and not how to strike.[9]

Hence, Sri Aurobindo's passive resistance was only a tool and not a creed to be followed in all circumstances.

Sri Aurobindo on Democracy

Sri Aurobindo looked upon democracy as an ideal which provided dignity and respect to man. While explaining the democratic ideal he has written that individualism has discovered the deeper truth that the individual is not just a social unit and that his existence, rights, claim to live and grow are not established solely on his social work and function. The individual is a soul, a being who not only has to fulfil his own individual truth and law but his natural and assigned part in the truth and law of the existence. This, according to Sri Aurobindo, is the basis of the democratic tendency of the world. Elsewhere he has said that spirituality is the only politics in India and the fulfillment of the *Sanatana Dharma* is its only *Swaraj*. Sri Aurobindo has pointed out that in *Sanatana Dharma* the rights and duties lose their artificial antagonism created by a world view which makes selfishness the root of action. As a result the deep and eternal unity of the nation is regained. According to him, the very first necessary element of democratic politics is difference of opinion which has to be frank, robust and held 'firmly' and 'passionately' while the first test of political capacity in a democratic country is to tolerate these differences of opinions—no matter how strong and vehement they are—without any disruption. Democracy demands free divergence of political opinions, open propagandas and debate. The advent of democracy can be hastened by the creation of freedom of speech and thought. Forceful attempts to silence the voice or evade significant differences of opinions are anti-democratic and therefore show an incapacity for democratic politics. Sri Aurobindo also tells us:

> The democratic tendency in humanity is and has long been pressing forward victoriously to self-fulfilment and the modern attempt of the banded forces of autocracy, bureaucracy, plutocracy and theocracy to turn its march can only result in its growing stronger by the check and urging forward with greater impetuosity to its goal. It is therefore the democratic tendency and the democratic capacity which aspires to go forward and be among the leaders of the world.[10]

He further adds:

> The credit is due much more to the people themselves than to the leaders on either side, and this itself is the healthiest sign of all and the guarantee of democratic development. When the people are wiser than their leaders and wise men, the democratic future of a country is assured. Men of great gifts and strong character are often carried away by their eager perceptions and at such moments it is the sound common sense of a capable democracy that sets right the balance.[11]

In democracy there should be an ample growth of parties for such growth hints at the approaching awakening in the national mind. The lack of political parties lead to political stagnation, 'death-in-life' for such absence denotes that the intellect of the country is torpid, its feelings feeble and flaccid, the passion of sincerity has not touched its aspirations, the fervour of hope is asleep and patriotism—being an inoperative sentiment—remains confined to the intellect only. Therefore, political parties are necessary provided they have a common end which overrides their specific differences as well as 'the freedom, greatness and splendour' of the country. Sri Aurobindo also remarks that self-government is impossible without a party and hence writes that socialism is an integral part of democracy because without it,

> ...democracy would remain a tendency that never reached its fulfilment, a rule of the masses by a small aristocratic or moneyed class with the consent and votes of the masses or a tyranny of the artisan classes over the rest. Socialistic democracy is the only true democracy, for without it we cannot get the equalised and harmonised distribution of functions, each part of the community existing for the good of all and not struggling for its own separate interests, which will give humanity as a whole the necessary conditions in which it can turn its best energies to its higher development.[12]

Sri Aurobindo has advocated grass-root democracy. He has written that *Swaraj* or self-government should commence from the villages of India and he considered the organisation of villages as an indispensable work for on this task depended the organisation of a mighty, single and compact democratic nationality. He also favoured the promotion of village *samitis* and considered them "not a mere council for deliberation" but a "strong organ of executive work".[13] Such *samitis*, he has said, should set up village schools and render education to young students, take up arbitration and recover control of justice, self-protection, village sanitation, local public works and to create socio-political awareness. It is noteworthy that the *Panchayat Raj* and the *Lok Adalats* in India have been planned and established based on the patterns of democracy advised by Sri Aurobindo.

However, Sri Aurobindo was not in favour of parliamentary democracy as he considered it unsuitable for Indians. During one of his talks with his disciples on 7 April 1926 he has said: "The parliamentary form would be hardly suitable for our people. Of course, it is not necessary that you should have today the same old forms [as in ancient India]. But you can take the line of evolution and follow the bent of the genius of the race...."[14] On 27 December 1938, we find him saying: "Parliamentary Government is not suited to India...there may be one Rashtrapati at the top with considerable powers so as to secure a continuity of policy, and an assembly representative of the nation. The provinces will combine into a federation united at the top, leaving ample scope to local bodies to make laws according to their local problems."[15]

Sri Aurobindo on the Hindu-Muslim Problem

Sri Aurobindo strived for the total liberation of India from British rule. India did achieve her freedom on 15 August 1947, that is, on Sri Aurobindo's seventy-fifth birthday but along with the joy of Independence came the pain of partition. Sri Aurobindo had dreamt of a united India—a unity which would be both cultural and spiritual. To quote his own words: "Each nation is a Shakti or power of the evolving spirit in humanity and lives by the principle which it embodies. India is the Bharata Shakti, the living energy of a great spiritual conception, and fidelity to it is the very principle of her existence. For by its virtue alone she has been one of the immortal nations; this alone has been the secret of her amazing persistence and perpetual force of survival and revival."[16] Therefore, he was quite unhappy with the creation of Pakistan which took place due to the partition. In the message he gave on 15 August 1947, he said that though India had achieved her freedom she did not achieve unity. In case the communal division remained, according to Sri Aurobindo, India could be seriously weakened and crippled and there would be possibilities of civil strife, new invasions and foreign conquest. He reiterated that if the partition was not annulled the internal development and prosperity of India could be impeded and her position among the other countries of the world could be weakened. To quote his own words: "...by whatever means, in whatever way, the division must go; unity must and will be achieved, for it is necessary for the greatness of India in future."[17] He has gone deep into the heart of the problem of Hindu-Muslim unity and dug out a feasible solution. According to him, the causes and remedies of Hindu-Muslim disunity lies in the regions of the heart and mind, hence, the unity needs to be sought in the said regions. Misunderstandings which cause mutual differences should be removed by a better mutual knowledge and sympathy. He further adds:

> ...we must extend the unfaltering love of the patriot to our Musulman brother, remembering always that in

> him too Narayana dwells and to him too our Mother has given a permanent place in her bosom; but we must cease to approach him falsely or flatter out of a selfish weakness and cowardice. We believe this to be the only practical way of dealing with the difficulty. As a political question the Hindu-Mahomedan problem does not interest us at all, as a national problem it is of supreme importance. We shall make it a main part of our work to place Mahomed and Islam in a new light before our readers, to spread juster views of Mahomedan history and civilisation, to appreciate the Musulman's place in our national development and the means of harmonising his communal life with our own, not ignoring the difficulties that stand in our way for making the most of the possibilities of brotherhood and mutual understanding. Intellectual sympathy can only draw together, the sympathy of the heart can alone unite. But the one is a good preparation of the other.[18]

In some quarters, however, it is believed that Sri Aurobindo was in a way responsible for the partition of India because he had emphasised highly on Hinduism, rather Hindu nationalism, which eventually led to the creation of Pakistan. According to many scholars and historians, Sri Aurobindo's *Uttarpara Speech* (which he delivered on 30 May 1909 soon after his release from Alipore Jail) is a living testament of his strong communal bent of mind. In this famous speech, Sri Aurobindo has said:

> We speak often of the Hindu religion, of the Sanatana Dharma, but few of us really know what that religion is. Other religions are preponderatingly religions of faith and profession, but the Sanatana Dharma is life itself; it is a thing that has not so much to be believed as lived. This is the dharma that for the salvation of humanity was cherished in the seclusion of this peninsula from of old. It is to give this religion that India is rising.[19]
>
> When therefore it is said that India shall rise, it is the Sanatana Dharma that shall rise. When it is said that India shall be great, it is the Sanatana Dharma that shall be great. When it is said that India shall expand

> and extend herself, it is the Sanatana Dharma that shall expand and extend itself over the world. It is for the *dharma* and by the *dharma* that India exists. To magnify the religion means to magnify the country.[20]

"That which we call the Hindu religion is really the eternal religion, because it is the universal religion which embraces all others.... This is the one religion that can triumph over materialism by including and anticipating the discoveries of science and the speculations of philosophy. It is the one religion which impresses on mankind the closeness of God to us and embraces in its compass all the possible means by which man can approach God. It is the one religion which insists every moment on the truth which all religions acknowledge, that He is in all men and all things and that in Him we move and have our being. It is the one religion which enables us not only to understand and believe this truth but to realise it with every part of our being. It is the one religion which shows the world what the world is, that it is the *lila* of Vasudeva. It is the one religion which shows us how we can best play our part in that *lila*, its subtlest laws and its noblest rules. It is the one religion which does not separate life in any smallest detail from religion, which knows what immortality is and has utterly removed from us the reality of death.... I say that it is the Sanatana Dharma which for us is nationalism. This Hindu nation was born with the Sanatana Dharma, with it it moves and with it it grows. When the Sanatana Dharma declines, then the nation declines, and if the Sanatana Dharma were capable of perishing, with the Sanatana Dharma it would perish. The Sanatana Dharma, that is nationalism."[21]

The aforesaid speech is misinterpreted by many historians. Sri Aurobindo considered nationalism as a religion or Sanatana Dharma because to him, it was an immensely significant act of sacrifice. To him, nationalism was not just a political programme but a religion which came from God and it was a creed which the Indians were required to live. Sanatana Dharma or Eternal Religion is not a synonym of Hinduism; by Sanatana Dharma he meant the universal religion (and not the traditional Hinduism) whose internal scripture was the voice of the eternal within the hearts of many whereas its external scriptures were as much as the holy books of the Hindus, Christians and Muslims. Sri Aurobindo's concept of nationalism was never pan-Hindu but pan-Indian. Though he (as well as Bipin Chandra Pal) had opposed separate Muslim representation in the legislative councils, he did so because he was reluctant to recognise the Hindus and Muslims as permanently separate political units which would preclude the growth of a single indivisible country.

To Sri Aurobindo, India was not a mere piece of earth. He considered India a spiritual entity, a mighty power, composed of the powers of all the millions of units that constitute the nation. To quote his own words:

> The work of national emancipation is a great and holy *yajna* of which boycott, Swadeshi, national education and every other activity, great and small, are only major and minor parts. Liberty is the fruit we seek from the sacrifice and the Motherland the goddess to whom we offer it; into the seven leaping tongues of the fire of the *yajna* we must offer all that we are and all that we have, feeding the fire even with our blood and lives and happiness of our nearest and dearest; for the Motherland is a goddess who loves not a maimed and imperfect sacrifice, and freedom was never won from the gods by a grudging giver.[22]

Sri Aurobindo's contribution in the field of politics and India's struggle for freedom has been aptly described by eminent scholars in the following words:

- Kireet Joshi: "...Sri Aurobindo's own life is a flaming example of Indian nationalism, not only in its uniqueness but also in its universality. If we study the history of Indian nationalism, we shall find that he stands out as the most heroic nationalist who formulated in the most inspiring terms the true aim of Indian nationalism, during the early period of nationalist struggle and accomplished the task of fixing it in the national consciousness within a short period of two years (1906-08) through blazing pages of the *Bande Mataram*. This miracle can be regarded as an unparalleled achievement in the entire world history of nationalism."[23]

- K.R. Srinivasa Iyengar: "Barely thirty months of active politics, yet Sri Aurobindo was destined to change the whole character of political activity in India and set the freedom movement firmly towards the goal of complete national independence."[24]
- Prema Nandakumar: "He [Sri Aurobindo] was verily the gift of the Divine to India, for he came to teach, to strive, to fulfil. He taught us the meaning of political freedom, the religion of patriotism, and the need to sacrifice everything at the altar of the Motherland. He came to teach us the Truth of the Spirit, the value of perfection in work, and the wisdom of offering our works to the Divine, unmindful of personal benefit or reward. He came to preach *sanatana dharma*, the universal religion of humanity, that is the true foundation of India's political, cultural and social history."[25]
- Som P. Ranchan and K.D. Gupta: "...the realisation of God through a nation distinguishes Sri Aurobindo from the Western political thinkers. Sri Aurobindo gives a spiritual colour to his concept of nation. While in his pre-Pondicherry days he looked upon the nation as a divine *shakti* to achieve national liberty, in his post-Pondicherry days (1910-50), he enlarged his spiritual vision and looked upon the nation as a milestone in the journey to a more integral, global consciousness and organisation."[26]

III
RELEVANCE OF SRI AUROBINDO'S THOUGHTS IN POST-INDEPENDENT INDIA

To Sri Aurobindo, India was not just a country but a Mother whom he worshipped and adored, hence, he tried to spiritualise politics and raise the plea for absolute freedom to the Vedantic level. However, his political thoughts and ideology met with little acceptance in post-Independent India. Historian like Sumit Sarkar,

Romila Thapar, Bipan Chandra, Amales Tripathi and Barbara Southard have criticised Sri Aurobindo's political philosophy. According to Peter Heehs, the Leftist historians were "united in their condemnation of the mixture of religion and politics they find in Bipin Chandra [Pal] and Aurobindo."[27] Amales Tripathi considered Sri Aurobindo's 'messianic nationalism' as an 'unnatural blend of religion and politics' which led to recoil and communalism. Barbara Southard opines that the Shakta-Vedanta imagery of Bipin Chandra Pal and Sri Aurobindo which was meant to appeal to an upper-caste Hindu constituency and their 'lack of concern with secular issues' led to the creation of circumstances 'conductive to counter-mobilisation among Muslims and some lower caste Hindus' eventually resulting in communal riots and lasting religious divisions.

Let's conclude by quoting a passage from Sri Aurobindo's article *The Hindu Sabha* published in the *Karmayogin* on 6 November 1909 in which we find him opposing the concept of Hindu nationalism and explaining the necessity of an absolute Indian nationalism:

> ...the country, the Swadesh, which must be the base and fundament of our nationality, is India, a country where Mahomedan and Hindu live intermingled and side by side. What geographical base can a Hindu nationality possess? Maharashtra and Rajasthan are no longer separate geographical units but merely provincial divisions of a single country. The very first requisite of a Hindu nationalism is wanting. The Mahomedans base their separateness and their refusal to regard themselves as Indians first and Mahomedans afterwards on the existence of great Mahomedan nations to which they feel themselves more akin, in spite of our common birth and blood, than to us. Hindus have no such resource. For good or evil, they are bound to the soil and to the soil alone. They cannot deny their Mother, neither can they mutilate her. Our ideal therefore is an Indian Nationalism, largely Hindu in its spirit and traditions, because the Hindu made the land and the people and persists, by the greatness of his past, his civilisation and

> his culture and his invincible virility, in holding it, but wide enough also to include the Moslem and his culture and traditions and absorb them into itself. It is possible that the Mahomedan may not recognise the inevitable future and may prefer to throw himself into the opposite scale. If so, the Hindu, with what little Mahomedan help he may get, must win Swaraj both for himself and the Mahomedan in spite of that resistance. There is a sufficient force and manhood in us to do a greater and more difficult task than that, but we lack unity, brotherhood, intensity of single action among ourselves. It is to the creation of that unity, brotherhood and intensity that the Hindu Sabha should direct its whole efforts. Otherwise we must reject it as a disruptive and not a creative agency.[28]

Notes

1. *Complete Works of Sri Aurobindo*, Vol. 6, p. 21, Sri Aurobindo Ashram Publication Department, 2002.
2. Prema Nandakumar, Sri Aurobindo, p. 15, Publication Division of Ministry of Information and Broadcasting, August 1972.
3. *Complete Works of Sri Aurobindo*, Vol. 7, p. 876, Sri Aurobindo Ashram Publication Department, 2002.
4. *Ibid.*, p. 906.
5. *Ibid.*, Vol. 6, p. 282.
6. *Ibid.*, pp. 278-79.
7. *Ibid.*, Vol. 19, p. 40, Sri Aurobindo Ashram Publication Department, 1997.
8. *Ibid.*, p. 42.
9. *Ibid.*, Vol. 6, pp. 294-96.
10. *Ibid.*, Vol. 8, p. 197.
11. *Ibid.*, p. 198.
12. *Complete Works of Sri Aurobindo*, Vol. 6, p. 684.
13. *Complete Works of Sri Aurobindo*, Vol. 7, p. 1049, Sri Aurobindo Ashram Publication Department, 2002.
14. A.B. Purani, *Evening Talks with Sri Aurobindo*, p. 291, Sri Aurobindo Ashram Publication Department, 2007.
15. *Ibid.*, p. 585.

16. *Complete Works of Sri Aurobindo*, Vol. 20, p. 57, Sri Aurobindo Ashram Publication Department, 1997.
17. Sri Aurobindo, *Autobiographical Notes and Other Writings of Historical Interest*, p. 479, Sri Aurobindo Ashram Publication Department, 2006.
18. *Complete Works of Sri Aurobindo*, Vol. 8, p. 31, Sri Aurobindo Ashram Publication Department, 1997.
19. *Ibid*., p. 6.
20. *Ibid*., p. 10.
21. *Ibid*., pp. 11-12.
22. *Ibid*., Vol. 6, p. 302.
23. Kireet Joshi, *Philosophy and Yoga of Sri Aurobindo and Other Essays*, p. 71, The Mother's Institute of Research, 2003.
24. K.R. Srinivasa Iyengar, *Sri Aurobindo: A Biography and a History*, p. 169, Sri Aurobindo Ashram, 1972.
25. Prema Nandakumar, *Sri Aurobindo*, p. 2.
26. Som P. Ranchan and K.D. Gupta, *Sri Aurobindo As a Political Thinker: An Interdisciplinary Study*, p. 69, Konark Publishers Pvt. Ltd., 1988.
27. Peter Heehs, *Nationalism, Terrorism, Communalism: Essays in Modern Indian History*, p. 104, Oxford University Press, 2005.
28. *Collected Works of Sri Aurobindo*, Vol. 8, pp. 305-06.

Bibliography

1. *Collected Works of Sri Aurobindo*, Vols. 1, 6, 7, 8, 19 and 20, Sri Aurobindo Ashram Publication Department.
2. Sri Aurobindo, *Autobiographical Notes and Other Writings of Historical Interest*, Sri Aurobindo Ashram Publication Department.
3. Prema Nandakumar, *Sri Aurobindo*, Publication Division of Ministry of Information and Broadcasting.
4. A.B. Purani, *Evening Talks with Sri Aurobindo*, Sri Aurobindo Ashram Publication Department.
5. Kireet Joshi, *Philosophy and Yoga of Sri Aurobindo and Other Essays*, The Mother's Institute of Research.
6. K.R. Srinivasa Iyengar, *Sri Aurobindo: A Biography and a History*, Sri Aurobindo Ashram.

7. Som P. Ranchan and K.D. Gupta, *Sri Aurobindo As a Political Thinker: An Interdisciplinary Study*, Konark Publishers Pvt. Ltd.
8. Peter Heehs, *Nationalism, Terrorism, Communalism: Essays in Modern Indian History*, Oxford University Press.
9. Sumit Sarkar, *The Swadeshi Movement in Bengal*, New Delhi, 1971.
10. Bipan Chandra, *Communalism in Modern India*, 1987.
11. Amales Tripathi, *Sri Aurobindo: A Study of Messianic Nationalism* in *The Calcutta Historical Journal*, 4 (1979).
12. Barbara Southard, *The Political Strategy of Aurobindo Ghosh: The Utilization of Hindu Religious Symbolism and the Problem of Political Mobilization in Bengal* in *Modern Asian Studies*, 14 (1980).

17

Jinnah's Political Thought (1876-1948)

Hitendra K. Patel

> "We are all sons of this land. We have to live together. We have to work together and whatever our differences may be, let us at any rate not create more bad blood.... Believe me there is no progress of India until the Musalmans and Hindus are united, and let no logic, philosophy, or squabble stand in the way of coming to a compromise." —*Saiyid*, 1945: 429

> "I am essentially a practical man; I have been in practical politics for over a quarter of a century. The words 'Nationalism' and 'Nationalist' have undergone many changes in their definition and significance... within the honest meaning of the term, I shall remain a nationalist."
>
> —Jinnah's Speech at Osmania University, Hyderabad, September 28, 1939

I
INTRODUCTION

Muhammad Ali Jinnah successfully campaigned to be the sole political spokesman of Indian Muslims. As a result of his campaign a new nation—Pakistan (which later became Pakistan and Bangladesh) came into existence which was unimaginable till 1930. This successful political campaign has a profound impact on the way the man has been seen after his death in 1948. In Pakistan, he is seen as the father of nation and in India he is no less than a political villain, who destroyed the vision of a powerful united, secular Indian nation which was espoused by the greats like Gandhi, Nehru and Maulana Abul Kalam Azad. It is an absorbing story of a life time in which a Western educated secular national man, who was deeply influenced by liberal and secular ideas of John Morley (a follower of John Stuart Mill) whom young Jinnah admired, who did not support the principle of separate electorates, and who refused to be a member of All India Muslim League till 1913 was to become a man who was the father of a nation which was founded on religious basis. A study of his political thought can be useful to understand how this transformation took place and how he allowed his earlier ideas to be subverted by his later political ideas guided by his political compulsions. As ideas should be understood in the contexts which generated them, the history of the context should be an integral to any study of political thoughts of Jinnah.

There cannot be any dispute that "Jinnah began his political career firmly inside the tradition of moderate politics" and till 1906 he was "steeped in the liberalism of Dadabhai Naoroji and Gopal Krishna Gokhale...in the liberal wing of the Indian National Congress." Ayesha Jalal, author of highly influential biography of Jinnah has correctly said that, "Jinnah began his political career firmly inside the tradition of moderate politics". This was natural for him considering his background.

He was born on 25 December 1876 in a family of a Khoja Shia merchant at Karachi which had migrated from Kathiawad (Gujarat). He was sent to London in 1892, at the age of sixteen, to get training in business by Graham Shipping and Trading Company where his father was associated. Before going there his mother, afraid of the probability of his son marrying an English girl, got him married to Emibai, a fourteen year old girl. The background of Jinnah was typically Gujarati. "His marriage procession was led by drumbeaters, women joining the procession, singing Gujarati wedding songs and sprinkling rice on the way, which was a typical local Gujarati Hindu tradition." Accounts of his early life reveal that his background had very little to make him a conservative person.

In London, after some time in apprenticeship of business, he switched to legal studies, but due to his indifferent schooling (he was taught Gujarati by a private tutor and had attended a *madarasa* and he had studied in an English medium school for some time) and weak grounding in the English language he had difficulties in qualifying for it, after three attempts. But, Young Jinnah adjusted with the new situation and he took to the English language, Western dress and Western mode of living. As B.R. Nanda has observed—"Jinnah's anglicism was uninhibited and permanent. He aspired to the lifestyle of an upper-class Englishman, achieved it and revelled in it." He changed his name from Jinnahbhai to Jinnah.

Young Jinnah was inspired by Dadabhai Naoroji and other liberal leaders. About Naoroji he spoke very highly all his life. He took keen interest in the political activities and the theatre in London during his three and half years stay there. He was so keen taking to the stage that he wrote to his father that he was leaving law career for theatre! Later, he took his law study seriously and did reasonably well. In London, he got the chance to listen to the speeches of great politicians like Gladstone, Lord Morley, Chamberlain, Balfour and others. He imbibed their style of parliamentary debate.

While Jinnah was in London his mother and his young wife died. He decided to return to India and settle down. At the young age of twenty, in 1896, Jinnah started his career as a lawyer of Bombay High Court. His early days were very difficult, but once he was noticed by an Englishman he moved ahead as a successful lawyer and his income rose to ₹ 20,000 per month during the war years. M.C. Chagla, his junior for six years, who later became the Chief Justice of the Bombay High Court has described him as a "poor lawyer but a superb advocate". Chagla admired Jinnah but he wrote about him, that, "I have never come across any man who had less humanity in his character than Jinnah. He was cold and unemotional, and apart from law and politics, he had no other interests. I do not think he ever read a serious book in his life. His staple food was newspapers, briefs and law books." By 1904, Jinnah has caught the attention of eminent Congressmen like Pherozeshah

Mehta. He came to prominence when he opposed the separate electorates for Muslims in 1906. In 1906, when Naoroji came from London to preside the session of the Congress, Jinnah acted as his secretary. It is important to note that in the session when a Muslim delegate demanded reservations for 'educationally backward classes', Jinnah insisted that the Muslims of India should be treated like the Hindu community, "the foundation upon which the Indian National Congress is based" to use his phrase. He criticised the formation of the All India Muslim League which made him a champion of unalloyed nationalism.

Although Jinnah was close to the moderates, he was also drawn towards the great extremist Congress leader Tilak. He acted as a legal support for Tilak and he filed his bail application when Tilak was charged with sedition. Jinnah expressed his displeasure over the judge's verdict by boycotting the dinner hosted in Judge's honour for receiving the knighthood. He believed that the judge obtained the honour by giving a "savage" sentence to a nationalist leader to please the government.

II
EVOLUTION OF JINNAH'S POLITICAL THOUGHT

There are two theories about Jinnah's political ideas of this period. One theory suggests that he was a liberal and he understood that the communal difference between the Hindus and the Muslims was against the national movement. To him, the national movement under the Congress was against the British imperialism and the communal differences posed a challenge to the secular and egalitarian foundations of a modern state which was dear to Jinnah. He remained with these ideas at least till 1916 when he tried to bring the Congress and the Muslim League together by Lucknow Pact. There is another theory which suggests that he was conscious of the fact that the Muslim leadership was overwhelmingly in favour of separate electorates and this had the crucial support of British officials. He was aware that once separate electorates were introduced he would have to fall back on the votes of the Muslims. So, by 1909 he was compelled to change his stand of 1906. He attended a meeting of the Council of the Muslim League and he was elected to the Imperial Legislative Council with Muslim leaders' support. And, once he entered the Imperial Legislative Council he sought to redress a long standing Muslim grievance on the validation of Muslim *Waqfs*. He further mellowed down in 1912 session of the Congress.

Both of these theories are based on solid evidences. By intent Jinnah was a liberal Congressman but his political compulsion made him keep Muslim League leaders happy. B.R. Nanda, who underlines his compulsions of this phase, has rightly mentioned that, "...while claiming to be a Congressman; he had to make a place for himself in the Muslim League." He did not attend the Congress sessions of 1909, 1911, 1912 and 1914. Meanwhile, in 1913 he enrolled himself as a member of the League.

Political thought of liberal Jinnah had now came face to face to the realities of politics. He wanted to become a 'Muslim Gokhale' but the reality was that he had to move ahead in politics as a Muslim leader and he had to get the support of the Muslims. He attempted to bring the League and the Congress between 1913 and 1916. He, along with Mazhar-ul-Haq, the Raja of Mahmudabad, Wazir Hasan (referred as "young group") and Fazl-ul-Haq, manoeuvred to get elected as the president of the League (earlier he was successful in getting the Raja of Mahmudabad the president replacing the Aga Khan) and convinced the Congress leadership to agree to Lucknow Pact which meant the Congress leaders conceded separate electorates and agreed to the principle of minorities being represented in such a way that they would not have to be afraid of the majority domination.

Jinnah was hailed as a nationalist leader and he was confident enough to say in his presidential address to the League session that, "The Mussalmans of India would be false to themselves and the traditions of their past if they do not share to the new hope that is moving India's patriotic sons today or had they failed to response to the call of their country."

Jinnah's growing reputation as a leader was being acknowledged now and he was articulating as a confident national leader who did not think in terms of a Muslim leader. In September, 1917, he said that the open competition should be the criteria and no community should be given any preference or reservation. At this stage Jinnah believed that the path of the Indians towards self-government was being blocked by three factors: the British bureaucracy, European commercial community and the military establishment. To him, the bureaucracy wrongly enjoyed the monopoly of power, the Europeans are wrongly enjoy the monopolistic control over Indian commerce and the military establishment unjustifiably denied Indians commissioned ranks.

At this stage, Jinnah was so confident that he did not hesitate to take head on collusion with Lord Willingdon, the Governor of Bombay, as a supporter of Home Rule movement, culminating in the anti-Willingdon demonstration and raising ₹ 65000 to build 'Jinnah People's Memorial Hall' in the compound of the Indian National Congress. Jinnah was seen by Willingdon as an "extremist" Congress leaders like Tilak and Annie Besant "who have no feeling of what is their duty to the (British) Empire in its hour of crisis (due to the World War)."

Jinnah opposed the drive to enlist the support of Indians for the British war efforts. He wrote to the then Governor General, Chelmsford:

> We cannot ask our Indian young men to fight for principle, the application of which is denied for their own country. A subject race cannot fight for others with the heart and energy with which a free race can fight.

Jinnah also vehemently opposed the Rowlatt Bill.

At this stage, his voice was anti-British and he was sincerely hoping to get more prominence at the national stage of Indian politics. Jinnah's status as a national leader reached to its height in the second half of 1918.

Coming of Gandhi changed the political environment and this change affected Jinnah immensely. Gandhi's approach to politics was qualitatively different from Jinnah and soon it became evident that the constitutionalism of Jinnah was no longer as attractive to common people as the non-violent popular politics of Gandhi. In December 1920, Jinnah faced the challenge of new politics of Gandhi. Gandhi moved a resolution "for the change of the creed of the Congress", proposing the *Swaraj* as the goal it meant to Jinnah an attempt of the Congress to sever the connection with the British government. He opposed this. He was heckled during his speech by people who cared little about his sentiments. It hurt Jinnah and he left the meeting in protest.

According to most of the historians this was the defining moment which made all leaders who dared to oppose Gandhi somewhat less influential in the coming years. Jinnah was one among them.

B.R. Nanda has very aptly summed up that, "he (Jinnah) had literally been hounded out of national politics. His labours of a decade had been destroyed in one day.... After the Nagpur session, Jinnah had literally become a political orphan."

Jinnah's opposition to Gandhian policies was largely principled. They respected each other, but the constitutional liberalism with which Jinnah had grown up with since his days in London did not approve of the populist activism Gandhi stood for. Jinnah was in favour of political class anchoring the political struggle at national level. He said in early 1920s why he found Gandhian approach unacceptable:

> If they (Gandhi and his supporters) were going to regulate everything in the country by the doctrine of non-violent non-cooperation, he (Jinnah) was afraid they were forgetting the human nature.... Gandhi's programme was based on the doctrine of soul force and it was an essentially spiritual movement.... It was not a political programme.

Jinnah's political thought guided him to believe that the movement like *Khilafat* was going to be unsuccessful as this was invoking religious and not political considerations. He was not off the mark on this, and historians must give credit for him to stand on his ground risking his political career against the tide of Gandhian wave.

Jinnah was opposed to Gandhian approach of giving religious leaders the centre stage in politics. To him, giving religious leaders preference over the political leadership of the Muslims was not a correct strategy. The policy of the Congress to woo the religious leaders for the national movement would lead to a situation where the leaders with obscurantist and pan-Islamic ideas would be more important. In Jinnah's view the modern national leaders like him should be given preference over them. He constantly sought to convince the Congress that he, not the leaders like Mohammad Ali or Abul Kalam Azad, needed to be seen the leader of the Muslims but, the Congress saw it differently. He tried to consolidate his position by asserting his leadership as a Muslim League leader. The League had gone with *Khilafat* movement and a new group of loyalists—Shafi group was up against Jinnah. But, Jinnah managed to keep his position intact and he was a key player as the leader of Independent Party which played a key role in the post-*Khilafat* Indian politics along with Swaraj Party, led by C.R. Das and Motilal Nehru. Jinnah's political ideas were different from Gandhi over communal problem of India. On this his ideas were very clear:

> What we want...is...mobilization of politically-minded people in India and it must be done purely on political lines and as far as possible religion should be separated from politics. Then alone it is possible for Hindus and Muslims and other communities to work together with one sole burning feeling of patriotism.

He was categorical that, he was "a nationalist first, a nationalist second and a nationalist last."

The changes taking place in the nature of Muslim politics had also affected Jinnah adversely. During the 1920s was a period of transition in Muslim politics. The emerging Muslim trading community of Bombay supported the leadership of Muslim community. Now, there emerged the politics of the Muslim majority (the Punjab and Bengal) and minority provinces.

The Majority provinces leadership was focussing on the regional politics and they were not eager to focus on national level politics of Muslims. The most vibrant politicians of Muslim community who were interested in national level politics were from the United Provinces. And, the leaders of this province were more comfortable dealing with the Congress leadership than their own community big landlords and elites. Jinnah was clearly the leader of the elites at this stage and hence he was at a disadvantage. The dislike of Jinnah for the mass politics was obvious. Jawaharlal Nehru has also made this observation that Jinnah did not like mass politics.

Jinnah continued with his political line of nationalism. Even in 1925 he expressed his dislike of separate electorates, but stressed the strength of Muslim feeling in its favour. He worked on the Hindu-Muslim accord for which he still had a political space left and in 1925 he somewhat changed his own stand of Lucknow Pact days. In 1927, he convened a conference of Muslim leaders in Delhi in which a joint electorate proposal was mooted. This was accepted by the Congress and the Hindu *Mahasabha*. Meanwhile, the Simon Commission came and Jinnah favoured boycott of the Simon Commission. In a way, 1927 brought back lime light on Jinnah once again.

One of the major landmarks in Jinnah's political career was his formulation of 'Fourteen Points', which remained the main plank of Muslim politics in India for the next ten years, came after the Congress' Nehru (Motilal) Report. Nehru report advocated full provincial status for the Muslim areas of the North Western Frontier and Sindh but it failed to satisfy the Muslim leadership. Jinnah's Fourteen Points demanded a federal system with complete autonomy and residuary powers vested in the provinces, separate electoral bodies and weightage for the Muslims and safeguards for protection and promotion of Muslim education, language, religion, personal laws and *waqfs*.

The Congress and the Hindu leaders like Malaviya did not accept these demands. During the Round Table Conferences held in London in 1930 and 1931 Jinnah got "disillusioned about the prospect of Muslims receiving a fair deal from the Congress" and he found himself and his ideas ignored. He was so dejected by the political developments and affected by the death of his second wife (who was a daughter of a Parsee layer) whom he was very attached that he left the country and settled in London in early 1930s. But, later, he was persuaded by the League leaders to come back and lead the Muslims of the country. After his return he was a different person politically.

The political situation had also somewhat changed. A historian has pointed out that, "With the increasing involvement of the industrial and mercantile class, the all India organisation became a possibility in the 1930s." The Muslim politics continued without Jinnah for some time but it was obvious that he was the only national leader of stature who could bring different sections of Muslims together at the national level.

After his return he did not get much time to make necessary political preparation and his party could manage to win 108 (about 23 per cent) seats out of total of 485 Muslim seats in the elections held in 1937. According to some scholars the differences between the Congress and the League might have been minimised had the Congress would have understood that the League could not be counted as a lost political force on the basis of their electoral performance of 1937. The Congress insisted to accept only such Muslims who would join the Congress was considered by the League as aimed at its elimination, and at the liquidation of independent Muslim political life in India.

The experiences of living under the Congress led governments backed by the Muslim League propaganda created bad blood between the Hindus and Muslims in many parts of India. This was seen as the failure of Jinnah's attempts to project the Muslim League as the party of the Muslims of India by the Congress and there was an air of confidence among the high command of the Congress not to negotiate with Jinnah at his terms. The negotiations of a share in government of the United Provinces and Bombay failed and these failures forced Jinnah to move towards the political line he followed for a decade: the campaign for a separate state for the Muslims of this country—Pakistan. Jinnah was not serious about the idea of a separate state when it was conceived, in ambiguous terms, by Mohammad Iqbal, the great poet, at Allahabad in 1930, but forced by his failure in 1937 elections and some related developments, he drifted towards the idea of Pakistan, an idea which was articulated by Rehmat Ali in 1933. The 'Two nation theory' was elaborated by Jinnah in January 1940 in an article in *Time Tide*. This was a defining moment of Indian history.

Jinnah's utterances after this point were qualitatively different from the earlier phase. He was not liked by the provincial leaders of the Punjab and Bengal which were Muslim majority states, but he, through his skilful political strategy and sheer force of his personality, managed to push forward his political agenda.

His change of ideas was pronounced in his utterances after 1937. Some of which can be considered here. After the failure of negotiations between the League and the Congress over power sharing in Bombay he said that the Muslim League would have no say in the government of any province in India where Congress was in majority. He said, "That is the end. There is nothing more to do except to get a state of our own for the Muslims of the country." Like a man possessed, he moved ahead on his new political agenda, he went against his own ideas of years. He said, "Religion alone is a cohesive for the idea of nationality."

He tried to rationalise his demand of a separate nation for the Muslims in following words:

> They [Islam and Hinduism] are not religions in the strict sense of the word, but are, in fact, different and distinct social orders, and it is a dream that the Hindus and Muslims can ever evolve a common nationality, and this misconception of one Indian nation has gone far beyond the limits and is the cause of most of your troubles and will lead India to destruction if we fail to revise our notions in time. The Hindus and Muslims belong to two different religious philosophies, social customs, literatures. They neither intermarry nor interdine together and, indeed, they belong to two distinct civilisations which are based mainly on conflicting ideas and conceptions. Their outlooks on life and of life are different. It is quite clear that Hindus and Musalmans derive their inspiration from different sources of history. They have different epics, different heroes, and different episodes. Very often the hero of one is a foe of the other

> and, likewise, their victories and defeats overlap. To yoke together two such nations under a single state, one as a numerical minority and the other as a majority, must lead to the growing discontent and final destruction of any fabric that may be so built up for the government of such a state.

He wrote:

> The British people...sometimes forget the religious wars of their own history, and today consider religion as private and personal matter between man and God. This can never be the case in Hinduism and Islam, for both these religions are definite social codes which govern not so much man's relation with his God as man's relation with his neighbor. They govern not only his law and culture but every aspect of his social life and such religions, essentially exclusive, completely preclude the merging of identity and unity of thought on which Western democracy is based and inevitably bring about vertical rather than horizontal divisions democracy envisages.

In 1940, at Lahore, Jinnah saw a future chance of peaceful coexistence only in the division of the subcontinent, for "the rivalry and the natural desire and efforts on the part of one to dominate the social order and establish political supremacy over the other in the government of the country will disappear."

In 1942, in Delhi, Jinnah declared: "Musalmans are a nation, and they must have their homelands, their territory and their state." He added, further, "that since the Indian Muslims constituted a nation by themselves, it was for them alone to determine their future."

He went on to accept that for Muslims the religious fraternity was more important than territorial nationalism. He said, that, "A Muslim of one country has far more sympathies with a Muslim living in another country than with a non-Muslim living in the same country."

Jinnah in his own way sought to argue that democracy and Islamic ideas were compatible. Somehow, he never really edit out the charm of democracy which he had admired since his London days, but his interpretation was different: "Islam and its idealism have taught us democracy." In 1946, he said, "What we are aiming at? It is not theocracy. It is not for theocratic state."

By 1943, the Muslim League had got control over the Muslim majority provinces and formed ministries. By 1945, the Muslim League had turned into a mass movement. In the Central Assembly the League won all 30 Muslim seats, and in 1945-46 elections 439 out of 494 seats reserved for the Muslims in the provincial assemblies. In the Punjab, the League got 75 seats and the opposition the Unionist Party got only 10 seats. In the minority province the League got 54 out of 64 seats. In Bombay it won all Muslim seats uncontested.

With the passage of time the chance of Muslim League and the Congress agreeing to a compromise to an idea of United India was becoming less and less. Still, a moment came when there could have been a way out, when Cabinet Mission came. Aziz Ahmad has noted that, "Jinnah went against the consensus of Muslim India in accepting the Cabinet Mission's proposal", but the Congress hesitated, due to Assam leaders' wish to get the region included in the Hindu zone, and Jinnah decided to change his position citing the Congress hesitation as an excuse. This was the last chance of reconciliation which was wasted, believe many. This commission had come in March, 1946 and it had proposed a three zone federation in All India Union Government, whereby India was to be divided into three zones—A (North West Provinces with Muslim majority), B (states with Hindu majority) and C (Assam and Bengal, with a slight Muslim majority).

The agreement could not be possible and, finally, in 1946, the League managed to get the necessary support from the Muslims of the country and the Congress and the British authorities were not favourable to him. On June 1947, the Congress and the Muslim League accepted Lord Mountbatten's plan for partitioning India into two sovereign states—India and Pakistan. Thus, the claim of Jinnah as the sole spokesman of the Muslims of India was finally accepted.

After Pakistan was created, Jinnah was hailed as undisputed leader of the new state. With no political adversaries ahead, Jinnah found himself in a situation where he could formulate his own policies without bothering about the pressures of keeping his claim as the sole spokesman of the Muslims. He came of his own, and tried to see the new Pakistan as a state which will be based on the democratic principles. He said that, "Pakistan was not going to be ruled by priests with a divine mission. We have many non-Muslims—Hindus, Christians and Parsis—but they are all Pakistanis. They will enjoy the same rights and privileges as any other citizen and will play their rightful part in the affairs of Pakistan."

He gave a secular speech in Pakistan parliament which amused people. If this was his aim why did he led the separate homeland for the Muslims, was the question for many. A part of his famous speech is worth consideration:

> ...if we want to make this great state of Pakistan happy and prosperous we should wholly and solely concentrate on the well-being of the people, and specially of the masses and the poor. If you will work in cooperation, forgetting the past, burying the hatchet, you are bound to succeed. If you change your past and work in a spirit that every one of you, no matter to what community he belongs, no matter what relations he had with you in the past, no matter what is his colour, caste or creed, is first, second and last a citizen of this State with equal rights, privileges and obligations, there will be no end to the progress you will make.

I cannot overemphasise it too much. We shall begin to work in that spirit and in course of time all these angularities of the majority and minority communities, the Hindu community and Muslim community...will vanish. Indeed, if you ask me, this has been the hindrance in the way of India to attain its freedom and independence and but for this we would have been free people long ago.

Therefore, we must learn a lesson from this. You are free, you are free to go to your temples. You are free to go your mosques or any other place of worship in this State of Pakistan. You may belong to any other religion or caste or creed; that has nothing to do with the business of the State.... You will find that in course of time Hindus will cease to be Hindus and Muslims would cease to be Muslims, not in the religious sense, because that is the personal faith of each individual, but in the political sense as citizens of the State.

Jinnah was a progressive man if we take his social ideas into consideration. He was one who did not hesitate to comment on the social problems for Hindu society as well. He supported social reform, opposed caste system (which he believed was given the legitimacy by Brahmanical ideology) and supported the Hindu Marriage Validity Bill which aimed to break the caste orthodoxy. Jinnah had supported Sharada Bill which some Muslim clericals was anti-Islamic. Scholars like Saad R. Khairi has written on his journey from Indian nationalism to Muslim nationhood and had underlined the influence of modern ideas in Jinnah's thoughts.

Stanely Wolpert, the biographer of Jinnah, has argued that, "(Jinnah) remained a great civil libertarian, always out-spoken in defence of individual rights and equal justice."

S.K. Alqama, a Pakistani scholar, has summed up that his political philosophy can be divided into four stages: First, the nationalist phase (till 1920); second, between 1920 and 1930; third, 1937-47; and, fourth, after 1947. In the first phase, he was influenced by four factors: nineteenth century liberalism, metropolitan flavour, mercantile milieu of Bombay of which Jinnah was a respectable member; and, his close contact with the Parsi community. Jinnah remained comfortable with the Congress politics till it remained true to liberal constitutional methods of protest, which gave primary importance to educated political class, he was hailed as a great ambassador of Hindu-Muslim unity, a nationalist Indian and he was seen as a 'Muslim Gokhale'. With the coming of Gandhi a new brand of popular politics began which put the old guards in discomfort. A new Muslim leadership also emerged, of which Jinnah was initially the leader, which went with the Gandhian mode of protests and this left to leaders of the earlier phase the option to either follow Gandhi or become somewhat irrelevant at national politics. Unlike some others like Motilal Nehru, Jinnah decided to oppose the Gandhian mode of agitational politics involving masses.

In the second phase, Jinnah remained an intelligent negotiator as the Muslim League leader with the Congress and the way the Congress and the nation gave importance to Jinnah's Fourteen Points as a response to Nehru's report showed that he was an important political figure in 1927-28. But, by 1930 Jinnah lost hope in the process of negotiation with the high command of the Congress and he left the politics of India and went to England. It was seen as the end of his political career. But, soon the Muslim League realised that without him the party could not go ahead, and he was persuaded to come back and take the command of the League. When Jinnah came back, the politics has changed, and the talk of a separate homeland of the Muslims for India was in the air. Jinnah, now a changed man was more determined and ready to take on the Congress on popular political level. After initial setbacks in the elections of 1937, Jinnah decided to mobilise the Muslim masses for the creation of a separate homeland for the Muslims of India. By the end of the War, he was powerful enough to claim that he was the leader of the Muslims of the land.

In the last phase, which witnessed extraordinary communal violence, which must have troubled Jinnah, he somewhat reverted back to his liberal ideas where the Pakistan which he had created was to follow the democratic path.

For people who loved and followed him, he was the father of the new nation. His death was mourned by millions. A million people joined when his death procession began. But he was seen as a man who caused the death of millions by cleverly mobilising the Muslims on the basis of religion. He was projected as a man who allowed himself to be used as a stooge of British, who opposed 1942 movement, who gave the dreadful call of 'Direct Action' giving licence to kill people of other religion, did everything possible not to allow the Congress leadership to come up with a plan to keep India united and who used his clout to make things difficult for the Congress when the interim government led by Nehru started working. The way he replaced Muslim leaders who favoured solution by leaders who followed him blindly during the negotiations clearly revealed that he was bent on dividing the nation. He allowed his liberal self to be completely dominated by his political ambition. He never liked religious ideas and people but he consciously used Islamic rhetoric, symbols and other tactics to gain political clout over the millions of Muslims who followed him.

These extreme views are not objective assessment of Jinnah's ideas. Ayesha Jalal has come up with a well-researched book to see Jinnah differently. She has argued that Muslim economic interests wanted a share of the surplus and did not necessarily favour the kind of "separatist" solution that was eventually imposed by the complex negotiation process which was dominated by the Congress. To Jalal, the Muslim League under Jinnah aimed to balance the conflicting interests of Muslims in majority and minority provinces in an effort to win a share of power at the all-India centre once the British quit. She puts the blame on the Congress for not conceding to the "real" demands of the Muslim League by calling for partition of Bengal and the Punjab and giving it exclusive control of the all-India centre. Jalal has forcefully argue that, "The fear of a powerful centre dominated by the Congress had been the main reason why the Muslim-majority province politicians had rallied behind Jinnah and the League." This line of argument has some merit also as the provincial leaders did not like Jinnah much. One should remember that in 1940 when the Lahore Resolution was introduced a Bengali leader Fazlul Huq had called for the formation of two Pakistan. It was the complex negotiation process which made Jinnah the sole spokesman of the Muslim community. Historians have argued that when Mountbatten came in 1947, it was not clear which way the tide would turn. The British had all three options open: first, they could transfer the power to duly constituted government of a united India; second, they could transfer power to India and Pakistan; and, third, could handover power to separate provinces. So, Ayesha Jalal makes a point that, "Jinnah's predicament was cruel. He had neither party organisation nor resources to direct a movement which the more formidable it looked the less he controlled." Jalal has brilliantly summed up the predicament of Jinnah: "Jinnah had his own priorities savaged tooth and claw by unthinking mob, fired by blood and lust, fear and greed. Ironically, and unfairly, horrors which lie so close to the surface of India have been laid at the door of this man of orderly constitutional advance, blamed upon his 'Pakistan' and upon the irreconcilable differences between Muslims and Hindus which his own career had consistently tried to bridge."

He was never a stooge of the British. Wolpert has rightly observed that he always believed in self-rule, reflecting perhaps, the interests of the Muslim industrialists, who felt constrained by colonial economic policies and preferred self-rule. Jinnah had a healthy respect for entrepreneurial skills of Parsis and he wished that Muslims should also learn from them. His sister, who was very close to him, and who looked after him, particularly after the death of his wife, has written an interesting article titled—'A Business Became a Barrister'. He started his career, as mentioned earlier, to become a businessman, and he was supported by the business community of Bombay. It is said that he was of the opinion that if some money comes to a Muslim's way he would spend that while a Hindu in his place would save the money.

Aziz Ahmad has made an interesting observation about Jinnah: "The secret of the success of Jinnah's leadership of Muslim India lay in essence in exactly the opposite of what appears to be the situation. He did not lead, but was led by the Muslim consensus. His role was that of a sincere and clear headed lawyer who could formulate and articulate in precise constitutional terms what his client really wanted."

Like a practical politician, he was able to use his skills to suit the political demands of his liking. It is true that he showed his basically democratic intent in his famous 'secular' speech which impressed people like Swami Ranganathananda, Lal Krishna Advani and scholars like Ajeet Jawed, a political scientist from Delhi University, who wrote *Jinnah: Secular and Nationalist* the fact remains that Jinnah allowed his politics to prevail over his ideas. Ramchandra Guha has written: "On his first visit to Dhaka, the governor general of Pakistan, Mohammad Ali Jinnah, told his Bengali audience that they would have to take to Urdu sooner or later." Jinnah said—"Let me make it very clear to you that the State Language of Pakistan is going to be Urdu and no other language.... Without one State language, no nation can remain tied up solidly together and function."

III
RELEVANCE OF JINNAH'S POLITICAL THOUGHT

Any study of Jinnah's political thought must keep the political context in which he operated. This speech, quoted below, will, however, keep scholars engaged thinking over why the "Muslim Gokhale", a liberal nationalist, became the father of an Islamic state by the historical forces.

One can say that Jinnah was able to achieve the Pakistan at the cost of going against his own ideology. He was too modern to be the architect of a *Sharia* led Islamic State of Pakistan after this new country came into existence. The Islamist leaders like Mausudi had all along maintained that there was nothing Islamic in Jinnah and the Muslim League. It was natural that Jinnah had to please his followers, which he managed to do for some time largely due to his stature as the creator of Pakistan, and not to go against his own modern ideology. These antagonistic forces could not go together and the Pakistan has not been able to resolve this in the last 67 years. For many, Pakistan, is a failed state. For this failure Jinnah has been criticised as he was the man who created Pakistan and tried to make it a democratic state. Rafiq Zakaria has rightly pointed out that, "If Pakistan was the culmination of the struggle for a Muslim nation, then clearly secularism was somewhat inappropriate ideology for it."

Jinnah failed at two levels: First, to believe that he would be able to guide his lieutenants would use the Islamic unity factor to keep the nation united; and second, the divisions within the new born country would be resolved in due course of time. He tried to dissolve the Muslim League and transform it into the Pakistan National League, convince the Indian Muslim League leaders and supporters to accept the national boundary, and try to follow the laws which the British had introduced in India and thus tried to follow the Turkish model of development of an Islamic state. But, he and his lieutenants failed. Many of his followers realised and privately confessed that Muslims were the worst sufferers of the partition. He, in a way, shared the wrong notion with the Indian leaders like Patel and Nehru that once the partition was accepted the Hindus and Muslims would not get involved in bloodshed. The Indian leaders thought that by conceding Pakistan to Jinnah they will hear no more of him and eliminate his nuisance value. Zakaria has mentioned in *The Man Who Divided India* that Nehru had put it privately that, "By cutting of the head we will get rid of the headache. They cut the head alright; but the headache persists to this day".

Jinnah also thought that after the partition things would be manageable. On two fronts his inability to visualise the scenario was very obvious: on the issue of the separation of the Muslim League along national lines and the language issue of East Pakistan. The Muslim League governing council meeting was convened on December 14-15, 1947 in Karachi. Jinnah was the president. In this meeting out of 300 members 160 were from divided India! Now, Jinnah advised the Indian Muslim League members to accept the separation of the League along national lines. This was resented by the Indian members. One of the members shouted—"We never thought this would be our fate; you have divided brother and brother. And, left us completely in the lurch." To this Jinnah replied—"This could not be avoided."

On the East Pakistan language issue his failure was more serious. The Bengalee Muslims of East Pakistan opposed the government efforts to make Urdu the national language of Pakistan. Jinnah visited Dhaka on 21 March, 1948, when about three hundred thousand people assembled to listen to him with the expectation that he would not go against the popular wish. Jinnah failed to read the situation and expressed his opinion that Urdu will be the official language of the East Pakistan, as we have already referred to. Jinnah failed to realise that language nationalism could be more powerful than the religious nationalism. After returning from Dhaka, seeing the inability of his lieutenants to control the situation the way he wanted them to, he said to his sister Fatima—"I have backed the wrong horse!" Rafiq Zakaria has observed that, "The Muslim brotherhood by which Jinnah swore, collapsed when the two wings of Pakistan fell apart." He has added further that, "he (Jinnah) had vowed that he would provide the Muslims a separate homeland to free them from Hindu domination. But what has really happened is that they have been permanently enslaved—two-thirds of them to the Hindus and the remaining one-third which constitute Pakistan to the power-brokers and drug dealers. As the noted Pakistani author, Ahmed Rashid has pointed out:

> Pakistan has become the hotbed of the biggest smuggling racket in the world...enmeshed with Pakistani smugglers, transporters, drug barons, bureaucrats, politicians and army officers....

In a nutshell, one can agree with Zakaria who says in 2002, "neither the religious fanatics nor the secular modernists are happy with what Pakistan has become fifty-five years after the passing away of their founder. Jinnah must be turning in his grave at what his much-trumpeted creation has turned out to be—'a failed state', as described by Najam Sethi, the distinguished editor of the prestigious Friday Times of Lahore."

Having said this, one can say that these failures must not take away the credit from the remarkable man called Jinnah who through his political acumen and leadership qualities created a nation by out manoeuvring the Congress leaders and the English Viceroy. His commitment to his ideas of modernity was too embedded in him that he did not allow the newly created state to become a theocracy. Even today, Jinnah is the most respected historical personality of Pakistan and historians and politicians in India are debating over the ideas of Jinnah whose ideas and politics had such a powerful impact on the modern history of South Asia.

References

Advani, L.K., *My Country My Life* (New Delhi: Rupa & Co), 2010 [2008].

Ahmad, Akbar S., *Jinnah, Pakistan and Islamic Identity: The Search for Saladin* (New York: Routledge), 1997.

Ahmad, Aziz, *Studies in Islamic Culture in the Indian Environment* (Oxford: Clarendon Press), 1964.

———, *Islamic Modernism in India and Pakistan 1857-1964* (London: OUP), 1967.

Ahmad, Syed Nesar, *Origins of Muslim Consciousness in India* (New York: Greenwood Press), 1991.

Akbar, M.J., *The Tinderbox: The Past and Future of Pakistan* (New Delhi: Harper Collins), 2011.

Alqama, S.K., "Four Stages of Jinnah's Political Philosophy", m-a-jinnah.blogspot.in/2010/11four-stages-of Jinnah-political.html (accessed in October 2014).

Guha, Ramchandra, *Patriots and Partisans* (New Delhi: Allen Lane), 2012.

Jalal, Ayesha, *The Sole Spokesman: Jinnah, the Muslim League and the Demand for Pakistani* (Cambridge: CUP), 1994 [1985].

Nanda, B.R., *Road to Pakistan: The Life and Times of Mohammad Ali Jinnah* (New Delhi: Routledge), 2010.

Sharma, Jai Narayna, *The Political Thought of M.A. Jinnah* (New Delhi: Concept), 2008.

Singh, Dinesh Kumar, "Jinnah: Liberal Constitutionalism and Islam" in M.P. & Roy, Himanshu, *Indian Political Thought: Themes and Thinkers* (Delhi: Pearson).

Wolpert, Stanely, *Jinnah of Pakistan* (New York: Oxford University Press), 1984.

Zakaria, Rafiq, *The Man Who Divided India* (Mumbai: Popular Prakashan), 2011 [2001].

18

Vinayak Damodar Savarkar (1883-1966)

Chittabrata Palit

I
INTRODUCTION

V.D. Savarkar is acknowledged as the author of the concept of the Hindu State. Its historical context will be discussed later. Savarkar was born in a village near Nasik in Maharashtra on 28th May 1883. His family was a well-known family of Chitpaban Brahmins. He was not only of high caste but also belonged to well to do family. Though he lost his parents early in life he was reared by his eldest brother. From his childhood says he dreamt of an armed insurrection against British rulers. To propagate his *Swadeshi* thought he formed the Mitramela in his boyhood days and Abhinav Bharat in his youth. He was closed to the extremists leaders of the Congress like Bal Gangadhar Tilak, Lala Lajpat Rai and Bipin Chandra Pal. Later he was sponsored by Shyamji Krishnabarma to study law in Britain. While in London he became an active member of the Indian League where all Indian Nationalists and revolutionaries used to meet. But Savarkar could not complete his studies as his friend Mohan Lal Dhingra was caught for assassinating some British officials and hanged by the British Government. He was chased by the British authorities. Though he temporarily went over to Paris and hid himself in the house of Madam Cama, he was soon found out and sent back to India. He was first imprisoned in Yervada Jail in Pune. Later he was sentenced to 50 years confinement and shifted to Andaman Cellular jail. Here he was physically and mentally tortured so much that he appealed to the British Government to release him on condition that he would no longer support the Armed revolutionaries. He was again shifted to prison in Ratnagiri Jail in 1921 and finally in 1924 he was conditionally released. Naturally he lived the life of a Political exile. But he secretly kept in touch with the Hindu Mahasabha. In 1937, he could come out of the jail due to relaxation of rules and was made the President of the Allahabad session of the Hindu Mahasabha. After this there is no turning back for the next consecutive years he continued to be the President of the sabha which functioned under his guidance and advice. On 30th January 1948 when Mahatma Gandhi was killed by Nathuram Godse, an RSS activists the Hindu Political Organization were all banned and their leaders were behind the bar. Savarkar was also arrested for the second time for his alleged conspiracy with Godse. The RSS under Golwarkar tried to reform itself as a socio-cultural organization since 1940. This was not endorsed by some extremist leaders of the Mahasabha. But Savarkar's guilt would not be proved as he was mainly the member of this sabha and not an activist. Though he was released he started fasting until death and left this world on 26th February 1966.

II
SAVARKAR'S CONCEPT OF HINDU STATE

The duality of Savarkar's life is often emphasized. In his early life he was a militant freedom fighter but later he became the inspirer of a Hindu State. His second image as a narrow Hindu crusader has over taken his real credential of a freedom fighter.

The controversy stems from his most controversial book *Hindutva: Who is a Hindu?* written during 1922-23 when he was in Ratnagiri Jail. Here is an extract from the book "so although the root meaning of the word Hindu like the sister epithet Hindu may mean only an Indian, yet as it is we would be straining the usage of the words too much—we fear, to the point of breaking if we call a Mohamed an a Hindu because of his being a resident of India."

The concept of Hindu state is a most misunderstood test of Savarkar. He was a Hindu Chauvinist or a staunch RSS man. In fact this book was inspired by his deep patriotism for a colonized India. Without the Colonial framework Savarkar's intention cannot be spelt out. We know him already as the author of *The Indian War of Independence 1857*, meaning the revolt of 1857. The book under discussion should also be read in the context of colonial rule and its root of escape. Written before 1947, Savarkar tried to find a viable alternative to British rule. For that a majorities was the only answer for the Indian solidarity. But it did not carry the baggage of communalism as in his scheme no such scheme is indicated. His use of the word Hindu was a synonym for India as much as it was for Rajnarayan Bose when he thought of Hindu Nationalism, the muslims of India had abstained from the Congress movement for Independence.

The concept of Hindu State should only be viewed as a strong challenge to colonial rule, designed to demolish the imperialist propaganda of India as a parochial pluralist society. Under the canopy of Hindu of epithet all Indians could comfortably assembled and together fight out the British ruler. No other religious community was under threat of Hindu Chauvinism. The RSS agenda was not an offshoot of Savarkar's Hindu State. The opponents of Savarkar depict him as an icon of RSS, but not Jinnah as an icon of Islamic fundamentalism or the Anglican State of Britain. The later is viewed as a sublime secular state and the pinnacle of democracy. Savarkar's Hindu State was born under the oppressive colonial rule and the root of the great escape from it. The purpose ended with Indian freedom.

III
SAVARKAR'S RELEVANCE IN CONTEMPORARY POLITICAL THOUGHT

Savarkar is much misunderstood in history. His Hindu State must be understood in the context of colonial rule. Therefore, he sought solidarity of the majority communities of Hindu as his bastion, and utilized his concept for the freedom struggle. He should therefore be regarded as an icon of patriotism and nationalism.

But his legacy has been variously interpreted by social scientist and political Pandits specially Marxist and muslim minorities.

Even a scholar like Ashis Nandy in his learned discourse has titled his paper on Savarkar as 'The Demonic and the Seductive in Religious Nationalism; Vinayak Damodar Savarkar and the Rites of Exorcism in Secularizing South Asia.' But Savarkar's Hindu state was not an expression of religious Nationalism, it was plain and simple Nationalism in terms of Hindu idioms of the majority to show strength to the British and not to the other religious sects of India. He had no intention to exercise other religious communities and negate secularism in South Asia. One has to understand that Hinduism is not necessarily communalism. It also had its legitimacy, to be promoted and protected; it becomes communalism when it starts becoming oppressive or even hostile to other religious. Unlike Islam and Marxism, it is a much more tolerant creed and should be accessed accordingly. This was Savarkar's legacy and no other. The post-colonial excess of the RSS or BJP cannot be soberly attributed to a Patriot like Vinayak Damodar Savarkar.

Let us know his mind state from his own writings particularly his definitive work Hindutva. To this category of names which have been to mankind a subtle of life and inspiration belongs the word Hindutva, the essential nature and significance of which we have to investigate into. The ideas and ideals, the system and societies, the thoughts and sentiments which have centered round this name are so varied and rich, so powerful and so subtle, so elusive and yet so vivid that the term Hindutva defines all attempts at analysis. Forty centuries, if not more, had been at work to mould it as it is. Prophets and poets, lawyers and law givers, heroes and historians, have thought, lived, fought and died just to have it spelled thus. For indeed, is it not the resultant of countless actions—now conflicting, now commingling, now cooperating—of our whole race? Hindutva is not a word but a history. Not only the spiritual or religious history of our people as at times it is mistaken to be by being confounded with the other cognate term Hinduism, but a history in full. Hinduism is only a derivative, a fraction, a part of Hindutva. Unless it is made clear what is meant by the latter the first remains unintelligible and vague. Failure to distinguish between these two terms has given rise to much misunderstanding and mutual suspicion between some of those sister communities that have inherited this inestimable and common treasure of our Hindu Civilization. What is the fundamental difference is the meaning of these two words, would be clear as our argument proceeds. Here it is enough to point out that Hindutva is not identical with what is vaguely indicated by the term Hinduism. By an 'ism' it is generally meant a theory or a code more or less based on spiritual or religious dogma or system. He talked about Hindu—although it would be hazardous at the present stage of oriental research to state definitely the period when the foremost band of the intrepid Aryans made it their home and lighted their first sacrificial fire on the banks of the Sindhu, the Indus, yet certain it is that long before the ancient Egyptians and Babylonians had built their magnificent civilization. The holy waters of the Indus were daily witnessing the lucid and curling columns of the scented sacrificial smokes and the valleys resounding with the chants of Vedic hyms, the spiritual fervor that animated their souls. The adventurous valour that propelled their intrepid enterprises, the sublime heights to which their thoughts rose all these had marked them out as a people destined to lay the foundation of a great and enduring civilization. By the time they had definitely cut themselves aloof from their cognate and neighbouring people especially the Persians, the Aryans had spread out to the farthest of the seven rivers, Sapta Sindhus and not only had they developed a sense of nationality but had already succeeded in giving it a local habitation and a name. Out of their gratitude to the genial and perennial network of water ways that run through the land like a system of nerve threads and wove them into a Being, they very naturally took to themselves the name of Sapta Sindhus an epithet that was applied to the whole of Vedic India in the oldest records of the world, the *Rigveda* itself. Aryans or the cultivators as they essentially were we can well understand the divine love and homage they bored to these seven rivers presided over by the River, the Sindhu, which to them were but a visible symbol of the common nationality and culture.

To sum up it has been clearly established in this essay that Savarkar was a prime patriot of India particularly in the colonial context. To counter British Imperialism he wanted to posit a strong India against it. His strong nation therefore had to be a Hindu Nation as Hindus were the majority people of India. But his Hindutva an integrative approach as shown from the quotation from his book Hindutva that it was a geographical and cultural concept where a Hindu who lived in India was naturally an Indian or connotatively a Hindu thus the various other religious people who have lived in India from time immemorial were all Hindus. His intention was to establish Indian solidarity in this way to challenge British mind. The spirit he had already shown in his earlier work *The Indian War of Independence 1857*. His Hindu strategy was therefore a political weapon which served its own purpose in the book. It was far from a communal ideology. It is sustainable even now but minorities who were more communal often feel threatened by it.

Bibliography

Ashis Nandy. "The Demonic and the Seductive in Religious Nationalism: Vinayak Damodar Savarkar and the Rites of Exorcism in Secularizing South Asia." working paper No 44 Feb. 2009 5th Edition South Asian Institution Department of Political Science, Heidelberg University.

Savarkar, Vinayak Damodar. *Hindutva* (Bombay, 1969 1st Publication 1923).

———. *The Indian War of Independence 1857* (London, 1909).

———. *Hindu Rashtra Darshan* in (Hindi) Bombay, 1969.

19

The Political Ideas of M.N. Roy (1887-1954): A Critical Analysis

Sobhanlal Datta Gupta

I
INTRODUCTION

Manabendra Nath Roy, a thinker and an activist, has remained an enigmatic and a somewhat marginalized figure in the annals of modern Indian political thought. As an activist he was largely a failure, since he could not leave behind any significant political party or organization which would carry forward his principles and ideas. As an ideologue, he was a suspect in the eyes of the nationalists and considered as an adversary by the Indian Left, since he began as a nationalist, embraced Marxism and, finally, espoused the philosophy of Radical Humanism, his very own kind of philosophy, for which there were few takers. He began his life as a militant political activist, while he ended up as a radical intellectual, cut off from politics altogether and deeply engrossed in philosophical pursuits. The transition from militant nationalism to Radical Humanism through a stint with Marxism is, however, inextricably linked with the complex trajectory of Roy's life, as he moved across the three continents of Asia, Africa and America virtually as a political fugitive.

Manabendra Nath Roy's original name was Narendranath Bhattacharya, who was born at Arabalia, a village in the 24 Parganas of undivided Bengal, on 21 March 1887. Born in a typical Bengali middle-class family, he passed the Entrance Examination and as a student came in contact with Aurobindo Ghose, Barin Ghose and Jatindra Nath Mukherji, the latter popularly known as Bagha Jatin (Tiger Jatin). It was a time of great political turmoil, as the Partition of Bengal took place in 1905, while *Anushilan Samiti* and other underground revolutionary groups began to be formed around 1902. Narendranath came in contact with them and when in March, 1915 a representative of the Indian Independence Committee at Berlin clandestinely reached Calcutta, promising military and financial support to the revolutionaries of Bengal young Narendra, under the assumed name Charles A. Martin, traveled to Batavia and then to Shanghai to negotiate a deal with the German authorities for transportation and delivery of arms to a secret group of Bengali revolutionaries who had, under the direction of Jatin Mukherji, masterminded a plan of armed uprising against the British authorities in Balasore. But this scheme of staging an assault on the Raj with German help did not materialize. The entire plan collapsed and Roy had to now choose the life of a political fugitive. Eventually, as the British police began trailing him, he clandenstinely reached Mexico in 1917 after a short stay at San Francisco, where he changed his name to Manabendra Nath Roy or M.N. Roy. In Mexico, he came in contact with the Socialist Party, was initiated in Marxism, primarily through his association with Michael Borodin, a Soviet emissary active in Mexico, played an important role in the formation of the Mexican Communist Party, reached Moscow in 1920, positioned himself in a very big way in the Third International, commonly known as Communist International or Comintern (1919-43), by reaching the highest echelon of leadership and, finally, ending up his Comintern career by subscribing to the views of the Communist Party of Germany (Opposition) [KPD(O)] in 1929. This happened because of his serious differences with the Comintern leadership on a number of issues, especially the colonial question, and he fell off the grace of the Third International. Thereafter he clandestinely returned to India in 1930, was arrested shortly thereafter in 1931 and after a long and hard prison life (1931-36) joined the Indian National Congress following his release in 1936. He was elected a member of the All India Congress Committee and in 1937-38 he travelled and lectured extensively in both North and

South India, advocating the need for an alternative democratic and modern leadership within the Congress. In 1939, on Roy's initiative the League of Radical Congressmen (LRC) was formed and, following the outbreak of War, under its auspices anti-fascist meetings and demonstrations were organized in different parts of India. By 1940, he became completely disillusioned with the nationalist politics of the Congress, as he failed to involve it actively in his campaign against the War and fascism. In 1940, he formed his own Radical Democratic Party (RDP) and between 1940 and 1946 he was engaged in the publication of a series of books and the journal *The Marxian Way* (together with Sudhindranath Datta). During this period, Roy also adopted a programme of organization of study camps under the auspices of the RDP and in May, 1946 he came out with the adoption of 'Twenty Two Theses' by the RDP, which constituted the essence of what eventually came to be known as Radical Humanism. In August 1946, he formed the Indian Renaissance Institute at Dehradun and became its Founder-Director. Henceforth his central pursuit became propagation of the philosophy of Radical Humanism which was considered as a break with liberalism as well as Marxism. In 1948, the RDP was dissolved and he spent the last years of his life in Dehradun till in his death on 25 January 1954 in a kind of philosophical and intellectual seclusion, while giving the final shape to his cherished project of Radical Humanism. It focused on the idea of rejuvenation of the masses through a kind of cultural renewal of their consciousness in the spirit of reason and scientific thinking.

II
EVOLUTION OF ROY'S IDEAS: FROM MILITANT NATIONALISM TO RADICAL HUMANISM

Broadly speaking, there were three main phases in the development of Roy's ideas. The first one refers to the period from 1918 to 1930, when Roy moved from nationalism towards Marxism, eventually turning out to be a dissident Marxist, as he dared question the claims of official Marxism, canonized as it was by the Soviet Communist Party and Comintern in the 1920s. The second phase dates back to 1931 and covers the period from 1931 to 1945 when he commenced his prison writings

(1931-36), which were the first stirrings of what came to be known as Radical Humanism in future. This was also the period that witnessed his brief, yet active, involvement in nationalist politics as well as his disillusionment with the Congress. The third phase which ranged from 1946 to 1954 is indicative of the crystallization of his philosophy of Radical Humanism. During this period, he became predominantly engaged in the exploration of profound philosophical questions underlying the study of human history, politics and society.

Phase One (1918-1930): In Roy's pre-Comintern phase, at least two of his writings deserve mention. One entitled *India: Her Past, Present and Future* (1918) and another article "Hunger and Revolution in India" (1919) demand attention for more than one reason. In the first piece, he defended the Indian tradition of tolerance and non-annexation and pointed out how prosperous and socially tranquil India was before the British conquest, pointing out that "The country developed not only a spiritual and moral civilization, but also perfected a social and political concept which contributed greatly to its material advancement and which has not yet been surpassed by any modern nation."[1] In the second article, while severely condemning the British exploitation of India, he focused on the idea that the English proletariat would gain nothing out of the World War I and would never be able "to overthrow his capitalistic oppressors so long as the workers of India are theirs to exploit at pleasure."[2] In this article use of such Marxist categories as "capitalism", "proletariat", "imperialism", read with his call for overthrowal of the Raj, provide the first clues to his understanding of India as a colonial problem which he subsequently developed in the Comintern period.

It is undeniable that from the political point of view the Comintern phase was certainly the most important as well as the most successful period in his life. He joined the Comintern, reached the highest level of its leadership and came to be recognized as a key spokesman of the colonial question in general and India in particular. His writings on India in this period, his organizational activities concerning the birth and growth of communist movement in India, his critique of the nationalist ideology and espousal of an alternative strategy of freedom struggle under the leadership of the working class and peasantry and, above all, his debate with Lenin on the colonial question and the official acceptance of his Supplementary colonial theses (after amendments made by Lenin) established Roy as a key theoretician of Comintern on the colonial question. Besides, as on Roy's initiative the Communist Party of India (CPI) was formed in 1920 at Tashkhent in Central Asia, his name has gone down in history as the founder of communist movement in India. In fact, in the 1920s, the leaders of the burgeoning communist movement in India like Muzaffar Ahmad, S.A. Dange and others were primarily guided by Roy's writings and he thereby came to be considered as the doyen of Marxist thought in India. Ironically, this was also the phase which generated major criticisms of his position within the Comintern, eventually leading to his break with the Communist International in 1929. It is this episode, namely, his differences with the official leadership of Comintern on a number of issues and his subsequent dissociation with the Comintern as its consequence which also established Roy as the dark horse of Indian communism in the eyes of the leaders of the Indian communist parties most of whom, ironically, had been groomed by Roy himself in the formative years of the Indian Communist Party.

It is a standardized understanding that the writings of this period constitute the core of Roy's Marxist thought, steeped as it was in the terminologies and idioms of the kind of official Marxism, namely, the Soviet brand of communism, which prevailed in the 1920s. This rather simplified view of Roy's thoughts on Marxism, however, demands a critical re-examination, if not reconceptualization, since this was Roy's rather early position on Marxism, which was essentially grounded in a somewhat mechanical and thereby determinist, reading of Marx. If one goes through some of Roy's representative texts of this period, i.e. his Supplementary Theses on the Colonial Question, which he prepared on Lenin's suggestion for the Second Congress of Comintern in 1920, *India in Transition* (1922), *The Future of Indian Politics* (1926), certain features of his analysis are quite evident. First, it is a kind of Marxism which is reflective of the spirit of economic determinism, his position being that under the aegis of colonialism industrialization had reached a certain level in India so much so that an industrial proletariat had emerged whereby it was possible to envisage the prospect of a proletarian revolution in India in alliance with the peasantry under the leadership of the Communist Party, almost on the model of the Russian Revolution. Second, Roy paid very little attention to the role of the peasantry in the anti-colonial struggle. Third, from his industrialization thesis he derived the idea of polarization of classes as in the West, and hence in his eyes bourgeois nationalism was a spent, virtually counter-revolutionary, force, which explains his ire towards Gandhi. Understandably, this reading of India and his project of an Indian revolution did not at all square with the ground realities of Indian society.

If one takes a closer look at Roy's writings on India in the Comintern period, one comes across a paradoxical element therein. On one level, in his reports and commentaries on India in the Comintern Congresses and various bodies of Comintern he repeatedly highlighted the fact that colonies like India needed to be studied and treated on their own terms and not in the typical Eurocentric perspective of the Communist Parties of Western Europe and it is exactly for this reason that he was deeply sceptical of the British Communist Party's CPGB's understanding of India as a colonial problem. On another level, however, Roy's own analysis of India as a colony hardly matched the ground realities of India. His perception of India as an industrialized colony, his dismissal of nationalism as a spent force, his almost total neglect of the peasant question, issues like caste, religion and untouchability, made his Marxist analysis largely Eurocentric in the sense that it was anchored in an optimistic and utopian vision that a proletarian revolution was imminent in India,—a left-extremist understanding shared by a number of West European Communist Parties as well as sections of the Comintern leadership. This was a deterministic, teleological view of Marxism, broadly endorsed by the Comintern and the dominant section of the Soviet Communist Party in which Roy's Marxism was grounded, as long as he enjoyed the confidence and support of the Comintern leadership. In fact, the essence of Lenin's disagreement with Roy centred around Roy's underestimation of the role of bourgeois nationalism notwithstanding all its limitations in the colonial countries, his neglect of the peasant question and his refusal to accept the idea of building up an anti-imperialist united front, as proposed by Lenin.

Broadly, around 1927, one notices the first signs of a shift in Roy's understanding of India as well as Comintern. Regarding India he began to take a more moderate view of the nationalist bourgeoisie in India and distance himself from the official position of Comintern following his return from China, where he was sent as the Comintern emissary to oversee the implementation of its line. It is now a well-known story that Roy was made a scapegoat for the failure of Comintern's adventurist line in China and he was blamed for his alleged revisionism. While this was the beginning of his marginalization in Comintern, his break with the Third International was complete in 1929 after he started writing in the organs of the Communist Party of Germany (Opposition) or KPD(O), which under the leadership of August Thalheimer and Heinrich Brandler had broken away from the Communist Party of Germany (KPD), the official affiliate of Comintern, by refusing to toe its pro-Stalinist line. This was more so, since Roy's position was now at variance with the severely ultra-left and sectarian position of the Comintern's Sixth Congress (1928), which branded bourgeois nationalism as a counter-revolutionary force in the colonial countries. Ironically, thus, as the Comintern was moving towards a left-extremist position on the issue of nationalism in the colonies, which, incidentally, was Roy's own position in his early years in Comintern, leading to his sharp differences with Lenin precisely on this question, Roy's position now stood considerably modified.

Roy's tryst with the KPD(O) was a turning point in his intellectual development. First, Roy now turned out to be a dissident Marxist, as he began to write for the KPD(O) press, and emerging thereby as a severe critic of Comintern's and thereby of the Soviet version of Marxism. Second, only after the recent availability of these materials in English, it is now evident that as he broke off with Comintern, he embraced a new brand of Marxism, with emphasis on openness and autonomy of Communist Parties. This is most strongly evident in his six-part article "The Crisis in the Communist International" and "The Russian Revolution: Its Place in History". Roy thus emerged as a heretic, critiquing not Marxism but the Comintern-inspired official Marxism yet by remaining within the camp of Marxism. During this phase his reflections on India too were reflective of a new spirit. In articles like "Tactical Problems of the Indian Revolution" (1930) and "Freedom Struggle in India and the Comintern" (1931), he moved away from his previous sectarian position on bourgeois nationalism and called for a broad-based alliance. Third, the new Marxism that Roy now embraced was quite different from the kind of Marxism which had been popularized by the Comintern, that is, the Soviet version of Marxism.[3] As against its determinist framework this new version of Marxism, which Roy now endorsed, was grounded in freedom, subjectivity and consciousness. It was thereby a kind of open Marxism which contested the claims of the Soviet version of closed Marxism.

Phase Two (1931-1945): Roy was arrested in July 1931, after he clandenstinely returned to India in December 1930 and he spent about six years (from July 1931 to November 1936) behind the bars. The years in prison and the prison writings constituted another turning point in his life. His prison writings merit serious attention and it's a pity that no attempt has yet been made to publish the complete prison manuscripts, which run up to 3750 pages.[4] It is in these writings that Roy made his intellectual position unambiguously clear, namely, his acceptance of science and materialism as the philosophical foundation of his thought, his dismissal of religion, since it does not square with reason and science, his reformulation but not rejection of Marxism essentially as a moral doctrine and not simply either as an economic doctrine or as an ideology based on narrow political practice. It is in these manuscripts that it is possible to discern the first stirrings of what later came to be recognized as

Radical Humanism. Some of the most representative writings of the prison period are *Materialism: An Outline of the History of Scientific Thought* (1931-33), *Science and Philosophy* (1934-36), *Heresies of the 20th Century* (1932-34, 1936), *The Ideal of Indian Womanhood* (1936) and *Fascism: Its Philosophy, Professions and Practice* (1933-34, 1935). As we will see, there is an integral connection between these writings and his core pieces which went into the making of the philosophy of Radical Humanism in the 1940s. For Roy the only yardstick that mattered in judging the relevance of a philosophy in human life was materialism, given his fierce opposition to irrationalism. His dismissal of religion, too, was a product of this understanding.

This explains his interpretation of Indian philosophy, which is at variance with the standard understanding that Indian philosophy is heavily oriented towards mysticism and theology. He refers to the early *Upanishads*, the *Shankhya* and *Vaisheshika* systems, the *Charvaka* system and, finally, the Buddhist tradition as torchbearers of rationalism, agnosticism and atheism in Indian philosophy, and thereby of materialism.[5] According to Roy's understanding, in India the materialist tradition was eclipsed with rise of Brahminism, because, except when the Buddhist tradition was dominant, the trading class was always weak, eclipsed as it was by the *Brahmins* and the *Kshatriyas*, who were hostile to trade. This led to the sustenance of a closed, self-sufficient village society in India, leading to the eclipse of the materialist tradition, despite its early promise, and the flourishing of spiritualism and religion under the aegis of Brahminism.[6] In India, he pointed out, unlike Europe, all schools of philosophy looked upon nature as a source of bondage, leading to a justification of self-mortification and pessimism, further solidifying the position of Brahminism in Indian society and strengthening the grounds of speculative philosophy, which, for Roy, was not real philosophy at all.[7] It is, again, in this spirit that Roy provided a masterly analysis of the role of Islam in history in his prison manuscripts. The triumphant march of Islam in the Arab world and its adjacent countries Roy attributes to the values of tolerance and egalitarianism that characterized the teachings of the Prophet. The decline of Christianity made the appeal of Islam extremely popular to the downtrodden masses, who felt that they had been betrayed by the initial promises of Christianity. For him, the triumph of Islam, therefore, was primarily due to its liberating and egalitarian principles rather than to its military valour. He regrets that the dogmatic Hindu mind failed to appreciate the fact how it was possible for small bands of predatory invaders from distant lands to make themselves rulers of such a vast country like India and find millions of converts who were attracted towards an alien faith. It could happen, Roy explains, because Islam was considered "as a message of hope and freedom to the multitudinous victims of the Brahminical reaction."[8] This simple truth the Hindus have failed to understand, Roy pointed out, wherein lies the failure of the Hindus to look upon the Muslims as integral parts of the Indian nation and thereby "appreciate the contribution they made towards the emergence of Indian society out of the chaos caused by the breakdown of the antique civilization."[9]

One major piece written by Roy in jail was "The Ideal of Indian Womanhood". He in a highly modernist and radical fashion pointed out that the so-called ideal of Indian womanhood was not conceived by women themselves—rather it was an image constructed by the patriarchal Hindu India for justifying the economic subjugation of women and the glorification of their status of "domestic chattel" and "breeding machines". Eventually, he argued, their subordination to man, their domestic slavery and concubinage were considered as voluntary, "inspired by some mystic ideal of womanhood."

A hard core materialist as Roy was, he was deeply anchored in the notions of science and reason, inspired by the philosophy of European Enlightenment. Materialism being his motto, he rejected all manifestations of irrationalism, be it religion or any ideology, that questions the claims of science and reason. This explains his unequivocal denouncement of Hinduism as well as fascism, *Heresies of the Twentieth Century* and *Fascism: Its Philosophy, Professions and Practice* being two classic illustrations. The first one is a series of essays, written in jail between 1932 and 1936, while the second one was written between 1933 and 1935.[10] In these works, Sibnarayan Ray rightly observes, Roy, while upholding his position as a philosophical materialist, however, "was very much a Marxist although not of the Orthodox variety."[11] For him, just as Hindu religious orthodoxy was unacceptable for its irrational foundations, similarly fascism, for Roy, was an ideology that thrived on irrationalism and was to be condemned in unhesitating terms. This irranationalism, in his opinion, was most strongly evident in nationalism. From his critique of fascism he moved on to its alternative. Closely resembling Tagore's uncompromising criticism of nationalism, Roy too advocated the cause of cosmopolitanism, which he distinguished, however, from internationalism. For him, cosmopolitanism was the highest form of humanism, since it believes in the idea of one world, and is, therefore, not compatible with internationalism, which believes in the coexistence and continuation of national states.[12]

Although M.N. Roy had a short stint with Congress politics, he soon became disillusioned with the Congress and in 1940 he launched his own Radical Democratic Party (RDP). But as he eventually realized that no political party could be the torchbearer of the philosophy that he stood by, the RDP was dissolved in 1948.

Phase Three (1946-1954): But his philosophical quest continued and deepened, *From Savagery to Civilization* (1940), *New Humanism: A Manifesto* (1947) and his magnum opus *Reason, Romanticism and Revolution* (1952, 1955) being its finest manifestations. The foundation of Radical Humanism, which was essentially a materialist philosophy, was grounded in the values of humanism, reason, morality and freedom and it was projected as a kind of alternative to the liberal notion of atomistic individualism as well as the conventional Marxist understanding of the regimented individual under socialism. Consequently, what he espoused in very definitive terms was the notion of a radical democracy, which would encourage neither elitism nor the notion of a collective ego. This was most clearly formulated in his programmatic document, namely, *New Humanism: A Manifesto*. Roy wrote:

> What is suggested is not the rule of the "intellectual elite", but such an organisation of society as will give

> unlimited scope for the unfolding of the creative genius of man, by placing the executive power of the State under the control of free individuals—free from the influence of vested interests and also from the vagaries of the collective ego, so very susceptible to demagogic appeals.[13]

Roy formulated the principles of what he considered to be Radical Democracy in the form of 22 Theses. He was sceptical of representative democracy and made a strong plea for what we describe today as participatory democracy. But in his understanding it was not just participation, since, as we know, it can also be very much passive. Rather he advocated conscious assertion of human subjectivity in exercising control over state power.

Theses Twenty Two stated the humanist spirit of Radical Democracy in explicit terms: "Radicalism starts from the dictum that "Man is the measure of everything" (Protagoras) or "man is the root of mankind" (Marx) and advocates reconstruction of the world as a Commonwealth and fraternity of free men, by the collective endeavour of spiritually emancipated moral men".[14]

Roy's idea of Radical Humanism, which he projected as a kind of third alternative to liberalism and the stereotyped notion of Marxism, based on the Bolshevik model, was deeply grounded in the interconnection of morality and autonomy of man. Therein also lie interesting clues to the understanding of a contentious question: Was Roy's notion of Radical Humanism opposed to and thereby an alternative to Marxism? Or, was it a modification of Marxism but in a radical direction, with focus on freedom and humanism? While his project of Radical Humanism was deeply rooted in materialism, he was uncompromisingly opposed to its determinist and teleological version, as his projected vision of the new man, the moral man, was deeply embedded in the ideas of autonomy and freedom, which rejected the notion of closure and boundaries. Anchored in materialism, Roy's Radical Humanism was in a way a restatement of Marxism too, keeping in mind the fact that he made a distinction between the original promise or vision of

Marxism and the degeneration that it underwent through its practice in the name of Bolshevism in Stalinist Soviet Union, which he himself witnessed as a leading Comintern functionary in Moscow in the 1920s. Thus, while endorsing the materialist view of history, he was opposed to any teleological/determinist interpretation. Thus, in Theses Four, while enunciating the principles of Radical Democracy, he pointed out that historical determinism does not exclude freedom of the will, since rational and scientific concept of determinism should not be confused with the teleological or religious doctrine of predestination.[15] Freedom and autonomy of the individual being one of the central concerns of Roy, he provided a novel interpretation of Lenin's doctrine of the party. Deviating from the standardized understanding of Lenin's *What is to be done?* (1902), he pointed out that Lenin envisaged the idea that proletarian culture as such means nothing, as it is unable to formulate its own ideology. Consequently, he pleaded for providing the impulse from outside, which would be actually provided by the middle-class intelligentsia, although he himself did not recognize it, resulting in the superimposition of the party on the class. The party thus never becomes a part of the class and this is how the cult of the party like a Leviathan is born, while the subjectivity of the class is eroded.[16] That Roy's notion of Radical Humanism had, theoretically speaking, no conflict with the original spirit of Marxism, which had its focus on reason and freedom of man, is evident in his deep appreciation of Marx's philosophy even when he embraced the philosophy of Radical Humanism.

Roy's notion of Radical Humanism envisioned the image of a man who combined freedom and the concern for the social,—both of them, interestingly, being traced to Marx. However, Roy's considered opinion was that the notion of the collective ultimately overshadowed the idea of autonomy in Marx, which was his original promise, and this happened, according to Roy, because of Marx's philosophical lineage. Roy explained this position very elaborately in his last work, his magnum opus *Reason, Romanticism and Revolution*. This analysis of Roy also provides clues to the understanding of the differences between Radical Humanism and Marxism. Thus, in a long chapter on

Marxism he argued that Marx's entire project of merciless exposure of capitalism was essentially a moral project and his defence of the cause of revolution was endorsement of the cause of the autonomy of man.

Roy's intellectual endeavour was aimed at effecting a fusion of rationalism and romanticism. Both the elements, he argued, were present in Marx, but eventually they were delinked. Marx's focus on the materialist view of history, his notion of morality, which, for him, did not exist in abstraction but was historically conditioned were manifestations of his emphasis on reason and materialism. Thus, while in the *Manifesto* it was pointed out that morality must be referred back to man's innate rationality, reason being the sanction for morality,[17] in *Reason, Romanticism and Revolution* he explained that although initially there was a connection between romanticism and revolution, there was eventually a rupture between reason and romanticism, as romanticism got priority in Marx's thought. In a long discussion on the history of European romanticism, Roy explained that, while focusing on will, subjectivity and freedom, it also gives birth to forces of irrationalism, when the meaning of will of the individual is transformed into a mythical will of the collective, as was done by Rousseau in his formulation of the concept of General Will. According to Roy, Marx, under the influence of Rousseau, was heavily drawn towards this idea, resulting in the eclipse of man by the masses.

It is this understanding which provides clues to the explanation of the difference between Radical Humanism and Marxism, despite their otherwise quite distinct similarities. For Roy, the original promise of Marxism, with its focus on freedom of the individual had been destroyed on one level by Marx's valorization of the masses and on another level by the practice of socialism, which replaced the will of the people by the will of the party. Roy's own experience in Europe, especially his long association with the Comintern, had made him deeply sceptical of the so-called notion of masses, since it is this collectivist notion which eclipses the individual and, moreover, in the long run it is hijacked by the party, which becomes the all-powerful Leviathan. Roy's ultimate concern, therefore, is the protection of freedom and autonomy of the individual vs. authority of the party as well as the masses. This fear of the collective and the threat posed by the party to the autonomy of the individual in the name of the people drew him away from the Marxist camp and, consequently, it became customary for his Left critics to associate his concept of Radical Humanism ultimately with liberalism, notwithstanding its deep affinity with Marxism on many counts.

III
RELEVANCE OF M.N. ROY IN CONTEMPORARY POLITICS

This has also been the chief source of misunderstanding of the relevance of Roy's ideas. While mainstream Marxists in India have criticized Roy's Radical Humanism for its alleged liberalism, the followers of Roy have defended his position for its critique of mainstream Marxism, which was a break with liberalism as well as orthodox Marxism. It is also very strange that among the Indian Marxists the popular notion is that Roy, if he has any relevance for the Left in India, should be remembered for his contribution to the organization of the Communist Party of India in its early years. What needs to be noted in this context is that this kind of assessment considers Roy as a Marxist only in the Comintern period and does not take into account his new interpretation of Marxism after his dissociation with Comintern and his association with the KPD (O) in 1929-30. This is explained by the fact that mainstream Indian Marxism, following the legacy of international communism that was nurtured by the Comintern, has always considered dissident Marxism as a deviation from Marxism proper. Consequently, Roy after his break with Comintern, was labeled as a "renegade" and his writings in the post Comintern period thus evoked no appreciative response from the mainstream Left in India. Among the Left intellectuals too, Roy's understanding of Marxism in the post-Comintern phase, his prison writings and his philosophy of Radical Humanism have evoked very little response. Leaving aside scholars like Sibnarayan Ray[18] who was a critical follower of Roy, in recent times Sumanta Banerjee has drawn the attention of the readers to these aspects of Roy's thought,[19] highlighting thereby the relevance of his ideas.

A further explanation of why Roy's new understanding of Marxism evoked no response from the Left was that, as distinct from the popular understanding of Marxism as economic determinism, which to a large extent was Roy's own understanding too in his Comintern phase, his later writings, focusing on the need for the birth of a new man and new civilization was reflective of his concern for the superstructure.

To understand why it happened, why his philosophy had no takers, why except through a handful of followers "Royism" virtually became extinct, why his radical philosophy could not elicit any response even from the new generation of radicals, there are several possible explanations. First, it is a truism that Roy's critiques of nationalism, his severely critical stance in regard to Gandhi made him a suspect in the eyes of the nationalists, despite his short stint with the Congress after his release from prison. Given his background, ideological orientation and, most importantly, his role in the Comintern as the chief spokesman of India, the Left could have been his natural ally. But this did not happen. One reason was the political compulsion of the CPI not to accept the return of Roy to the party, once his ties with Comintern were snapped. It is an irony of history that although Roy expressed his desire to return to the fold of the CPI after 1935, when the Comintern virtually embraced Roy's position by discarding ultra leftism, the CPI rejected his request. Besides, the outlook of alternative Marxism that he shared with the KPD(O) was anathema to the Communist Party of India. The other reason was his steady shift from organizational politics, which engaged his attention in the early period of his life, to philosophy, the journey from political activism to pure intellectualism, manifest as it was in the disbanding of his own Radical Democratic Party in 1948. It goes without saying that his growing political apathy towards organizational politics, his journey from concrete to abstract irked the Left, resulting in his political isolation from mainstream politics in general and Left politics in particular.

Second, Roy being a radical intellectual par excellence, it needs to be recognized that he was essentially rooted in the tradition of European modernity, the two poles of which were the Renaissance and Enlightenment respectively. His attraction towards Marxism, especially his endorsement of the revolutionary-humanist essence of Marxism in the post-Comintern phase and his eventual espousal of Radical Humanism, notwithstanding its differences with Marxism, can all be explained in this spirit. The values that he cherished, namely, reason, science, materialism, together with morality and humanism, were essentially elements that constituted the core of European modernity. Some of his representative writings like *From Savagery to Civilization* and *Reason, Romanticism and Revolution* bear testimony to it. For him the march of history is the march of civilization and progress, a story of the triumph and glory of man towards his own self-emancipation. This does not simply fit in with the intellectual moorings or lineage of India's Marxists, who have been largely guided by a stereotyped understanding of Marxism.

Finally, despite the intellectual prowess that Roy displayed as a thinker, it is undeniable that, after all, his idea of Radical Humanism, his vision of the future man was a Utopian project, untranslatable in reality. His optimistic vision of the future was a philosophical enterprise, unintelligible to the common man, to any political party. More importantly, his entire understanding was based on the assumption that it is the rational faculties of the individual which would ultimately triumph over what is profane in man,—a proposition that hardly squares with the realities of the world. May be, completely disillusioned with the world in which he was living, he took refuge in a world of utopia, just as in the last days of his life he chose almost a life of intellectual seclusion in the hills of Dehradun. It is perhaps an irony of history that, while the projection of his utopian vision was his marker as a first-rate intellectual, this, again, was also the weakest dimension of his thought,—a thought that nobody shared with him except a handful of his followers.

Notes

1. Sibnarayan Ray (ed.), *Selected Works of M.N. Roy*, Vol. 1: 1917-1922 (Delhi: Oxford University Press, 1987), p. 98.
2. *Ibid.*, p. 158.
3. For Roy's writings of this period see Sibnarayan Ray (ed.), *Selected Works of M.N. Roy*, Vol. 3: 1927-1932 (Delhi: Oxford University Press, 1990). These writings of Roy published in the KPD(O) press were totally unknown to the English-speaking readers till the publication of this volume.
4. See in this connection the editor's note on Roy's Prison Manuscripts in Sibnarayan Ray (ed.), *Selected Works of M.N. Roy*, Vol. 4: 1932-1936 (New Delhi: Oxford University Press, 1997), pp. 313-16.
5. See chapter 3 of "Materialism: An Outline of the History of Scientific Thought" in *ibid.*
6. *Ibid.*, pp. 342-44.
7. *Ibid.*, pp. 339-40.
8. *Ibid.*, p. 400.
9. *Ibid.*
10. See editor's note in *ibid.*, pp. 405 and 429.
11. *Ibid.*, p. 406.
12. M.N. Roy, *New Humanism: A Manifesto* (Delhi: Ajanta, 1981), p. 37.
13. "Principles of Radical Democracy, 22 Theses" in *ibid.*, p. 44.
14. *Ibid.*, p. 62.
15. Roy, *New Humanism*, p. 54.
16. *Ibid.*, p. 29.
17. *Ibid.*, p. 36.
18. See Sibnarayan Ray's multi-volume intellectual biography of Roy, *In Freedom's Quest: Life of M.N. Roy*, Vols. I-IV (Kolkata: Minerva Associates, 1998-2007).
19. Sumanta Banerjee, "Remembering M.N. Roy", *Economic and Political Weekly*, 3 July 2004, pp. 2957-58.

References

Bhattacharya, G.P. *Evolution of the Political Philosophy of M.N. Roy* (Calcutta, 1971).

Haithcox, J.P. *Communism and Nationalism in India: M.N. Roy and Comintern Policy 1920-39* (Princeton, 1971).

Karnik, V.B. *M.N. Roy: Political Biography* (Pune, 1978).

Ray, Sibnarayan. *In Freedom's Quest: Life of M.N. Roy,* Vols. I-IV (Kolkata, 1998-2007).

———. *M.N. Roy: Philosopher-Revolutionary* (Kolkata, 1984).

——— (ed.). *Selected Works of M.N. Roy,* Vols. I-IV (New Delhi, 1987-1997).

20

Abul Kalam Azad (1888-1958): Politician, Theologue and Educationist

Rajasri Basu

I
INTRODUCTION

Abul Kalam Azad was an Indian scholar and a leader of the Indian national movement, who after Independence became the first education minister of the Union Government. In 1992, he was posthumously awarded the highest Indian civilian order "Bharat Ratna". He was an extremely erudite person having a great scholarship on Islamic culture and civilization, a great public speaker and debater, a man of highest integrity and a great visionary.

Abul Kalam Azad was born on November 11, 1888 at Mecca in a very orthodox Muslim family. His name at birth was Firoz Bakht. He was, however, known more as Muhiyuddin Ahmad. In his teens, he began to use the pseudonym Abul Kalam Azad. Azad's family descended from a line of eminent *Ulama* or scholars of Islam, hailing from Herat, Afghanistan. His forefathers came to India in early 15th century and settled first in Agra and then at Delhi. Azad's grandfather died at a time when Azad's father was very young and as such Azad's father was brought up by his maternal grandfather. In 1855, Azad's father's maternal grandfather decided to leave India and to settle at Mecca. However, he could not do so, first due to the outbreak of India's first war of Independence in 1857 and then due to his illness and he ultimately died in Bombay. Azad's father Maulana Khairuddin, however, shifted to Mecca and there he married

Sheikh Mohammed Zahir Watri's daughter. Sheikh Mohammed Zahir was a great scholar at that time in Medina. Maulana Khairuddin had also become well-known after a ten-volume work in Arabic came out in Egypt.

Azad's family migrated to Calcutta, in 1890 primarily for a medical treatment which was needed for Azad's father but decided to settle here. His mother died in 1891, when Azad was just three years old. In Calcutta, Azad was not sent to any school, nor to any Madrasa, although the Calcutta Madrasa was there, but he learnt from his father and other Arabic scholars. Azad's father was very much against Western education and a firm believer in the old ways of life. Azad's progress in his studies was phenomenal and took only four years to complete *Darse Nizami*, which is a full course in Arabic and Persian consisting of languages, philosophy, logic, arithmetic, geography and history. By the age of sixteen, he mastered several languages like Urdu, Persian, Hindko, Arabic and Hindi. Meanwhile at the age of thirteen, he was married to a young Muslim girl, Zuleikha Begum.

The then intellectual life of Calcutta gradually started influencing Azad and he began to doubt the traditional ways of his father and secretly diversified his studies. Azad learned English through intensive personal study and began learning Western philosophy, history and contemporary politics by reading advanced books and modern periodicals. There is an interesting story regarding Azad's learning of English. The chief examiner of the Oriental Course of Studies at that time, Maulavi Mohammad Yusuf Jafri taught Azad the English alphabets and gave him Peary Charan Sarkar's *First Book* and Azad thereafter learnt English all by himself. Azad grew disillusioned with Islamic teachings and was inspired by the modern views of Sir Syed Ahmed Khan. Increasingly doubtful of religious dogma, Azad entered a period of self-described "atheism". However, all these happened only after the death of his father in 1909.

It was actually since 1908 that the minds of the young Maulana began to undergo changes. He noticed that India was presenting two faces to the world: One, the face of the Hindus, which was fired with patriotism and dreams of a new,

Independent India; and the other, the Muslim face, which was basically loyalty to the British. And against this backdrop was the Indian colonial state, in the hands of the British, which was bent on dividing the two communities, creating suspicion in both against one another. He made up his mind to play a different role in the political scenario, of uprooting from the Muslim mind the loyalty to the British and of fostering Hindu-Muslim unity, from which he never deviated from his life.

The period was also a period of great mental strain and stress. Azad was born into a family where religious beliefs and traditions were accepted without any question and the family did not like the idea of deviating a bit from the orthodox ways of life. But Azad at that time was not prepared to accept all without questioning and in fact could not reconcile himself with all the religious traditions and customs. His mind was a full of a new sense of revolt. For two to three years, this unrest continued and finally he was able to break himself from all bonds imposed on him by his family and his upbringing. It was at that time that he decided to adopt a pen name 'Azad' meaning 'Free' to indicate that he was no longer tied to any inherited beliefs.

II
POLITICAL THOUGHT OF AZAD

The most important turning point in Azad's life took place when he was initiated into politics by Shyam Sundar Chakravarthy, a Bengali revolutionary. Chakravarthy was a close friend and aide of Sri Aurobindo Ghosh, one of the most fiery revolutionaries of that time in Bengal. K*armayogin,* his paper became a symbol of nationalist awakening and revolt. Azad joined the revolutionaries, and at first there was some amount of mistrust amongst the revolutionaries regarding Azad as most of the revolutionary groups at that time were anti-Muslim. This is not completely without reasons. Azad, however was slowly able to gain trust and confidence from them. Moreover, Azad was able to convince the fellow revolutionaries that although some Muslims, no doubt sided with the British government, it is wrong to generalize about the Muslim *community* on the basis of the deeds of certain individuals.

During this period Azad had an opportunity of visiting Iraq, Egypt, Syria and Turkey. There also he met some revolutionaries and developed a firm conviction that Indian Muslims should also take a leading role in India's nationalist struggle. After returning to India, he thought that what is most needed is to develop a strong public opinion amongst the Muslims and for that he himself took upon the pen for editing an Urdu weekly newspaper from Calcutta called Al *Hilal*. It is noteworthy both from the standpoint of its get-up as also from its content. The weekly brought out a new line of journalism by including pictorial illustrations as permanent features in its columns. But more than that people were attracted to its nationalist tone and temper. It achieved unprecedented popularity within a very short time. Meanwhile, war broke out and the publication was banned in 1914 and the press was confiscated in 1915. Azad bought a new press and started a new journal called *Al Balagh*. Soon the government externed Azad in 1916 and he was sent to Ranchi, where he remained in detention till December 31, 1919.

In 1920, a meeting with Gandhi at Delhi left a deep impression upon him and a transition from a fiery editor to a great revolutionary took place. At this time, Azad became actively involved in the *Khilafat* movement. Azad saw this as an opportunity to energize Indian Muslims and achieve major political and social reform through the struggle. Gandhiji was also chalking the programme of non-cooperation and boycott against the British. Formally Gandhi presented the programme of non-cooperation for the first time from a public platform at the All India Khilafat Conference held at Meerut. Initially, leaders of the *Khilafat* movement like Mohammad Ali, Shaukat Ali, Hakim Ajmal Khan and Congress leaders like Lala Lajpat Rai, C.R. Das did not endorse Gandhi's programme. But Azad, from the very beginning, gave his unqualified support to Gandhi. Finally, the nation-wide non-cooperation movement was launched, which drew an unprecedented public response. The Government retaliated by arresting the leaders and after most of the leaders' release from prison, Azad was elected President of the Congress in 1923 at the age of 35. Azad took over the reins of Congress at a time when Congress was going through a very critical phase between the pro-changers and no-changers. The pro-changers led by C.R. Das. Motilal Nehru and Hakim Ajmal Khan were in favour of 'entry programme', that is gradual entry into the legislative councils for sharing and exercise of power; while the no-changers led by Rajagopalachari, Dr. Rajendra Prasad, who were staunch Gandhiites were in favour of direct action and no change in their tactics.

Azad, during his presidency did not side either of these two lobbies, instead, tried to reconcile the two groups by judging the merits of each group's arguments. This is one of his characteristic features, to which I will come, in details, in the next section. He was never hesitant in accepting a proposal, if he found substantial merit in that, and while doing so he never fumbled in distantiating or even alienating an old friend or ally.

In 1928, Azad endorsed the Nehru Report and called for an Independent India committed to secularism. At this time, Azad developed a close friendship with Nehru and began espousing socialism as the means to fight inequality, poverty and other national challenges. In fact, Azad was quite close to Motilal Nehru and treated Jawaharlal Nehru as his friend's son, and the same feeling was also reciprocated by Jawaharlal toward Azad. In 1929, he was elected President of the All India Muslim Nationalist Party and in his presidential address expressed views on Hindu Muslim solidarity. In 1930, Azad joined the greatest upheaval of the time—the Salt Satyagraha, launched by Gandhi and was again imprisoned. At the 1936, Congress session in Lucknow, Azad was drawn into a dispute with right-wing Congressmen Patel, Prasad, and Rajagopalachari regarding the espousal of socialism as the Congress goal. Azad had backed the election of Nehru as Congress President, and supported the resolution endorsing socialism. In fact, Azad throughout had some reservations with respect to Patel, Rajendra Prasad, whom he considered to be right-wing Hindu leaders, and who, according to Azad, did not develop any independent reasoning and backed what Gandhi told and proposed.

The year 1935 was quite important as a new Government of India act came into force, which introduced a hazy federation in India, with some sort of provincial autonomy. Elections were held in 1937 following this act, Congress took part in administration as it was able to get majority of seats in seven of the eleven provinces. Azad was then a member of the Congress Parliamentary Board, and in that capacity he tried to reconcile the differences between the rightists and the leftists within the Congress, without aligning himself to any particular group. Azad supported dialogue with Jinnah and the Muslim League between 1935 and 1937 over a possible Congress-League coalition and broader political cooperation. Azad stood by Gandhi with most other Congress leaders, but reluctantly endorsed the Congress's exit from the assemblies in 1939 following the inclusion of India in World War II.

Azad was again elected Congress President in 1940 at its Ramgarh session, the very year, when the Muslim League adopted a resolution calling for a separate Muslim state in its session in Lahore. From 1939 onwards, Azad played a very important role; first in negotiating talks with Sir Stafford Cripps at a somewhat informal level in 1939, then in negotiating with Cripps Mission in 1942 and in ultimate rejection of Cripp's Proposal as Congress President, in voicing India's stand vis-à-vis World War II, in finding a solution to the communal problems. In all such roles what is remarkable is his identity as an Indian and it is from this identity that he looked, analysed and commented on every proposal. While performing this role, he had at times serious differences with Gandhi, but he remained committed to his views and tried to convince Gandhi, sometimes with success and sometimes without.

At this juncture, Azad's severe criticism regarding Jinnah's two nation theory must be mentioned. Azad lambasted religious separatism and exhorted all Muslims to preserve a united India, as all Hindus and Muslims were Indians who shared deep bonds of brotherhood and nationhood. In his presidential address, in Ramgarh Azad said:

> ...Full eleven centuries have passed by since then. Islam has now as great a claim on the soil of India as Hinduism. If Hinduism has been the religion of the people here for several thousands of years Islam also has been their religion for a thousand years. Just as a Hindu can say

> with pride that he is an Indian and follows Hinduism, so also we can say with equal pride that we are Indians and follow Islam. I shall enlarge this orbit still further. The Indian Christian is equally entitled to say with pride that he is an Indian and is following a religion of India, namely Christianity.

A brief mention about Azad's opposition to undertake a mass movement at this stage is required. Azad was of the opinion that at a moment when Japan was knocking at the door and was almost in a position to acquire Andaman and was dangerously close to Bengal, the British Government would not tolerate any mass upsurge by the Indians, be it violent or not. Gandhi, on the other hand, firmly believed that since the war was on the Indian frontier, the British would come to terms with the Congress as soon as the movement was launched and even if this did not take place, the British would hesitate to take any drastic steps against the Indians and this would give Congress the time and opportunity to start an effective movement. Nehru was also not much in favour of Gandhi's proposal and after much debate and discussions, the Quit India Resolution was undertaken and passed by the Congress Working Committee.

The "Quit India" movement in 1942 ultimately saw the entire Congress leadership in jail. Within the prison, the Congress leaders were initially totally cut-off from the outside world and were not in a position to know what was happening outside as no newspaper or radio were allowed inside. But soon, they were given *Times of India* and got to know that after their arrest violent incidents of protest took place. Communications were disrupted and factories were closed down. Police stations were attacked and burnt. Railway stations were attacked and in some cases destroyed. Military lorries had been burnt. And all these incidents were taking place without a leadership as all the leaders were languishing in different jails of the country. Thus, Azad's apprehensions about the futility of a non-violent mass upsurge in the war situation almost proved to be correct and leaders were kept in captivity for about four years, that is, till the time when the victory of the Allied was certain and imminent. In his captivity, personal losses occurred to Azad, as he lost his wife as well as his sister. Azad began working on his classic Urdu work, the *Ghubhar-i-Khatir*, (24 letters) in urdu on contemporary events which he used to write everyday in the afternoon.

After his release in 1945, Azad in his sixth year of Congress presidency led the Congress delegation in the Simla Conference. The Conference was attended by the Congress, the Muslim League and members of the scheduled caste, Sikhs, Christian community, and some other smaller political parties. The Conference proposed, which is popularly known as Wavell Plan the reconstitution of the Viceroy's Executive Council in which the Viceroy was to select persons nominated by the political parties. Different communities were also to get their due share in the Council and parity was reserved for caste Hindus and Muslims. While declaring the plan, the Secretary of State for Indian Affairs made it clear that the British Government wanted to listen to the ideas of all major Indian communities. Yet he said that it was only possible if the leadership of the leading Indian political parties agreed with the suggestions of the British Government. However, differences arose between the leadership of the Congress and the Muslim League on the issue of representation of the Muslim community. The Muslim League claimed that since it was the only representative party of the Muslims in India, it has the sole prerogative of nominating the Muslim representatives in the Viceroy's Executive Council. Moreover, Jinnah insisted that the Congress should nominate only Hindu members. This, to the Congress delegation was a strange demand and unreasonable one, as first, how could the League interfere in the nomination of the Congress, which is surely an internal matter of the Congress, and secondly, if the Congress nominates any Muslim member, then the Muslim representation would increase and the League should be delighted for that. Ultimately, it so happens that out of the five members that the Congress nominated, two were Hindus—Nehru and Patel, one Muslim, the Congress president, one Parsee and one Christian. The Congress delegation projected their party as one representing all the communities living in India; it had approached all political problems from a national standpoint and recognized no distinction between the Hindus and Muslims on political issues. Ultimately, it so happened that the Viceroy's Executive Council had two Muslim members not nominated by the League—Azad, and Khizir Hayat Khan, the Premier of Punjab, who was nominated by the Viceroy and his candidature was backed by Congress. Congress also opposed the idea of parity of representation of between the caste—Hindus and the Muslims. All this resulted in a deadlock leading to the failure of the Conference. But, this is, perhaps, the first time in the history of the Indo-British relations when the talks failed not due to political reasons but for communal reasons.

After the conclusion of the War and the victory of the Labour Party in England, Atlee, the then British Premier made a categorical statement in the Parliament that situations have been changed completely in India and Indians as a nation are demanding freedom. And it requires a new approach from the British Government too. A high level Cabinet delegation was sent to India to find out a plan for a possible transfer of power to India. The cabinet mission came out with a proposal on May 15, 1946 advocating a federation with a weak Central Government and greater autonomy for the states. Actually, this proposal was Azad's brain-child, who thought that in order to thwart Muslim League's two nation theory and the Pakistan proposal, a federal type of government for entire India would be the best answer. He pointed out that only three subjects, namely, defence, communications and foreign affairs would be given to the Central Government and all the other subjects would be vested to the provinces. It was also decided that that the Union would be grouped—the Muslim dominated Baluchistan, Sind, Punjab and NWFP would form one group; Assam and Bengal would form one group while the Hindu majority provinces would form another group. There were problems regarding Punjab and Bengal as Punjab had a mixed population, while Bengal also had both Hindu and Muslim population. There was also problem in placing Assam and Bengal in the same group as Assam was a Hindu dominated province. This proposal was ultimately endorsed by both the Congress and the League, although there were serious reservations in both the parties.

However, on 10 July Nehru held a press conference in Bombay declaring that the Congress had agreed only to participate in the Constituent Assembly and regards itself free to change or modify the Cabinet Mission Plan as it thought best. This disturbed the League and Jinnah argued that the declaration from the Congress President that the Congress could change the scheme through its majority in the Constituent Assembly meant that the minorities would be placed at the mercy of the majority. The Muslim League rejecting the Cabinet Mission Plan decided to resort to direct action for the achievement of Pakistan. The 'Direct Action day'—August 16, 1946—unleashed communal violence in an unprecedented way in Calcutta and other parts of Bengal, in particular and throughout the country in general. This day ultimately turned out to be crucial in deciding the country's destiny as it showed to the Congressmen that sharing a peaceful solution by agreement with the Muslim League is almost an impossibility.

To end the disorder and rising bloodshed, Wavell encouraged Nehru to ask the League to enter the government. While Patel and most Congress leaders were opposed to conceding to a party that was organizing disorder, Nehru conceded in hope of preserving communal peace. The League leaders entered the council under the leadership of Liaquat Ali Khan, the future first Prime Minister of Pakistan who became the finance minister. But the council did not function in harmony—separate meetings were held by League ministers, and both parties vetoed the major initiatives proposed by the other, highlighting their ideological differences and political antagonism. Meanwhile, Atlee wanted to fix a date for transferring power to India, which Lord Wavell did not think to be a politically correct decision. Lord Wavell believed that unless the communal disturbances were controlled, it would not be proper to lay the foundation of transfer of power. These differences ultimately led to Wavell's resignation as Viceroy of India, paving the way for the arrival of the new (and proclaimed the last) viceroy, Lord Mountbatten in early 1947. Congress leaders expressed the view that the coalition was unworkable. This led to a new proposal called the Mountbatten proposal paving the way for the partition of India.

Before the acceptance of the proposal of partitioning India, it was hotly debated in the AICC and Azad realizing the increasing popularity of the League and the probable unworkability with the League abstained from voting, remaining silent most of the time and ultimately the Resolution was accepted by 29 to 15 votes.

The Constituent Assembly, which came into existence in December, 1946 for drafting the Constitution of free India saw Azad working in tandem with Nehru, Prasad, Patel and Ambedkar in drafting the Constitution. In the sovereign, democratic, republican India, Azad became the first minister in charge of Education. He was also the Minister of Education in the Interim Government from January 1947. As Education Minister of India, Azad played an important role in framing India's national policies. He raised the issue of the National System of Education which is today the bed-rock of the National Policy on Education (1986) updated in 1992. The concept implies that, up to a given level, all students, irrespective of caste, creed, location or sex have access to education of a comparable quality. All educational programmes, he said, must be carried out in strict conformity with secular values and constitutional framework. He stood for a common educational structure throughout India. The wealth of the nation, according to Azad, was not in the country's banks but in primary schools. The Maulana was also a great votary of the concept of neighbourhood schools and the Common School System. Although he was a great scholar of Urdu and Arabic, he was not averse to imparting education in English. However, he was in favour of imparting primary education in mother tongue.

Among the new institutions he established were the Indian Council for Cultural Relations (1950), the three National Academies namely, the Sangeet Natak Academy (1953), Sahitya Academy (1954) and Lalit Kala Academy (1954). ICCR is basically a cultural Institute devoted to the promotion art, literature, music and dance, and also involved in dialogue with other nations in these matters. Azad felt that the cultural content in Indian Education was very low during the British rule and needs to be strengthened through curriculum. As Chairman of the Central Advisory Board of Education, an apex body to recommend to the government educational reform both at the center and the states including universities, he advocated, in particular, universal primary education, free and compulsory for all children up to the age of 14, girls education, vocational training, agricultural education and technical education. If Azad were alive today he would have been the happiest to see the Right to Free Education Bill getting cabinet approval for the approval of Parliament. The Right to Education Bill seeks to make free and compulsory education a fundamental right. He established University Grants Commission (UGC) in 1956 by an Act of Parliament for disbursement of grants and maintenance of standards in Indian universities. He firmly believed that if the universities discharged their functions well, all will be well with the Nation. According to him the universities have not only academic functions, they have social responsibilities as well. He was pioneer in the field of adult education. On the technical education side he strengthened All Indian Council for Technical Education. The Indian Institute of Technology, Kharagpur was established in 1951 followed by a chain of IIT's at Bombay, Madras and Kanpur and Delhi. School of Planning and Architecture came into existence at Delhi in 1955. He gave a new life to 'Anjamane-Tarrqui-e-Urdu-e-Hind'. During the partition riots when the 'Anjamane-Tarrqui-Urdu' suffered, its Secretary Maulvi Abdul Haqq decided to leave for Pakistan alongwith the books of the Anjaman. Abdul Haqq had packed the books but Azad got them retrieved and thus saved a national treasure being lost to Pakistan. He also helped the Anjaman to revive by sanctioning a grant of ₹ 48,000 per month from the Ministry of Education. Likewise he increased the grants of Jamia and, Aligarh Muslim University in their days of financial crisis. He paid particular attention to the Archaeological Survey of India's efforts to repair and maintain the protected monuments. Azad spent the final years of his life focusing on writing his book *India Wins Freedom,* mainly on the requests of Humayun Kabir, his personal secretary. He died on February 22, 1958, and his dream of releasing the book on his seventieth birthday remains unfulfilled.

Azad's Views on Secularism and Nationalism

After a discussion on the life and works of Azad, it would be easier to focus on his political thought. As can be understood from what has been already said, Azad was a secular person to the core to whom distinctions and differences of men on the basis of religion is totally irrelevant. He worked tirelessly to achieve not only Hindu-Muslim unity but for the unity of all religious communities. One example will illustrate it very well. When according to the Wavell plan at the Simla conference, Congress was allowed to nominate five representatives—one choice was obvious, Azad himself, and two others are almost decided, that is Nehru and Patel. But regarding the two others, Azad thought that a Parsee and a Christian should be nominated as although both the communities were numerically small, both have a nationalist outlook and have always supported the Congress. Moreover, there was no platform from where these two communities could represent themselves. The Sikhs and the Scheduled Castes got their representation separately and to make the Viceroy's Executive Council a pan-Indian outlook consisting of all the religious communities, he devised this plan. This showed his commitment to communal harmony.

In fact, secularism constitutes the basic core around which Azad's idea of nationalism revolves. This should be understood in a greater detail, in the sense that Azad was not an atheist or indifferent to personal religion. Although, he himself proclaimed that he leaned toward 'atheism' between his age of 14 and 22, he came out of it and remained a Muslim. I have a personal feeling that it is easier for a person to become secular if he/she does not believe any religion. But this is not the case with Azad. He was a practicing Muslim, who was a great scholar in Urdu and Arabic. In fact, his translation of Quran from Arabic into Urdu in six volumes is indeed his "Magnum Opus". This commentary can be regarded as his most definitive, though controversial, theological statement on how Indian Muslims could live out their religion in a religiously pluralist and politically secular environment. It was a landmark effort to inject a liberal ethos into Islam. This pluralist and multicultural ethos inform Azad's political thinking, though from the religious standpoint, he was essentially a believer in oneness of religion, *Wahdat-i-deen,* From this respect, he seems much closer to Gandhi.

The influence of Gandhi could also be noticed from the lifestyle that he led. He led an austere life. At the time of his death he had no property and his bank balance shows a meager ₹ 2800. In his personal *almirah* were found some cotton *achkans*, a dozen *khadi kurtas* and *pyjama*, two pairs of sandals, an old dressing gown and a used brush. But there were lots of rare books which are now a property of the nation.

But it should also be mentioned that the influence of Gandhi did not colour Azad's rational judgements and the reading of political situation on the basis of his own judgement. There were several occasions, when he differed with Gandhi. One such occasion was the question of India's participation in the World War II. Gandhi was totally opposed to the idea of India's inclusion in the war, as being the champion of non-violence, he could not tolerate the occurrence of the war. In fact, Gandhi, at that time, was under terrible mental strain and even contemplated of committing suicide as he could not do anything in stopping the war. Patel, Rajendra Prasad and Rajagopalachari also supported Gandhi about India's position vis-à-vis the war. Azad and Nehru, on the other hand, were also against India's participation in the war. But the reasons are different. To them, as long as India is under Britain, there is no question of India participating in the war. Azad took the view, that India could support Britain's war efforts if Britan took positive steps toward India's demand of self-determination. They believed that if India wanted to join the war, it should be decided by India, not by the alien power. In fact, both of them and Nehru, in particular had all the sympathies with the forces of democracy, that is the Allied Power, but they pointed out that if a man's hands and feet are tied, can he work for the forces who are the enemies of those who have tied his hands and feet? Thus apparently it may show that the entire Congress leadership was against India's participation in the war, the reasons are different for Gandhi and his staunch followers, on the one hand and Azad and Nehru, on the other. To Gandhi, non-violence was a creed; while to Azad, it was a strategy which was offering the best results under the circumstances. To Gandhi, India's non-participation in the war was based on India's commitment to non-violence; to Azad, India's non-participation in the war was a strategy to get freedom. Thus, the war, itself, did not disturb Azad, as was the case with the Mahatma; it was the issue of India's unwilling participation in the war that bothered Azad.

Azad's political thinking, unlike many of his contemporaries including Gandhi is marked more by consistency than by internal contradictions. It is well-known, that unlike Western political thought, where almost all the thinkers were theoreticians and not active politicians, India political thought develops surrounding the thinking of those, who were active politicians. As a result, the thinker or the politician has to shift many a times in consonance with the changing political events. This is true in case of Gandhi; this is also true in case of Rabindranath, who was certainly not a politician, but had intense writings on several political issues. But unlike them, Azad's thinking is remarkably consistent. One can get a consistent account in Azad's political and intellectual development: his induction in the orthodox Islamic education, his reading of Sir Syed Ahmed Khan, his revulsion at his father's religious prejudices, his precocious career as a journalist; his remarkable erudition in Arabic sources; his disdain for the conservative '*ulema* as well as westernised Muslims; and finally, his career as a secular and national leader of Indian National Congress. In fact, Azad was so much a nationalist and secular leader that he personifies the aspirations of Congress which is a party of all religions, caste and creed. His status was thus the focal point of Gandhi's clash with Jinnah, who maintained that politically no one but a Muslim Leaguer could represent Muslim interests. Some of the Congress leaders talked from a majoritarian Hindu standpoint, while the strident Muslim Leaguers decried Azad as a 'renegade'. Yet he remained, until the end, consistent in his loyalty to a unified Indian nation. Time and again, he repudiated Jinnah's two-nation theory. He reaffirmed: "It is one of the greatest frauds on the people to suggest that religious affinity can unite areas which are geographically, economically, linguistically and culturally different." With an insight rare for those from his background, he pointed out that the real problems of the country were economic, not communal. The differences related to classes, not to communities.

This aspect is another important facet of Azad's political thinking. Although, we have noticed that in 1928, Azad endorsed the Nehru Report and called for an independent India committed to socialism in opposition to many of the then Congress right-wing leaders, but nowhere, do I come across the fact that he was under the influence of Marxist political thought. But without being a Marxist as such, he understood that the problems relating to Muslims of India are not based on the fact that they profess a different religion from that of the Hindus, but is related to their relative deprivation with respect to the sharing of economic resources and educational facilities. In this respect, a somewhat closeness may be noticed between Azad and Sir Syad Ahmed Khan, who called for Western education of the Muslims and started the Aligarh movement.

The affinity of thinking between Nehru and Azad could be found in some other aspects too. He was also committed to a liberal political framework wedded to parliamentary democracy. This can be noticed from the fact that he was actively involved in the making of the Indian Constitution. He was a firm believer in the freedom of thought and expression, which could be noticed from his *Al Hilal* days. He took up his pen to preach nationalist views in the weekly, for which his weekly was ultimately confiscated.

Azad's View on Education

A few words about Azad's thinking on education may now be mentioned. As the first education minister of independent India, Azad played a crucial role in building the foundation of education in India, which was elitist and colonial at that time. From his young days, Azad understood the importance of science and technology, not just as tools for developing a modern nation but more importantly as vehicle for establishing the foundation of modern education. At the same time, Azad's educational perspective was fundamentally Islamic in inspiration, yet he was able to synthesize happily anything of value anywhere. He was not exclusively an "Islamic" mind or even an "oriental" mind, unacquainted with, or insensitive to, the rich streams of influences emanating from other sources. Regarding the medium of instruction, Azad realized that either Sanskrit of Persian was not suited; but at the same time he was critical of English, which was introduced as the medium of instruction as that would lead to artificial shaping and thinking of children's minds. He firmly believed that only provincial languages need to be developed to serve the purpose of medium of instruction. Another important issue for Azad was democratization of education. Azad was inspired by the values of our freedom struggle and he was convinced that those values should come in handy for nation building, where education should be seen as a right for all the citizens of this newly independent nation. In this context, Azad also emphasised on education of women, which was almost marginalized at that time.

III
RELEVANCE OF AZAD'S THOUGHTS

The cornerstones of Azad's political thought, which are of immense relevance today may now be discussed. First, although Nehru and Azad remain true friends not only during the days of struggle, but also after independence, it is quite clear from the full text of Azad's autobiography *India Wins Freedom* although Azad dedicated this book to Nehru, friend and comrade that he developed some strong reservations about Nehru in late 1946 and early 1947. When Muslim League first accepted the plan of the cabinet mission and later withdrew from it and resorted to direct action on August 16, Azad noted that: This was one of the greatest tragedies of Indian history and I have to say with deepest regret that a large part of the responsibility for this development rests with Jawaharlal. His unfortunate statement that Congress was free to modify the Cabinet Mission plan reopened the whole question of political and communal settlement. Azad had also very strong opinion vis-a-vis Patel. This is, however, nothing but quite obvious. Azad stated that it was Gandhi, who built Patel step by step and naturally on all occasions, he merely echoed Gandhi's wishes.

Second, it seems Azad was quite a loner particularly in the last years of nationalist struggle. He always spoke of a composite Indian culture committed to pluralistic ethos, but he was not much accepted by his community. Even his colleagues of Congress opposed him particularly during 1947, when Congress was keen in accepting Mountbatten Plan and Azad still tried to cling to the Cabinet Mission Plan. In fact, since 1946, Azad was almost sidelined and as stated earlier was forced to accept the partitioning of the country in silence. On the other hand, Muslim League, for obvious reasons did not have any regard for Azad, which can be shown by two very oft-quoted incidents: One, Jinnah called Azad a Muslim "show-boy" Congress president, and second from the fact that Jinnah refused to shake hand with Azad after the Simla Conference. What is more disheartening is that even in India, Azad has not been an attractive subject to the scholars and researchers of Indian political thought. A British historian of South Asia noticed how differently those who supported the movement for Pakistan have come to be remembered and compared with those who devoted themselves to Indian nationalism. Mohammad Iqbal's tomb of sandstone and white marble is a place of pilgrimage. Mohammed Ali Jinnah's *mazar* is a symbol of Pakistan's identity and one of the first places to which the visitor to Karachi is taken. Maulana Abul Kalam Azad's mausoleum before the Jama Masjid in Delhi, on the other hand, is not greatly frequented.

Third, Azad was really as Nehru said "a finished product of culture." From a reading of his autobiography, it seems to me that he deliberately drops the curtain in places, where he could have said more. This deliberate silence no doubt points to a man of great culture and refined taste and prevents us from not only knowing a particular time period, in details but also prevents us from knowing the man completely. It is also said about his autobiography in Urdu *Tazirka*, which is although written much earlier in 1919, that he spoke little and concealed more.

Fourth, he was, no doubt a great orator. But as he preferred to speak in Urdu, it was difficult to organize people on a mass scale. As Prof. Mushirul Hasan said: He was not somebody who traversed the dusty political terrain to stir the masses into activism. But he had a remarkable rational mind full of logical consistency that had the ability of convincing those, who at first did not share his views. This happened in umpteen times in various meetings with Gandhi, Nehru and the several British delegations.

The Indian nation should wake up and should try to embrace at least a few remarkable traits of this great son of India—who mixed scholarship and inwardness; integrity and belief; support and opposition nonchalantly and with great ease. With respect to education, 21st century India is recognizing now the right to education; but it was in the first decade of post-colonial India that Azad talked about the necessity of providing basic education to all. The same can be said about Azad's emphasis on women's education as he believed that it was necessary for two purposes: One, as citizens of free India, women should have education, and second, educated women could teach the next generation young people. We have now understood how education is related to human development. Herein lies the great contribution and relevance of Azad's vision and political thinking.

Further Reading

Azad, Abul Kalam. (1958, reprint: 1989). *India Wins Freedom*. Orient Blackswan, New Delhi.

Habib, S. Irfan (ed.) (2010). *Maulana Abul Kalam Azad and the National Education System* (National University of Educational Planning and Administration), New Delhi.

Hasan, Mushirul. (1991). *Nationalism and Communal Politics in India, 1885-1930*, Manohar, New Delhi.

21

Acharya Narendra Deva (1889-1956): Ethical Socialist

Sarbani Guha Ghosal

I
INTRODUCTION

Acharya Narendra Deva (October 31, 1889-February 19, 1956) is one of the revered names in the history of Indian socialist thought as well as in the history of freedom movement and anti-colonial struggle in India. He was born in a family of eminent intellectuals in Faizabad of Uttar Pradesh. His father Babu Baldeva Prasad was a renowned lawyer of his time and wanted to make his brilliant son Narendra a lawyer of high repute. Gradually Narendra also became a lawyer of high status as well as he became well conversant in a number of languages and a great scholar of politics, economics and sociology. He was a magnificent orator and writer in Hindi and English. In 1926 became the principal of Kashi Vidyapith and became known as Acharya Deva. From 1951 to 1954, he also served as the chancellor of the Lucknow University. He started to champion openly the cause of socialism within the nationalist movement since the nineteen thirties.

II
POLITICAL IDEAS OF NARENDRA DEVA

Acharya Deva started his political career as a believer in the extremist nationalism of Bal Gangadhar Tilak and Aurobindo Ghosh. He was the secretary of the Home Rule League of his locality. He also took active part in the Gandhian Non-cooperation Movement. In the young age of Narendra Deva the Indian National Congress was suffering from the ideological battle between the moderates and the extremists. He had deep faith on the extremist ideals and armed with those he actively got involved in the nationalist and anti-imperialist struggle of his time. He presided over the inaugural meeting of the All India Congress Socialist Conference in 1934. He realized that unless the farmers of the country were imbibed with nationalistic sentiments it was very hard to secure freedom. He vigorously participated in organizing the peasantry of the country under All India Kisan Sabha and also elected its secretary twice. He was also closely associated with the pro-socialist bloc of the Indian National Congress and was a member of All India Congress Working Committee for a considerable period. His inclusion in the Working Committee was proposed by none other than Pandit Jawaharlal Nehru after the Lucknow session of INC in 1936. In 1947 his name was suggested for Congress presidentship but was opposed by Sardar Vallabhbhai Patel.

Gradually he was deeply attracted toward Jayaprakash Narayan and with the efforts of this duo in particular the socialist wing of the Congress became powerful which ultimately led to a split in the mainstream Congress movement. However, Deva was not at all in favour of severing ties with Congress. The pro-socialist group under them was quite enthusiastic about the idea of transforming Congress into a socialist political organization by inducting the workers and peasants more in the leadership and by going in direct confrontation with the Britishers regarding Swaraj. As a result in the Nasik Conference of Congress, 1948 the socialists were ultimately compelled to sever their ties with Congress. Later on this Socialist Party became the Proja Socialist Party (PSP) and in the post-independent days it gave up its revolutionary ideas and started following the principle of democratic socialism. Furthermore in 1952 at Mumbai with the initiative of Narendra Deva the Krishak Mazdur Proja Party (KMPP) and Congress Socialist Party merged together with the intention to give new direction to the socialist movement in India.

Socialist theoretician and political leader Narendra Deva was greatly influenced by Buddhism and Marxism and was considered as an eminent Buddhologist (not Buddhist) of the country. He was not a Buddhist by conviction but the anti-transcendentalist orientation of Buddhist thought attracted him a lot. He believed that not theism but the acceptance of moral governance of the world was the essence of Indian culture. The writings of Bukharin, particularly his famous book Historical Materialism influenced him a lot. He accepted Bukharin's criteria and classification of classes and agreed with him in holding that besides two main social classes of the bourgeoisie and the labourers there are found in society other classes too like the middle classes, the transition classes and the mixed classes. He also deeply detested the idea of bureaucratic interference in state. He was a firm believer in the idea of class struggle and believed that the management of industry should be controlled by the workers as a class. Being a believer in the materialistic interpretation of history he thought that capitalism had exhausted its all creative potentiality and growth of monopolies further worsened the exploitative face of capitalism. In this context adoption of scientific socialism is the only way to save humanity from unending conflict and severe wars (Varma 1996: 512-13).

III
NARENDRA DEVA'S RELEVANCE IN INDIAN POLITICAL THOUGHT

Narendra Deva is often identified as an ethical socialist because of his strong belief in the primacy of moral values. He considered socialism as a part of cultural movement and emphasized upon the moral foundations of socialism. To him, truth was primary and basic entity. Yet he refused to adhere to the Gandhian concept of *ahimsa* (non-violence) in its entirety and also refused to give up the theory of class struggle. In this context it is worthwhile to remember that though Narendra Deva and Jayaprakash Narayan were Marxist in their ideology they were in close touch with Gandhi and won his personal affection as well.

In his famous writing *Socialism and the National Revolution* Acharya Deva tried to view the socioeconomic problems of India from the perspective of class struggle. He called for an alliance between the lower middle classes and the large masses of peasantry and workers. He was aware of the fact that the theoretical basis of socialism would not have much appeal for the general masses and they could be made class-conscious only by appealing straight to them in economic terms which had direct bearing on their daily lives. Following Leninist formulation he believed that socialist revolution would occur not necessarily in the industrially advanced countries but where "the chain of imperialism is the weakest". To him the working class was the vanguard in the struggle for liberation and peasantry and intelligentsia were the "auxiliaries of the anti-imperialist struggle". He strongly held that constitutionalism and reformism would not bring any good for Indian masses and active mass mobilization based on economic orientation could bring true democracy in India. Inculcation of socialism in nationalist struggle was of utmost importance for Deva. With this intention he tried to merge the nationalist movement and the socialist movement of the country together.

According to Narendra Deva India was passing then through the stage of bourgeois democratic revolution. He cautioned the Marxist socialists of his time against any kind of dogmatism and urged them to form alliance with the petty bourgeoisie of the country in the freedom struggle. The socialists, to him, for their own interest and for the interest of establishing socialism in the country, must actively got involved in the widespread nationalist struggle. Political freedom from colonial oppression was "an inevitable stage on the way to socialism". Thus he showed his complete support to the famous August Resolution of the INC on 1942 and said that it "defined the social dimensions of freedom". He regarded that August Resolution was a great example of mass solidarity and its aim was to establish the supremacy of the common man. In his analysis British imperialism in the country had strengthened its foundation with the help of native princes, feudal oligarchs and the native capitalists. This counter-revolutionary alliance had to be challenged by broadening the basis of freedom with definite constructive works among the masses and thereby winning their confidence. It required serious programming towards political and economic emancipation of the country. A united front of workers, peasantry and petty-bourgeois elements could be of help in this regard as it could both widen and strengthen the base of mass struggle. Deva hoped that after the World War II a series of mass revolution in India would draw its new future. Unfortunately his expectation failed in materialization test.

Acharya Deva took keen interest in agrarian reconstruction of India. He favoured mobilization of all sections of peasantry together under the aegis of the Kisan Sabhas. He felt that emancipation of peasantry was deeply tied up to the rural literacy campaign and mass education. Appalling poverty was the most immediate crisis for the Indian peasants and so agricultural reconstruction should primarily be directed toward poverty alleviation. This demanded radical scheme for rural reconstruction which to him in reality was nothing other than organizing and strengthening of rural cooperative societies and imbuing the peasants with socialist ideology together. He formulated some very specific schemes for agrarian reconstruction and prominent among those were cancellation of debts of the peasants and availability of cheap credit for them. He also called for rearrangement in the land distribution pattern. Abolition of the middleman system which stood in several layers between the actual tillers and the state was also within his formulation. However, he denounced peasantism or narrow agrarianism as that would increase unnecessary the rural-urban conflict. He propagated the idea of instilling grass-root democracy in the villages by introducing cooperative commonwealth (Varma 1996: 515). This would be instrumental in removing the cultural backwardness of the rural people as well as that would infuse new ideals and aspirations among the rural masses.

Famous French philosopher and protagonist of syndicalism Georges Eugene Sorel's idea of general strike had considerable impact upon Deva. He had faith in the emotional, tactical and ideological benefits of general strikes. For India, Narendra Deva thought that a general strike would paralyze the entire economy and would ultimately force the British colonial exploiters to leave the country. Moreover, if the general strike could be made successful then that would be a great prelude for a socialist revolution in the country.

Narendra Deva was a protagonist of secularist nationalism. But his secularism did not emanate from indifference toward the religions. He was ready to give religion its due place in social life but strongly believed that transcendental and theological concerns must not overcast the process of rational social planning. He believed true nationalism in India was neither antagonistic to socialism and not to secularism.

Throughout his political career Acharya Deva tried to expand the basis of the nationalist struggle. Generally the socialists of his period used to prioritize international socialist revolution over nationalist struggle. But in spite of being a socialist by conviction nationalist struggle was never a second preference for him. He believed that true emancipation of the people of the country was possible only by successfully combining nationalist freedom struggle with the struggle of the workers and peasants. He was strongly attracted to the Marxist tradition of class struggle rather than to the Leninist idea of capturing political power with an armed party by violently overthrowing the authority. In other words, his main thrust was on the humanist foundations of socialism as that would help India to traverse through a completely new path. It was for this in the post-independent period also he was not in favour of dissociating the socialist movement of the country completely from the agenda of the Congress which staunch socialists like Dr. Rammanohar Lohia followed. In the 1950s thus Deva supported the theory of "Compulsions of Backward Economy and Responsive Cooperation" propagated by another noted socialist Dr. Ashok Mehta.

Acharya Narendra Deva belonged to that genre of political theorist and activist who believed in continuously exploring the real lives of the masses instead of leading or preaching from a high altar. His practical politics was well complemented with his incessant studies of international and national conditions. Though his ideas were often criticized for being contradictory and unrealistic in nature but his contribution towards the growth of Indian socialist political thinking can never be forgotten. The uniqueness of the Indian condition and the adaptation of the socialist ideology to suit its needs were quite aptly understood by him. Rajni Kothari, the great master of Indian Political Science identified that Narendra Deva, Jayaprakash Narayan, Vinoba Bhabe, Achyut Patwardhan, Aruna Asaf Ali as institution builders of India who stayed away from party politics and concentrated on building institutions of a truly voluntaristic kind without which the more official efforts at institution-building would have lacked depth and a grass-root anchorage (Kothari 1997: 109).

References

Kothari, Rajni. 1997. "Institution Building in India: Retrieving Lost Ground" in *India International Centre Quarterly*. Vol. 24. No. 1. Spring 1997.

Lal, Shiv. 1989. *Indian Political Thought: Secular Politics*. New Delhi: Election Archives.

Varma, V.P. 1996. *Modern Indian Political Thought*. Agra: Lakshmi Narain Agarwal Educational Publishers.

22

Jawaharlal Nehru: An Architect of Modern India (1889-1964)

Lopamudra Sengupta

I
INTRODUCTION

Jawaharlal Nehru, India's first Prime Minister reminds us of a man with a multifaceted personality. The smile on his face, the red rose on his button-hole, and the easy enchantment of his manner, whether with children or with adults, and his love for the sights and sounds of Nature, reveals his aesthetic bent of mind.

He was an ardent nationalist and freedom fighter during the colonial period and in the post-independence period, for almost two decades (1947-64) he tried to secure the position of India in the history of world politics.

His uniqueness as noted by eminent Parliamentarian Hiren Mukherjee lay in the unobtrusive opulence of endowment, which gave him, the thick of politics and in the face of frustration a peculiar refinement and grace of spirit.[1]

In order to grasp the essential elements of the political thought of one of the most notable political actors and world's statesman of the twentieth century, it is important to discuss briefly his life in the early childhood and the environment in which he had grown up that largely shaped his personality.

Jawaharlal Nehru born in 14th November 1889 in Allahabad was the son of the eminent lawyer—politician Motilal Nehru and was brought up in the midst of wealth. Prosperity in the family was so pronounced that Jawaharlal one said "I am a typical bourgeois brought up in the bourgeois surroundings with all the early prejudices that this training has given me."[2] His father was a great admirer of English and he appointed English tutors for his son, who studied at home till the age of fifteen. As a boy he was exposed to the study of theosophy which was introduced by his residential tutor Ferdinand T. Brooks, a Theosophist and a disciple of Annie Besant.

In May 1905, Nehru was sent to Harrow for education. In England, he studied metaphysical arguments and discussed about reincarnation and the doctrine of *Karma*, and referred to the writings of Madame Blavatsky, the Hindu Scriptures and the Buddhist '*Dhammapada*' and other philosophers and mystics. His admiration for the great book like *Upanishads* and the *Bhagavata Gita* grew when he was a young boy about twelve or thirteen years. He joined the Theosophical Society at the age of thirteen and was initiated by Mrs Besant herself. Two years later he went to Trinity College at Cambridge, where in 1910 he obtained a degree in natural science.[3]

In the childhood Nehru was much closer to his mother, than his father Motilal Nehru. Though he admired his father's strength, and courage and cleverness', he feared him for his terrible temper and domineering attitude.[4]

Later however Nehru carried much further his father's rationalism and agnosticism. Motilal Nehru was not a religious man though he had respect for the Hindu Religion and had considerable knowledge on Hindu inheritance as a lawyer. He did not like many of Hindu social customs, and dejected them for which he later came into conflict with the orthodox Hindu section of the society. This points out that Nehru was not raised in an orthodox Kashmir Brahmin Family. The family had come down to Delhi from Kashmir, in the eighteenth century at the insistence of the Mughal emperor, Farukhsiar, who recognised the eminence of Pandit Rajkaul (one of Nehru's ancestors) as a Sanskrit and Persian scholar. Nehru's descendants were thus known as *Kaul-Nehru's* as they lived on the bank of the canal, *Nahar*. Later on Jawaharlal's father dropped *Kaul* and they came to be known as 'Nehru's'. Nehru thus grew up in the cosmopolitan culture being much influenced by Mughal manner of life and Islamic culture. Jawaharlal wrote "I grew up in the North India, where there is a mixture of what is sometimes called moslem culture in language, in ways of living in food etc." Nehru thus grew up in a composite cultural life.[5]

Later in life Nehru was married to Kamala, a simple lady who had greatly inspired him to join in the nationalist politics.

II
NEHRU'S CONTRIBUTION TO POLITICAL THOUGHT

Ideas of Gandhi and Nehru

After the completion of his studies in England Nehru returned to India in 1912, at the age of twenty-three, 'with a culture that imbibed values both from the east and the west.' In 1917, he was elected both as the Secretary of his Home Rule League, Allahabad, and also as the member of the All India Congress Committee. Finally in 1929, he was elected as the President of the Congress.

Though Nehru was largely influenced by Mahatma Gandhi who had initiated and indoctrinated him into active politics he largely differed from Gandhiji in his vision in re-building the nation. For Gandhiji, there was no separation between religion and politics. Gandhi believed in astecism, renunciation and non-violence. By contrast, Nehru was secular in his outlook and approach. Being secular in approach, Nehru insisted on using reason in the solution of moral and political problems.

Secondly, Gandhi was nostalgic about the self-sufficient villages of the past. Nehru thought that the idea of decentralisation should not be confused with the self-sufficiency of the village resting on old rather primitive methods of production.

Thirdly, Nehru was discontented with Gandhiji's idea of Trusteeship which cannot significantly ameliorate the social and economic condition of the masses. Nehru believed in largest scale industrialisation of the country and for higher standard of living for the people.

Fourthly, Nehru did not subscribe to Gandhiji's concept of party-less village democracy which according to Nehru was to be exploited by some vested interests. He also felt that Gandhiji's conception of democracy has nothing to do with numbers or majority or representation in the ordinary sense. It is based more on service and sacrifice and uses more moral pressure. Nehru was more keen to Western democracy which believed in representative democracy based on universal suffrage. Nehru thought that the organised parties were essential for its functioning.

Nehru looked upon science and technology as great creative forces but Gandhi had a great suspicion of the large application of science and technology. Thus Nehru and Gandhi differed fundamentally in their outlook on their life, politics and economics. Thus while Gandhiji sought to change people's mind and heart and tried to build up the socio-psychological infra-structure of the democratic society Nehru was more interested in Institutions and he sought to change economic social and political relationship and build social institutions of democratic and just polity.[6]

Amidst various differences between Gandhi and Nehru they shared essentially certain things in common one being essentially the desire and ability, to set down the ideas on the printed page. Nehru's literary ability can be found out from his three major publications.

(i) *Glimpses of World History* (1934)

(ii) *An Autobiography* (1936)

(iii) *The Discovery of India* (1946)

all of which acclaimed him as a writer before Indian Independence. After Independence his letters to his Chief Ministers which he wrote from October 1927 and continued till December 1963, was published in V volumes as "Letters to Chief Ministers", and had thrown light on all most all the major subjects that Nehru had thought about from economic development and religious politics the ethics of governance, the cold war, etc.

From all these books we get a clear vision of Nehru's vision and dreams about India which he wanted to translate into reality. But Nehru's dreams were not easy to be realised. After

Independence, he was left with a disintegrated economy with problems related to local aspirations or local sense of identity that were under the foreign control, and the princely state like Hyderabad and Kashmir.

Nehru's vision of 'New India' was fashioned out of the urgent realities of Indian political experience and socio-economic conditions, as well as his own intellectual and moral commitments.[7]

Nehru's Idea of Nationalism

Nehru's nationalist spirit can be discerned from his various writings. He did not propound any new theory of nationalism. He had a strong belief in fundamental unity of India based on its cultural foundations. In his *The Discovery of India* which he had written in his prison days in Ahamednagar Fort in 1944, he discussed various aspects of past and present day India, the coming of the Aryanas, Indus valley civilization, etc. Apart from the civilization he also discuss the various religious scriptures that depicts his deep yearnings for his country. His frequent utterances of names like the great monk Buddha, and emperor Ashoka reveals his faith in Indian culture and that he was proud to be an Indian.

Nehru all along had a driving force for freedom and independence. It gave a certain degree of unity, vigour and vitality to many people all over the world.[8]

Nehru's nationalism is also reflected in some of the attitudinal arrogance which he showed towards the British rulers. He criticized their racial arrogance and blamed them for the ruthless exploitation of this country. He was also against the imperial powers who took political and administrative decisions.[9]

By virtue of being a nationalist Nehru, was also a crusader against imperialism. Nehru's anti-imperialism was largely the product of his own understanding of the historical evolution of the laws of social change. Nehru was clear in his mind that so long as imperialism was not rooted out, mankind would continue to suffer both exploitation and oppression.

Nehru's Socialist Ideas

The beginning of Nehru's interest in socialist ideas can be traced back to days of Cambridge when he was attracted to Fabian socialist ideas of Bernard Shaw the Webbs and also of Bertrand Russell.

In keeping with his rationalist and secular attitude, Nehru was in search of a political Ideology in India. In 1920 hearing of a march on Allahabad by some peasants he decided to visit their encampment on banks of the Yamuna. Looking at them and their misery Nehru's heart was filled with shame due to his easy going life and also with sorrow due to his ignorance of vast multitude of semi-naked sons and daughter of India, and the overwhelming poverty of India which he had witnessed. He therefore became keen in adopting socialism.

However, Nehru himself noted that is outlook of socialism was much wider and his approach to socialism was idealistic, ethical, humanitarian, scientific, technological, pragmatic as well as Marxian.

Nehru tried to evolve a social philosophy for the construction of Indian society on the basis of equality, social justice and security. In order to achieve the goal of classless society, he emphasized the necessity of "total transformation" of social life through democratic methods. He was of the view that the process of the rich becoming richer and the poor poorer has to be stopped by planned methods.

Nehru was also greatly impressed by the efforts of Soviet Union, to bring about a total change in the social life by planned methods after the revolution. But he could not accept thc practical form of communism.

In 1933 in '*Whither India*' Nehru said that a purely nationalistic approach, which had no economic or social content, was incomplete and that a progressive ideology of social revolution was essential. If an indigenous government took the place of the foreign government and kept all the vested interests intact, that would not be even the shadow of freedom. Therefore, politically freedom would mean independence and severance of the British connection, and economically and socially it would mean the ending of class privileges and the establishment of socialism.

Writing to his daughter in 1933 Nehru attempted to define socialism. He said that socialism was of many kinds, but there was general agreement that it aimed at control by the state of the means of production; that is, land and mines and factories and the lime, and the means of distribution, like railways, and also banks and similar institutions. The idea was that the individual should not exploit any of these institutions or the labour of other of his personal advantage.[10]

For Nehru socialism much more than an economic doctrine. It was the philosophy of life. He saw no way of ending the poverty, the vast unemployment, the degradation and subjection of Indian people except through socialism.

In 1929, Nehru as Congress President Nehru categorically declared himself as a socialist. In 1936, Nehru again as Congress President spoke of socialism in an economic and not in a merely humanitarian sense. In the thirties Nehru spoke of socialism. But after 1937 and till the early fifties Nehru was preoccupied with questions relating to freedom struggle, the Quit India movement, transfer of power and partition rather than with socialism; and during this period socialism was not as prominent in his speeches as it was before.

Thus it is important to note the Nehru's view of socialism kept changing, his views greatly differed from around the years 1935 and 1955. It has to be admitted that this change was probably due to the rapid change in circumstances where Nehru who had been in the role of a political agitator was then acting in the position of Prime Minister of India.

Nehru's Idea of Democracy and Secularism

Nehru was a firm believer of human equality and social justice in all aspects of human life. Based on this belief parliamentary democracy according to Nehru was the most suitable form of government. He said that parliamentary democracy is not something which can be created in a country by some magic wand. Parliamentary democracy naturally involves peaceful methods of action, peaceful acceptance of decision taken, and attempts to change them through peaceful ways again.

Nehru's experience of British imperialism during the long years freedoms struggle, had contributed to strengthen his love and deep attachment to civil liberties. He was a great defender of freedom which constitutes the basis of democracy.

Nehru realised the goodwill of the people and their co-operation a needed for the successful working of democracy.

According to Nehru, democracy is the best form of government as it preserves the highest human values. Nehru was confident about the success of democracy of India. He said "We will resist the imposition of any other concept here or any other practice."

Thus Nehru was a firm believer of Parliamentary system, free election, free press, freedom of speech, of religion and assembly, political parties and constitutional safe guards for individual rights.

We have earlier noted that Nehru was brought up in a cosmopolitan culture. It was because of this liberal cultural up bringing that Nehru adopted a secular approach. He condemned the leaders of the Hindu Mahasabha as reactionaries and upholders of upper-class interest. He was never satisfied with the generally prevalent religious explanation of Hindu-Muslim tensions in pre-independent India. Nehru's devotion to *scientific methodology*, with its emphasis on *rationalism* helped the evolution of his nationalist political ideology which, in its emphasis on secular's democracy, opposed medievalism, obscurantism and religious dogmatism.

Nehru's secularism found expression officially for the first time in the resolution draft by him on 'Fundamental Rights and Duties' which was adopted by the Karachi Congress in 1931. Clause (1)(ix) of the resolution read: 'The State shall observe neutrality in regard to all religions.' The secular state did not in any sense imply that religion ceased to be significant in the life of the individual. It only meant the separation of the state from religion—a cardinal principle of modern democratic practice. Nehru was vehemently opposed to the idea of a theocratic state which, in his view, was both medieval and anti-democratic in character and had no place in the mind of a modern individual.

Nehru favoured a strong secular base for the state primarily for the maintenance of social stability and religious harmony among diverse groups. It was his firm conviction that a secular state alone could better serve a community divide by diverse religious creeds and faiths. With the state pledged to secular way of life, the Constitution of India guaranteed the right to freedom of religion as a fundamental right. Nehru was specially interested in the enumeration of the 'Directive Principles of State Policy' which suggested the creation of a uniform civil code for all in India. In order to maintain national unity and thereby to ensure orderly progress, a secular approach was considered to be an imperative need.[11]

Nehru: Ideas in Liberalism Humanism and Rights

Brought up in the liberal culture of British legacy, Nehru greatly stressed emphasis on individual rights. He was attracted to the ethical norms of Western humanism, and later to the precepts of the *Vedanta*, the ancient system of Hindu philosophy, but stripped of its purely metaphysical and religious beliefs. He spoke for nationalism and racial equality which were nothing but reflections for his live for human beings while referring to Soviet society, some of whose achievements he admired he remarked: *I am too much of an individualist and believer in personal freedom, to like over much regimentation.* Although conscious of the powerful pressures limiting the scope of individual action, he also professed his belief in free will. Within limits, and in the worth of the individual. He was acutely sensitive to the sufferings of the masses.

It is difficult to place Nehru in an ideological spectrum. He was a liberal and a democrat, a socialist and an individualist. However, one need not be confused about these because all the above ideologies barring the 'means' of attaining it spoke actually of greater humanity and the emancipation of mankind.

Nehru declared, "I suppose I am temperamentally and by training an individualist, and intellectually socialism does not kill or suppress individuality; indeed I am attracted to it because it will release innumerable individuals from economic and cultural bondage".

As K.R. Narayan (Member of Indian Foreign Service) pointed out from his own experiences that Nehru's sensitivity to the little things of life brought out more vividly than anything else the humanist in him.

President of India, R. Venkataraman, also talked of Nehru as a great humanist. Extraordinarily sensitive to human needs and demands of humanism, he ever ignored human factors in his advocacy of modernization of the Indian economy, scientific and technological progress and unremitting efforts towards world peace and opting for human betterment.

On December 11, 1963, he said we should think more of the very poor countrymen of ours and do something to improve their lot as quickly as we can.

Action speaks louder than words. Nehru's attitude was not to think too much about fundamental intellectual problems but rather to concentrate on the immediate urgent and concrete problems of life. This is, indeed, the core of Nehru's approach, to merge thought and action in the achievement of social goals. "The call of action has long been with me," he wrote in 1944, "not action divorced from thought, but rather flowing from it in one continuous sequence."[12]

Rights of Underprivileged

This humanistic appeal led Nehru to evolve a philosophy and policy for development and growth of the tribal people, culminating in the early fifties in the well-known Panchasheel of tribal development. Nehru's sensitivity about human beings can be sensed when in 7 June 1952, Nehru said: there are generally two ways of approaching the problem of the tribal people. One might be called the anthropological approach of treating these people and not as living human beings with one could work and play. The other approach is of rather ignoring that they are something special and different and trying to absorb them into normal pattern of society elsewhere. Both these approaches according to Nehru were wrong. He believed that a measure of protection in their areas is needed so that no outsider can interfere with them except with the consent and goodwill.

Nehru thus touched the tribal psyche when he called for their advancement along with the preservation of their identity.

His strong belief in retaining one's own culture and his rejection in imposing one's culture on the tribal's are clearly surfaced when he pointed out that "I would prefer being a nomad in the hills to being a member of stock exchanges, where one is made to sit and listen to noises that are ugly to a degree. Is that the civilizations we want the tribal people to have? I hope not. I am quite sure that the tribal folk with their civilization of song and dance, will last till long after stock exchanges have ceased to exist."[13]

Nehru also championed for the peasantry. It was only in June 1920, his interaction with the Kisans who came to Allahabad from interior of Pratapgarh to draw the attention of prominent politicians of their woeful conditions that helped Nehru is developing his 'human face' which was already lying latent in him.

Nehru was not only man of great vision but he was also man of action. After independence he had realised that there has to be specific planning and policies that will form the basis of good institutions required to perform the basic structural functions required for the State. With aim in mind he set out to build the Planning Commission and also formulated an unique system of mixed economy which according to him could have save the economically ravaged country and will build it systematically along its own needs at that time.

According to Nehru more and more it is being realized in other parts of world that we in India are engaged in a mighty adventure. To build up this country and to solve the problems of poverty and unemployment in a democratic way on this scale is something that has not been done any where.

According to Nehru the Western world had either paid in sufficient attention to economic liberation or acquired it at the cost of individual rights. Without socio-economic freedom the departure of British rule would have little impact on the quality of life of India's millions. Planning was at the heart of Nehru's effort as to marry of welfare State with democracy. Although his disagreed with Russia's curbing of political liberties, he took great inspiration from its determinations and resolve towards economic self-sufficiency.

Nehru's Ideas on Planning and Mixed Economy

Nehru considered planning as the application of science to national problems. He took active part in the proceedings of the National Planning Committee, of which he was the chairman, and which was set up by Subhas Bose as Congress president in 1938. The Planning Commission contained the Five Year Plan.

After independence the question arose whether Nehru would introduce planning and fully implement socialistic politics. Indeed, there was a crisis in business confidence because an avowed socialist had become the prime minister, and there was a "strike of capital" pending announcement of the government's industrial policy. This policy, announced in 1948, contemplated public ownership of munitions, atomic energy, and railways; and in certain other industries, namely, coal, iron and steel, aircraft manufacturing, shipbuilding, telephonic and telegraphic materials, and minerals, the government reserved the exclusive right to start new ventures, though the existing concerns in these industries were to remain free from governmental control and were not to be nationalized for at least ten years. The rest of the industrial field was left open for free enterprise.

India's First Five-Year Plan (1951-56) was moderate as compared to subsequent plans. Under it about two-thirds of the expenditure of the public sector were allocated for agriculture, community development, irrigation, power projects, transport and communications. Only 10 per cent of the expenditure was allocated for industrial development.

In the second plan Nehru insisted that more importance be given to industry so that India could attain economic self-reliance and develop along modern lines.

The third plan was more ambitious, and its targets were more than double the targets of the second. Its object was to take India to a stage where he national economy would become self-sustaining.

Planning under Nehru was based on the concept of a mixed economy. In 1952 the Planning Commission stated: "In a planned economy the distinction between the public and the private sector is one of emphasis. The two sectors are and must function as parts of a single organism. But Nehru said that it was obvious that an undeveloped country like India could not progress except by enlarging the public sector and except by controlling the private sector at important points. The private sector would have to function under certain broad strategic controls, but otherwise with freedom and initiative.

He wanted to follow the middle path. In 1958, he said that he did not want state socialism of that extreme kind in which the state was all powerful and governed practically all activities. He wanted decentralization of economic power, where possible. He conceded that one could not decentralize iron and steel and locomotives and other big industries, but it was possible to have small units or industries, particularly on a cooperative basis, in various sectors.[14]

Nehru's concept of a mixed economy envisaged the simultaneous participation of the public and private sectors in developmental activities. Key sectors of the economy were to be wholly under state control while the private sector would operate in other spheres. However, the private sector must be subject to state control so as to make it function within the objective of the national plan. While commenting on the role of the private sector, Nehru observed: "The control over the private sector will relate not only to its, dividends and profits but will extend to all the strategic points in the economy of the country". He envisaged gradually more and more state control over the private sector in order to make the mixed economy sufficiently capable of adapting itself to changing conditions.

Nehru's arguments in favour of a mixed economy might sound logical in the peculiar Indian conditions. According to him, he choice before the country lay essentially between the socialist and capitalist systems. But he was not prepared to exercise the choice in view of the limitations inherent in both. Argued Nehru:

> Western economics, though helpful, have little bearing on our present-day problems. So also have Marxist economics which are, in many ways, out of date even though they throw considerable light on economic progress. We have thus to do our own thinking, profiting by the example of others, but essentially trying to find a path for ourselves suited to our own conditions.

Thus, it was clear that Nehru did not want to imitate any economic model of other countries. India must evolve a system which suited her own requirements and genius. The ideal of a mixed economy was thus considered to be the best. Stressing this point rather heavily, Nehru declared:

> ...(economic) change will have to be in the direction of a democratically planned collectivism.... A democratic-collectivism need not mean an abolition of private property, but it will mean the public ownership of the basic and major industries.... In India especially it will be necessary to have, in addition to the big industries, cooperatively controlled small and village industries. Such a system of democratic collectivism will need careful and continuous planning and adaptation to the changing needs of the people.[15]

Nehru and His Vision of India in World Affairs

An article on Nehru's political thought should also portray Nehru's vision about independent India in world affairs. It should not be forgotten that in January 1950, when India became a republic, Nehru became both prime minister and India's foreign minister. As a foreign minister he had great vision for the country. After the liberation of the country Nehru dreamt of freedom from poverty and distress. According to Nehru India gained political freedom at last but he was aware that there are other freedoms that still remain for India to achieve.

According to Nehru, India is the member of the family of nations and had no wish to shirk any of the obligation and burdens of that membership. India accepted the obligation of membership in the United Nations and intended to abide by them. Nehru was also willing to be associated with the Commonwealth of the Nations. As he felt that India will have real advantages. He also made it clear that India's policy does not adhere to policy of lying up with any power bloc. Nehru knew that India's immediate needs were economic betterment and raising the standard of people. According to Nehru the more we can succeed in this, the more we can serve the cause of peace in the world.

Nehru pointed out that India is a very old country with a great past. But she is a new country also with new urges and desires. Since August 1947, she has been in position to pursue a foreign policy of a own. India was limited by the realities of situations which she could not ignore or overcome. Thus, India tried to combine idealism with national interest. The main objectives of the policy are: the pursuit of peace, not through alignment with any major power or group of powers but through an independent approach to each controversial or disputed issue, the liberation of subject people, the maintenance of freedom, both national and individual, the elimination of racial discrimination and elimination of want, disease and ignorance which afflict the greater part of world population. Nehru pointed out that India cannot effort to align with any particular nation or a group because India was going through times of crisis, and in times of crisis it is non-unnatural for those who are involved in it deeply to regarded calm objectivity in others as irrational, short-sighted, negative, unreal or unmanly.

Nehru made it clear that the policy India has to pursue should be a neutral policy. It is a positive and a vital policy that flows from our struggle for freedom and from the teaching of Mahatma Gandhi. Peace is not only an absolute necessity for India in order to progress and develop but will also serve as of paramount importance to the world. On question how that peace can be preserved Nehru pointed out, that it will not be by surrendering to aggression, not by compromising with evil or injustice but also not by talking and preparing for war. Nehru believed that the maintenance of this detachment is not only in India's interest but also in the interest of world peace and freedom.

Thus, Nehru had chosen the policy of mutual understanding and peaceful co-existence, to reduce the tensions of the world. He often said: "It would be totally unrealistic to suggest that India possesses some magic or *mantra* to end these evils, but it is our responsibility as members of the human family to advocated a course of action which might lesson international tensions and ultimately remove the sources and cause of conflict". He further stated that we could not escape some responsibilities of an international nature, and we should try to discharge them to the best of our ability. In his opinion, this approach and philosophy which we have inherited from Asoka, Gandhi and other great rulers and thinkers, the philosophy of "live and let live," of non-violence, toleration and co-existence, could be the only panacea for the problems of our times.[16]

Nehru was an exponent of *Panch Sheel* or the five cardinal tenets of international amity and understanding. In June 1954, the fundamental concepts of *Panch Sheel* were laid down in the course of a joint declaration by Nehru and Chou En Lai, The *Panch Sheel* was the basis of Nehru's foreign policy. An analysis of *Panch Sheel* shows that it was based on the principles of international policy. The *Panch Sheel* included principles such as (1) mutual respect for each other's territorial integrity and sovereignty, (2) mutual non-aggression, (3) mutual non-interference in each other's internal affairs, (4) equality and mutual advantage, (5) peaceful co-existence and economic co-operation.

The principles of *Panch Sheel* are akin to the principles of the United Nations Charter. The first four principles embodied in different provisions of the United Nations Charter. Although the fifth principle on peaceful co-existence has not been written down in the Charter, it is implied in it if we read the Charter with all its provisions together.

According to Nehru, *Panch Sheel* was a peaceful and constructive strategy. He remarked: "The *Panch Sheel*, or five foundations of peaceful co-existence, offers the correct approach". Nehru strongly pleaded in favour of *Panch Sheel* a policy of co-operation and co-existence not only for reducing international tensions but also for solving many international problems. He insisted on a policy of constructive co-operation and peaceful co-existence, both for India and the outside world.

Nehru was firm believer in the principles of the United Nations and was opposed to the bipolarisation of world politics and refused to join any Power Bloc. He pursued the policy of non-alignment which form the core of Indian foreign policy. It was the result of Nehru's belief in democratic socialism. Nehru had been careful to point out that he sponsored a dynamic concept of non-alignment and not a passive one of neutrality. If liberty was endangered and the security of the country threatened, he would not hesitate to modify the concept of non-alignment.

Nehru made constant efforts to seek peaceful solutions for international disputes. He had great faith in the course laid down by Gandhiji for solving tension—national and international.[17]

III
IDEAS OF NEHRU AND ITS CONTEMPORARY RELEVANCE

Nehru's ideas can only be justifiably summed up against the domestic constraints and external factors in world affairs that were present in India at that time. Nehru has repeatedly been drawn into the cauldron of debates, which has pointed out that it was his highly ambitious political aspirations that eventually led to the partition of India.

According to the critics Nehru has been blamed for his attitude of 'sycophancy', which has created more problem for him than good. In an article "Where Caesar Faltered", *Essay towards an Assessment of Nehru's Legacy*, H.N. Bali pointed out that Nehru, pursued policies like the great Mughals. He continued the tradition of a durbar of sycophants who were ever ready to endorse his views and fancies. Nehru was a poor judge of human beings and relied on people who did more harm to him and his country than he ever realized.

Moreover though he repeatedly spoke of secularism yet his refusal to lay the real foundation of a secular polity through a uniform civil code and other necessary measures creates great confusion.

It should be reconsidered, that these 'follies', are a result of historical past. To remember Voltaire, "the history of the world's great leaders is often the story of human folly". Political scientist should be able to scientifically analyze the underline conditions of *real-politik* and view them objectively before focusing on any contemporary issue.[18]

But under no circumstances we can ignore the visions that have been propounded by these great thinkers.

It cannot be denied that Nehru, was brought up in the Western liberal culture at a very impressionable age. Fortunately for India, Nehru could infuse the fresh air of liberalism, democracy and spirit of individualism and humanism into this archaic, feudal society. Both Gandhi and Nehru despite struggles against the British could usher in the feeling of necessity to safeguard the interests of "the individuals". The need to fight against domination and stand up one's own rights which were grossly curbed during the British rule is an essence that dominates human rights paradigm today.

Moreover Nehru's scientific temperament and importance of technology invokes great respect even today. He was the prime mover in setting up the National Laboratories, the Council of Scientific and Industrial Research and those centres of excellence called the Indian Institute of Technology. While delivering the first convocation address of IIT, Kharagpur in 1956—'Here stands fine monument of India representing India's urges, India's future in the making.'

As regards secularism Nehru remained convinced that in a multi-religious, pluralist and democratic country like India, a secular framework was imperative. Nehru was aware that creating a just State by just means and creating a secular State in a religious country, was probably the most difficult task to be achieve after Independence.[19]

The true measures of Nehru's humanism, his tolerance and his liberalism, is perhaps best revealed in the following in the following extemporaneous reflections on 'What constitutes good society and the good life?'

> ....Broadly speaking, apart from the material things that are necessary, obviously, a certain individual growth in the society, not only the corporate social growth but the individual growth.
>
> For I do believe that ultimately it is the individual that counts. I can't say that I believe in it because I have no proof, but the idea appeals to me without belief, the old Hindu idea that if there is any divine essence in the world every individual possesses a bit of it...and he can develop it. Therefore, no individual is trivial.....
>
> ....I do believe in certain standards. Call them moral standards, call them what you like, spiritual standards. They are important in any individual and in any social group. And if they fade away, I think that all the material advancement you may have will lead to nothing worthwhile.... So while I attached very considerable value to moral and spiritual standards, apart from religion as such, I don't know how one maintains them in modern life.
>
> It's a problem.[20]

It is difficult to assess Nehru's achievements and contribution in the Indian political thought in a few words. In the words of veteran communist leader and brilliant Parliamentarian Hiren Mukherjee, Nehru was described following the oft-quoted words of Shakespeare as the "Gentle Colossus", which surely describe him aptly.

> His life was gentle, and the elements
> so mixed in him that Nature might stand up
> And say to all the world
> 'This was a man!'[21]

Notes

1. Mukherjee, H. (1986). *The Gentle Colossus: A Study of Jawaharlal Nehru,* Walton Street, Oxford, Oxford University Press, p. 212.

2. Ghosh, S. (1984). *Modern Indian Political, Thought,* New Delhi, Allied Publishers Private Ltd., p. 286.
3. Ghosh, S.C. (1984). *Nehru's Idea of Socialism,* Calcutta, Oceania Publishing House, pp. 14-15.
4. *Ibid.*, p. 13.
5. *Ibid.*, p. 11.
6. *Ibid.*, pp. 40-43.
7. Brown, J. (2003). *Nehru—A Political Life,* India, Oxford University Press, p. 341.
8. Pillai, R.C. (1986). *The Political Thought of Jawaharlal Nehru In Pantham and Deutsch ed(s) Political Thought in Modern India,* p. 260.
9. Das Patra, H.H. (1995). *Indian Political Traditions,* New Delhi, Sterling Publishers, p. 209.
10. Ghosh, S. (1984). *Modern Indian Political Thought,* op. cit., p. 304.
11. Pillai, R.C. (1986). *Political Thought in Modern India,* op. cit., p. 272.
12. Devaraja, N.K. (1988). *Humanism in India Thought,* New Delhi, Indus Publishing Company, p. 144.
13. *Ibid.*, p. 49.
14. Ghosh, S. (1984). *Modern Indian Political Thought,* op. cit., pp. 300-01.
15. Pillai, R.C. (1986). *The Political Thought of Jawaharlal Nehru in Pantham and Deutsch ed(s) Political Thought In Modern India,* New Delhi, Sage Publications, p. 268.
16. Das, H.H. Ptro P.S.N. (1995). *Indian Political Traditions,* New Delhi, Sterling Publishers Private Ltd., p. 213.
17. *Ibid.*, p. 214.
18. Bali, H.N. (2014). "Where Caesar Faltered", *The Sunday Statesman*, 7, December, p. 6.
19. Gupta, G. (2014). *The Magnitude of Nehru's Achievement,* The Statesman, 10, December, p. 6.
20. Brecher, M. (1962). *Nehru: A Political Biography,* Great Britain, Oxford University Press, pp. 607-08.
21. Mukherjee, H. (1986). *The Gentle Colossus—A Study of Jawaharlal Nehru,* New Delhi, Jawaharlal Nehru Memorial Fund, p. 212.

Suggested Readings

Ali, Tariq (1985). *The Nehru's and the Gandhis: An Indian Dynasty,* Great Britain, Pan Books.

Guha, Ramachandra (2012). *Makers of Modern India,* New Delhi, Penguin Books.

Khosla, Madhav (ed.) (2014). *Letters for a Nation from Jawaharlal Nehru to His Chief Ministers* (1947-1963), New Delhi, Penguin Group.

Mushirul, Hasan (ed.) (2007). *Nehru's India: Select Speeches,* New Delhi, Oxford University Press.

Nehru, Jawaharlal (1989). *An Autobiography*, New Delhi, Oxford University Press.

23

B.R. Ambedkar (1891–1956)

Debi Chatterjee

I
INTRODUCTION

Dr. B.R. Ambedkar has been one of the greatest leader's to have come up in modern India. Few would match his stature. His mastery over jurisprudence, his constitutional expertise, political finesse and outstanding knowledge of political philosophy, history, economics and western and Indian political thought all added up to make him the outstanding statesman and that he was. He had his analyses of India that was sharp and intricate, his vision of the future and a blueprint of action. At the centre of it all was his uncompromising commitment to social justice and his condemnation of the Hindu Brahminical social structure. Protest against caste, casteism and the Brahminical system probably reached its peak in the modern era under the influence of Dr. Ambedkar. To many, particularly the socially downtrodden, he was the 'Great Man', referred to as 'Babasaheb' Ambedkar. It was with the coming of Ambedkar on the scene, and under his able leadership, that religious and social struggles of the low castes of the earlier years were supplemented by the articulation of their demands in terms of the modern language of politics from the first half of the twentieth century.

Bhimrao Ramji Ambedkar was born in 1891 in the British-founded town and military cantonment of MHOW. It was a place near Indore that was in the then Central Provinces (now in Madhya Pradesh). He was the fourteenth and last child of Ramji Maloji Sakpal and Bhimabai. His family was of Marathi background hailing from the town of Ambavade in the Ratnagiri district of modern-day Maharashtra. They belonged to the Hindu, Mahar caste—a caste that was deemed to be low in terms of the Hindu social hierarchy and its members were treated as untouchables. Mahars were, because of their caste, subject to intense socio-economic discrimination. A Mahar's conventional place in the village community was that of a *balutedar* or *watandar*, i.e. a village servant whose duty was to the village and whose recompense came from the village. With the advent of British rule, however, new work opportunities and exposures opened up to them new avenues of economic and social progress. It was in such a caste and in such a milieu that Ambedkar was born.

Though he was born in an untouchable Mahar caste family, overcoming the many hurdles that he had to encounter because of such birth, Ambedkar was able to obtain a very high level of education. First he secured a college education in India and subsequently obtained law and doctorate degrees from Columbia University and the London School of Economics. Through financial assistance received from the Maharaja of Baroda, Ambedkar was able to graduate from Elphinstone College in Bombay (1905-12), spend three years at Colombia University (1913-16), and one year at the London School of Economics (1916-17). He was awarded an M.Sc. degree in 1921 for his thesis "Provincial Decentralization of Imperial Finance in British India." In 1922, he submitted another dissertation, "The Problem of the Rupee," for which he later managed to get a D.Sc. degree from London University. He was called to the Bar in 1923.

Ambedkar's ideas developed as a clear synthesis of Indian philosophical ideas and Western liberal thinking. His in-depth knowledge of Hindu philosophy that he acquired over years starting from a childhood routine of daily recital of the Hindu scriptures and exposed under the light of Kabir and Buddha's dicta, unraveled to him the many and diverse facets of Indian society. The liberal democratic influence on Ambedkar was strong and in his writings it repeatedly came up for acknowledgement. To him, Western liberal thought seemed to hold out the panacea for the ills of his own caste-ridden society, of which he was so much a victim. Underlying the entire gamut of Ambedkar's demands there was a strong unwavering belief in liberal democratic institutions and their capabilities of bringing about social justice. In his *Annihilation of Caste*, Ambedkar acknowledged his indebtedness to John Dewey, referring to him as "my teacher, and to whom I owe so much". Apart from Dewey, intellectually Ambedkar was much influenced by Western stalwarts such as Edwin Robert, Anderson Seligman, Edwin Cannan, John Maynard Keynes and Bertrand Russell, among others.

II
AMBEDKAR'S ACTIVISM IN THE POLITICAL ARENA

Testimony before the Franchise Committee, 1919

Ambedkar's maiden entry into the Indian political field took place in 1919 with his testimony before the Franchise Committee or the Southborough Committee, as it is popularly known.[1] By the time that the Southborough Committee hearings took place, Ambedkar was a graduate of Elphinestone College and had spent three years at Columbia University and one year at the London School of Economics (Zelliot, 1995: 97). In November 1918, Ambedkar had joined Sydenham College of Bombay as a Professor of Economics but he could not serve there for long in view of the humiliating social treatment that he received from his colleagues. He resigned his post on 11th March, 1920 and resumed his studies in law and economics in London (Kuber, 1978: 17). It was during this period of his stay in India that Ambedkar made his representation before the Franchise Committee. Ambedkar did not make his presentation on behalf of any group. He simply spoke as a college graduate from amongst the Mahars of Maharashtra. His presentation was lengthy and sophisticated, bearing ample evidence of his awareness of the Indian social scenario on the one hand and his knowledge of Western political philosophy on the other.

In his testimony Ambedkar argued that any scheme of franchise that fails to bring about the representation of opinions as well as persons falls short of the requirements of a popular government. He enumerated the real social divisions of India as those of (i) touchable Hindus, (ii) untouchable Hindus, (iii) Mohammedans, (iv) Christians, (v) Parsees and (vi) Jews, pointing out that "it will not do good to ignore these real divisions in devising a system of policy, if the policy is to take the form of popular government". Refuting the oft given arguments in favour of mere territorial constituencies and proportional representation, Ambedkar held that under the peculiarities of the Indian context, "the importance and necessity of communal and adequate representation of untouchables is beyond question". He argued that the Depressed Classes were 'slaves', 'de-humanised' and 'so socialised as never to complain'. So they should be given communal representation in such numbers as will enable them to claim redress.

Ambedkar's petitioning was significant as an early step towards articulation of the Depressed Classes demands in the modern idiom of politics. His use of the public platform of the Governmental Commission, then independently and confidently, fully supportive of any extension of democracy to India, was in stark contrast to that of other untouchables. He was not bound to the Non-Brahmin movement; his English was fully equal to the situation; he believed in the political process and was only anxious that the Depressed Classes get a share in it according to their numbers and needs (Zelliot, 1998: 68).

Statement before the Simon Commission, 1928

The Indian Statutory Commission was a group of seven British Members of Parliament that came to India in 1928 to study the issue of constitutional reforms. It was commonly referred to as the Simon Commission after its chairman, Sir John Simon. On 29 May 1928, Ambedkar submitted a statement before the Simon Commission on behalf of the *Bahishkrit Hitakarini Sabha*, or the Depressed Classes Association, an organisation which he had founded in 1924 to work for the social and economic betterment of the Depressed Classes. His statement was titled *'Statement Concerning the Safeguards for the Protection of the Interests of the Depressed Classes as a Minority in the Bombay Presidency, and the Changes in the Composition of and the Guarantees from the Bombay Legislative Council Necessary to Ensure the Same under Provincial Autonomy*'. While he did not renew his 1919 demand for separate electorates, he spoke in favour of adult franchise and seat reservations of up to twenty two in the Bombay Legislative Assembly of one hundred and forty members. He called for special guarantees for the Depressed Classes (Zelliot, 1998: 101).

At the Round Table Conferences, 1930-32, and the Gandhi-Ambedkar Debate

Between 1930-32 the British Government held three Round Table Conferences in London to determine Indian opinion regarding the proposed new constitution of India. At these Round Table Conferences Ambedkar, along with Rao Bahadur Srinivasan, represented the Depressed Classes. At all these Conferences, Ambedkar strongly argued in favour of Separate Electorates for the Depressed Classes. It was a viewpoint that was vehemently opposed by M.K. Gandhi who was the representative of the Indian National Congress.

It may be noted in this context that the First Round Table Conference had been boycotted by the Indian National Congress because of the ongoing Non-Cooperation Movement; as such a direct confrontation with Gandhi did not take place. But, by the time of the Second Round Table Conference, the Gandhi Irwin Pact had been effected and the Civil Disobedience Movement called off. This brought Gandhi to the negotiating table. As such, at that Conference Ambedkar directly confronted Gandhi. Ambedkar did not hesitate to cross swords with Gandhi and firmly argued his viewpoint regarding the rights of the untouchables. It was Ambedkar's acid test as the world was looking on to the two gigantic leaders vying with each other for the right of recognition as the leader of the Indian masses. Ambedkar claimed to speak for the untouchables, a claim which Gandhi contested in seeking to represent the totality of the Indian people, including the Depressed Classes. The *Indian Daily Mail* of July 21, 1931 noted:

> Dr Ambedkar made a tremendous impact at the Round Table Conference, and his speech at the opening session

> was of the finest bits of oratory delivered during the whole conference. (Kadam, 1991: 40)

In taking up the cause of the untouchables, who over time came to be known as the Depressed Classes and later Scheduled Castes, Ambedkar was in a position to go much further than Gandhi and adopt a distinctly more radical and activist stance.

Till the 1950s, Ambedkar devoted much of his energies towards finding a political solution to the untouchables' woes. On the one hand, he concentrated on bargaining with the British Government and the Indian National Congress for the incorporation of safeguards for the Depressed Classes in the Constitution. On the other hand, he strove to politically organize the Depressed Classes through the formation of first the Independent Labour Party (1936), then the Scheduled Castes Federation (1942) and finally visualizing the forming of the Indian Republican Party (1956).

In the Constituent Assembly

Ambedkar is probably best known as the 'Father of the Constitution' in view of his role in the drafting of the Indian Constitution. He was a member of the Constituent Assembly, elected to it originally from Bengal. Ambedkar became the Chairman of the Committee that drafted the Constitution, commonly termed the Drafting Committee. He played a decisive role in the process of constitution-making and emphatically sought to safeguard the interests of the low untouchable castes, technically referred to as the Depressed Classes. In fact, he went so much as to assert that he had agreed to be a part of the Constituent Assembly keeping in mind their interests. The Constituent Assembly approved the Constitution on November 26, 1949. The Constitution thus drafted was, however, not the perfect picture of what Ambedkar wanted to see. In fact, he had to accept many compromises in the course of its drafting. This becomes clearly evident from a reading of *States and Minorities: What are Their Rights and How to Secure them in the Constitution of Free India* which incorporated Ambedkar's own vision of the Indian Constitution as he ideally wished to see it. It was published in May 1947 and widely regarded as his alternative to the formal constitution. In several respects it was a major departure from the actual constitution that Ambedkar, as Chairman of the Drafting Committee, played a crucial role in drafting. It was undoubtedly a more socialistic, egalitarian and collectivistic state that Ambedkar was projecting in that document. It also included explicit economic and social provisions and special facilities for the deprived Scheduled Castes.

As India gained independence, in August 1947 Ambedkar became the first Law Minister of the country. He was all in favour of empowerment of women and wished to ensure that women were in no way treated as inferior to men. As law minister, one of the major initiatives taken by him towards reforming the Hindu social order was in the form of drafting the Hindu Code Bill. It was aimed at enhancing gender equality in Hindu society. However, in the face of stiff orthodox resistance the bill was abandoned, following which Ambedkar resigned from the ministry in 1951.

On the Social Plane

On the social plane, Ambedkar launched several struggles to counteract the unequal treatment meted out to the untouchables by the caste Hindus. The Mahad *Satyagraha* (1927), burning of the *Manusmrti* (1927) and the Kala Ram Mandir *Satyagraha* (1930) were among the major movements launched by Ambedkar in this spirit.

The Mahad Tank *Satyagraha* was illustrative of the mass preparedness for action on the one hand and Ambedkar's leadership abilities on the other. It was the first mass rally organised by the *Bahishkrit Hitakarini Sabha*[2] (Kadam, 1991: 80). The 1920s had been witnessing a sustained campaign for the opening up of public places, particularly wells and tanks, for the access of the untouchables. An unimplemented resolution of the Mahad Municipality opening up the Chowdar Tank to the untouchables was already there when the initial crowd of over 1,500 marched ahead to establish their rights to draw water from the tank. Drinking of the tank water, rioting, police complaints and the subsequent cleansing of the tank by caste

Hindus, were enough to create a furore. Even before the heat died down, Ambedkar planned a second '*Satyagraha* conference' in December to re-establish the *Mahar's* right to the water. This time ten to fifteen thousand people assembled! Although the decision to take water from the tank was suspended in deference to the request of the District Magistrate, it was not without a clear demonstration of the *Mahar's* mood and acclaim for Ambedkar's leadership. The campaign had been partly spontaneous and partly planned. Mahad, the chosen movement place was one where Ambedkar had a significant measure of caste Hindu support, where a tenant movement uniting the *Mahar* and *Kunbi* peasants was in the offing—a movement which was to develop into the largest anti-landlord movement of *Mahar*ashtra in the 1930s. It was also a place where the municipality had already passed a resolution opening public places to the untouchables (Omvedt, 1995: 44). The Mahad *Satyagraha*, widely acclaimed as the first untouchable liberation movement did not succeed in getting water, but did succeed in the public burning of the *Manusmrti* (Omvedt, 1995: 44).

Ambedkar was both a theorist and activist. The two identities nurtured and reinforced each other—none being of lesser importance than the other. He was indeed a prolific writer. And, in his writings he linked up his theoretical expositions with the realities of the struggles. In 1920, Ambedkar launched a Marathi journal, *Mook Nayak* (Leader of the Dumb), to champion the cause of the untouchables. The journal was short-lived. In 1927, he made another attempt and started a fortnightly *Bahishkrit Bharat* (*The Outcaste India*), which also failed to survive for long. Ambedkar's major writings include, amongst others, *Annihilation of Caste, Who Were the Sudras, The Untouchables, Mr. Gandhi and the Emancipation of the Untouchables, States And Minorities,* and *Thoughts on Pakistan.*

Rejection of Hinduism and the Conversion Movement

Initially, Ambedkar sought to awaken the good sense of the caste Hindus and reform Hinduism. But, by the mid-thirties, he did not hesitate to challenge Hinduism as such. As the conflict with Gandhi over the issue of Separate Electorates for the untouchables climaxed between 1930-32 in the context of the three Round Table Conferences, Ambedkar was convinced that Gandhi and the Indian National Congress were simply holding brief for Hinduism and seeking to safeguard the interests of upper caste Hindus, and that Hinduism itself had to be discarded. Ambedkar's journey to Buddhism that culminating in the great conversion ceremony of 1956 along with thousands of his followers, was in fact a continuum of this thought process.

It may be noted in this context that Ambedkar was a believer in religion. Religion, he believed, was a necessity of human existence. It was, to him, a part of one's "social inheritance"; a matter of right living and a framework for a moral life. He conceptualised it as a system of moral values, a system of injunctions and prohibitions designed to promote a harmonious human life.

Religions, Ambedkar insisted, should be judged by social standards and be based on social ethics. He identified four basic characteristic of religion. First, he felt, religion in the sense of morality must remain the governing principle of every society. Secondly, religion, if it is to function must be in accord with reason which is merely another name for science. Thirdly, its moral codes must acknowledge the fundamental tenets of liberty, equality and fraternity. Fourthly, religion must not sanctify or ennoble poverty.

Hinduism failed these tests. "What is called religion by the Hindus", he noted in his *Annihilation of Castes*, "is nothing but a multitude of commands and prohibitions". The *Philosophy of Hinduism, Revolution and Counter-revolution, Riddles of Hinduism* were just some of the many places in which he critiqued Hinduism. The core of the Hindu scheme of governance, he noted, is enshrined in a written constitution and "anyone who cares to know it will find it laid bare in that sacred book called the *Manusmrti*, a divine code which lays down the rules which govern the religious, ritualistic and social life of the Hindus in minute detail and which must be regarded as the Bible of the Hindus and containing the philosophy of Hinduism." This Hinduism fails against the yardstick of utility and justice. Justice, he points out, is simply another name for liberty, equality and fraternity. But, in Hinduism "you will find both social inequality and religious inequality". By denying social equality and economic security Hinduism, he showed, denies liberty. Hinduism fails even the test of fraternity as fraternity can arise only where there is a sentiment of fellow feeling and with the existence of nearly two to three thousand castes this sentiment cannot grow. As for utility, he noted that the very structure and ideology of caste destroyed social utility and by denying justice, Hinduism *ipso facto* denied utility. Thus viewed, Hinduism he asserted "is Superman's heaven and the common man's damnation."

The idea of conversion was kept alive for twenty years during which Ambedkar explored the various options, till, on 14th October 1956, he renounced Hinduism along with an estimated half a million other Dalits to embrace Buddhism. In an open letter written in 1936 he had set out the choice of conversion as being between Islam, Christianity and Sikhism. In course of time, his preference appeared to be for Sikhism, which still later on he gave up in favour of Buddhism. According to his biographer, Dhananjay Keer, Ambedkar had started working on his magnum opus, The *Buddha and his Dhamma* from 1951. In it, he spelt out the details of his path. Ambedkar's path of Buddhism was not the path of ancient or medieval Buddhism; it was neither Theravada, nor Mahayana or Vajrayana Buddhism. It was referred to as fourth path—Navayana.

Basic Tenets of his Ideas

With the arrival of Dr B.R. Ambedkar on India's political scene, the untouchables' demands for justice came to be articulated in terms of the modern language of politics. His academic acumen, extensive knowledge of both Indian and Western philosophical thought, expertise in economics and law placed him in an undoubtedly strong position in bargaining for the rights of the untouchables, called the Depressed Classes. His personal experiences of pain and the trauma as a member of an untouchable caste stimulated him to take up their cause for social justice. This he did with firm determination and unmatched skill. For the first time in modern Indian history, the untouchables began learning the use of political tools for protecting their rights.

Ambedkar relied heavily on the nuances of parliamentary politics. It is a matter of serious debate as to whether Ambedkar had any other alternative to parliamentary politics for political practice. Perhaps, given the constraints of his resources, adversarial environment and to some extent his personal limitations, he had none. Whatever may it be, he expected much from the State. He was convinced that goods and services, rightly apportioned under democratic pressure, could go a long way towards ameliorating the plight of the socially oppressed. As such, he emphasised on the centrality of the state and recognised the possibilities arising out of using it as leverage for ensuring social justice. It was necessary not only for the Depressed Classes, but for the development of democratic India as a whole. Ambedkar had a vision of Independent India. It was a democratic India. A democracy that was not merely politically defined, but that which was firmly rooted in social and economic values of equality; his belief in democracy was holistic. Social exclusion whether on the basis of caste or gender was simply not acceptable to him. Ambedkar's ideal system that had to be put in place through the commitment of the state, ensured by the struggles of the people. For the advance of that India, he urged for the annihilation of the caste system. And, in attaining it, the political tool was considered to be of vital importance.

Whilst politically, Ambedkar relied heavily on Western liberal tradition, the influence of the Soviet Union in terms of economic thought was no less significant. In economic terms his stance was basically socialist, though he did not develop any long term alignment with any socialist party.

Ambedkar's acceptance of Buddhism shortly before his death was not simply a matter of a religious choice; it was essentially a social choice and was inextricably linked to his political struggle. Together, the political and religious struggles were like two pillars of the single effort to attain social justice for the untouchables. It was a unique example of welding together two distinct languages of struggles, the traditional language of religious protest and the modern language of participatory democracy.

He contributed significantly to the process of nation building as he vigorously countered the notion of the fragmentation of the Indian people along caste lines which prevented India from constituting itself as a unified and a modern nation.

III
AMBEDKAR'S LEGACY AND CONTEMPORARY RELEVANCE

The effects of the conversion movement initiated by Ambedkar have been variedly evident. Its greatest impact was on Maharashtra and Uttar Pradesh. Whilst scholars like Wilkinson and Thomas[3] tend to suggest that conversion has not made any major difference in the social and occupational life of the converts to Buddhism, according to others, certain advantages have accrued to the dalits who converted to Buddhism. These neo-Buddhists as they are called, appear to have improved significantly over the Hindu Dalits in terms of several parameters such as the sex ratio, literacy and work participation.[4]

Economic and educational considerations apart, most importantly conversion has emerged as a rallying call for identity formation of the dalits particularly in western and northern India. Special occasions for celebration of events have been identified in terms of the Buddhist conversion tradition. The *Diksha bhoomi* has virtually come up as a place of regular pilgrimage of dalits and the *Viharas* have developed as gathering grounds for the community. Eva-Maria Hardtmann noted in her work the minute details of the contemporary functioning of the *Viharas* in U.P. observing that "taking part in the Buddhist ceremonies in the Viharas seemed to be a way for the dalit Buddhists to learn more about Buddhist rituals and about Ambedkar. It was also a way to introduce Ambedkar and Buddhism to their children" (Hardtmann, 2011). As observed by the reputed Ambedkarite scholar Eleanor Zelliot, "The psychological impact of Buddhism, the matter of changed identity, cannot be judged by visible signs" (Zelliot, 1998: 212). As the same author notes, "psychological freedom from the sense of being a polluting person is a major achievement of the Buddhist conversion" (Zelliot, 1998: 219).

Not that all, or even a majority, of dalits chose to accept the Buddhist option. In fact, a sizeable portion of the Ambedkarites stayed outside the Buddhist fold. Nonetheless, the impact made on the dalit political movement by those who chose to become Buddhists is noteworthy. It undoubtedly contributed to the rise of a new awareness and a new elite. In the rise of the Dalit Panther Movement in Maharashtra in the 1970s, for example, the impact of Buddhism was clearly evident. Leaders like Namdeo Dhasal and Raja Dhale, belonging to different factions of the movement, recognized the liberating significance of Buddhism. In mainstream dalit politics of the Bahujan Samaj Party, Kanshiram spoke of Buddhism and his proposed conversion. It was reported in the newspaper *The Hindu* (10.10.2006) that his last rites were done along lines of Buddhist rituals. In 1996, in the meetings aimed at reviving the Republican Party of India in U.P. many spoke about Buddhism as the philosophy that should guide the party and quoted Ambedkar's *Buddha and his Dhamma* (Hardtmann, 134-35).

The greatest significance of the conversion movement of Ambedkar lay in his attempt to weld together two very different lines of struggles in ensuring social justice for the dalits. One line of struggle rested on the traditional language of protest—the religious struggle. The other, rested on the modern language of parliamentary politics. He was probably the first to attempt this bonding of the two very diverse languages of protest at the national level. Even as he suffered setbacks in his political struggles using the modern language of politics, he turned to the other language, the religious. The implications of this were to unfold in the decades to come.

Ambedkar taught the Mahars, nay the untouchables, to effectively articulate and aggregate their interests. While during his own lifetime efforts to transcend the limits of Mahar politics and bring forth larger working alliances between different oppressed groups met with limited success, his image as leader of the Depressed Classes as a whole was established beyond doubt. 'Educate, agitate and organise' was the slogan that inspired and still inspires—a slogan that Ambedkar had given to the socially down-trodden masses. Mark Jurgensmeyer in his book *Religious Rebels in the Punjab: The Social Vision of Untouchables* describes how in Punjab, the emancipation process among untouchables in the 1940s was due to the 'Ambedkar Alternative', while Lynch speaks of the impact of Ambedkar's ideas on the Jatavs of Agra as a 'turning point' in their socio-political mobilization. The impact of his ideas across the country was such that it would perhaps not be an overstatement to say, with Christophe Jaffrelot that "he was arguably the first pan-Indian Dalit leader" (Jaffrelot, 2005: 143).

Dr Ambedkar's able political leadership was reflected in his presentations before the Simon Commission in 1928, at the Round Table Conferences between 1930-32 as well as in the Constituent Assembly debates where he was the Chairman of the Drafting Committee. At all these levels he put in his utmost efforts to see that the Depressed Classes were assured certain minimum safeguards which he felt to be essential for their security under the new constitutional system. He believed that minus certain safeguards their plight would be deplorable as on transfer of power, power would almost certainly go into the hands of the upper castes who would be ill disposed towards the Depressed Classes.

Through sustained political mobilization and hard bargaining Ambedkar had succeeded in establishing the Scheduled Castes as a politically relevant category and made future generations of the downtrodden people conscious of their legal rights and the political weapons for carrying forward their struggles. His life and vision have continued to inspire Scheduled Caste activists long after his demise. A whole spectrum of dalit (Scheduled Caste) activists over the years have turned to his ideas for sustenance. Whether it was the radical Dalit Panthers of the 1970s or the different factions of the Republican Party, or even the Bahujan Samaj Party today, Ambedkar remains the icon-projected differently, but acceptable to all. The dalit movement today draws much of it's inspiration from Ambedkar's legacy. No single strand of dalit movement can claim to be the sole inheritor of Ambedkar's ideas and struggles. From the purely political claims to the Ambedkarite legacy as manifest in the struggles of the Republican Party or the Bahujan Samaj Party to the neo-Buddhist converts in search for an alternative identity of dignity, the entire spectrum of Ambedkarite following is indeed mind-boggling. Today, bearing the legacy of Ambedkar, attempting to cope with pressures of globalizations, dalits have moved beyond the borders of India in search of support for their human rights demands. Their activism leading up to the Durban Conference against Racism in 2001, at the time of the Conference and subsequently has no doubt opened up a new chapter in the history of dalit struggles.

A total assessment of Ambedkar is yet to come. Ambedkar has frequently been seen in a fragmented way—either as a leader of the Scheduled Castes or Mahars, or as the maker of the Indian Constitution. Yet, he was much more than either. He was simultaneously a social activist, a political thinker, an economist and over and above all a true democratic Indian.

Notes

1. The Committee had been constituted for the purpose of gathering material for determining the franchise for the Montagu Chelmsford Reforms. It examined representatives of different interests and communities and thereafter submitted its report on 22 February 1919.
2. The decision to set up the *Sabha* had been taken in 1924 with the professed intent of (a) promoting the spread of education amongst the Depressed Classes by opening hostels; (b) promoting the spread of culture among the Depressed Classes by opening libraries, social centres and organising study circles and classes; (c) advancing the economic conditions of the Depressed Classes by setting up industrial and agricultural schools; (d) representing the grievances of the depressed classes.
3. T.S. Wilkinson and M.N. Thomas (ed.), *Ambedkar and the Neo-Buddhist Movement*, The Christian Literature Society, Madras, 1972.
4. Dr Shura Darapuri, "Dalit Buddhists Far Ahead of Hinduised Dalits", *Dalit Voice*, June 1-15, 2008, p. 12.

Select References

Chatterjee, Debi (2004). *Up Against Caste: Comparative Study of Ambedkar and Periyar,* Jaipur: Rawat Publications.

——— (2010). *Ideas and Movements Against Caste in India: Ancient to Modern Times,* Delhi: Abhijeet Publications.

Dr Babasaheb Ambedkar: Writings and Speeches, Bombay: Government of Maharashtra, Vols. 1-17.

Hardtmann, Eva-maria (2011). *The Dalit Movement in India: Local Practices, Global Connections,* New Delhi: Oxford University Press.

Jaffrelot, Christophe (2005). *Dr Ambedkar and Untouchability,* New Delhi: Permanent Black.

Kadam, K.N. (1991). *Dr Babasaheb Ambedkar and the Significance of His Movement: A Chronology.* Bombay: Popular Prakashan.

Kuber, W.N. (1973). *Dr Ambedkar: A Critical Study.* New Delhi: Peoples Publishing House.

Moon, V. (1995). *Dr. Babasaheb Ambedkar.* New Delhi: National Book Trust.

Omvedt, Gail (1994). *Dalits and the Democratic Revolution: Dr Ambedkar and the Dalit Movement in Colonial India.* New Delhi: Sage.

Wilkinson, T.S. and M.N. Thomas (ed.) (1972). *Ambedkar and the Neo-Buddhist Movement,* Madras: The Christian Literature Society.

Zelliot, E. (1998). *From Untouchable to Dalit: Essays on the Ambedkar Movement.* New Delhi: Manohar.

24

Subhas Chandra Bose: Nationalism, Socialism, Pragmatism

Sumit Mukerji

In the history of India's freedom struggle, the name of Netaji Subhas Chandra Bose occupies a prominent place particularly because of his spectacular exploits as the commander of the Indian National Army which expedited, though indirectly, the process of transfer of power in 1947. Since this final phase in the life of Bose is surrounded by an aura of romance, most historians tend to magnify it as the sole index of his importance as a historical figure and the phenomenon that was the I.N.A. However, ever since his entry into active politics in 1921, Bose was able to make a sensational impact both as a prominent leader at the national level for a considerable length of time encompassing nearly two decades (1921-41). He also distinguished himself as a thinker of acumen and insight.

I
INTRODUCTION

Born on January 23, 1897, Bose since his early life was an idealist. The inspiration of Swami Vivekananda in his life was pervasive in developing his spirit of idealism. Nationalist sentiments had also started to surface in him and while he was a young student in Ravenshaw Collegiate School, Cuttack, he participated in the programme dedicated to the memory of Bengal's first martyr Khudiram Bose under the inspiration of the Headmaster Benimadhav Das. After passing the Matriculation examination with flying colours standing second, he took admission in Presidency College. At this point of time, Subhas had pronounced religious proclivities and once left his home in search of a Guru only to return disillusioned. His results in the Intermediate Examination were not up to expectations. He was determined to compensate for this in his Graduation but his alleged complicity in a student's strike in protest against the misdemeanour displayed by Prof. E.F. Oaten towards the students followed by an assault on the professor, led to his rustication from the college and the university. After the lapse of one year which he devoted to social work in Cuttack, Subhas was permitted to resume his studies from Scottish Church College with honours in Philosophy thanks to the intervention of Sir Asutosh Mukherji. He stood second in the B.A. examination and went to England to compete for the Indian Civil Service Examination. After only eight months preparation, Bose ranked fourth in the I.C.S. examination. However, his intensely sensitive nationalistic mind stood in the way of his accepting the lucrative Government service. After tendering his resignation largely under the inspiration of the noted leader of Bengal Aurobindo Ghosh, now exiled in Pondicherry, Subhas returned to India and was initiated into active politics through his apprenticeship under Deshbandhu C.R. Das, the prominent leader of Bengal who was also Mayor of the Calcutta Municipal Corporation. Bose's tenure as Chief Executive Officer of the Calcutta Municipal Corporation was short lived because of his imprisonment and deportation to Mandalaya. In the meantime, C.R. Das had expired and Bose after resumption of his political life after an interruption of three years, found himself promoted from the stature of a lieutenant to that of a national leader. He became a prominent leader of the Left Wing of the Congress and espoused the cause of complete independence from its platform. He was affiliated along with Jawaharlal Nehru to the Independence of India League. He also became Mayor of the Calcutta Municipal Corporation and articulated the cause of Municipal Socialism. His closeness with the revolutionaries of Bengal had already earned him a suspicious reputation in the eyes of the British Government and he was again imprisoned in 1932. His health broke down and he was allowed to go to Europe for treatment. He was in Europe from 1933 to 1937 which marked his emergence as a political thinker. This was the time when he wrote his book *The Indian Struggle* where he enunciated his political ideas in a cogent form and articulated his doctrine of *New Samyavada* based on a synthesis of Communism and Fascism. He toured a number of countries like Austria, France, Italy, Ireland, Turkey and Germany and acquainted himself with the political system prevalent there and also familiarized himself with important political developments. His sojourn in Europe was a turning point in the evolution of his political thought. After his return to India he was again placed under arrest and subsequently released. In 1938, he became President of the Indian National Congress on the recommendation of Mahatma Gandhi at the Haripura session in 1938. However, his differences with the Right wing leadership intensified to a point of no return and in 1939, he contested Gandhi's nominee Dr. Pattavi Sitaramayya in the Presidential election and defeated him. By now, indications of the Second World War had become very clear and Bose in his short address at the Tripuri session of the Congress in 1939, which he attended in a state of serious illness, clearly declared his policy of utilizing the international situation to India's advantage. Gandhi at this point of time had become an inveterate opponent of Bose and wanted him out of the Presidential chair. In the face of determined opposition from the Right wing, Bose resigned and formed his own party, the Forward Bloc. He was soon expelled from the Congress on disciplinary grounds but he continued to propagate his programme of action throughout the lengths and breadths of India with unabated energy. He set up the Left Consolidation Committee with the objective of rallying all the radical leftist forces under one single banner. This however did not materialize. His forecast about the imminent outbreak of the Second World War proved correct and he felt that this was India's golden opportunity. Gandhi however felt that the opportune moment had not yet arrived. Bose now began to contemplate the idea of going abroad and organizing an armed struggle against British imperialism with the help of some foreign power. His logic was that this was the propitious moment to capitalize on the war situation which would leave England smashed and emasculated. Bose was arrested again after leading the Hollwell monument agitation in Calcutta. He commenced a fast unto death in the prison and the government removed him from prison and placed him under house arrest. On January 16, 1941, he escaped dramatically from his house and moved first to Peshawar, then to Kabul from where he tried to contact the Russian embassy but failed. He then went to Germany and set up the Indian Legion. He also met Hitler and tried to persuade him to provide assistance to the cause of India's independence. Here he was destined to be disappointed. In the meantime, the war situation had worsened particularly after Hitler's attack on Russia. While Bose was convinced that this act would prove disastrous he resolved to make a final bid for the freedom of his country with the help of another axis power, Japan. When Japan occupied Singapore, the war prisoners of the British Indian Army were freed. The Indian Independence League comprising the non-resident Indians of South East Asia with its military unit the Azad Hind Fouj was formed by General Mohan Singh and Pritam Singh. Japan wanted to use it as a fifth column against the allied powers and when pressurized by the Japanese Government to provide military aid, Mohan Singh and Pritam Singh revolted and were taken into custody. Rash Behari Bose, the exiled Indian revolutionary now assumed leadership and procured assurance from the Japanese that they would help in the cause of the Indian freedom struggle. However he was ageing and therefore invited Subhas to come over to Singapore and assume charge of the Indian National Army. After a perilous submarine voyage from Germany, Bose reached Madagascar and then a Japanese submarine took him to Saigon. Thereafter he went to Tokyo by a military aircraft and impressed the Japanese premier Tojo who was fascinated by his personality and promised to help him. He assumed charge of the I.N.A. from Rash Behari Bose and established the provisional Azad Hind government on October 21, 1943. He came to be acclaimed as "Netaji" and moulded the I.N.A. for a total mobilization for a massive armed assault on the citadel of British imperialism. He persuaded Tojo, Premier of Japan to provide material, financial and logistical support to the I.N.A. without any kind of compromise on the question of honour. The Azad Hind Fouj advanced up to Kohima and Imphal, penetrated nearly 250 square miles and hoisted the tricolour flag on Indian soil. The untimely advent of monsoon forced it to retreat and after the surrender of Japan, the position of the I.N.A. was hopeless. The irrepressible Bose boarded a plane to Manchuria with the intention of soliciting the support of Russia for the Indian cause. On August 18, 1945, news of his death in an air crash at Taihoku was transmitted. However even today, the truth of the story is shrouded in mystery and there is every reason to believe that the air crash story was a Japanese concoction.

II
THE IMPACT OF THE I.N.A.: MISADVENTURE OR PRAGMATISM?

Bose subscribed to the official Congress policy of non violence under duress. In the heart of hearts he was convinced that an armed struggle alone could liberate India from British rule. He also thought in terms of inciting a spirit of revolt in the British Indian Army. His decided view was that passive resistance must give way to active resistance and in the last phase, armed revolution would be inevitable. For though weapons like non-violent *Satyagraha* could embarrass the British government, they were not capable of forcing the British to quit India. Seizure of power by force was thus the only option. When all his efforts to induce Gandhi to launch an all out struggle against British imperialism failed, he took his decision to strike at the British citadel from outside. This idea has been criticized as dangerous as it might have invited a Japanese invasion of India. The fact of the matter is that Bose did not expect a military victory but his calculation was that once the I.N.A. entered India, a revolution would break out not only among the civilian population but also the Indian Army. In none of the Gandhian movements was any attempt made to infiltrate the armed forces. This was the agenda of militant nationalists like Jatin Mukherjee and Rashbihari Bose who were the predecessors of Subhas. The I.N.A. nearly captured Imphal after launching a massive offensive alongside the Japanese in the Arakan Front on February 4, 1944. Had

Imphal been captured, history would have been different. A secret despatch by the Army headquarters admitted that the conquest of even a single Indian state would have widespread repercussions upon morale and politics.[1] The untimely arrival of the monsoon caused the I.N.A. to retreat despite fighting a gallant and heroic battle. The surrender of Japan on August 14, 1944, laid the last nail on the coffin of the I.N.A. However, the trial of three I.N.A. Officers Maj. Gen Shah Nawaz Khan, Lt. Col. P.K. Sahgal and Lt. Col. G.S. Dhillon, unleashed a wave of protest throughout the lengths and breadths of the nation. On September 2, acting Viceroy Colville reported to the Secretary of State that "Bose has come in for much praise as a national hero and the nationalist press is suggesting that under international law Bose and his followers are entitled to all the honours of war and are not liable to punishment."[2] Army men without caring for military discipline sympathized with the I.N.A. soldiers by attending meetings in support of the I.N.A. prisoners and also by sending contributions to support their defence.[3] Lt. Gen. Francis Tuker the G.O.C. of then Eastern Command noted apprehensively that "The I.N.A. affair was threatening to tumble down the whole edifice of the Indian Army."[4] The naval revolt of February 18, 1946, which was inspired the I.N.A. Court Martial, resulting in the Royal Indian Navy being renamed as Indian National Navy, jolted the citadel of imperialism further. The message was now loud and clear that the strongest bastion of loyalty to British rule, could no longer be relied upon. A Defence Committee report of June 12, 1946, said that the Royal Indian Navy and even the Royal Indian Air Force could not be relied upon. The reliability of the Indian Army as a whole, was open to serious doubt. This even applied to the Gurkha units.[5]

In retrospect it appears that Bose's idea was pragmatic rather than utopian. Recent testimony by Japanese historian like Akashir and Nagasaki, have revealed that Japan had no intention to occupy India. Moreover, Japan never included India within its Co-prosperity sphere. Japan probably did not have any agenda of aggrandizement with respect to India because the distance at which India was located would make it difficult for

Japan to subjugate and control India. It is however an interesting speculation as to whether India's freedom would have been expedited had Bose gone to East Asia a year earlier when the war situation was more in favour of the Axis Powers. In terms of its immediate results, the I.N.A. was a disaster but its long term repercussions were far reaching. It infected the colonial masters with a fear psychosis for the first time which testifies to the correctness of Bose's final and desperate bid for India's freedom. It has been rightly stated that the attempt to make the army and the Police disloyal, was a method seldom tried by the Congress. Real success was achieved in Malaya in 1944-45 by Netaji Bose. The last mutinies by cadets in Bombay and Karachi made the British authorities feel that their defence forces could not be relied upon.[6] This was the first time since 1857, that Indian soldiers had become disloyal. The I.N.A. legend captured popular imagination and was a realistic adventure rather than a suicidal misadventure. It was an indirect catalyst behind the transfer of power.

III
SUBHAS ON NATIONALISM AND SOCIALISM

Subhas Chandra Bose confessed in 'My Personal Testament' written on November 29, 1940, that "I was originally fashioned by nature to be first and foremost, a thinker, but circumstances have forced me into a life of hectic political activity with the result that I have not been able to make my contribution to the thought life of India and of the world. But I have certain definite ideas on philosophic, social, economic and political problems and should like them to be amplified and worked out by the generation that follows ours. I have this much to claim for myself that my ideas do not float in the air. They are intimately related to reality as we know it."[7] Thus Bose disowned any utopian streak and averred to be a practical idealist. He was not a theoretician or system builder but articulated his vision of future India with clarity and perceptiveness.

In all his speeches and writings, Subhas Chandra Bose expressed his strong commitment to Socialism. Here however he was not in favour of blind imitation of any model but was firm in his advocacy of an Indian brand of Socialism. In his presidential speech at the Rangpur Political Conference of March 30, 1930, he said that “This Socialism did not derive its birth from the books of Karl Marx. It has its origin in the thought and culture of India. The gospel of democracy that was preached by Swami Vivekananda has manifested fully in Deshbandhu Das who said that Narayana lives amongst those who till land, prepare our bread by the sweat of their brow.”[8] He added in a note of caution that “New ideas of Socialism are nowadays travelling to India from the west and they are revolutionizing the thoughts of many, but the idea of Socialism is not a novelty in this country. We regard it such only because we have lost the thread of our own history. It is not proper to take any school of thought as unmistakable and absolute truth. We must not forget that the Russians, the main disciple of Karl Marx, have not blindly followed his ideas. We have therefore to shape society and politics according to our own ideals and according to our needs.”[9] In the earlier year he had said in his presidential address at the Maharashtra Provincial Conference, Poona on May 3, 1928, that “Communism is not a Western institution. Among the Khasis of Assam private property as an institution does not exist in theory even today. The clan as a whole, owns the entire land. I am sure that similar instances can still be found in other parts of India and also in the past history of the country.”[10] His point was that artificial transplantation of any alien system would be counterproductive. As his ideas began to mature, he interpolated the issue of fascism in his visualized framework. As the Mayor of Calcutta Municipal Corporation, Bose said on September 27, 1930, that he envisaged a synthesis of what modern Europe called the synthesis of Socialism and Fascism that is to say a combination of the attributes of justice, equality and love which were central to Socialism and the efficiency and discipline of Fascism.[11] It should be clarified here that Subhas was never ideologically inclined either towards Socialism or Fascism but talked of a synthesis of their positive features. He reiterated this in his address at the All India Naujawan Bharat Sabha on March 27, 1931, saying that, justice, equality, freedom, discipline and love, were the five principles which should constitute the basis of India's collective life.[12] The emphasis on love clearly indicates that any system which curbed individual freedom was an anathema to Bose. Far from visualising a Fascist dictatorship in India, Bose affirmed his faith in a Socialist Republic. However, he was of the decided view that India must evolve her own brand of Socialism in consonance with her tradition, history and culture.

Here, he saw an opportunity for India to make her own original contribution to the thought life of the world. Thus in his presidential address at the All India Trade Union Congress on July 4, 1931, he said that, "I have no doubt in my mind that the salvation of India, as of the world, depends on Socialism. India should learn from and profit by the experience of other nations but India should be able to evolve her own methods in keeping with her own needs and her own environment India should evolve her own form of Socialism. It may be that the form of Socialism which India will evolve will have something new and original about it which will be of benefit to the whole world."[13] By now the stage was set for the comprehensive and authentic articulation of his ideas in his famous book *The Indian Struggle* published in 1935 during his period of exile in Europe. This book symbolises the culmination of his ideas developed over the years and an exposition of his theoretical concept of Socialism.

Bose wrote that, "Whether one believes in the Hegelian dialectic or the Bergsonian or any other theory of evolution, in no case need we think that creation is at an end. Considering everything, one is inclined to hold that the next phase in world history will produce a synthesis between Communism and Fascism. And will it be a surprise if that synthesis is produced in India?"[14] Elucidating his point, Bose said that Communism and Fascism had certain common features like supremacy of the state over the individual, denunciation of parliamentary democracy, belief in party rule, planned industrial reorganization and suppression of dissenting minorities. These common features would constitute the new synthesis which Bose called *Samyavada* or the doctrine of equality and it was India's task to work out this synthesis.[15] He listed five reasons why Communism would not succeed in India. Firstly, he was of the opinion that while the Indian movement was a nationalist one, Communism had no sympathy for nationalism. Secondly, he felt that Russia had no interest in a world revolution. Thirdly, many of the economic ideas of Communism would make a strong appeal to Indians but some of its other aspects would have a contrary effect because Russian Communism was anti religious and atheistic while in India there was no feeling against religion as such. Fourthly, the materialistic interpretation of history was not likely to find unqualified support in India. Fifthly, while Communism had made some remarkable contributions in the domain of Economics like the idea of state planning, it had made no original contribution to the solution of the monetary problem.[16] Bose ended saying that India would not become a new edition of Soviet Russia and the various modern socio-political movements and experimentations being conducted in Europe and America would have considerable influence on India's development.[17] The vision expounded by Bose reveals continuity in his thought process because he had been expressing the same ideas for quite some time in the past. The proposed synthesis of Communism and Fascism however came to be heavily criticized for his inability to appreciate the fact that Fascism was the most aggressive phase of imperialism and through it the crisis of Capitalism became manifest. He was also taken to task for his eclecticism and vagueness of conception of both Fascism and Communism. The contending logic was that any synthesis of Communism and Fascism was theoretically untenable since one stood for the emancipation of humanity from bondage while the other stood for the annihilation of individual freedom. The similarities between the two which he highlighted were superficial rather than real.

Bose partially modified his stand in an interview to R.P. Dutt in London on January 24, 1938, where he admitted that his expression had not been a happy one and clarified that what he had meant that after winning freedom, India would move in the direction of Socialism. He also defended himself saying that when he wrote his book, Fascism had not yet started on its imperialist expedition.[18] In his famous speech at the Tokyo Imperial University Bose restated his stand. He considered the similarities and differences between National Socialism and Communism. Both in his opinion were anti democratic and anti capitalistic. However National Socialism, despite its success in creating national unity and solidarity, had failed to reform the economic system which was capitalistic. Communism had to its credit, the great achievement of planned economy but it was not able to appreciate the value of national sentiment. India needed a synthesis of Nationalism and Socialism.[19]

In his projection of a synthesis of Nationalism and Socialism, Bose remained firm in his denunciation of aggressive nationalism of Nazi Germany and Fascist Italy. In a letter to Dr. Thierfelder on March 24, 1934, he wrote, "When I first visited Germany in 1933, I had hopes that a new German nation which had risen to a consciousness of its national strength and self respect, would instinctively feel a deep sympathy for other nations struggling in the same direction. Today I regret that I have to return to India with the conviction that the new nationalism of Germany is not only narrow but also arrogant and selfish."[20] He also severely criticized Mussolini's conquest of Abyssinia saying that "Since Mussolini came to power in 1922, Italy has been thinking aggressively in terms of expansion, of a revival of the Roman empire."[21] He also castigated Great Britain for its policy of appeasement saying that it first challenged Italy and then beat a retreat before the bluff and bluster of Mussolini.[22] He was thus most vocal about any manifestation of imperialist self aggrandizement. His admiration for Italy and Germany related only to the disciplined foundation of national life they had ensured and consolidated. This was what he wanted India to emulate, not the reactionary features of the former. The proposed synthesis was relative, not absolute.

IV
RELEVANCE OF SUBHAS CHANDRA BOSE TO MODERN INDIA

The relevance of Subhas Chandra Bose to modern India can be established only in the light of the free India visualized by him and the ideals which he wanted to constitute the bedrock of her national life. Subhas never envisaged a dictatorship in India though he preferred a strong party with dictatorial powers for some time after independence. He had no faith in mid Victorian democracy but did not think of introducing a Fascist dictatorship in India at any time. In his Haripura speech, he clearly spoke of a multi-party system. His overall bent of mind was not dictatorial and what he wanted was a disciplined democracy. At the same time he wanted the state to be a servant of the people as he mentioned in his Tokyo speech. Bose was always in favour of individual freedom but felt that some kind of forced march might be necessary to arouse the people from their inertia and torpor. This is worth experimenting with in modern India where unbridled democracy is the other name of licence and anarchy. Doubts have been expressed as to the time limit of authoritarian rule and the process of switch over to democracy. For once dictators are entrenched in power, they perpetuate their authority. Subhas thus laid emphasis on the training and preparation of the nation builders of free India and believed that with the inculcation of requisite idealism, they would not behave like self seekers and usurpers. It was enlightened despotism which Subhas spoke of, not Hitlerism.

The modernist outlook of Subhas manifested in his advocacy of post independence reconstruction of India along scientific lines was endorsed by Tagore who preferred a scientifically tempered person as Congress President. It was Subhas who initiated National Planning as an integral feature of Congress policy and appointed the National Planning Committee. He was in this sense the precursor of the Five Year Plans of independent India which were a vindication of his ideas.

In view of the Feminist Movement operative in India, one may appropriately recall the role Subhas assigned to women in his I.N.A. He organized the Jhansi Rani Regiment and inspired women in East Asia to come out of the drudgery of kitchen life and perform the role of soldiers on the battlefield. He had an abiding faith in *Nari Shakti* or power of the women folk and espoused gender equality most emphatically. His new role definition for women makes Subhas Chandra Bose strikingly modern in the present Indian context.

The example of national unity and secularism set by the I.N.A. where there was not a trace of caste or religious distinctions, where all communities intermingled freely, and there was a common kitchen deserves to be emulated in modern India. The I.N.A. was truly a Nation in Making. It was the epitome of the ideology of Indianness which Bose injected in each soldier. The I.N.A. was thus significant not for what it did but for what it was. Subhas was dead against the partition of India and affirmed that "My Divine Motherland shall not be cut up." It is believed by many that had Subhas returned to India, the partition of the country would have been prevented. Today when forces of disintegration are threatening to sap at the roots of unity, this inspiring clarion call reverberates resoundingly in our ears. Nationalism was the foremost ideal championed by Netaji Subhas Chandra Bose who was a nationalist first and last. Unity, Faith and sacrifice were the ideals of the I.N.A. and in modern India, adherence to them alone can enable us to combat the centrifugal forces which are threatening the country with the spectre of fragmentation.

V
THE MYSTERY OF DISAPPEARANCE OF NETAJI: A NEVER ENDING STORY

After the reported air crash at Taihoku on August 18, 1945 where Subhas Chandra Bose was reported to have been killed, a large segment of his countrymen refused to believe that he was dead. Subsequently the Government of India appointed two enquiry commissions, first under the chairmanship of Shah Nawaz Khan in 1956 and thereafter another one in 1970 one with Justice G.D. Khosla the chairman. Neither of these commissions was able to prove conclusively that the air crash story was true. In the meantime the publication of *The Dissentient Report* by Suresh Chandra Bose and *Netaji, Dead or Alive?* by eminent parliamentarian Prof. Samar Guha exposed the contradictions in the air crash story. In 1998, the Government of India appointed another enquiry commission chaired by Justice Manoj Mukherjee who submitted his report on May 17, 2006. In this report, the air crash story was conclusively repudiated and it was also stated that the ashes preserved at the Renkoji temple were not those of Netaji. The report conclusively established on the basis of investigations in Taihoku that no plane took off from the airport on the day of the reported air crash. However, Justice Mukherjee observed that in all probability, Netaji was no more alive. This evoked adverse criticism from many quarters because without affirming the date and time of any person's death, there can be no declaration of even his probable death. Some fascinating researches by Anuj Dhar in his books *Netaji, Back from the Dead* and *History's Greatest Cover Up* have produced revelations of Netaji residing in India at Faizabad in the guise of ascetic Gumnami Baba who was declared dead in September 1985 but subsequently the report was found to be unsubstantiated. The researches by the noted scholar Purabi Ray in the Russian archives articulated in her book *A Search for Netaji* sought to establish the fact of his death in Russia. There is however no conclusive proof of this though it is possible that Netaji was in Russia for a certain period of time. After the surrender of Japan, he wanted to go to Russia to seek her help for India's freedom. Even after his great escape from India, he initially wanted to go to Russia but was repulsed by the Russian embassy and forced to go to Germany. When Hitler was pushed to a tight corner in the face of the massive counter attack by the Red Army after his invasion of Russia, Netaji steadfastly refused to allow his Indian Legion in Germany to be used against Russia. Despite being castigated by Indian Communists as Quisling, he had an enduring faith in Russia as a potential ally for achieving India's emancipation. There is however no clinching proof of his death in Russia. The question that continues to confront historians, scholars and the countrymen of Netaji, is why did he not return to India if he did not die in the air crash? Did he opt for spiritual life? It is true that Bose had pronounced spiritual proclivities and sacrificed his essentially spiritual urge for the sake of liberation of his enchained motherland. Many find it difficult to accept the idea of his seeking refuge in the world of spirituality considering the fact that his life was one of ceaseless activism. They also feel inclined to ask why a nationalist like Subhas should choose to remain hidden from public eye when he was sure to be greeted with rapturous acclamation by his countrymen had he returned to India? How could he choose the life of a recluse when his motherland needed his services? Those who believe in the spiritual orientation of Bose, subscribe to the view that after India's independence, Bose had no stomach for politics. He had no aspiration to rise to the seat of power in independent India and assigned priority to spirituality over politics at this stage of his life. While no final answer to the question of his disappearance can be given, it is an indisputable fact that Subhas Chandra Bose still continues to captivate the imagination of a large number of his countrymen even in the new millennium.

The interest in the Netaji Mystery is in evidence in the recent initiatives taken by both the government of West Bengal as well as of the government of the centre. In September 2015 the government of West Bengal released 64 files on Netaji. Though they did not shed any light on the mystery of his disappearance yet they did provide some information about the political life of Netaji and also of I.N.A. Currently the Honourable Prime Minister of India Mr. Narendra Modi has also expressed his resolve to ensure that all other files pertaining to Netaji which are in the custody of the different countries are released speedily. This proves beyond the shade of doubt that Netaji is still of enduring relevance and significance to India in the New millennium.

His charisma, dynamism, patriotism and qualities of leadership continue to inspire and fascinate the people even today. Thus interest and curiosity about Netaji is still undiminished. What happened to him is still shrouded in mystery and future alone can tell whether it will be unravelled.

Notes

1. T.R. Sareen, "The Indian National Army", Ram Dayal ed., *We Fought Together for Freedom,* Oxford University Press, New Delhi, 1995, p. 207.
2. N. Mansergh ed., *The Transfer of Power 1942-47,* Vol. vi, London, 1973, p. 197.
3. B.C. Dutta, *Mutiny of Innocents,* Sindhu Publications Pvt Ltd, Bombay, 1971, p. 107.

4. Lt. Gen. Sir Francis Tuker, *Where Memory Serves,* London, 1950, p. 48.
5. *Defence Committee Paper* D.O. (46) 68.
6. Wilhem Von Ponchhammer, *India's Road to Nationhood: A Political History of the Subcontinent,* Allied Publishers, New Delhi, 1981, p. 461.
7. Subhas Chandra Bose, *Crossroads,* Netaji Research Bureau, Calcutta, 1980, p. 334.
8. *Selected Speeches of Subhas Chandra Bose,* Publications Division, Government of India, New Delhi, 1983, p. 47.
9. *Ibid.*
10. *Ibid.*, p. 30.
11. Sisir Kumar Bose and Sugata Bose, eds., *Netaji: Collected Works,* vol. vi, Netaji Research Bureau, Calcutta, 1987, p. 128.
12. Bose, n. ix, p. 58.
13. *Ibid.*, p. 64.
14. Subhas Chandra Bose, *The Indian Struggle,* in Sisir Kumar Bose ed., *Netaji: Collected Works,* vol. ii, Calcutta, 1981, p. 351.
15. *Ibid.*, p. 352.
16. *Ibid.*, pp. 352-53.
17. *Ibid.*, p. 353.
18. Bose, n. i, p. 30.
19. *Ibid.*, n. iv, p. 12.
20. Sisir Kumar Bose and Sugata Bose, eds., *Netaji: Collected Works,* vol. viii, Oxford University Press, Delhi, 1994, pp. 165-66.
21. Subhas Chandra Bose, "Europe Today and Tomorrow", *Modern Review,* August 21, 1937.
22. *Ibid.*

Reading List

Bose, Pradip. *Subhas Bose and India Today,* Deep and Deep Publications, New Delhi, 1998.

Bose, Subhas Chandra. *The Indian Struggle,* Netaji Research Bureau, Calcutta.

———. *Cross Roads,* Netaji Research Bureau, Calcutta.

———. *Fundamental Questions of the Indian Revolution,* Netaji Research Bureau, Calcutta.

———. *An Indian Pilgrim,* Netaji Research Bureau, Calcutta.

Das, Sitangshu. *Subhas: A Political Biography,* Rupa, New Delhi, 2006.

Jog, N.G. *In Freedom's Quest*, Orient Longman, New Delhi, 1969.

Mukerji, Sumit. *Subhas Chandra Bose: The Making of a Warrior Philosopher 1921-41,* N.E. Publishers, Kolkata, 2006.

Mukherjee, Hiren. *Bow of Burning Gold,* Peoples Publishing House, New Delhi, 1993.

Toye, Hugh. *The Springing Tiger,* Jaico, Calcutta, 1959.

25

Political Ideas of Jayaprakash Narayan (1902-1979)

Sibranjan Chatterjee

I
INTRODUCTION

Jayaprakash Narayan, a man of great personal charm and moral integrity, was a commanding figure in Indian public life for almost two generations. He had an immense ability to influence others through a combination of personal fearlessness, clean personal life, physical and moral daring, and love for his fellow countrymen.

Jayaprakash Narayan was born on October 11, 1902, in a small village Sitab Diyara, which at the time of his birth belonged to Chhapra district of Bihar. He claimed his descent from a respectable *Kayastha* middle-class family. His father Hansu Dayal was a government servant in the Revenue Department and mother Phulo Rani was simple religious-minded woman, having a deep imprint on young Jayaprakash's mind. Unlike other children he was not so much interested in games, but was quite and thoughtful. From his childhood he developed a feeling of love and sympathy for the poor peasants of his village. Having completed his primary education in his native village, he was admitted to Class VII of Patna Collegiate School. On the results of his Matriculation Examination he was awarded a scholarship and was admitted in Patna College. At that time the extremist and revolutionary movements radiated outwards from Bengal to Bihar and other provinces of India. As the Patna Collegiate School had no hostel, the students lived in a building called Sarasvati Bhavan, where many future prominent leaders including Rajendra Prasad, the first President of India, lived. In that building the student leaders organized regular meetings for spreading nationalist ideals and Jayaprakash regularly attended there. Thus, even as a school student, he came into contact with the nationalist and revolutionary ideas of the period. In response to Mahatma Gandhi's call in the early months of 1921, Jayaprakash, along with a group of bright students, left Patna College and joined Non-Cooperation Movement, just a few weeks before his Intermediate Examination. Subsequently he took his Intermediate Degree from Bihar Vidyapith. He continued his science studies under the guidance of Professor Phuldeo Sahay Verma of Benaras Hindu University. In May 1922, he obtained a scholarship and proceeded to the USA for higher studies. In the meantime in 1920 (at the age of eighteen) Jayaprakash married Prabhavati, the daughter of Brajkishore Prasad, a lawyer by profession and a nationalist leader of Bihar close to Gandhiji. After marriage Jayaprakash came into intimate contact with Gandhiji who treated Prabhavati as his daughter. After Jayaprakash sailed from Calcutta for the USA in 1922, Prabhavati, with the permission of her husband, went to Sabarmati Ashram. There she undertook the vow of celibacy and became a staunch devotee of Gandhi and his philosophy.

During his stay for eight years in the USA, Jayaprakash took formal education in both science and arts, particularly in Mathematics, Chemical engineering, Bacteriology, Philosophy, Economics and Sociology. At Wisconsin he changed his course of study from natural science to social science. In 1929, his thesis entitled "Cultural Variation" and submitted for the Master's Degree of Ohio University, was adjudged the best dissertation of the year by the said University. When Jayaprakash was in the USA, the omens of the impending world-wide depression of 1930s were becoming increasingly visible on the surface of the American economy. Moreover, the new socialist state of Russia threw a challenge to capitalism by posing an alternative socio-economic and political system. For survival, side by side academic pursuit, he had to work in various places including factory and face the curse of depression and apartheid. In Chicago, he was maltreated by racially prejudiced factory owners who hated 'coloured people' or 'Asiatics'. He also painfully noticed the brutal treatment meted out to the Negro people in various spheres of American life. At this time in Chicago he came into contact with Manuel Gomez, a man of Mexican origin, who was in charge of the oriental section of the Communist Party of the USA and was largely influenced by him. In different factories where he worked from time to time, he actively participated in demonstrations and strikes which had been organized by the socialist labour unions. The writings of M.N. Roy also had an impact on his political mind. In 1929, he returned to India with radical socialist ideas on Marxist model.[1]

After his return to India, Jayaprakash joined Indian National Congress and was appointed Secretary of the Labour Research Department of the party. He had an intimate relation with Jawaharlal Nehru. Jayaprakash, along with his wife Prabhavati, joined the Civil Disobedience Movement led by Gandhiji in 1930 and both were arrested. After their release from the jail at the end of the Movement, Prabhavati went to Wardha Ashram to profess and practise the Gandhian ideals and Jayaprakash became deeply engrossed in forming the Congress Socialist Party. With the effort of some young radical Congressmen and under the leadership of Jayaprakash and Acharya Narendra Dev Congress Socialist Party was formed in 1934. This platform within the Congress was based on three propositions: (1) the primary struggle in India was the national struggle for freedom, (2) nationalism was a necessary stage on the way to socialism, (3) the socialists must work inside Indian National Congress because it was the primary body leading the national struggle. As Jayaprakash said: "We Socialists do not want to create factions in the Congress nor do we desire to displace the old leadership of the Congress and to establish rival leadership. We are only concerned with the policy and programme of the Congress. We only want to influence the Congress decisions."[2] Jayaprakash was the guiding star in making Marxism the base of the ideology of the Congress Socialist Party. In his book *Why Socialism* he observed that "today more than ever before it is possible to say that there is only one type, one theory of Socialism-Marxism."[3]

Under the influence of Gandhiji the Marxist Jayaprakash was soon turned into the Gandhian Jayaprakash. In this transformation his wife had also a role to play. It has already been noted that in connection with his marriage, he came in touch with Gandhi. Following the former's return to India from the USA, he was welcomed by the latter and treated by him as a son-in-law. Particularly, after coming back from the USA, Jayaprakash became very close to Gandhiji and was greatly influenced by the latter's way of life, personality and view on non-violence. He felt that the Marxist theories of class struggle, violent revolution and dictatorship of the proletariat were not in conformity with the Indian tradition and culture. Gandhiji's view that means must be as pure as end had a deep imprint on Jayaprakash. Besides, he was shocked to see that the Indian Communists were denouncing the national movement as bourgeois.

In 1938, Jayaprakash was nominated to the Congress Working Committee when Jawaharlal Nehru was the Congress President. In 1940, he was imprisoned for six years. In 1942, he managed to escape from jail accompanied by five comrades. Departing from Gandhi's theory of non-violence for the time being, he organized an armed guerilla band and kept up the 'August Revolt' (Quit India Movement of August 1942) from the underground. He was then known as 'August Hero'. He was rearrested in September 1943 and released in April 1946. At this time he and other socialists realized that the Congress leaders seemed to be more interested in power politics rather than in anything else. He and Rammanohar Lohia worked hard to form "Socialist Party" in 1948, of which Jayaprakash became the General Secretary and Acharya Narendra Dev the President. In the First General Elections of 1952, the results of the "Socialist Party" were not satisfactory. Moreover, Jayaprakash had difference of opinion with other front-ranking leaders of the "Socialist Party" and ultimately in 1955 he retired from politics and devoted himself to the task of social and moral reconstruction of the society on the Gandhian line. In the last part of life, in spite of ill-health, he started anti-corruption movement from Bihar in 1974 and gave a clarion call to the masses for total revolution in the non-violent way. All non-Congress parties stood behind him. The movement spread to all parts of India, the intensity of which was so deep-rooted that in June 1975 the President of India had to proclaim Internal Emergency during the Prime Ministership of Indira Gandhi. Under his guardianship all non-Congress and non-Communist parties merged into a single party, Janata Party, and in the Lok Sabha elections held in March 1977 Janata Party came to power at the Centre. It was, however, a short-lived government owing to difference, quarrel among the leaders of the party and the government without any ideological base. In the meantime, Jayaprakash was bed-ridden and died on October 8, 1979, with a frustrated and disappointed mind.

II
POLITICAL IDEAS

Concept of Socialism—It has already been noted that during his stay in the USA, Jayaprakash was attracted towards the Marxist ideology. As an architect of the policy of the Congress Socialist Party, he said that there was only one type of socialism, that is, Marxism. But soon he was disenchanted with the Marxian Socialism and developed his socialist ideology in the context of Gandhian principles. To him, both socialism and Gandhism aim to abolish feudalism and capitalism and establish a classless, casteless, non-exploitative society. Both stand for preserving individual freedom, ensuring the dignity of the individual and using the democratic means to reach the socialist goals.

Jayaprakash pointed out that socialism and democracy are complementary concepts. To quote him, "socialism could not exist, nor be created, in the absence of the democratic freedoms."[4] He further stated that his "picture of a socialist India is the picture of an economic and political democracy. In this democracy man will neither be slave to capitalism nor to a party or the state. Man will be free."[5] Inspired by Gandhi, Jayaprakash emphasized that not only material development, but the moral and intellectual development of the individual would be the goal of democratic socialism. Further, unlike the Marxists, he found no conflict between nationalism and socialism. One of the basic propositions of the Congress Socialist Party, as noted, was to recognize nationalism as a necessary stage on the way to socialism.

Jayaprakash rejected the Marxist theory of "ends justify the means." According to him, if by socialism we mean the material as well as the moral improvement of the individual, then it logically follows that this goal cannot be attained without commitment to certain human values and standards of conduct. Thus comes the question of pursuing good means to reach good ends. To quote Jayaprakash, "the greatest thing Gandhi taught us was that means are ends, that evil means can never lead to good ends and that fair ends require fair means."[6] He further argued that disregard for good means and a total eclipse of moral values were major factors responsible for the failure of socialist construction in Soviet Russia.

Several socialist programmes as outlined by Jayaprakash are stated as follows:

1. Complete independence, in the sense of separation from the British imperialism.
2. All political and economic power to the producing masses, i.e., to those engaged in producing goods or rendering services either by hand or by brain. Jayaprakash pointed out that throughout human history power never rested with the working people, but with the capitalists and elite enjoying all privileges.
3. Development of the economic life of the country to be planned and controlled by the state.
4. Socialization of key and principal industries (such as, Steel, Cotton, Jute, Railways, Shipping, Mines, etc.), banks, insurance and public utilities, with a view to the progressive socialization of all instruments of production, distribution and exchange.
5. State monopoly of foreign trade.
6. Redistribution of land to the peasants.
7. Elimination of princes and landlords and all other classes of exploiters without compensation.

8. Liquidation of debts owned by the peasants and workers.
9. Recognition of the right to work or maintenance by the state.
10. Encouragement and promotion of co-operative and collective farming by the state.
11. Adult franchise on a functional basis.
12. No support to or discrimination between religions by the state and no recognition of any distinction based on caste and gender.
13. Representation of the workers in the management of the state-owned and state-managed enterprises through their elected representatives.
14. Reorganization of the village life so that the villages can be made self-governing and self-sufficient units as far as practicable.[7]

In 1953, there were discussions between Jawaharlal Nehru and Jayaprakash regarding increasing co-operation between the Congress and the Praja Socialist Party (PSP) in the spheres of national reconstruction and development. But the talks failed to produce any concrete result mainly owing to the opposition of other socialist leaders. At the Betul Conference, the compromise formula of Jayaprakash was rejected by a majority of the socialists. This made him frustrated and he decided, as already stated, to retire from politics.

From the academic viewpoint, his socialist programmes, as placed in the aforesaid Conference, are worth-noticing. In addition to the above programmes as outlined by him, some other programmes of Jayaprakash may be referred to:

1. Abolition of Second Chamber of the legislature.
2. Administrative reforms at all levels, including decentralization of political power and administrative authority.
3. Reform of law and legal practices.
4. Effective machinery to deal with corruption.

5. Suitable legislation to prevent fragmentation and bring about consolidation of holdings.
6. The rural economy to be transformed into a co-operative economy through compulsory multipurpose societies.
7. Demarcation of spheres of large and small-scale industries, and establishing, encouraging and protecting small-scale industries.
8. As a first step towards achieving economic equality in the country higher salaries and emoluments of government officials shall be scaled down.
9. The spirit of *Swadeshi* to be promoted and made to pervade all walks of life.[8]

Unlike the Marxists, Jayaprakash argued that socialism is not opposed to the dominant values of the Indian culture. In a word, Jayaprakash is the most well-known and recognized personality in the field of Indian socialism. Mahatma Gandhi regarded him as the greatest Indian authority on socialism.

Democracy and Partyless Democracy—Jayaprakash was a democrat. He was a passionate lover of individual liberty throughout his life. To him, democracy is a creed as well as a way of life. He emphasized upon the moral values of democracy. The problem of democracy is essentially a moral problem. Constitutions, systems of government, political parties and elections—all these are relevant to the business of democracy. Unless there is development of the moral and spiritual virtues of the people, the best Constitutions and political systems would not make democracy work. Jayaprakash, like Gandhiji, believed in the concept of "inner swaraj" which means the capacity of an individual to control his desire and impulse in the light of an ideal. It further implies the willingness and ability of a person to sacrifice his personal interest for the sake of the common interest.

Jayaprakash suggested several qualities for the proper functioning of democracy: (1) concern for truth, (2) aversion to violence, (3) the spirit of co-operation, (4) love of liberty and the courage to resist oppression, (5) respect for the opinion of others, (6) the sense of duty or responsibility, (7) belief in human equality, and (8) ability to lead a simple life.

Jayaprakash did not find any conflict between socialism and democracy. To him, as already referred to, socialism cannot exist nor be created in the absence of the democratic freedoms. At the same time, democracy cannot be effective without socialism. We have earlier noted that in his early life he had faith in Marxism, but gradually he realized that India must evolve her own brand of socialism suited to her needs and conditions and should be brought about through democratic and non-violent means. In another place he said: "In a fully democratic India the transition to socialism can be and should be a peaceful democratic process."[9] Moreover, Jayaprakash stood against the growth of centralization in the political and economic spheres and regarded centralization as a menace to democracy. As a part of decentralization, he emphasized that the villages should be made self-governing and self-sufficient units.

Jayaprakash was a critic of democracy in its present form. He said: "The party system as I saw it was emasculating the people. It did not function so as to develop their strength and initiative nor to help them establish their self-rule and to manage their affairs themselves."[10] Certain drawbacks of Western model of parliamentary democracy were highlighted by him:

(1) Parliamentary democracy is found to be resting on a very narrow base. "It is like an inverted pyramid that stands on its head." In this connection Jayaprakash referred to the defect of our electoral system which has led to the minority government. Instead of the majority, it is the minority that rules the country. In elections, a number of candidates contest for one seat and the candidate, who secures more votes than his rivals, is declared elected even though he secures less than fifty per cent votes. Owing to heavy expenses of elections, only the rich and affluent persons can contest the elections. Hence, the plea that elections enable the people to take part in the functioning of government is, according to Jayaprakash, myth and an eye-wash.

(2) Parliamentary democracy, to Jayaprakash, leads to atomization of society. In a parliamentary democracy the voter feels a sense of power only once in every five years when elections take place.

(3) To Jayaprakash, the real interests of the people are often sacrificed at the altar of demagoguery. The need to catch votes creates an unlimited scope for indulging in half-truths, for provoking the popular passions and for arousing false hopes by making false, but pleasing promises.

(4) A major defect of parliamentary democracy is its tendency towards centralization. He observed: "At one extreme of its political spectrum is the nation state and at the other the individual voter, with a blank in between."[11] The individual is reduced to abject helplessness. A natural outcome, to Jayaprakash, of centralization is the growing power of bureaucracy, and the solution of this problem lies in more and more decentralization.

(5) Parliamentary democracy cannot exist without political parties, that is, small caucuses of politicians, who create false notion of democracy and self-government and reign in the name of the people.

In his thought-provoking pamphlet "A Plea for Reconstruction of the Indian Polity" Jayaprakash explained his idea of partyless democracy. The highest political institution of the local community should be the General Assembly—the 'gram sabha'. All adult persons should be considered members of the 'gram sabha'. The selection of the executive body—the 'panchayat'—should be by general consensus of opinion in the 'gram sabha'. No person can occupy the same post for more than a fixed period. It will be the responsibility of the 'gram sabha' and 'gram panchayat' to ensure that the village becomes self-sufficient in food, clothing, shelter, primary education and primary medical care. The 'gram panchayats' will have to be integrated into the 'panchayat samiti'. Jayaprakash wanted that the 'panchayat samitis' should play a significant role in the economic and political life of the country, particularly in the spheres of planning and development. The 'panchayat samiti' is to be elected by the 'gram panchayats' as a whole and not by individual members. 'Gram panchayat' as a body, not its individual members, will represent the village community. The next storey, to Jayaprakash, above the 'panchayat samiti' will be the district council which will be elected by 'samitis' as such and not by the individual members. Likewise, all district councils of a State would come together to elect the 'Vidhan sabha' or the State Legislature. In like manner, the State 'Vidhan sabhas' would bring into existence the 'lok sabha' or the Central Legislature. Thus, the political institution at each level is an integration of all the institutions at the lower level.[12] The partyless democracy starts from the bottom and is based on two principles—replacement of the party-politics and election by community consensus and secondly, replacement of the principle of majority by unanimity. Subsequently, however, Jayaprakash partially modified the election system of 'Vidhan sabha' and 'lok sabha'. But the essence of the concept of partyless democracy has remained unchanged.

Total Revolution—The call for "Total Revolution" was the last revolutionary quest of Jayaprakash Narayan. The origin of total revolution lay in the students' movement of Bihar which was initiated by the Bihar Students' Struggle Committee with twelve initial demands in March 1974. Eight demands related to educational matters. The remaining four demands included the removal of corruption, bringing down prices, removal of unemployment among both the educated and uneducated, and basic changes in the educational system. Subsequently, the movement included the demand of the resignation of the Bihar ministry and the dissolution of the Legislative Assembly of Bihar. The direct involvement of Jayaprakash Narayan in the movement added to it a new dimension and the political demands of the students became the universal demands of the people.

Total revolution, according to Jayaprakash, aims at changing society in all its aspects. The goals of total revolution are to "create a new order of social and economic equality, genuine democracy and moral values within the Gandhian framework."[13]

The word 'total' does not mean complete, as is sometimes interpreted wrongly. On several occasions, Jayaprakash explained that the revolution was not complete or over. The total revolution was a continuous process. By 'total revolution' he made it clear that he wanted to initiate a revolution that would cover the total life.

The people's struggle, as prescribed by Jayaprakash, will be peaceful and will never assume violent method. As a follower of Gandhiji, he emphasized upon non-violent and peaceful methods to bring about total revolution.

It is true that Jayaprakash explained the aspects of his total revolution largely in the background of the Bihar movement. But his revolution was not limited to the Bihar movement only. It would be an all-embracing process. Further, this total revolution is not just a temporary arrangement for the fulfilment of some temporary and local demands. It is rather a guideline for the future also. It may be noted that Jayaprakash did not explain his concept of total revolution from the viewpoint of class character of the Indian society. But his total revolution aimed at a classless, casteless society. Further, the meaning of total revolution, as explained by Jayaprakash, is relative and flexible. In his own words, "at different times a total revolution might take different forms, even different meanings in the sense that its contents might also be different."[14]

This idea of total revolution was mooted long before 1974. Once while addressing the students of Kanpur, he had given his mind to the students to start a movement of Quit India type. When the students of Gujarat started the movement and became successful in their demand for dissolution of Gujarat Assembly, Jayaprakash met them at Ahmedabad and said dissolution of the Assembly should not be the objective. It should have a larger objective—changing society in all its aspects. Total revolution, to Jayaprakash, is a combination of seven revolutions—economic, social, political, cultural, moral-spiritual, ideological or intellectual, and educational. A brief analysis of these categories of revolution may be made.

Economic Revolution

(i) To Jayaprakash, the aim of economic development should be man and as such, he desired such economy which provides for minimum standard of living of every person.

(ii) The reduction of gross inequalities in the socio-economic system.

(iii) The formation of planning cells at regional, block and village levels.

(iv) The balancing of prices of agricultural and industrial goods.

(v) Development of rural-based industries. The manufacture of consumer goods for domestic use should be the task of small rural industries.

(vi) Saving the villages from urban exploiters.

(vii) Urgency of the development and modernization of agriculture.

(viii) The concept of social ownership is to be applied to the large industrial establishments. The workers employed therein may act as trustees for safeguarding their interests and the greater interests of the consumers and the community.

(ix) Guarantee of full employment, provision for need-based wages and effective steps for checking price rise.

Social Revolution

(i) Prohibition of unjustified and irrational customs and conventions which thwart social progress.

(ii) Encouragement of inter-caste marriage. To Jayaprakash, caste system has been an obstacle to social and economic growth.

(iii) Building up a classless society where there will exist no class distinctions.

Political Revolution

(i) Not more than two terms for any political office holder are to be permitted.

(ii) The candidates for elections should not be imposed by the central or provincial parliamentary boards. The people's committees should set up candidates after prolonged popular consultation at the local level.

(iii) A combination of the German List system and the majority system may be experimented with to reduce the drawback of mere majoritarianism.

(iv) There should be a comprehensive Act against defection.

(v) All incumbents of high posts in the legislature, government, Universities and private sector should declare their assets periodically.

(vi) The legislators who have ceased to command the confidence of a majority of the voters and have betrayed the trust reposed in them are to be recalled.[15]

Cultural, moral-spiritual revolutions—The aim of cultural revolution, to Jayaprakash, is to bring about a radical change in the values of human life and the general attitude of man towards his fellow-beings in the society. Thus, cultural revolution is a kind of moral or spiritual revolution which is interlinked with cultural revolution. As Jayaprakash has pointed out, human life must fulfil both material and spiritual requirements. A man has to be provided with food, clothing, shelter, etc. But there should be no extravagance, wastefulness or luxury. There should be voluntary restriction on consumption. Jayaprakash was of the view that unlimited greed for material needs ultimately kills the moral virtues of man and gives rise to economic inequality and injustice in society. He advised man to rise above his animal nature and become worthy of his moral and spiritual capabilities.

Ideological or intellectual revolution—Jayaprakash firmly believed that no revolution for reconstructing the social set-up could be brought about successfully without making the people aware of its utility. For this what is required is ideological or intellectual revolution for building up a new social order.

Educational Revolution

(i) Jayaprakash regarded education as a vital component of the new social order and urged for a thorough change of the present educational system.

(ii) Special efforts should be made to educate the parents and guardians.

(iii) Co-ordination of knowledge with the actual experience of life, in other words, correlation of teaching with real life-situation.

(iv) Following the ideals of Gandhiji, Jayaprakash wanted a system of education which will make the students self-sufficient and create self-confidence in them.

(v) To Jayaprakash, the Universities of our country are following the system introduced by the British Government and only a few changes have been made. The Universities as a whole are suffering from the worst forms of nepotism and corruption and are more and more ceasing to perform the functions assigned to them. He stood for thorough restructuring of University education.[16] He referred to the instance of China and said: "Here we might follow the example of China in which all the schools and colleges were closed down and the students were sent out to the villages and slums of the towns to impart the rudiments of education to every citizen, young or old."[17]

III
RELEVANCE

(1) Jayaprakash died in 1979. He was actively involved in and acquainted with post-independence political and social conditions of India. Mahatma Gandhi rightly regarded him as the greatest Indian authority on socialism who wanted to bring about socio-economic transformation of society through peaceful, non-violent and democratic methods. His several socialist programmes have been implemented by the Government of India and various State Governments.

(2) To Jayaprakash, the present democratic set-up rests on a narrow base. It is difficult to understand how a system built on adult franchise and the responsibility of the executive to the popular branch of the legislature can be criticized as resting on a narrow base.[18]

(3) Jayaprakash's concept of partyless democracy as an alternative to parliamentary democracy does not appear to be realistic. How is it possible to hold elections without political parties at the national or provincial levels? It may be feasible, to a limited extent, at the village level. At the same time, it must be admitted that democracy can be made meaningful through community participation which is possible only through decentralization of political machinery. As an ideal, the theory of partyless democracy is unique. But its real success demands social and economic equality, greater political consciousness, faith in the purity of means, and above all, a classless society. Needless to say, presently all these conditions are absent. Hence, the idea of partyless democracy appears to be a distant future ideal.[19]

(4) Jayaprakash accorded priority to the principle of consensus in democracy. But he could not altogether ignore the 'majority' principle. He suggested that it might be provided that the villagers first try the method of selection by general agreement, and failing therein, recourse to drawing lots. It is true that parliamentary democracy and majority principle have some drawbacks. But for this election and party system cannot be dispensed with.

(5) Jayaprakash failed to give any clear definition of his concept of total revolution, as a result of which a clear-cut programme did not emerge from the concept. His call for total revolution was fundamentally a movement for the people. But he did not define the word "people", and as such, all kinds of persons irrespective of their class, caste, creed and everything else came within the definition of people. The lack of political and ideological unity among the participants of the movement may frustrate the main objective of the movement. Moreover, Jayaprakash wanted total revolution to be peaceful, non-violent and without disturbing the democratic structure of society. According to the critics, the conception 'revolution' and simultaneously commitment to peaceful democratic norms appear to be somewhat contradictory.

Notes

1. Das Gupta, Nitis, *The Social and Political Theory of Jayaprakash Narayan* (New Delhi: South Asian Publishers, 1997), pp. 8-13.
2. Chandra, Bipan and others, *India's Struggle for Independence, 1857-1947* (New Delhi: Penguin Books, 1998), p. 306.
3. *Ibid.*, p. 307.
4. Narayan, Jayaprakash, *From Socialism to Sarvodaya* (Kashi: Akhil Bharat Sarva Seva Sangh, 1958), p. 13.
5. Quoted in Das Gupta, Nitis, op. cit., p. 69.
6. *Ibid.*, p. 57.
7. Varma, V.P., *Modern Indian Political Thought* (Agra: Lakshmi Narain Agarwal Educational Publishers, 1971), pp. 520-23.
8. *Ibid.*, pp. 524-25.
9. Chaudhuri, Alok Narayan, *Evolution of the Political Thought of Jayaprakash Narayan* (Kolkata: Pragatishil Prokashak, 2004), p. 87.
10. Narayan, Jayaprakash, op. cit., p. 197.
11. Narayan, Jayaprakash, *A Plea for Reconstruction of the Indian Polity* (Varanasi: Akhil Bharat Sarva Seva Sangh, 1959), p. 50.
12. *Ibid.*, p. 71.
13. Chaudhuri, op. cit., p. 171.
14. *Ibid.*, p. 74.
15. Varma, V.P., op. cit., pp. 530-32.
16. Chaudhuri, op. cit., pp. 173-78.
17. Narayan, Jayaprakash, *Total Revolution* (Varanasi: Sarva Seva Sangh Prakashan, 1975), p. 33.
18. Jayapalan, N., *Indian Political Thinkers: Modern Indian Political Thought* (New Delhi: Atlantic Publishers, 2012), p. 243.
19. Chaudhuri, op. cit., p. 169.

26

Rammanohar Lohia and Socialist Thought in India

Chitrita Chaudhuri

INTRODUCTION

Rammanohar Lohia (1910-1967) was a dynamic and colorful personality in the socialist movement of India that began its journey at the backdrop of Indian struggle for independence. Socialist movement started in an organized form with the formation of Congress Socialist Party (CSP) within Indian National Congress. It was led by a group of young intellectuals like Jayaprakash Narayan, Acharya Narendra Dev, Achhyut Pathavardhan, Minoo Masani, Ashok Mehta and Rammanohar Lohia.

Though these leaders had a more or less general agreement on the major principles of Marxism and Leninism, they were not blind supporters of communism, particularly in respect it was being practiced in the then Soviet Union. Rammanohar Lohia and other socialist leaders started to express strong reservations against the way communism was being practiced in Soviet Union. Russian experience drove the leaders in different directions. New ideas were generated. In spite of internal dissension, CSP maintained its organizational cohesion during the freedom struggle.

After India became independent the socialist leaders stood for a third force in Indian politics, but they could not retain their unity. They tried to follow a line of Democratic Socialism—eschewing the path of capitalism of Congress and totalitarianism of Communists. Lohia gave a new shape to this doctrine of socialism.

I
BIOGRAPHY

Rammanohar Lohia was born on 23rd March 1910 at Akbarpur village in Faizabad district of UP. His father Hiralal was a staunch follower of Gandhiji and Congress. Lohia's father took him to Gandhiji at a very young age.[1] In fact Lohia's interest in politics was inherited from his father.

After his primary education in village Lohia was admitted to a school in Bombay, called Marwari Vidyalaya from where he passed high school examination in 1925. Lohia's interest in politics took a radical shape during his college life. He had his college education first in Benaras (1925-27) and then in Calcutta (Vidyasagar College between 1927 and 1929).

After completing graduation from Calcutta University he went to Europe for further studies. While in abroad he never dis-associated himself from the politics of his country. Lohia was in Berlin, Germany during the period 1929-32 to carry out his Ph.D thesis, the title of which was "Salt and Satyagraha". It indicates how Lohia kept himself fully conversant with the developments in the country.

Lohia came back to India in 1933 with burning faith in socialism but with a critical attitude towards communist politics. He retained his old regard for Gandhi and found a new ideal in Jawaharlal Nehru who had already introduced socialist ideas in the national movement.

With the formation of the Congress Socialist Party within Congress in 1936 by some vibrant young intellectuals like Jayaprakash Narayan, Minoo Masani, Acharya Narendradev, Ashok Mehta and others, Lohia found an organization close to his ideals. He played an important part in CSP. He became the editor of the weekly journal *Congress Socialist*. In this connection it would not be out of the way to mention that it was mainly because of his strong writing power and clear vision of world politics Pandit Nehru chose him as the secretary of foreign policy department of Indian National Congress in 1936. It was during this period Lohia wrote his book *The Struggle for Civil Liberties* with a forward by Jawaharlal Nehru.

In 1939 when the Second World War broke out in Europe Lohia wanted Congress to resist all attempts to involve India in any war waged by Imperialist Britain. He was in favour of implementing the policy of 'War Resistance.'

Lohia played a very crucial role during Quit India Movement in 1942. When most of the leaders of Congress including Gandhi were arrested Lohia along with JP and others went underground. He conducted independent radio station from Bombay and Kolkata while in underground. In 1944, he was arrested and sent to Lahore Jail where he suffered inhuman torture by the British Police. After his release in 1946, Lohia joined freedom struggle in Goa and courted arrest as a *Satyagrahi*. Lohia opposed the proposal of India's partition in Congress Working committee meeting in 1946. He also participated in the people's movement against Nizam of Hyderabad in 1947.

Immediately after the killing of Gandhi, Lohia along with others left Congress and formed Socialist Party. The decision was taken in the Nasik Conference in March 1948. Lohia organized a huge rally of workers and peasants and marched towards Delhi for a people's charter. The first Asian Socialist Conference was held in Rangoon in 1951 under the leadership of Lohia.

The independence of India encouraged the people of Nepal to start a democratic struggle led by Nepali Congress against the autocratic rule of the Ranas. Lohia was closely and actively associated with this struggle. He championed the cause of political freedom in Nepal.

The result of first general election to parliament held in 1952 was not very encouraging for the Socialist Party. To remove its ideological weakness the Socialists met in a Special Convention at Panchmari in May 1952 under the Presidentship of Dr. Rammanohar Lohia. It is here Lohia gave his famous theory of equidistance from both capitalism and communism and gave socialism a clear ideological foundation. With the merger of

Socialist Party and Kisan Mazdoor Praja Party (KMPP) a new party was born, called Praja Socialist Party in 1953. Lohia was elected its general secretary.

In 1954 a crisis occurred regarding the PSP ministry in Travancore-Cochin. Police fired upon unarmed crowd which gathered for an agitation against the government. Lohia who was then detained in prison for leading a farmer's movement in UP, sent a telegram asking PSP government to resign. However his proposal was rejected by the party in a special convention of PSP at Nagpur in November 1954. Due to internal difference in opinion regarding party's attitude towards Congress Lohia was ultimately suspended from the party in July 1955.

In December 1955, Lohia laid the foundation of his new socialist party in Hyderabad. He became its president. English monthly journal *Mankind* and Hindi journal *Jan* started its publication under his editorialship from 1956.

After the failure of his 'Seven Years Plan to Power' Lohia's politics entered into a new phase of Anti-Congressism. In 1963, Lohia entered Lok Sabha from Farooqabad, UP by defeating a congress candidate in a by-election. For the first time in the history of parliament 'No confidence motion' was moved against Nehru government. There he raised voices against the inhuman living conditions of the common people as against the luxurious life led by a handful of people. In the meantime, he courted arrest several times while launching protest movements against government's policy of price rise, language, reservation, etc. He gave the slogan 'Congress Hathao Desh Bachao'.

In 1964, Samyukta Socialist Party emerged with the merger of Socialist and Praja Socialist Party but this also could not last long due to the rivalry of two old groups. However in the election of 1967 Congress was defeated in eight states and non-congress government sworn in. Lohia's dream was successful to some extent.

The colourful journey of Dr. Lohia came to an end on 12th October 1967 when Lohia breathed his last at the Wellington Nursing Home, New Delhi.

II

Though widely considered as a hardcore political activist and leader, Lohia wrote extensively to give his political ideas a solid foundation. Keeping in mind the space constraint here I will touch on to some of his basic thoughts and ideas.

LOHIA'S SOCIALISM AND PHILOSOPHY OF HISTORY

In order to find a justification for his new socialist civilization Lohia felt the necessity of a philosophy of history. Instead of regarding history as a mere enumeration of events Lohia always tried to find out some laws, purposes or patterns behind historical developments. According to Lohia those who believed in the philosophy of history could broadly be divided into two categories—one group stood for linear concept of history and another group for cyclical view. The first group regarded human history in terms of continuous progress in a straight line. In the 18th and 19th century linear view became so popular that many European scholars maintained that human history after passing through its ancient and medieval periods have entered the modern phase and reached its highest development in the Western countries. Even 'historical materialism' of Karl Marx was no exception. Marx also believed that history of human civilization is a story of continuous progress from primitive communism to slave society, from slave society to feudal society, from feudal to capitalist society, from capitalism to socialism and finally at the highest stage of socialism would come communism.

Lohia could not accept this linear view of history as it always placed the Western countries of Europe in an advanced position in the ladder of civilization. Rather he maintained that it was a very simplistic and generalized attempt to divide the world history into three or four stages. It was an attitude to hold various multi-dimensional patterns of development of human history into a simple frame.

Moreover Lohia noticed that in course of last one hundred years or more, due to various archaeological excavations men had come to know about the existence of many civilizations which flourished in the past at different regions of the world and then disappeared, as for example Indus Valley Civilization of Harappa and Mohenjo Daro, Chinese civilization, Mayan civilization, the Egyptian civilization and the Aztecs in central America. The linear view had no answer to this.

Lohia found an answer to this in a cyclical view of history. The cyclical theorists like Spengler, Toynbee and Pitirim did not think in terms of one civilization continuously rising upwards but with reference to the rise and fall of various civilizations. According to them each civilization after passing through a period of progress would reach it highest position which would again be followed by a period of decline, leading ultimately to its extinction. A new civilization then would arise or several civilizations might also come into existence in some other places. This civilization would also pass through the same process of rise and decline. Though Lohia accepted the cyclical view of history as it was consistent with his dream of socialist civilization, he did not fully agree with the interpretation given by its major exponents. Lohia also pointed out that one civilization would not influence the development of any subsequent civilization. Every civilization is self-contained. In other words, he did not accept the spiral view of progress as supported by Toynbee and Sorokin.

At the back of his mind Lohia always had the concern for the present backward countries constituting about two-thirds of the world. With their large population and scarce resources and with no colonies in their possession they would never be able to reach the present highly developed industrial civilization of Europe. Having accepted this superior position of Western Europe, Lohia believed that the people of the present backward region were destined to remain forever in a inferior position. Lohia wanted a change. This political compulsion drove Lohia to search for a new theory of socialist civilization which would be completely different from all other previous civilizations.

Problem of Efficiency

The exponents of the cyclical view had simply stated the fact of the rise and fall of civilization, but never tried to find out the reason why all civilizations had passed through the process of rise and fall. Lohia believed that if one could understand the cause of rise and fall, it might be possible for mankind to build-up a new civilization that would not suffer the same fate.

According to Lohia the main cause of the rise and fall lay in their tendency to develop 'Efficiency in a limited and particular direction only'. "Every society hitherto", he wrote "has been able to practice efficiency alone in a specific and limited direction."[2] However it might have deluded itself that it was practicing 'total efficiency'.

By total efficiency Lohia understood all sided development of society and individuals, their development in all directions. In contrast by partial efficiency Lohia referred to their development in one direction only. According to him the character of a civilization was determined by the particular efficiency it sought to promote. The Greek civilization attained efficiency in art, literature and philosophy and the Romans showed their genius in the field of empire building and jurisprudence. The Athenian civilization trained the mind while the Spartan trained the body. According to some scholars the Asian civilization was mainly spiritual while the Western civilization was materialistic. The efficiency that a particular civilization promoted, would depend to a large extent on the characteristic feature of the region and its surrounding conditions within which it rose. According to Lohia each civilization would promote to the maximum possible extent only such potentialities and efficiency among its individuals as it would be necessary for its collective life and were in conformity with its basic character. The talents and potentialities, not considered necessary, would remain largely ignored. Lohia also believed that a civilization once developed would not be able to change its character by changing its emphasis from one type of efficiency to another. Thus according to Lohia, a civilization would live the full course of its life seeking to attain its special efficiency to the maximum possible extent and then would gradually lead to decline.

Two Motions of History

In its initial stage when the civilization would continue to grow in its own direction there would remain in society a healthy and vigorous life. According to Lohia internally during this period different sections of the people would remain involved in class struggle to improve their economic position. Everyone tried to get a share in this prosperity. Externally also such a civilization would be in a state of rising power in its relationship with the outside world. It would be able to combat any aggression or threat of aggression from any other foreign country. After reaching the maximum level of growth in one direction (partial efficiency) the civilization then would enter into a period of decline and would lose its former health and vigour. Then the civilization would be confronted with two major setbacks. Internally, in its declining stage the civilization would fail to tolerate class struggle and therefore the class system would be replaced by caste system. Externally again the civilization would not be in a position to defend itself from outside threat. Then a new civilization would emerge in a different part of the world with a new focus and direction, resulting in 'regional shift' of civilization. Lohia wrote "internally all human history has been an internal movement between classes solidifying into castes and castes loosening into classes."[3]

Class and Caste

Concepts of class and caste have attained a new dimension in Lohia's writing. Caste in Hindu society refers to a system of hierarchically divided society into four groups, i.e. *Brahmin, Kshatriya, Vaishya* and *Shudra* based on fixed social status and occupation determined by birth. In the opinion of Lohia, in its period of growth and prosperity every civilization would pass through class struggle by which different classes of people would try to better off its position or status in society. The idea of class struggle was inspired by the ideal of equality. But when maximum efficiency was reached in one particular direction, civilization, Lohia believed, would enter into a period of stagnation and a deadlock ensured. The internal class struggle became unbearable and therefore an attempt would be made to resolve it into an apparently just system of caste. Caste system justified by the principle of justice was invoked here as an attempt to maintain *status quo*. Explaining the relationship between class and caste Lohia observed, 'Class is mobile caste. Caste is immobile class.' Every society had known this movement from class to caste and vice versa. What distinguished class from caste was its mobility and in that sense caste was an universal phenomenon like class.

Apart from this internal movement between class and caste. Lohia spoke of another kind of external conflict between regions as a result of which the centre of civilization shifted from one region to another. Lohia called it 'continental shift'. According to Lohia when a civilization started declining it was unlikely that a new civilization would occur in the same region with maximum efficiency in another direction. It would break up in a new region or in a new area.

So far the world has seen a number of civilizations at different times at different parts of the world. But instead of promoting total efficiency or all round development of mankind they had sought for 'partial efficiency'. After attaining maximum efficiency in one particular direction and ignoring all other aspects, these civilizations had collapsed like dinosaurs.

Third Motor of Historical Development

The two motors of history, according to Lohia, were the internal oscillation between class and caste and the regional shift of civilization. But these two forces of history could not bring before mankind the promise of a better civilization free from the menace of a struggle between class and caste and also between regions—a civilization which would be free from the cycle of rise and fall and would be based on world unity.

Lohia fortunately found a new driving force, a 'third motor' of historical development. By third motor he meant a process of approximation and integration both among the nations as well as within the nations. One was external integration and the other was internal integration. By external approximation Lohia meant gradual process of coming together of diverse elements or unity among different peoples of the world. By internal approximation he referred to the process by which different sections of the people within a country coming closer to each other. Lohia justified his point by making reference to the role played by agencies like language, religion, education, various cultural and artistic activities, various scientific discoveries, techniques of production, various articles of consumers' use, food habit, dress code and many others. A tendency towards equality had begun, both horizontally and vertically. Therefore, the third motor of historical development which had brought some sort of world unity, Lohia believed, would be able to build up a new civilization of total efficiency. The present modern civilization had already entered into its declining stage. Hence, according to Lohia, man stood before the stage of walking into a state of total efficiency by breaking the 'wheel of history'. The birth of a new civilization based on world harmony and total efficiency would be achieved through a purposeful, intelligent and willed human design.

After the inevitable breakdown of the existing Western civilization, new socialist civilization would arise in the present underdeveloped third world countries of the world. Lohia wrote, "When a civilization flickers, the torch generally passes into the hands of its outcastes. The outcastes are the underdeveloped two-thirds of the world."[4]

Capitalism and Imperialism—The Theory of Twin Origin

Another very significant critical analysis of Marxism, written by Lohia, needs mention in this connection. Marx thought that with the growth of capitalism there would be concentration of capital in the hands of a few capitalists. Labour would be socialized and more and more exploited by the capitalists of their own countries. With increasing poverty of the proletariat there would arise an open confrontation or class struggle between them and the capitalists. Finally, the proletariat through socialist revolution would capture power and establish control over the means of production by driving out the capitalists from power.

Lohia was never in total agreement with this theory of Marx. He accepted the fact that huge concentration of wealth was taking place in capitalist states of the West through exploitation of the proletariat. But he could not accept the fact that the poverty and the misery of the proletariat was deteriorating day by day in the west. Rather in countries like England and Germany the condition of the working class was improving and thereby diluting the case of acute class struggle. Lohia was of the opinion that the rate of impoverisation and discrimination was much much higher in the third world countries like India.

In fact Marx had considered capitalism only in the context of Western Europe. He predicted communist revolution to break out in countries with developed capitalist civilization. But in reality the first socialist revolution took place in the comparatively backward region of Russia. This experience urged Lohia to re-examine the laws of capitalist development as analysed by Karl Marx and his subsequent followers like Lenin.

The factor behind the development of capitalism in the west, according to Marx, was the exploitation of the workers in the form of private profit. But Lohia was confirmed that apart from this internal factor there was another external factor which was equally responsible. Lohia pointed out that the Western European countries had acquired their initial capital or huge resources through the exploitation of the colonies. Lohia observed, "in order, therefore, to understand capitalist development, it will be necessary to think of capitalist economy as consisting not alone of an internal circle represented by the west European economy, but of two circles, an internal west European circle and an external world circle, from which the internal west European circle draws its dynamic, surplus value, its exploitation, its sucking and so on."[5] Without this colonial exploitation Lohia firmly believed capitalism could not have developed so much. Not that Marx was not aware of this stage of colonial exploitation, but as Lohia said "it acts as an addendum to his main doctrine."[6]

Lohia also could not accept Lenin's explanation that imperialism was the highest stage of capitalism. The capitalist countries at their initial stage used to sell their products within their national markets. But with the huge increase in industrial products national market was not enough. It was only then the large capitalist countries in an attempt to extend their market became engaged in colonial rivalry and as a result came imperialism.

Lohia on the other hand was convinced that capitalism and imperialism developed side by side as twins. Industrial revolution started its journey from the middle of eighteenth century and it was during this period capitalism reached its height side by side with imperialism. In the wake of great geographical discoveries in the sixteenth and seventeenth centuries, the west European merchants went to different parts of the world outside Europe and acquired huge amount of wealth and fortune which facilitated the rise of capitalism in the west. Referring to the development of British capitalism, he wrote, that the British capitalists built up their huge capital more by exploiting the resources of India than by exploiting the British labour. "If capitalism has extracted surplus value from its home labourers by paying them less than what they produce", Lohia wrote, "upon this extraction has continually acted the far greater surplus value derived from the colonial toilers."[7]

Lohia and the Theory of the Weakest Link

The success of proletarian revolution in Russia, instead of in highly developed west European states, had called for several febrile attempts to explain this stubborn fact in accordance with Marxism. The most well-known theory that the communists developed on this issue was the 'theory of weakest link'. Explaining the theory of weakest link Lenin and other communists pointed out that revolution might break out in any country and that would depend on the strength of the capitalist forces and organization of the revolutionary party of the country. The imperialist rivalry might make a particular capitalist country weak and exhausted and that would provide the revolutionaries of that country with an opportunity to overthrow the capitalist regime.

This view that the proletarian revolution would take place where capitalism was weakest, was outright rejected by Lohia because it had nothing to do with the Marxist view that with the growth of capitalism the workers of a country would bring about the revolution. Lohia wrote, "Marx himself says that it (capitalism) will break at its strongest point"[8] and therefore the theory that capitalism would break at its weakest point was not regarded by him as consistent with the general laws of Capitalist development as explained by Marx. On the other hand, Lohia believed, that the weakness in the chain of world capitalist system and in the ability of the ruling classes to cope with the revolutionary movements were likely to arise more in the backward regions of the world than in advanced capitalist countries. Hence revolutions against capitalism would likely to take place in the predominantly agrarian and the under-developed countries of the modern world.

Capitalism and Communism—Two Parts of the Same Civilization

According to Lohia capitalism and communism were not fundamentally different from each other. They were not antagonistic to each other. Rather Lohia regarded capitalism and communism as two major expressions of the same existing civilization. The only major difference between the two was one of ownership of the means of production. Capitalism was based on private ownership whereas communism on social or state ownership. Apart from this apparent difference both the systems, in the opinion of Lohia, were motivated by the principle of more and more material prosperity through large scale production, increasing standard of living for people within the nation, craze for efficiency and technological innovation, increasing centralization and subordination of all aspects of life to economic activities. Both capitalism and communism, Lohia pointed out, believed that general aims of the society would flow from the economic aims.[9] Those were the driving forces of modern civilization and there capitalism and communism remained at the same position. The basic character of a modern civilization, Lohia pointed out, must be understood with reference to its basic features and vital impulses and not simply by their economic and political systems. It "cannot be understood in terms of democracy or totalitarianism, private or state property alone."[10] In that sense Karl Marx and Adam Smith had ample similarities. Lohia was surprised to see that both capitalism and communism claimed to have a world view, both tried to solve the economic problems of the world. But Lohia observed that they were only concerned about their own people. They never tried to take into account the problems and the misery of the entire world, particularly the third world. Not only that but the Western world in their demand for more and more material happiness and rising standard of living had lost their peace of mind, 'life of poise and tranquillity'. In order to fulfil their economic aims man had sacrificed all other aspects of life. Uncertainty, unhappiness, tensions, worries and frustration had become a part of their lives. For this one sided development of material prosperity this civilization like all other previous civilizations would sure to face death and disaster.

Basic Features of Lohia's Socialism

Both capitalism and communism, Lohia felt, had developed in the context of West Europe characterized by highly developed productive forces, mass scale industrial production, widespread use of science and technology, huge capital with of course very low density of population. On the other hand, situation is completely different in the poverty stricken two-thirds area of the world. They did not have the necessary capital (private or state owned) for large scale industrial production. Nor did they have any colony from where they could collect external resources. In addition they had the burden of feeding huge population. That is why Lohia was in favour of the theory of equal irrelevance for both capitalism and communism particularly in the context of the third world which was the prime concern of Lohia.

The new civilization which Lohia expected to rise in that part would stand for a harmonious development of all the human potentialities and also would not try to increase efficiency in one particular direction only. It would not restrict itself within the internal oscillation between class and caste. It would also be able to put an end to regional shift externally. Lohia called it socialist civilization. This would not be a part of the existing capitalist or communist civilization, but a completely different one covering the entire humanity. Lohia was in search of new ideas, new methods and new techniques for his proposed new civilization.

Two Aims

In the opinion of Lohia there existed two sets of aims in society—(a) general aims which included values like democracy, truthfulness, good conduct, world peace, peace of mind, etc.

and (b) economic aims meaning thereby material prosperity and happiness. Lohia pointed out both Adam Smith and Karl Marx were of the opinion that general aims would automatically flow out of the fulfilment of economic aims. On the other hand, Gandhian sociologists felt economic aims to flow out of general aims. This effort of treating the two sets of aims as separate and delinked appear to Lohia 'thoroughly futile', rather they should be treated as autonomous. One set of aims would have its impact on the other, but one would not depend on or flow from the other. Lohia wrote "a new socialist theory of autonomous relationship between economic and general aims is what might reconstruct the world."[11]

Doctrine of Immediacy

Another novel contribution of Dr. Rammanohar Lohia was his doctrine of immediacy. Lohia used this concept as a standard of judgment in the context of direct relation between the ultimate objective or aim and the immediate aim or the present means through which the ultimate aim would be accomplished. It was largely a theory regarding harmonious relation between ends and means. Explaining his views Lohia wrote, "Means are ends in the short run and ends are means in the long run. Whatever method one employs in order to achieve one's desired aims tends to become the end in the long run.... Means are piecemeal achievements of that end."[12] To Lohia the 'end' was an ideal to be realized in future and 'means' were measures taken immediately at present. Illustrating this point Lohia observed that it was not possible to achieve the victory of truth through falsehood, of democracy through dictatorship. Lohia was very much opposed to the communist method of class struggle as it completely failed the test of immediacy. It was justified by the ultimate rise of communism in future which provided a sanction for the use of all immoral and undemocratic methods. Lohia's immediacy was an acceptance in a different language of the Gandhian doctrine that no good end could be realized by bad means. The socialists in their struggle to power, Lohia believed should not adopt such means or measures which would not be consistent with the socialist ideals.

Four Pillar State

To Lohia neither parliamentary democracy nor proletarian dictatorship could prevent concentration of power and tyranny. He therefore stood for decentralization, for federalism, but not in the way it was being practiced in the modern world. Federalism normally means distribution of powers between the centre and the states by the constitution. This two fold division was not acceptable to Lohia. "Sovereign power", he wrote, "must not reside alone in centre and the federating units. It must be broken up and diffused over the smallest region where a group of men and women live."[13] Instead of dividing power between the centre and the states he sought to divide it into four units—the village, the district, the province and the centre. The village and the district bodies should not be treated as mere local government institutions. They would have well-defined executive and legislative powers with substantial part of state revenue to their credit. And, to Lohia, only then the democracy of first grade would be established.

Lohia wanted this decentralization to spread even in the economic field—such as production, ownership, planning where it would prevent the concentration of economic power. So he pointed out "not through the mixed economy of social and private ownership but through spreading social ownership over the four pillars of the state will it be possible to diffuse economic power."[14] Lohia gave emphasis of the autonomous character of village government. By this he wanted the village to stay in close relationship with numerous other villages and the nation as a whole. He said "I have deliberately used the term 'autonomous' rather than 'independent'."[15] Lohia feared that the concept of village self-sufficiency or independent village might hamper the unity and the integrity of the country.

Small Unit Machine Technology

As per the law of history Lohia expected his socialist civilization to rise in the present backward regions of the world, not in west Europe. Referring to the driving forces of Western civilization of large-scale industrial production and ever increasing standard of living Lohia wrote that, "It is a patent fact that these driving forces are no longer applicable to the world as a whole. Two-thirds of the world has no use for them."[16] Therefore, instead of running after the objective of higher and higher standard of living Lohia stood for a decent standard of living for all the people based on small unit machine technology. This was necessary because of the scarcity of resources and density of population in most of the third world countries. The economy based on small unit machine would provide opportunity for employment of a large number of people. With small unit machine it might not be possible to reach the high standard of living now existing in the Western developed countries. But it would enable them to solve their present problems of dire poverty and unemployment and assure for their people a decent standard of living. Further, this technology, Lohia believed, would enable a country to develop all its sectors and regions simultaneously instead of concentrating on a particular part or sector. Not only that, but this small unit tools would also be favourable for democratic principles as well as help in the achievement of general aims of society. Lohia considered the modern 'leviathan' state economy based on heavy machinery as very complicated and constantly violating the principles of democracy and decentralization.

By small unit machine technology Lohia never meant of using tools like spinning wheel which he called as 'dead or dying out'. He was in search of small but multi-purpose tools run by electricity or oil, tools which would be relatively simple and inexpensive, available in every village and city. It would not require large capital investment. Lohia therefore called for the invention of new such tools that would be a complete breakthrough from the existing modern tools. Thus a new process of industrialization would begin. It would develop all the areas of the country simultaneously and would ultimately lead to a decentralized economic order throughout the world.

Like Gandhi Lohia also hated concentration of power from the core of his heart. To him democracy could be successful only when the commonest person at the lowest level would be able to express his opinion and participate wilfully in the affairs of the state. Though Gandhi had tremendous impact on Lohia but he was never a blind supporter of that great personality. He accepted many of Gandhi's basic principles, but modified them in the light of his own experience and judicious considerations.

Spade, Vote and Jail

Spade vote and jail—these were the terms used by Lohia to describe the method of establishing socialism. By spade he meant constructive work. Vote stood for parliamentary democracy through electoral process while jail or prison referred to *satyagraha* or protest movement against injustice. Lohia gave stress on all these three types of activities to inspire and invigorate his party workers for capturing power for socialism.

In his famous speech at Panchmari in May, 1952 Lohia pointed out that the doctrine of socialism would not be able to thrive except through constructive action. He called upon his party workers to take up programs for digging minor canals, wells and tanks, for building roads and dams and similar other projects even while in opposition. He firmly believed that a party could not grow by neglecting constructive work because it was this intention of doing good, would bring them closer to the people.

Lohia did not share the Marxist view that parliament was essentially a bourgeois institution and therefore a useless instrument for a revolutionary transformation of the society. He gave sufficient importance to the will of the people as expressed through parliamentary election. "The majesty of vote", Lohia stated "should never be derided, for there is no alternative to it."[17]

But even this parliamentary democracy was not enough. In a backward country like India where the people were the victims of misery poverty, corruption and all sorts of injustices, Lohia felt, could never be asked to wait for the next election to bring any change in the system. Slow method of parliamentary democracy would not suffice. Here Lohia's solution was that under such circumstances people should try to redress their grievances by organizing non-violent civil disobedience or what Gandhi called *satyagraha*—a weapon to fight out injustice inflicted on people. Otherwise people would lose faith in democratic method and resort to insurrectional violence.[18]

Party and Power

M.N. Roy, Jayprakash Narayan and Acharya Vinoba Bhabe—all advocated for a partyless democracy. They believed that the party system and the craze for power were largely responsible for the rise of all immoralities in politics. But Lohia had a completely opposite view. To him as long as injustice and exploitation would prevail in society there would remain the necessity of a band of men and women "organized in a political party with a clearly held motivation and mode of action."[19] The party would combat the evil forces through election and civil resistance. In 1952 at the formation of Praja Socialist Party, Lohia categorically stated that the new party must be inspired by the will to power for socialism.[20] At the foundation conference of Socialist Party in December, 1955 Lohia gave the call of 'Seven years will to power'. With all his emphasis on civil disobedience and decentralization Lohia felt very the much the need of a party in order to come to power. The politics of good men, instead of parties, he thought, would ultimately end in a political dictatorship.[21]

World Outlook

Inspired by the ideal of establishing a civilization covering the whole world, classless and casteless in composition Lohia's socialism would have an independent career of its own and would not be founded on the achievements of the present modern civilization whether capitalism or communism. Both had failed to eliminate poverty and war from the world or remove regional inequality. "They have enveloped the world with fear and hate", wrote Lohia. "Man is no longer at peace with himself."[22] Lohia's vision was not confined within the national boundary, but spread far beyond to dream of a 'world state', a fifth pillar added to his concept of 'Four pillar state'. Lohia realised that UN had failed in its duty as it had come to be dominated by the big powers. So Lohia was determined to give a shape to his ideal of 'World State' to whom the states would surrender a portion of their sovereignty for the greater interest of the people. The process of integration, according to Lohia, had already started among the people in terms of 'internal and external approximation'. Even government level cooperation between the states was not acceptable to him as it hardly created any field of cooperation among the people at their wider level—rather a sense of 'donor-recipient' attitude prevailed. And that was why Lohia called for the establishment of a 'World Parliament' based on universal adult franchise. He was in favour of setting up 'voluntary international brigades' for carrying out various activities for the cause of humanity. With this world outlook Lohia started to edit his famous journal *Mankind*.

In international politics Lohia conceived of a new foreign policy which would help in the rise of a new socialist civilization. He stood for a positive foreign policy, a third camp of socialism. It would not be a policy of avoiding alignment with either block in cold war, capitalist block led by USA and communist block led by Soviet Union. Lohia could not accept Nehru's policy of nonalignment as an impartial and ideal foreign policy for the backward third world countries. To him it was a policy of reaction rather than action. Instead his 'Third Camp' would be a policy of independent action and initiation with a purpose to create an ideal socialist civilization.

III
RELEVANCE OF LOHIA'S THOUGHT

Lohia was never an academician in the way Marx, Hegel or Green was. He never intended to formulate a theory as such. He was basically an active politician, a political leader. The socialist civilization which Lohia potrayed, was an outcome of his long experience of political struggle. To establish a classless and casteless egalitarian society was the dream of Dr. Rammanohar Lohia. He was a great supporter of democracy and liberty throughout his life. Hence instead of following the Western path of socialism Lohia gave it a completely different shape. He wanted to provide a new doctrinal foundation to his concept of socialist civilization.

The problem of the backward third world countries, particularly India constituted the central concern of his entire political thought and consciousness. Therefore neither capitalism nor communism was considered to be an acceptable solution to Lohia. To him both were European weapons against Asia. But the question remains that not all the problems of the third world countries are of same nature. Barring some major common issues like poverty, illiteracy, unemployment, malnutrition they have their own separate necessities. So the critics argue that Lohia was more guided by emotion rather than reality, particularly when he felt that his dream of socialist civilization would also be acceptable to prosperous Western countries just because they would prefer peace and tranquillity in place of war and tension.

The fact is that Lohia never claimed to have solved all the problems of the third world countries by one single stroke. He was also aware of their peculiarities. What he tried was just to provide some guideline, a new line of thinking in support of his belief. The relevance of Lohia's socialist thought should be judged with reference to the common problems of the third world.

One of the major features of Lohia's socialism was his anti-elitist view. Lohia believed that the elitist structure of the present society whether in the form of language or caste or dress or living style had created a wide gap between the ruling class and the common people. It had instilled a sense of inferiority complex among the masses whom the rulers sought to govern and exploit. Lohia regarded this situation as a great obstacle to the establishment of a true democratic and egalitarian society. Lohia's anti-caste movement and 'banish English' movement were guided by this motive only. Lohia actually wanted to break this elitist structure of the society.

The toughest criticism against Lohia was that he was arrogant and destructive. He knew what was to be destructed, but not what was to be built up. He had no clear vision of his ideas. That was because of his political image. He could not compromise with his stand. And that is why he constantly broke away from one party and built up another one. He was hostile and arrogant towards his opposition. All this turned him into a disputed or controversial character in contemporary politics. He was out spoken and thoroughly independent, not a man to be controlled.

But all this did not apply to Dr. Rammanohar Lohia as a political thinker where he was very clear, reasonable and systematic. His analysis of capitalism and communism as Europe's weapon against Asia, his philosophy of history, his ideas of socialist civilization are the unique expressions of his deep analytical mind. His contribution in the development of Indian socialist thought is beyond dispute.

Notes

1. Indumati Kelkar, *Lohia: Siddhant aur Karma* (Hindi), Navahind Prakashan, Hyderabad, 1963, p. 27.
2. Rammanohar Lohia, *Wheel of History*, Hyderabad, Rammanohar Lohia Samata Vidyalaya Nyas, 1974, p. 35.
3. *Wheel of History*, *ibid.*, n. 2, p. 38.
4. Rammanohar Lohia, *Marx Gandhi and Socialism*, Hyderabad, Rammanohar Lohia Samata Vidyalaya Nyas, 1978, p. 339.
5. *Ibid.*, p. 96.
6. *Ibid.*
7. Rammanohar Lohia, *Fragments of a World Mind*, Allahabad: Maitrayani, p. 192.
8. Rammanohar Lohia, *Marx Gandhi and Socialism*, n. 4, pp. 99-100.
9. *Ibid.*, p. 334.
10. Presidential address of Rammanohar Lohia to the special convention of Socialist Party, Panchmari, M.P., 23rd May, 1952, p. 14.
11. Rammanohar Lohia, *Marx Gandhi and Socialism*, n. 4, p. 112.
12. Presidential address of Rammanohar Lohia at Panchmari, n. 10, p. 173.
13. R.M. Lohia, *Fragments of a World Mind*, n. 7, p. 70.
14. *Ibid.*, p. 73.
15. R.M. Lohia, *Marx Gandhi and Socialism*, n. 4, pp. 131-32.
16. *Ibid.*, p. 132.
17. Presidential address of Rammanohar Lohia at Panchmari, n. 10, p. 29.
18. R.M. Lohia, *Marx Gandhi and Socialism*, n. 4, p. 127.
19. Socialist Party, Foundation Conference, Hyderabad, Presidential address, December 28th, 1955, p. 8.

20. Rammanohar Lohia, *Will to Power and Other Writings*, Hyderabad: Navahind Prakashan, 1956, p. 4.
21. *Ibid.*, n. 19, p. 129.
22. Presidential address of Rammanohar Lohia to the special convention at Panchmari, n. 10, p. 2.

Suggested Readings

Books and Pamphlets written by Lohia

Marx, Gandhi and Socialism

Wheel of History

Fragments of a World Mind

Will to Power and Other Writings

Interval During Politics

Caste System

Foreign Policy

Notes and Comments

The Struggle for Civil Liberties

The Mystery of Sir Stafford Cripps

Works on Rammanohar Lohia

Indumati Kelkar—*Lohia: Siddhant aur Karma* (Hindi).

Annis Mukhtar and Vijaykant Dixit (ed.). *Lohia: Many Faceted Personality*.

M. Arumugam—*Socialist thought in India: Contribution of Rammanohar Lohia*.

N.C. Mehrotra—*Lohia: A Study*.

V.K. Arora—*Rammanohar Lohia and Socialism in India*.

Karuna Kaushik—*Russian Revolution and Indian Nationalism: Studies of Lajpat Rai, Subhas Chandra Bose and Rammanohar Lohia*.

Prakash Shastri—*Socialist thought in India with special reference to Lohia's quest for indigenous socialism*.

B. Chakraborty and R.K. Pandey—*Modern Indian Political Thought*.

Index

D

E

F

G

H

I